CHEESE

CHEESE

EXPLORING TASTE
AND TRADITION

Patricia Michelson
OF LA FROMAGERIE

PHOTOGRAPHY BY LISA LINDER

GIBBS SMITH
TO ENRICH AND INSPIRE HUMANKIND

First U.S. edition
14 13 12 11 10   5 4 3 2 1

First published in 2010 by Jacqui Small,
7 Greenland Street, London NW1 0ND

Published in the United States by
Gibbs Smith
P.O. Box 667
Layton, Utah 84041
1.800.835.4993 orders
www.gibbs-smith.com

Editorial Manager Kerenza Swift
Art Director Lawrence Morton
Production Peter Colley
Main photography Lisa Linder/Wil Edwards
Illustrator Kate Michelson

Printed and bound in China

Library of Congress Cataloging-in-Publication
Data
Michelson, Patricia
Cheese : exploring taste and tradition /
Patricia Michelson ; photographs by Lisa Linder.
— 1st ed.
p. cm.
ISBN-13: 978-1-4236-0651-2
ISBN-10: 1-4236-0651-5
1. Cookery (Cheese) 2. Cheese. 3. Cheese—
Varieties. 4. Wine and wine making. l. Title
TX759.5.C48M534 2010
641.6'73—dc22
                                    2010000669

CONTENTS

Foreword 6

What Is Cheese? 8

The British Isles & Ireland 14
Southwest & Southern England 16
The Midlands & Wales 24
Northern England & Scotland 32
Ireland 38
   FEATURES:
   Keen's Farmhouse Cheddar 20
   Montgomery's Cheddar 20
   Colston Bassett Stilton 28
   Stichelton 29
   Ardrahan 42
   Durrus 43
   Gubbeen 43

France 44
Northern France 46
Central France 58
South & Southwest France 72
   FEATURES:
   Mimolette 50
   Époisses 60
   Soumaintrain 61
   Ami Du Chambertin 61
   Langres 61
   Fleur de Chèvre 64
   Cendré de Niort 64
   Mothais 64
   Bonde de Gâtine 64
   Chabichou 64
   Salers d'Estive 70
   Cantal Laguiole 70
   Roquefort Carles 77
   Papillon 77

Alpine 82
French Alpine 84
Swiss Alpine 94
Italian Alpine 98
German & Austrian Alpine 106
   FEATURES:
   Beaufort Chalet d'Alpage 86
   Fontina 104

Italy 110
Northern Italy 112
Central & Southern Italy 124
   FEATURES:
   Gorgonzola Naturale 119
   Gorgonzola Dolce 119
   Parmigiano Reggiano 122

Spain & Portugal 134
North & Northeast Spain 136
Central & Southern Spain 142
Portugal 146
   FEATURES:
   Picos de Europa 140
   Manchego 144

The Rest of Europe 150
The Netherlands 150
Scandinavia 152
Poland, Greece, & Germany 154

USA & Canada 156
West Coast 158
Central United States 172
The East 184
Canada 204
   FEATURES:
   Andante Farm: Cavatina, Cadence, Minuet,
    & Figaro 164
   Bleu Mont Dairy: Bleu Mont Cloth Cheddar
    & Lil Wil's Big Cheese 172
   Capriole Farmstead: Old Kentucky Tomme,
    Julianna, Sofia, O'Banon, Mont St. Francis,
    Piper's Pyramide, & Wabash Cannonball 181
   Jasper Hill Farm: Constant Bliss & Bayley
    Hazen Blue 185
   Rawson Brook Fresh Chevre 196
   Three-Corner Field Farm: Battenkill Brebis,
    Shushan Snow, & Feta 200

Australia & New Zealand 208
Australia 209
New Zealand 212

Appreciating Cheese 214

Recipes 224

Directory of Cheeses 296

Acknowledgments 304

FOREWORD

by Jamie Oliver

If you've bought this book, or are thinking about buying it, chances are you're a person that already understands the joy that good food can bring to your life. My dear friend Patricia certainly is, and in another life we'd probably be married with a hundred cheese-loving children by now! Her passion for sourcing, buying, maturing, selling, and promoting quality cheese is unrelenting, and I honestly believe her customers (of which I am one) are some of the luckiest in the world.

Over the past 50 years, a lot of the artisan love, care, and attention that has traditionally gone into cheesemaking has started to flitter away as trends move more and more toward mass production. But thanks to people like Patricia, traditionally made domestic cheeses, as well as wonderful imported foreign varieties, have managed to keep their place in the food market and even raise their profile. Hopefully this beautiful book will help that to continue.

The world of cheese is so damn exciting and—without sounding too pretentious— life is too short to eat plasticky processed cheese week after week! If you feel a bit unsure or scared by the huge variety, this book is for you. Along with beautiful pictures that will help you next time you're faced with a well-stocked cheese counter, there's also loads of excellent and relevant information. Patricia tells you which animal each cheese comes from, as well as how and in which area of the country it is produced. She also profiles producers who are at the top of their game, so you can look for their cheeses. More importantly, she gives you an idea of what each tastes like, and what sort of things you can make or serve with it. It's really a kind of cheese encyclopedia and, hand on heart, I couldn't think of any better person to guide you through this wonderful world than Patricia.

When I flick through these pages I want to get straight in my car, drive to La Fromagerie, and pick up some of the varieties she has featured here. But if you're outside of Britain, the wonderful thing is that you can still have access to many of the types discussed here, thanks to mail order and the Internet. I can guarantee that the guys producing them really want you to try their stuff, and you won't be sorry you did.

Like wine, each cheese has its own special personality. One person might walk the long way home to pick up a certain type of blue cheese, while his best friend might think it stinks and is repulsive. That's one of the things I love about cheese, and it is something Patricia really understands—it's so individual. I think when you read this book, you'll end up with the ability to hunt down certain cheeses, whatever their character, and make them a part of your life.

What is cheese?

I came to love cheese not by a thoughtful evaluation over many years, but by way of a fall down a mountain and a piece of cheese at the end of the day. It was more like what the French would term a *coup de foudre*, or love at first sight. I often bless the fact that my skiing ability is less than athletic, and having lost track of my partner and consequently having to trudge down the mountain through the village of Meribel in Savoie, exhausted and hungry, I was drawn to the golden glow of the cheese shop. I bought a nugget of Beaufort, to nibble on my way back to the chalet, and that delicious piece of cheese changed my life and my livelihood. Today, Beaufort Chalet d'Alpage is still the signature cheese at La Fromagerie.

The simple beginnings of just one cheese brought home after the skiing vacation slowly turned into a business, first by selling from my shed, then with a market stall in Camden Town, followed by a tiny shop in Highbury, before moving to a larger premises opposite, and finally adding the beautiful shop and café in Marylebone, all in London. Of course, it has taken nearly 20 years to be where I am now, and along the way I have learned and honed my trade, met many wonderful people, and, above all, appreciated the fact that the land gives us so much. I am lucky to be able do the work I love and to pass on my enthusiasm to others who share a similar desire to eat well and respect the land, our animals, and, above all, our future. My shops are an extension of me. The Cheese Room is unique—a walk-in cooled and humidified room where cheeses can be seen and tasted at a temperature that enhanced their ripening and keeping qualities. It has often been described as a "library of cheese" because you can walk around the room, read the tasting labels, and then, instead of taking down a book and flicking through it, you can have a sliver taken from the cheese to taste, or chat with one of the enthusiastic assistants about what you would like to try next.

In this book, the cheeses are arranged as on a journey of discovery, with maps to denote approximately where the cheeses are found. Use this book to inspire you on your own journey. There are many of my own photographs from my travels dotted throughout the book. When I set out on my little foraging trips, I simply take a region and divide it into grids, then find the local towns and go from there. I look to see if there is a market, often calling the local tourist information center for addresses of the local artisans. It is amazing what you can glean, and before you know it you have several people to call and visit.

What is cheese? You would think the answer would be straightforward, wouldn't you—it is milk turned from its liquid state into curds, then formed into cheese. The steps a cheesemaker has to take in order to get to the end product, however, are not so straightforward.

The milk must be heated in a careful progression, and an active yeasty-style starter must be added to the milk at just the right moment to bring the acidity levels up so that it will accept the rennet coagulant. The rennet (produced either from a calf stomach lining* or a vegetarian alternative, both of which are high in acidity) helps to separate the watery whey from the solids. The solids are then cut into small pieces, before being scooped into molds or presses, salted or brine-bathed, then matured and ripened.

Along the way, cheeses can have additional molds added to produce white bloomy rinds, or sticky orange coats, blue veins, charcoal ash, or charcoal ash mixed with *Penicillium roqueforti* blue molds or pinky-washed crusts. There is alchemy and science mixed with skill in cheesemaking, but none of this would be possible without that wonderful gift of nature: milk.

Patricia Michelson

---

* The reason why the baby calf fourth stomach lining is used for rennet is because the animal has to be suckling from its mother to obtain the right high acidity level in the fourth stomach. Calves are culled because, if a dairy herd has a surfeit of male animals, the farmer tries to sell them to beef herds, as well as keep some for steers, but any others have to be slaughtered and the meat is sold and the fourth stomach kept for rennet. The same goes for beef herds with their female animals. The historical connection probably lies in when milk was kept in animal stomach pouches for transporting from one place to another, and it was found that the liquid changed to a lumpy curd when the acidity within the lining mingled with the milk.

Molds

Geotrichum candidum is a fungus that grows on surface-ripened cheeses during the early stages of ripening. On some cheeses, such as St. Marcellin, it is an evenly spread white and gray patchy mold. On soft cheeses such as Camembert and semihard cheeses such as St. Nectaire, the fungus can prevent the *Penicillium candidum* molds from overtaking and leading to bitterness. In washed-rind cheeses, it is used to deacidify the surface of the cheese, creating a welcoming environment for *B. linens* to grow.

Brevibacterium linens (*B. linens*) is a mixture of introductory bacteria cultivated on the surface of washed-rind cheeses, which create the orange or pinkish color and the high aroma. *B. linens* requires a low-acid environment, moisture, and oxygen to flourish.

Penicillium candidum (*P. candidum*) is a variant of the mold *Penicillium camemberti* (a typical white bloomy mold that turns off-white to gray after several days). The *P. candidum* remains white and is the trademark of a bloomy rind cheese. This surface mold, given the right amount of salt and moisture, will develop a rind that breaks down from the outside in, creating an increasingly soft, buttery texture with time.

Penicillium roqueforti (*P. roqueforti*) or *P. glaucum* is a mold that is added to the curds, before the cheese is pressed and formed. This mold is a decomposing toxin that is activated by air. The air is introduced during the maturing process by piercing the cheese with needles, to allow the spores within to grow and spread.

Styles of Cheese

Soft cheese has no discernible rind and high water content—ricotta, quark, cottage cheese, curd cheese, and mascarpone are all good examples. Soft cheeses are very delicate and should be consumed soon after purchase.

Fresh cheese has no discernible rind, but may have a little more structure than a soft cheese. A high water content keeps it from drying out, and its shelf life is limited. Good examples are the very light and frothy Primosale, fresh goat cheese, and nonbarrel-aged feta.

Bloomy cheese has a white fluffy rind from *Penicillium candidum*. Cheeses such as Brie and Camembert have a little of the culture mixed into the curds, then more coated on top of the cheeses once they are in their molds or forms, to help with the process of rind development. Brillat-Savarin is a triple-cream cheese from Normandy, where the coat gently grows on the outside of the cheese and needs careful supervision to let the molds adhere to the cheese and not become too furry. If the outside rind becomes too dry or too wet, this triggers aromas and flavors that can be very unsavory. Check that the rind looks "perky" before buying one of these cheeses. With some matured goat cheeses, the white rinds are flecked with golden molds, too.

Washed cheese is produced when a soft cheese has a *lineum* smear, which is encouraged by washing the cheese in a saltwater solution, white wine, or Marc de Bourgogne (a very fiery alcohol made from distilling vine pressings after winemaking). After about three weeks, the reaction of the washing creates a surface color change from white to orange. Some good examples of washed cheeses are Époisses, Langres, Munster, Livarot, and Taleggio.

Brevibacterium linens on a rind is the same bacterium found on human skin.

Semihard (uncooked) cheese is made when the moisture is squeezed out before forming, and includes such cheeses as Mimolette, Cheddar, Ossau, Cheshire, and pecorino. Cheeses such as Ossau ewe's milk from the Pyrénées are pierced with fine needles in the same way as Cheshire, to encourage the whey to drain out.

Semihard & hard (cooked) cheeses are made when the milk is heated to a high temperature, to encourage the draining process because the large size of the cheese requires this. When the curds are placed in their hoops or molds, a weight is pressed down to assist the process. These include the big cheeses, such as Parmesan, Gruyère, Comté, Beaufort, Gouda, and fontina.

Pasta filata cheese is one that has spun or stretched curds, such as provolone, mozzarella, provola, burrino, and scamorze. After draining, the fresh cheese rests for a while, then is placed in hot-water baths, where pieces are pulled off, then stretched and kneaded until a soft, elastic, stringy texture is obtained.

Persille or Blue cheese *Persille* means "parsley," and in the old days cheeses were pierced so that the airborne bacteria could penetrate the cheese and create the feathery blue molds. In the case of Roquefort, the outside of the cheeses were rubbed with a fine crumb of sourdough bread that had become moldy and dry, and even today this process is used; however, injection and piercing with *Penicillium roqueforti* in a more structured format are the way in which most blue cheeses are made.

Fat Matters

Determining the amount of fat in cheese is shown as a percentage of fat in the total "dry matter" (defined as fats plus solids that are not fats). This percentage is constant throughout the life of the cheese after maturity; however, the percentage of fat in the whole cheese increases as moisture evaporates with maturing and, therefore, detailing this would not provide an accurate definition for the consumer.

A cheese that is 45 percent fat matter does not actually contain 45 percent. The fat is calculated on the whole cheese nutrients minus the water. This is specific to French cheeses, but in other countries the fat lipids are calculated on the total weight of the cheese, which will also include water. The list of figures here (see right) should be taken into account when assessing or calculating the nutritional value of cheese.

Cheese	% of actual fat
Fromage frais or any other fresh curd 0% fat	0
Fromage frais or any other fresh curd 20% fat	3
Fromage frais or any other fresh curd 30% fat	5
Fromage frais or any other fresh curd 40% fat	8
Fresh semisalted cheese (i.e. Primosale fresh cheese)	13
Fermented cheeses, such as Camembert	16–22
Fermented washed-rind cheeses, such as Livarot	20–23
Fermented pressed uncooked cheeses, such as Cantal, Reblochon, Mimolette, Cheshire, Cheddar	20–26
Fermented pressed cooked cheeses, such as Comté, Gruyère, fontina, Parmesan	26–30
Fermented blue cheeses, such as Roquefort	34–35
Cheese that is creamed like a fondue based on 45% fat	22
Goat cheese	15–25

Nutritional Value

Once a cheese is drained and pressed, then matured, the harder and more aged it becomes, and also the richer it becomes in nutrients. So if you want to calculate your nutrient intake from the following list, base it on about 1–1½-ounce (30–40-g) portions. If you are following a very strict low-cholesterol diet, you may not be able to eat cheese, but for most of us it is important to obtain calcium from cheese. To have your quotient of calcium every day—even if you are on a diet—use the list here (see right) or stick to low-fat fromage frais or goat cheese.

Cheese	Protein %	Fats %	Calcium mg
White bloomy rind cheeses	15–20	16–22	180–200
Washed-rind soft cheeses	20–30	20–23	200–500
Pressed uncooked cheeses	25–30	20–26	650–800
Pressed cooked cheeses	30–35	26–30	900–1,350
Blue cheeses	24	34–35	500–700
Creamed cheeses, such as fondue	18	22	750
Goat	16–35	15–25	180–200

Gluten Intolerance

Hard and aged cheeses are gluten-free—the time taken to mature releases sugars and salts that are naturally part of milk, but retains proteins and caseins that are easy to digest. Cheddar, Parmesan, and pecorino are fine, as are other cheeses in the same style.
Blue cheeses, such as Roquefort, are not gluten-free because bread that is allowed to turn moldy is used to help create the bacteria that produce the blue veins.

Goat's and ewe's milk cheeses are easier to digest, too, and can be eaten softer and creamier, but watch out for bloomy rinds because they may cause concern with their bacterial makeup.
Fresh cheeses, such as fromage blanc, fromage frais, and Petit Suisses, are fine as long as you read the label to make sure that no additives or preservatives, such as gum, have been used to thicken their consistency.

The British Isles
& Ireland

What do Jervaulx monks and Wensleydale cheese have in common? In the IIth century, the Norman Conquest had a major impact on life in Britain. It brought far-reaching changes—some would say order, wealth, landowning, and agriculture—to an island that had been run largely in an unruly way. It was during this period that the religious order of Jervaulx monks came from Normandy and Flandres to Britain—in particular, Yorkshire—with their desire to be self-sufficient, as well as to spread the word of their faith in a positive way. Their capabilities included sheep farming, cheesemaking, and horse breeding, and they are widely acknowledged as the original makers of Wensleydale cheese.

During the time of Henry VIII and the dissolution of the monasteries, the Jervaulx abbey was destroyed, but the monks' legacy remains in its influence on many of the traditional cheeses produced in Britain today.

This brief explanation encapsulates how this group of islands is partly defined by its history of farming and the skills and techniques that help to produce traditional foods, including cheese, many of which have been passed down through the generations and by communities despite centuries of war and conflict. This in turn reflects the history of cheesemaking throughout Europe and the New World, too.

There are literally hundreds of cheeses in the British Isles and Ireland, and there is now a thriving and exciting cheese movement that has not been seen since the start of the Industrial Revolution. Two world wars almost finished the dairy industry in Britain, but like Philippe Olivier, who revived cheesemaking in Normandy after it had been devastated by the same conflicts, Britain's own Randolph Hodgson of Neal's Yard Dairy championed specialty cheesemakers and helped to build their recognition and reputation all over the world.

I have very firm views about the cheeses of the British Isles. Nothing is more exciting than the crumbly, wet texture and grassy flavor of a traditionally made Wensleydale, the nutty intensity of Cheddar, the herby sharpness of Cheshire, and the mineral-rich buttery texture of Stilton. These represent all that is fine and good about British cheese. I like to choose cheeses that represent their region, and I am fascinated by the way in which they evolve due to variations in soil, weather patterns, and minerals. The amazing range of flavors experienced when tasting a Stilton (see page 28) or Stichelton (a new cheese developed by Joe Schneider with Randolph Hodgson, see page 29) is magical. The flinty minerals are synonymous with Derbyshire; the creamy rich intensity of the cheese develops slowly and the crust, the crucial part of the maturing process that can make or break the taste, has a stonelike crumb made possible by the damp, cool aging rooms. In Ireland, the microclimate and soft, sweet water in the south produce wonderfully rich, aromatic cheeses, both washed rind and hard. From the north of Ireland comes one of my favorite goat cheeses, Ryefield (see page 39); it is light and airy, with a salty freshness to be enjoyed first thing in the morning on toast.

Every region of the British Isles has something to offer, from Wales with Caerphilly (see page 30) to Scotland with its delicious Dunsyre Blue (see page 34). Ireland has so many different styles of cheese that I am overwhelmed by the choice, but it is a relatively new cheese from the wild and dramatic coast of Kerry that has caught my heart. Called Dilliskus (see page 41), the cheese is made by Maja Binder and uses dillisk, or dulse, seaweed in the curd. It has all the makings of a fine territorial, utilizing traditional techniques, such as the inclusion of dillisk, to give the cheese its unique flavor. The farm is very close to the sea, where the salty spray finds its way into the milk through the pastures, while the maturing caves are in old stone farm buildings with well-seasoned wooden shelving. All these factors contribute to the tastes and textures of this cheese.

The British and Irish are island races. They may be small in comparison to other countries and continents, and they may not have the extremes in temperature to produce different styles of cheese, but what they do have in bucketloads is a quality that is highly defined and, at last, recognized as being worthy of greatness.

The following selection features cheeses from all over the British Isles that are representative of their regions. This may seem like a small selection, and I wish I could include more, but it is my way of starting the journey that gives a real view of life through cheese.

Within every region of England there are plenty of weekend farmers markets, and this is a great way of seeing and tasting at first hand the local produce. The markets are always the first place I visit on my travels, wherever I go, because this is an excellent way to meet the producers, chat, and taste their wares. Sitting down in the market square, with a glass of locally made beer and a chunk of cheese, is not a bad way to pass the time and soak up the atmosphere.

TOP Cows grazing on the Colston Bassett fields, Nottinghamshire. BOTTOM Apple orchards in southern England.

Southwest & Southern England

The south and southwest of England enjoy good weather patterns throughout the year, enabling farm animals to graze outdoors. If asked what cheese is made in the south of England, most people would say Cheddar. The Southwest is the largest region in England—the area extends from Gloucestershire and Wiltshire to Cornwall and beyond to the Isles of Scilly. The majestic chalk cliffs of Dover over to the southeast indicate land that is well drained and gritty. Although this area is not as well known for its cheeses as the Southwest, there are plenty of stylish individual cheeses being produced by small-scale cheesemakers. As well as goat's, cow's, and ewe's milk, there are also buffalo-milk cheeses being pioneered in Hampshire and other counties in the region. The landscape of the Southwest is romantic with rocky coastline, moorland, and green rolling hills, while the Southeast is flatter, divided into arable and pastoral farming, with grazing for sheep still maintained on the coastal marshes. The Sussex and Kent regions have vineyards with award-winning wine production and Kentish hops to make distinctive beers, which are perfect accompaniments for the crumbly regional cheeses.

Devon, Beenleigh, and Harbourne Blue

TOTNES, DEVON

Robin Congdon's farm overlooks the Dart Valley in a very picturesque part of Devon. The three blue cheeses made on the farm are Devon Blue with cow's milk, Beenleigh Blue with ewe's milk, and Harbourne Blue with goat's milk. All three weigh about 6½ pounds (3 kg) each.

Devon Blue The unpasteurized Jersey cow's milk is partly responsible for Devon Blue's fresh grassy, earthy, buttery flavor. It has a rich and creamy close texture, with tangy blue veins that gently bleed into the cheese.

Beenleigh Blue is made with unpasteurized ewe's milk and vegetarian rennet. The texture of the cheese is more chewy and dense than Roquefort, and the blue veins are well spread, with threads rather than the pockmarked craters often found in the former. The flavor has a flinty mineral sweetness, with a slightly aggressive briny hit. One would not imagine that a British blue could taste like this, and it is much to Robin's credit that he has achieved such an individual style to his cheeses. Beenleigh is at its best between midsummer and midwinter.

Harbourne Blue is made with unpasteurized goat's milk and vegetarian rennet. The cheese's texture can be very crumbly, and the contrasting colors of pale, almost alabaster curd and dark, inky blue veins give this cheese an almost delicate ethereal quality. However, its flavor dispels all of this. Strength and power are uppermost in the flavor ladder.

Many believe this to be Robin's best cheese, and it is at its optimum between early summer and late fall. The sharp, tangy flavor that comes through with the early summer cheese is stunning. Try serving Harbourne Blue alongside a chilled full-bodied white wine on a warm summer's evening—there could not be a more ideal way of enjoying this cheese. At La Fromagerie, we also love serving quince "cheese," or paste, with all of Robin's cheeses because they complement each other so well.

ABOVE LEFT The fields of southern England.

ABOVE RIGHT Grazing pastures in Devon.

OPPOSITE, TOP CHEESE Devon Blue, MIDDLE CHEESE Beenleigh Blue, BOTTOM CHEESE Harbourne Blue

Cornish Yarg 🐄 LISKEARD, CORNWALL

The original cheesemakers were Alan and Jenny Gray (the name "Yarg" is actually "Gray" back to front), and this was one of the first new specialty cheeses to come onto the market around 1980. The recipe is based on an ancient Caerphilly, which they brought with them from their home in Wales, with a nod to Cheddar. Instead of a crust being allowed to form on the outside, it is covered with nettles found growing wild in the area. The cheese is made by hand in open vats, using pasteurized milk from local Holstein and Friesian cows and vegetable rennet. After pressing and brining (dipping the cheese in a saltwater solution), it is wrapped in wild nettle leaves in a beautiful lacy relief pattern of blue and green, giving the finished cheese its unique appearance. The nettles impart a citrusy tang to the cheese, which mellows after maturing, and the aroma is gentle and subtle. A very popular cheese, especially with children who prefer a mild taste, Cornish Yarg also finds favor with pregnant ladies because it is very easy to digest.

Ticklemore 🐐 TOTNES, DEVON

This cheese was originally made by Robin Congdon, who has a true understanding of the variables in making handmade cheese in this part of the country. He has since passed on the technique and recipe to Debbie Mumford at Sharpham Creamery. This area of Devon is truly magnificent, with the river Dart meandering through the farmland, and the hills as a backdrop to the green fields rolling down to the water's edge. The semihard unpasteurized goat's milk cheese is made with a vegetarian rennet and is formed into an oval, which is actually achieved by placing the curds in kitchen colanders. The bloom on the crust grows during the maturing process, and tiny eyelet holes are scattered throughout the flaky pâte. This produces a young cheese with a slightly open texture, but during maturation the texture becomes closer and flakier. The taste is fresh, light, and gentle, with hints of fresh, grassy woodland and only the faintest goaty aroma. These flavors make it perfect for cooking, as well as for presenting as part of a cheeseboard.

Alderwood 🐄 ASHMORE, DORSET

Cranborne Chase Cheese, the maker of Alderwood, is part of the Manor Farm estate in the hilltop village of Ashmore, north Dorset. The microclimate in this particular region is quite different than that of nearby areas, with a warm breeze rippling over the land. The sweet and savory minerals in the grass also influence the milk and finished cheese, making Alderwood very

different than the Cheddars from this part of England. It is based on a Bel Paese or St. Paulin using unpasteurized cow's milk and a traditional rennet, resulting in a rather mild, sweetly nutty-tasting cheese. It has a brine-washed rind, however, which creates a warm apricot-colored jacket and enhances the cheese's flavor.

The fine grazing pastures of this beautiful estate cross Cranborne Chase and Blackmore Vale, an area of outstanding natural beauty reserved as the hunting grounds for monarchs from the Norman Conquest until as recently as the 20th century. From the 18th century until 2007, the estate was owned by the same family, but the new owner has since totally revamped the dairy, bringing it up to date. The farm's flint, stone, and brick buildings have been converted for cheesemaking and maturing, and the original recipe has been slightly reworked, but still retains all the relevant requirements for a handmade cheese, using milk from their next-door neighbor's herd of Holstein-Friesian cattle.

The cheese curds are placed in their molds on day one, brined on day two, and then the first washing occurs on day three. The cheese is then taken to the ripening room and kept at a low temperature with a high humidity, to encourage the development of the rind. During the maturing period—about 12 weeks—natural molds develop, giving a mottled orange-brown appearance to the rind. The stone maturing buildings also impart their own minerals and flora from the air, which influences the flavor of the cheese.

Although Alderwood can be eaten young, I always like to give it a few extra weeks, with several washings in a local hard cider to further enhance the flavor.

Cardo 🐐 TIMSBURY, SOMERSET

This semihard washed-rind goat cheese uses cardoon thistles as a coagulant (rennet), to separate the curds from the whey. The washed, naturally bloomed rind is the result of a saltwater solution that is brushed onto the cheese, leaving a thin sticky "film." The aroma is not too strong, but there is an earthy, mossy vegetal perfume that comes through, while the taste is fruity without being aggressive. There is also a lovely herbal mineral element, which comes from a combination of the milk and the brine washing. This is a wonderful, relatively new cheese from cheesemaker Mary Holbrook, whose very successful truncated pyramid Tymsboro has won many prizes at the British Cheese Awards and is made along the lines of the French goat cheese Valençay. With Cardo, she took inspiration from the Portuguese mountain cheeses that also use thistle as a coagulant, but I think that the cheese is also not dissimilar to the Corsican Casinca or a Tomme de Cléon from Vendée in France. The window of opportunity to sample Cardo is very limited, mainly due to the way in which Mary rears her animals, allowing them time for rest and play, as well as kidding.

OPPOSITE, TOP LEFT Ticklemore
OPPOSITE, TOP RIGHT Alderwood
OPPOSITE, BOTTOM LEFT Cardo
OPPOSITE, BOTTOM RIGHT Cornish Yarg

Somerset Cheddars

The temperate climate and wetlands of the Somerset levels, together with the limestone of the Mendip Hills, are ideal conditions for growing lush pastures and producing Cheddars of outstanding flavor and texture.

Keen's Farmhouse Cheddar

WINCANTON, SOMERSET

The Keen family has farmed at Moorhayes, which is both arable and dairy, since 1899. The rather majestic 16th-century gabled farmhouse sits proudly on a hill overlooking the farmland, which in this part of Somerset is low-lying and prone to wet. The unpasteurized cow's milk cheese is made by hand using a traditional rennet, and what differentiates this Cheddar from, say, Montgomery's is its texture. Keen's has a heavier texture, with a spicy, deep, almost tingling sensation on the tongue, a nutty, fruity tang, and a rich, vigorous finish. The method of heating and pressing also differs from that of Jamie Montgomery's, but I think that in this little pocket of Somerset the *terroir* shows the way. I like Keen's Cheddar for its weighty chewiness, and the fact that it is a great cooking cheese.

Montgomery's Cheddar

NORTH CADBURY, SOMERSET

Jamie Montgomery makes a superb farmhouse Cheddar with immense skill, using unpasteurized cow's milk and traditional rennet, and every part of the cheesemaking process is overseen by him. What I love about this cheese are its fruity complexity and its elegance—a combination that makes the perfect cheese sandwich! The grassy aroma of the cheese is offset by its mellow, rich taste, which lingers gently on the tongue. The wines of Bordeaux are an obvious partner, with their austere first impression, building up to a full-bodied flinty taste. Bordeaux and Somerset have comparable regional patterns.

Manor Farm, situated in North Cadbury, is in the heart of Camelot country and the epicenter of Cheddar. Jamie's family has been making cheese for three generations, utilizing milk originally from their pedigree Ayrshire herd, but latterly switching to Friesians because they have a higher milk yield. He has been careful to breed cows that retain as much of the Ayrshire characteristics as possible.

Montgomery's Cheddar is aged on wooden shelving in barns for a minimum of 12 months, but additional aging of 14–18 or even 24 months gives the cheese an even greater depth of flavor. The making of Cheddar is quite complex, requiring several stages of draining, cutting, milling, and final pressing. Jamie uses an old peg mill for the milling process, to produce a less even result; the cheese then develops a texture that breaks down with a crumble in the mouth. Jamie's cheeses have a texture and flavor that are somewhat different than other West Country Cheddars because he monitors the fat and protein levels carefully—too much leads to a much sharper taste—and he always aims for a drier, earthy, sweet hay flavor. His smoked Cheddar is cut into sections and smoked over oak chips, to create a really fruity, bosky taste. The cheese has a fine aroma that is both sharp and tangy.

Cheddar produced by members of the West Country Group, who make cheese using milk from local herds, if not their own, and who apply traditional methods to all aspects of production, now have a Protected Designation of Origin (PDO), to separate their cheeses from other cheddars made elsewhere in the world. It was not possible to protect the name "Cheddar," but at least the West Country Group's cheesemakers have accreditation.

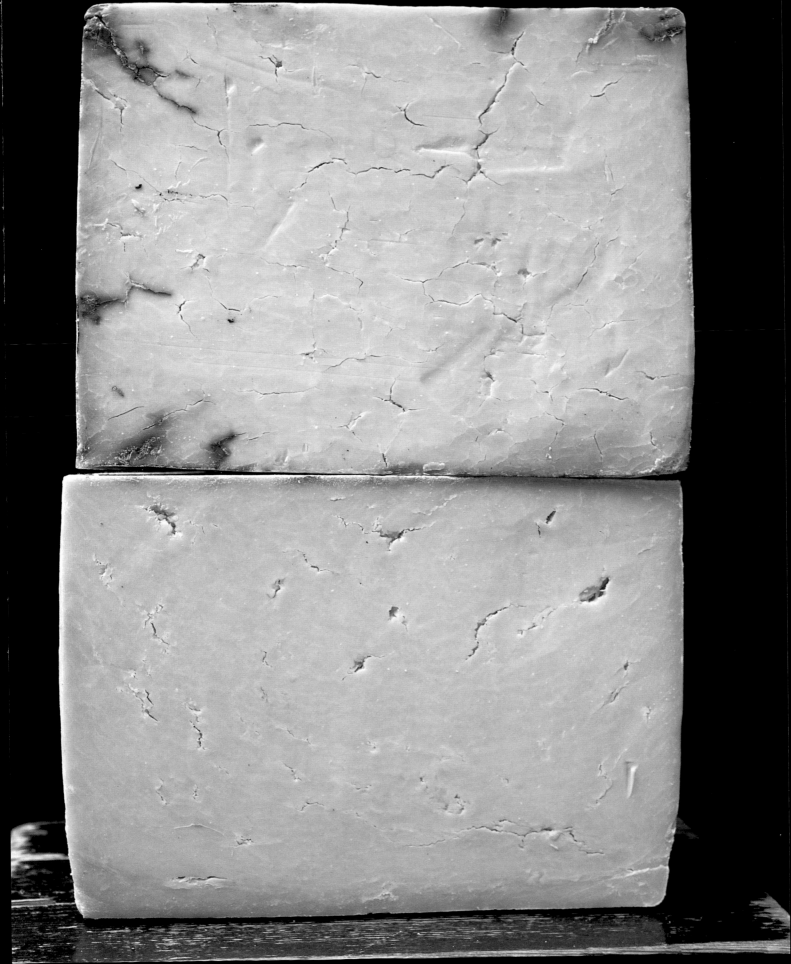

Waterloo & Wigmore 🐄 🐑 RISELEY, BERKSHIRE

I am often asked why handmade cheeses are so different from those made in larger dairies. I believe it comes down to a particular knowledge of how to treat the milk and turn it from its raw state into cheese. The intricate stages of production are fascinating and as much an art as a science. Wigmore and Waterloo are both washed-curd cheeses, as opposed to washed-rind ones.

The washed-curd method involves replacing the whey with water and washing the curds to reduce the number of starter bacteria and sugars (lactose). This in turn moderates lactic acid levels and helps to retain valuable moisture. The starter bacteria—a sort of yogurty mixture that encourages the formation of curds—feed on the lactose and convert it to lactic acid. All of these thingss influence the final taste and texture of the cheese.

It is all a matter of balance. If not enough of the starter bacteria is washed away as the curds form, then the cheese will be too dry and acidic; yet if too much is washed away, the result is a very soft, sloppy cheese, with little flavor and a low acidity. Also, there is a risk that low acidity could allow the growth of harmful bacteria; it is therefore vital for Wigmore and Waterloo to contain a good level of acidity, but it does take much longer to reach this perfect balance, before salting in order to retain the soft texture and the good flavor.

Once the curds are at the salting stage, a preparation of *Penicillium candidum* is used to produce the white bloomy rind (the same as for Brie and Camembert); again, however, it is essential to get the acidity, or pH, correct so that the white mold will grow properly. It is also very important to turn the cheese every day during maturation, to achieve an equal growth, because the mold relies on oxygen to grow. This is where a "refiner" or cheese "maturer" takes over, and his or her skill can turn the rind into a soft, satinlike finish.

Even though Anne and Andy Wigmore have been making Wigmore and Waterloo for more than 18 years, they are still tweaking things here and there to improve flavor and texture. Originally, they made the cheeses with unpasteurized milk, but they have turned to "thermizing," to improve consistency. Thermizing milk for cheeses with rinds, such as Camembert, Livarot, and Pont l'Évêque, is more common now in France and other European countries. The milk is heated before chilling, which kills off any harmful bacteria in the raw milk (if there are any), but leaves a significant number of good lactic acid- and enzyme-producing bacteria (thermophiles) usually killed off by pasteurization.

Waterloo is made with Guernsey cow's milk and Wigmore with ewe's milk. Wigmore has a fruity iron flavor that develops with maturing to become a velvety and mellow-tasting cheese. Waterloo, however, has a buttery, slightly salty taste, which is balanced by a more acidic center.

Tunworth 🐄 HERRIARD, HAMPSHIRE

The South Downs has long been associated with hop growing and agriculture, and vineyards are now bringing in another line of business. There are a few cheesemakers in the Southeast, producing a variety of styles, including goat's and ewe's milk cheeses, but Tunworth has attracted a vast amount of interest in its bloomy rind cow's milk cheese.

Julie Cheyney and Stacey Hodges are two friends who decided to go into business together, making cheese using milk from a neighboring farm. From simple beginnings making cheese in the kitchen, they have built a modern dairy in an old wooden barn to create the right conditions to progress their

LEFT, LEFT CHEESE Tunworth, TOP RIGHT CHEESE Wigmore, BOTTOM CHEESE Waterloo

cheesemaking. Their interpretation of a soft, mellow-tasting cheese with a thin bloomy rind has been achieved by adding a little *Penicillium candidum* (white mold) to the milk during heating, then quickly draining off the whey, before forming the cheese by hand and placing it in the drying room for a few days. Almost magically, the soft, downy bloom starts to appear, and temperature and humidity levels then have to be carefully maintained to continue the development. This results in a cheese with an almost melting rind that clings to the fudgy center.

Tunworth is also a great leap forward for British cheesemaking because it takes on a French style, but with a distinctly English flavor. Perhaps not as nutty or earthy as a Camembert because Tunworth uses whole milk, giving it a slightly heavier texture, it is nevertheless a delightful addition to a cheeseboard, to be best enjoyed at around five to six weeks. You will see this cheese at farmers markets in Hampshire, as well as at specialty cheese shops and served in restaurants.

Stinking Bishop 🐄 DYMOCK, GLOUCESTERSHIRE

This cheese is in much demand, especially because such a limited amount is made. The farm is small, and the commitment to rearing Gloucester cows means that the milk yield is not as high as, say, from Holsteins.

Stinking Bishop has several similarities to French cheeses, such as Époisses (see page 60) and vacherin (see page 90). The aroma is pungent, but that does not necessarily mean that the flavor is equally strong. On the contrary, the prepared curds are not drained, milled, and salted, but instead are washed in perry (hard pear cider) made from a particular variety of pear called Stinking Bishop, hence the cheese's name.

As with vacherin, the curds are ladled directly into molds, to increase the moisture content and encourage bacterial activity. Salting takes place when the cheeses are turned out of the molds, then wrapped in a bark collar, again as is done with vacherin.

The flavor of the cheese is not too strong when young, but, given a little time in a high-humidity cool aging room, it develops to become more complex and rich.

Single Gloucester 🐄 CHURCHAM, GLOUCESTERSHIRE

Diana Smart started making cheese in her sixties and wanted to keep to a very traditional recipe using milk from her herd of Gloucester cattle, although the paucity of cows in her herd has meant that she has had to supplement milk from Holsteins for her cheeses other than the Single Gloucester. She first made the cheese in her kitchen, lining the molds with cut-down old sheets that she had boiled first to sterilize. The cheese has a deliciously light texture with a savory, nutty flavor, which I prefer to eat on the young side.

ABOVE, TOP CHEESE Stinking Bishop, BOTTOM CHEESE Single Gloucester

The recipe for Single Gloucester uses low-fat milk, and Diana's cheeses are a true example of a traditionally made cheese of this type. The evening milk is skimmed of its cream, then combined with the whole morning milk. Very little starter is used, and rennet is added 30 minutes later. Once the milk has set, the curd is cut, heated again with continuous stirring, then allowed to settle before the whey is drained off. The curd is then cut into 16 squares, turned, and then rested, before being cut again into smaller squares, turned again, and rested once more. Additional cuttings are made before the almost pea-size curd is finally salted, milled, pressed, and matured for a minimum of three weeks; additional aging of up to four months produces a denser, more crumbly cheese.

Traditionally, Single Gloucester was made solely for family consumption and is, therefore, less well known than Double Gloucester, mainly because of its size, flavor, and texture, which is somewhat different from the Double, whose character is more in line with Cheddar and seemingly more popular.

In 1997, Single Gloucester received Protected Designation of Origin (PDO) status, which means that it must now be produced only on farms in Gloucestershire with pedigree Gloucester cattle.

The flavor of Single Gloucester is very typically British, so I would say that English varieties of apple and pear are wonderful accompaniments to enjoy with this cheese.

The Midlands & Wales

The mineral-rich coal seams of the Midlands filter into the pastureland, which produces fine dairy and beef cattle and great regional cheeses. The Great North Road was the first main link into England's bustling capital city, London, and brought fortune to the region, but the Industrial Revolution and the onslaught of manufacturing and mining reduced the pastureland and affected the substructure of the soil. Land has been reclaimed and nurtured back to life, however, and dairy and beef farming continue to flourish. Wales, located on a peninsula to the west of the Midlands, boasts 746 miles (1,200 km) of coastline and a varied landscape of mountains and outstanding natural parkland, dissected by rivers of clear, clean water. The wet and windy weather and often cold winters encourage cattle rather than arable farming. This climate produces the delicious Caerphilly cheese, with its distinctive mineral quality and soft crumble.

Berkswell 🐑 BERKSWELL, WEST MIDLANDS

Half-wooden stone houses, a medieval church, and lush green pastures surround Ram Hall Farm in this delightfully picturesque corner of middle England, not too far from Shakespeare country.

Sheila, Stephen, and Tessa Fletcher started making ewe's milk cheese in the mid-1980s, experimenting with a Caerphilly recipe, then tweaking it until they found a formula that was unique to them. The curds are heated, vegetarian rennet is added, and then they are left to rest. The milk soon starts setting, and looks similar to a wobbly blancmange when it is cut and then heated again, before being placed in molds in the shape of woven baskets, rather like a pecorino or Manchego. The finishing touch, before placing in the maturing rooms, is to paint the outside of the cheese with whey, to ensure that the rind stays firm but also thin.

The taste on first impression is fresh, becoming fruity and nutty as it warms in the mouth. We love the young cheeses for their sweetness, but it is only when we allow ourselves to hold back selling them and to mature for an extra five months that the texture becomes denser and the complexity of flavors more intense and rewarding.

LEFT Berkswell
ABOVE Tal-y-Llyn Lake, West Wales.

Innes Button 🦌 TAMWORTH, STAFFORDSHIRE

Simplicity is key to this cheese: "fresh," "light," and "acidic" are the only words necessary to describe the Innes Button goat cheese. The dairy and farm are meticulously run by Stella Bennett and her son Joe, who is now at the helm. One of the highlights for me is when I arrive at the shop early enough to say hello to Joe, who delivers the cheeses sometimes. His shock of curly red hair and cheery demeanor are a welcome start to our day!

The recipe is simple, and the process starts immediately after milking, with the warm unpasteurized milk being quickly transformed with vegetarian rennet to produce soft and fragile curds, as well as to preserve the flavor synonymous with Innes' cheeses. Since 1987, when it started with 100 goats, the herd has grown to 350, mostly crossed Saanen and Toggenburg. Around 220 nannies are milked morning and evening, each producing on average 3 quarts (3 liters) of milk per day. To maintain production of the cheeses, kidding continues throughout most of the year, and the diet is carefully calculated, in order to produce milk of the highest quality and also without any additives or pesticides. The delightful fresh, mousselike tiny cheese is free of any rind. As well as the plain version, there are those with a coating of charcoal ash or fresh rosemary, or a topping of pink peppercorns.

THIS PAGE, TOP LEFT CHEESE Innes Button Pink Peppercorns, TOP RIGHT CHEESE Innes Bosworth Ash Log, MIDDLE LEFT CHEESE Innes Button Rosemary, BOTTOM LEFT CHEESE Innes Button French Salted Ash, BOTTOM RIGHT CHEESE Innes Bosworth Leaf

Appleby's Cheshire 🐄

WESTON-UNDER-REDCASTLE, SHROPSHIRE

It is hard not to be bowled over by Shropshire, a region of exceptional beauty, with its lush pastures, thick hedges, undulating hills, and great spreads of thickets and woodlands. The farm is on the edge of the river Dee and the Mersey basin, where the soil on top is sandy, before changing to clay lower down, then marl and sandstone, breaking down to form an underlying rock salt, which all help to explain the character of the cheese.

It is believed that Cheshire is Britain's oldest cheese, dating back to Roman times and mentioned in the Domesday Book. Records show that it was transported to all the major cities in Britain from around the mid-17th century, either by road or canal. It was also the cheese of choice for ships' rations during times of war in the 18th century. (Records from Admiral Nelson's ship HMS *Victory* mention Suffolk cheese, which was a very basic, hard acidic Cheddar-style cheese, as well as Cheshire.) The cheese is very similar to that of Cantal (see page 70) from the Auvergne, France, which may mean that, during the crusades of the 11th and 12th centuries, the recipe for Cheshire could well have traveled to France and Spain.

The Cheshire from the Appleby's farm is handmade, cloth-wrapped, and made with unpasteurized milk using vegetable rennet. The addition of annatto (a natural red food coloring, see Shropshire Blue, below) gives a beautiful salmon-pink color to the cheese. The texture is crumbly and surprisingly light, and the taste is mild and mellow when young, becoming more savory and herbal with maturing. It is also a surprising match for the lighter, sweet styles of single-malt Scotch.

Shropshire Blue 🐄 NOTTINGHAMSHIRE

AND LEICESTERSHIRE

The name of this cheese does not actually identify its provenance. Originating in Scotland in the 1970s, its production moved to Leicestershire, then Nottinghamshire via Cheshire, when the Scottish dairy closed. Its orange color is due to the addition of annatto, a natural coloring from the pulp surrounding the seeds of the South American achiote tree, and it was probably originally added to differentiate the cheese from Stilton. The cheese is very similar in style to Stilton, with a sharp, metallic edge coming from the blue veining. It is more mellow in flavor than Stilton, however, making it a good snacking cheese at any time of day, especially with a stick of crisp winter celery.

LEFT Appleby's Cheshire
OPPOSITE Shropshire Blue

Stilton & Stichelton

The mineral-rich soil in Nottinghamshire is said to encourage the bluing in Stilton, and the well-drained pastures encourage dense, creamy milk. These elements combine to produce the superb Stiltons of this region.

Colston Bassett Stilton  COLSTON BASSETT, NOTTINGHAMSHIRE

First served in local coaching inns for travelers, this famous cheese found its way to London in the 18th century, as recorded by Paxton & Whitfield, the famous cheese shop in Jermyn Street, which organized deliveries.

The land around Colston Bassett is devoted to grazing, and the soil is rich in minerals, which undoubtedly influences the flavor of the milk. The cheese is made using pasteurized cow's milk, with either traditional or vegetarian rennet. I prefer the traditional (animal) rennet because I believe that the slower method of maturing and ripening the cheese with this coagulant produces a more complex flavor and a richer texture.

The cheese made with traditional rennet is also treated a little differently than the vegetarian alternative. It is left undisturbed for longer, and piercing with thin stainless-steel needles begins at around 12 weeks, rather than the usual 5–7 weeks. Once the air enters the holes, the added *Penicillium roqueforti*, which has so far been dormant, starts to

ABOVE Grading Colston Bassett.

ABOVE Salting Colston Bassett.

grow, forming as it does the typical blue veins associated with Stilton. This method also influences the texture of the cheese, which ideally should be crumbly and richly buttery, rather than dense and claggy. The blue, with its forthright metallic minerality, is a good foil to the creaminess of the cheese.

Once the cheese has been pierced, the outside crust also starts to change as the calcium is released from within the cheese and starts to mingle with the molds found on the rind.

With careful brushing and controlling of the growth of the molds, the crust starts to develop and resemble a craggy rock face, and the aroma at this point is similar to that of a damp basement or cellar.

OPPOSITE Colston Bassett Stilton
BELOW Stichelton

Introducing the blue at a slightly later stage means that the cheese has already begun the maturing process before the veins start to thread their way through. This encourages development of a spicy tang to the rich flavor.

Weather patterns play a big part in how all blue cheeses develop, and for Stilton the perfect conditions are during early fall, when the grass is dry and sweet, and the air is warm during the day, cooling considerably in the evening. At this time of the year, the cows are content because they can stay outside all the time and do not have to shelter from the elements. That is why we always look forward to Christmas, when Stilton is one of the most sought-after traditional treats in Britain.

Stilton is often served with a glass of port, viewed as the perfect partner, but wines from southwest France and some Spanish reds, such as Priorat, with a bold structure, work very well, too.

Stichelton WELBECK ESTATE, NOTTINGHAMSHIRE

Joe Schneider, an American who ventured first to the Netherlands to make Greek cheese for a Turk, finally found his feet in Britain. With the help and friendship of cheese guru Randolph Hodgson, Joe and Randolph became partners and together created a raw milk regional blue cheese. Their recipe uses a tiny amount of starter at the heating stage, then a very small quantity of traditional rennet, meaning acidity is slow to progress and making the curd very fragile. Everything is done by hand, including the careful ladling of the curds, and the milling and salting take place the day after the milk is set. The cheese is not pressed, but is left to sit in hoops in a warm room to settle over the next five days, when it is removed. The outside of the cheese is smoothed by hand using simple kitchen knives, and a minimum of three months passes before piercing with a three-pronged fork implement takes place. Taste Stichelton alongside Stilton and note the difference—there is a definite richness to Stichelton, with a dense and creamy pâte, and the blue is spicier. The fragility of the various stages of making and maturing means that the flavor and texture can be markedly different, especially with seasonal variations, too, but it is really exciting to see the progress made with each batch.

Gorwydd Caerphilly 🐄 TREGARON, CEREDIGION

Todd Trethowan, whose family moved to Wales from Sussex, first got the cheesemaking bug when he worked on Dougal Campbell's farm (see Lincolnshire Poacher, page 31) during his vacations from university. After graduating, he decided to learn more about cheese and spent time with Chris Duckett in Somerset, whose recipe for Caerphilly he has utilized, including the type of starter. It is not so strange that Caerphilly is made in Somerset; the cheese was first made near the mining communities of South Wales, but due to its popularity over time it crossed over the Bristol Channel into Avon and Somerset. The generosity of cheesemakers!

As with other young cheesemakers, Randolph Hodgson of Neal's Yard Dairy was influential in giving Todd the encouragement he needed, and since the mid-1990s he has helped and advised in the development of the cheese.

Gorwydd Farm overlooks the Teifi Valley, where the afternoon sun warms its pastures. Pastures located in temperate climates are at their best from midmorning until midafternoon, when the soil's goodness, warmed by the sun, is sucked up by the blades of grass, making the grass sweetly fragrant and juicy. The farm is rather remote, and its grazing pastures have an underlying structure of lead, coal, and lime. Todd buys milk from neighboring farms, and every stage of the cheesemaking process is done by hand. The molds, which have been made for him by a local blacksmith, are a traditional cake-pan shape with a separate metal disk lid.

The Caerphilly takes about four hours to make. The fresh milk is first warmed, before the starter is added, then heated again to a slightly higher temperature. It is left to ripen for two hours and reheated for the rennet to be added. The curd is left to set for about 45 minutes, before being cut and scalded. It is then stirred for an additional 45 minutes, until it forms a smooth, elastic texture that indicates that the acidity level is correct and the curds are ready for draining. Unlike Cheddar, which is piled into blocks and milled, this cheese is pushed into a heap, cut into 2-inch (5-cm) cubes and then into 1-inch (2.5-cm) cubes. Salting follows, then the cheese is placed in cheesecloth-lined molds and pressed for 30 minutes, before another top-surface salting. The final stage is a 16-hour pressing and brining for 24 hours. The maturing time on the farm is around two months before being sold, although the cheese can be aged for longer.

The difference between a Duckett's Caerphilly and Todd's is the crust. The softer, velvety gray molds are allowed to grow on Gorwydd, rather like those on the French Sainte-Nectaire. These form in the cold, high-humidity maturing rooms, and the lime, lead, and coal minerality also plays a part in the way the rind turns. The cheese has that familiar crumbly texture, yet tastes fresh and creamy, with earthy mellow tones. A very versatile cheese, it can be used in baked dishes, crumbled over vegetables, or, better still, served as part of a cheeseboard, with crunchy spring radishes dipped in a little sea salt.

There is a bright acidity to the cheese that marries well with white wines, such as Chablis or Riesling. I often pair this cheese with crumbly goat cheeses, and also a Comté d'Estive (see page 84) and a Bavarian Blue with rich, deep flavors. What is so likable about Gorwydd is its versatility, allowing it to be placed on the cheeseboard with soft, washed, and hard cheeses. Whereas the modern versions of Caerphilly lean toward a Cheddar style, this old-fashioned softer crumble embraces its origins.

LEFT Gorwydd Caerphilly
OPPOSITE Lincolnshire Poacher

Lincolnshire Poacher ALFORD, LINCOLNSHIRE

The Fens are not an obvious location choice for cheesemaking because the land is mostly arable. Simon and Tim Jones' farm is situated at the southernmost part of the Lincolnshire Wolds, where the land has a little more character other than the usual flat vista found in the Fens. The chalky, limey soil is a definite plus for the flavor of the cheese; this is counteracted by the fact that rainfall is low in this part of England, signifying that the quality of the grass in summer is not great. Consequently, cheesemaking takes place between mid-fall and late spring, when the rainfall is greater, and the smaller quantities of summer milk are sold to the main local milk distributor.

The grazing pastures are not sprayed with nitrates, pesticides, or fertilizers (which leave a telltale taste of bitterness in the milk and consequently the cheese), and are carpeted with clover, which is a natural way of adding nitrogen into the soil and encouraging good grass growth and other nutrients in the soil, thereby benefiting the cattle. The Jones' overall organic approach and land management encourage wildlife and flora, which again contribute to the quality of the soil on their land, as well as to the environment.

The cheeses made in spring have a sweeter milk taste, and, if you compare the flavors of, say, the four- or five-month cheese with ones aged for 18 months or longer, you will taste how a cheese evolves from this sweet acidity to a long, lingering fruity flavor.

Simon Jones was taught cheesemaking by the late Dougal Campbell, whose famous Welsh cheese T'yn Grug is greatly missed. T'yn Grug was a cross between Cheddar and Swiss Gruyère, and this has influenced Simon's cheese. Poacher is made with unpasteurized cow's milk and traditional rennet, and while in appearance it looks like a Cheddar, when you cut into the cheese, the way it cracks and crumbles makes it different. This is due to the fact that the milk is heated with a fast-reacting culture, unlike a West Country Cheddar, which uses a slower starter. Furthermore, the curds are cut in the vat, and the flavor, while meaty, has a distinct savory–sweet acidity, acquired through the chalky minerals that infiltrate the grazing pastures. There is a richness, too, from the milk of the Holstein cows, which is the same milk used for the Auvergne Cantal cheeses. I always insist on cheeses aged for 18 months plus for their structure and depth of flavor—they partner beer perfectly.

Northern England & Scotland

The stone mining tradition in the rugged Dales landscape has had a distinct effect on the soil and in turn on the structure and flavor of the cheeses produced in this area. Weather patterns also play a big part: winters are bleak, and the sudden change when spring appears shows directly in the cheeses that follow on. Scotland's cheese styles have associations with Suffolk due to the migration of cheesemakers, and also with Ireland. The landscape and force of the weather determine the flavors and textures of the harder and blue cheeses. They have a bite and sting, and sometimes can appear aggressive on the tongue.

THIS PAGE,
LEFT CHEESE
Sliced Doddington,

RIGHT CHEESE
Richard III Wensleydale,

BOTTOM CHEESE Doddington

Richard III Wensleydale 🐄

BEDALE, NORTH YORKSHIRE

The Yorkshire Dales have a long history of cheesemaking. Suzanne Stirke, whose Wensleydale has a wonderful crumble and limestone mineral tang redolent of the local soil, was an academic lecturing in history before she tried her hand at cheesemaking. At first, she made the cheese with ewe's milk from her farm, but it proved almost impossible to get a sufficient amount of milk, so she turned to cow's milk from a neighboring farm.

Rather like a double-curd Lancashire, this is a semi-hard crumbly cheese with a nutty, creamy texture and taste, and a salty tang. Serve the delicious young cheese with a slice of fruit cake for a lovely afternoon treat.

To achieve the cheese's characteristic moist crumble, after heating and draining, the curds are block-piled to drain further, followed by milling, salting, and breaking up the curd by hand. The curds are then placed in molds and left for a day, before being turned and wrapped in cloth. They are left for another day before being turned again, brined, then closely wrapped in cheesecloth to inhibit molds from growing. I receive the cheese after three weeks because it is really delightful as a young cheese. If I want a more aged version, however, then Suzanne sets aside a cheese for us that has not been block-piled, but that is milled directly after draining, then brined for two days, to encourage the blooms on the rind. In this way, the cheese stays moist and crumbly. If you are wondering why the cheese is named Richard III, it is because Middleham Castle, the childhood home of the once king of England, is in the vicinity.

Doddington 🐄 WOOLER, NORTHUMBERLAND

The Maxwell family, with its herd of Friesian and Normande cows, have been making cheese on its farm for more than 12 years—first very hesitantly at the kitchen sink, before moving into production and changing the original recipe based on Leicester cheese to a Cheddar type. The result is Doddington, which definitely suits the Normande cows because their milk has a higher protein content than the Friesian; the proportion of fat in the Friesian milk helps to balance this out.

The semihard cheese made with unpasteurized milk and animal rennet follows a traditional recipe with a few tweaks, one being that the milk is scalded similar to that for a Leicester. Next, to "cheddar" it, the curds are cut and stacked, resulting in an acidity quite similar to a Montgomery's Cheddar (see page 20). The cheese has a dense yet crumbly texture, with a pleasing gentle aroma, while the taste is initially fresh and salty, then mellows to a rich, earthy fruitiness.

The salty, spicy tang is partly due to the farm's proximity to the coast—the briny sea air permeates the pastureland. It is often thought that the taste and texture are similar to a Dutch Gouda, but this may be due to the use of fresh whole milk from the morning milking. The sweetness of Doddington is apparent as it ages, rather like a mature Gouda, especially with cheese made from milk from spring, summer, and the last flush of grass growth in September. The cheese is covered in a beet-colored breathable wax brought in from the Netherlands, which also helps to prevent unwanted furry molds appearing on the rind during the long maturing process.

Kirkham's Lancashire 🐄

GOOSNARGH, NEAR PRESTON, LANCASHIRE

The Kirkham family has been farming for three generations, and the Goosnargh area—although close to the city of Preston, and with the highway only 2 miles (3 km) away from the farm—is in unspoiled green rolling countryside and is deeply entrenched in agriculture.

The meadows have an abundance of wildflowers and herbs, such as meadowsweet, which loves the damp conditions, and dandelion and clover, and they all assist the acidity levels in the milk. They also encourage the development of the cheese's flavor and texture because very little starter is added to the first heating. These plant aromas, as well as a light lemony tang, can be detected in the finished cheese, which is nothing like the industrially made versions. The main reason for this is that the traditionally made cheese uses a blend of six milkings (from two days' production), which gives a unique flavor and texture—crumbly and savory, without any aggressive sharpness or acidity. The young cheese would be delicious made into a thick savory cream, then spread onto the bottom of a pastry crust and topped with apples to make a pie; alternatively, the apples could be sprinkled with shaved shards of cheese set underneath a pastry lid. The more mature cheese is really delicious grilled on toast under the broiler until light golden and bubbling.

The cheesemaking process starts with heating of the morning and evening milk. When the curd has set, it is cut into cubes and left to stand, before being drained off into a cloth-lined drainer, where it is crumbled by hand three times over one and a half hours. The next day some of it is added to the previous day's curd, before proceeding to milling, salting, and molding, then pressing and wrapping in cheesecloth. Once the rind is dry, the cheese is lightly rubbed with melted butter, to seal it and prevent any unwanted molds from developing.

There is a rather poignant story about the Kirkhams' plan to increase the size of the dairy in 2008, due to demand for their cheese always exceeding supply. They spent a small fortune building a new, state-of-the-art dairy, which replaced the old stone dairy house they had used for years and years. They found that the cheese reacted badly to the new surroundings, however, and developed a bitter flavor and an unpleasant grainy texture.

Interestingly, what they had not realized was that the cheese made from a traditional family recipe would take time to become familiar with the new building. The flora and bacteria had not had time to develop in the air, and the temperature inside the cheeseroom was too cold and was killing what little cultures were present.

The new building needed time to "bed-in," and drastic action was taken to warm up the area and introduce new flora and bacteria. By the end of the year, things were more or less back to normal, and the cheese is again tasting as it should, with a buttery, grassy sweetness and a citrus freshness to the flavor. It just goes to show how important it is to understand the vagaries of nature and go with them, rather than against them.

Dunsyre Blue 🐄 CARNWATH, LANARKSHIRE

It is only since the 1960s that we have seen a real revival of Scottish cheeses, especially softer creamy styles that definitely have their own flavor profile quite unlike those south of the border in England. Humphrey Errington is one such cheesemaker who has adapted old recipes, and for the past 25 years he has worked tirelessly perfecting his methods. His 300-acre (120-ha) farm overlooks the Pentland Hills, with their austere, remote landscape, underlined in sandstone and with peat, heather, and abundant water, all of which give the soil and pastureland very particular qualities that are beneficial to dairy farming.

Humphrey is also noted for his work with EAT, the European Alliance for Artisan and Traditional Raw Milk Products, which offers help, advice, and support to producers and creators of raw milk products.

Milk from Ayrshire cows is used to make Dunsyre Blue, a cylinder-shape rich and creamy-textured cheese. The flavor is neither too aggressive nor overly salty. Made to a traditional recipe, the cheese was originally mentioned in *The Cook's and Housewife's Manual*, written by Meg Dods and published in 1826. It has a moist white rind, with blue-green spicy-flavored veins running through the cheese. During production, Dunsyre Blue is wrapped in foil and aged for 6–12 weeks. The cheese weighs about 6½ pounds (3 kg).

ABOVE Dunsyre Blue
OPPOSITE Kirkham's Lancashire

All of Humphrey's cheeses are made with raw milk and animal rennet. Alongside Dunsyre Blue, Humphrey also makes his famous ewe's milk cheese, Lanark Blue, which is Scotland's answer to Roquefort (albeit more forceful in taste), and a crumbly cow's milk cheese, Maisie's Kebbuck, named after Humphrey's mother-in-law, who does not eat blue cheese. This is an unpressed cheese in the style of traditional cheeses of Scotland. There is a sharp lactic edge reminiscent of a Wensleydale, and a "peaty" taste and aroma; Scotch whisky is an ideal drinking partner.

In addition to his cheeses, Humphrey also produces Fallachan (Gaelic for "lost treasure"), which is a rather interesting fermented alcoholic (13 percent) drink made from whey, a by-product of the cheesemaking process. Originally called "Blaand," the revived recipe is made following traditional methods and is aged for a year in oak casks. Fallachan's taste is not unlike a dry sherry, and it is actually rather good with his cheeses.

Caboc  TAIN, ROSS, AND CROMARTY

This is Scotland's oldest cheese, dating from the 15th century. Originating in the Scottish Highlands, the cream cheese was first made by Mariota de Ile, the daughter of the chieftain of the Clan MacDonald of the Isles. At 12 years of age, Mariota was in danger of being abducted by the Clan Campbell, who planned to marry her to one of their own and seize her lands. Mariota escaped to Ireland, reputedly taking refuge in a nunnery (in line with the clan's leanings toward Catholicism), where she learned how to make cheese. On her return, she married (within the family constraints) and passed the recipe to her daughter, who in turn passed it on to her daughter. The recipe is still secret and has been handed down from mother to daughter ever since; the current descendant of the clan and owner of the recipe is Susannah Stone.

Caboc has a deep, buttery color and a mild, sour flavor. During production, the cheese is formed into logs and rolled in toasted oats.

According to legend, the tradition of coating Caboc in oats started by accident. A cattle herder stored the day's cheese in a box that he had used to carry his oatcakes earlier in the day. When he opened the box to eat the cheese, he found that it had been covered in the crumbs from the oats. He liked it so much that, from then onward, Caboc has been made with an oat coating.

To make your own version, simply mash a whole soft cow's milk curd cheese or a triple cream Explorateur or a goat curd cheese with a little crème fraîche to lighten and soften the mixture, add crumbled coarse sea salt or kosher salt to heighten the flavor, then form into small balls, before coating in toasted fine oats.

Isle of Mull  TOBERMORY, ISLE OF MULL

Sgriob-ruadh Farm (Gaelic for "red furrow" and pronounced *ski-brooah*) is on the Isle of Mull on the west coast of Scotland. The farm's owners, the Reades, could not have found a more different way of farming from their origins in Somerset than this wind-, rain-, and sea-lashed landscape. The herd is mainly Friesians, with the odd Jersey and Ayrshire, and they have also recently introduced Brown Swiss cows, which creates an interesting cheese.

Many lessons had to be learned while building and restoring the farm, which had been abandoned for 16 years. During the rebuilding and renovation work, which they did themselves, they designed an innovative underground cheese room, the roof of which now looks like a grassy mound. It was incorporated to assist with controlling humidity levels and temperature because for half of the year the island receives more than its share of extreme weather.

The cows spend seven months in a shed due to the weather conditions on the island. This is no ordinary shed, however, but rather a warm retreat with a thick rubber carpet flooring, which is then strewn with shredded recycled paper (collected from all over the island), rather than the usual straw.

The farm grows hay to make into silage for winter feed, and in the spring the herd is able to graze outside until early fall. The Reades had originally

sold just their milk in Somerset, but Chris decided with the move that she wanted to make cheese. Before leaving she took lessons and made cheese with Cheddar makers. I often look for Somerset Cheddars made in the warmer months for the more complex flavors; however, the Mull winter cheeses, which are paler in color, have a better flavor because the controlled feeding of hay and mashed barley residue from the local whisky distillery allows the distinct spicy, herbal, almost alcoholic tastes to come into play. The summer cheeses can have really aggressive herbaceous spiky notes, and sometimes it is hard to actually eat the cheese as part of a mixed cheeseboard because the flavors are so dominant.

I have often paired these summer cheeses with Scotch whisky served with a splash of water because they really work well together. The cheese is made with unpasteurized milk using a traditional rennet.

Although the Reades' expertise in cheesemaking started with Cheddar in Somerset, they do not consider Mull to be a Cheddar. The paler cheese has a lighter crumble, with unique briny, tangy flavors, and the small amount of blue veining that sometimes runs through the edges of the rind into the cheese is a sign of its maturity and is something to be savored.

Ireland

Ireland has become a force to be reckoned with in the cheese world. There are links to Brittany and the west coast of France in the landscape and soil of the west and south coasts of Ireland, with the sandstone ridges and the high Carrantuohill in Co. Kerry, together with the Upper Lake in Killarney, helping with the movement of rain and drainage to fertilize the pastureland. There are granite and lime in the soil, with peat-covered uplands and rich clay. Combined with the Gulf Stream warming the west coast, they create a landscape that is bright green and luscious. The rockier coastline of the south and southwest encourage dairy farming, rather than arable farming, and there is a concentration of cheesemaking in the south, taking in washed-rind styles, as well as hard, soft, and creamy cheeses. The air is clean and clear, the rain soft, and the climate temperate. The peaty bogs give the whiskey a lighter flavor due to its three-phase distilling process (Scotch whisky has two phases), and these sweeter styles are really delicious and easy drinking with the cheeses, especially the washed-rind semisoft varieties and the majestic Desmond and Gabriel (see page 41).

THIS PAGE, LEFT CHEESE Ryefield, RIGHT CHEESE Cashel Blue, BOTTOM CHEESE St. Tola

Ryefield ☞ BAILIEBORO, CO. CAVAN

Ryefield is a rindless goat cheese made by the Fivemiletown Creamery Cooperative, owned and run by local dairy farmers. The co-op is situated in the rolling hills and lakes of Co. Cavan, and the cheesemaking facility is at the top of Stone Wall, which is 820 feet (250 m) above sea level and has spectacular views over almost half the county. Every day, fresh batches of cheese are made after pasteurizing the milk slowly, giving the cheese a light, frothy texture and a really gentle milky, nutty taste. Ryefield is a perfect introduction to cheese for children and can be used in salads, spooned on top of soups, and made into fillings for pasta and pancakes.

St. Tola ☞ INAGH, CO. CLARE

The weather in Ireland, especially in the south with its microclimate, gives the grass a vivid green quality that is unique. The clouds scud by at a rate of knots, and the rainfall is soft and silky, all contributing to the production of fine cheese.

Meg and Derrick Gordon were the original cheesemakers of St. Tola, and in 1999 their neighbor, Siobhan Ni Ghairbhith, took over the farm and eventually brought it to full registered organic standards. The farm is not far from the west coast, about 10 miles (16 km), and the soil is peat and sand, producing lush meadowland. Meg is the sole cheesemaker, using milk from her herd of Saanen white goats with a few brown Toggenburgs, and her tiny cheesemaking unit is a haven of pristine cleanliness and good housekeeping practices. The milk is organic and unpasteurized, and vegetarian rennet is used.

The best season for St. Tola is mid-spring to midwinter, although the early spring cheeses arrive in the shop without their bloomy rind, and we leave them for a few weeks in our cold room with high humidity, to allow the wrinkled white rind to develop.

The cheese is light, with a velvety texture that is fine and smooth. There is hardly a hint of goatiness in the taste, but there are subtle flavors of sweet peat and the sea. The goats love to roam and forage, and, even though there is all that lovely grass available, they prefer to chew on bracken, wild flora, and leaves from the bushes. This is a very elegant, fine goat cheese, to be enjoyed with dry white wines, as well as light reds.

Cashel Blue ☞ FETHARD, CO. TIPPERARY

Husband and wife team Louis and Jane Grubb have perfected their distinctive whole blue cheese by first heating the rich milk provided by their pedigree Friesian cows in a hundred-year-old copper vat. Once the milk is pasteurized then cooled, a starter with *Penicillium roqueforti* is added, before heating again. Rennet (traditional or vegetarian) is then included, and it is left to set for one hour. The curd is cut and left for another hour, before being removed from the vat in linen cloths and left to drain. The curds are then dropped straight into the molds and left for the next two days to drain further, with occasional turnings. As soon as the cheese is dry enough, salting and piercing take place.

At this point the cheese is creamy white, but after two weeks in a cold room molds begin to appear on the outer surface, showing that the blue is growing. The cheese is washed of this outer mold, dried, and wrapped in foil to inhibit additional mold growth. It is then placed in a very cold room for at least two to three months, although at four to five months it reaches its full potential.

Cashel Blue has a rich and creamy texture. The cheese is well marbled, with nutty blue molds that have a hint of sweet earthy saltiness. Maturing this cheese in the coolest part of the cellar with high humidity gives the texture an almost melting consistency and a very enjoyable and satisfying taste.

ABOVE Crozier Blue

ABOVE, LEFT CHEESE St. Gall, TOP CHEESE Desmond, RIGHT CHEESE Coolea, BOTTOM CHEESE Gabriel

Crozier Blue 🐑 FETHARD, CO. TIPPERARY

This is a relatively new cheese, produced seasonally (it is not available from midwinter through mid-spring) from the milk of a flock of Friesland sheep recently established on the limestone pasturelands. Throughout the milking season, the ewes are allowed to graze freely on the fertile grasslands of Tipperary, producing the distinctively flavored milk that gives Crozier a smooth, buttery texture, countered by the salty grittiness of the blue veins.

Henry and Louis Clifton Browne are nephews of Louis and Jane Grubb, makers of Cashel Blue, and the farm is actually next door. Cheesemaking is interlinked, with the Grubbs overseeing the production of the cheese, while the Clifton Brownes take care of the day-to-day running.

The story of Crozier Blue began in 1993, when Henry, using the milk from six sheep, began experimenting with blue cultures. Over the following five years, he played with the cheese recipe while also increasing the flock, including importing the high-yielding Friesland ewes from Britain. Making of the cheese has since been taken over by his aunt and uncle.

The pasteurized vegetarian cheese has a similar flavor and texture to Roquefort, but is maybe a little sharper and slightly drier. Crozier Blue is slow to mature and can be eaten young, when it is crumbly and tangy (around two months), although for a more strident flavor and a creamier texture it is best matured for at least four months in a refrigerated cold room.

St. Gall 🐄 FERMOY, CO. CORK

Gudrun and Frank Shinnick's cheesemaking skills are rooted in Switzerland. Named after the monastery of St. Gallen near Appenzell, this brine-washed unpasteurized cow's milk cheese has all the characteristics of a fine Swiss cheese in its salty, caramel, fruity sweetness, but with a rich, earthy creaminess redolent of the Irish countryside. The recipe includes traditional rennet and skim milk, which produces a firmer texture. The cheese is pressed in a traditional style.

Coolea 🐄 MACROOM, CO. CORK

Helene and Dick Willems, who originally hail from Limburg, in the Netherlands, started making cheese on their farm in the late 1970s. The herd is made up of Meuse Rhine Issel cows, well known in the Netherlands and Germany for being sturdy and long-living and for producing an abundance of milk; they were first introduced to Britain in the 1970s. The farm is situated a few miles along very winding roads off the main Killarney highway, and has a lovely aspect overlooking a valley. Helene and Dick, on retiring, handed over the cheesemaking reins to their son Dicky, who then brought on board his wife, Sinead, to help him run the business.

The cheesemaking process for Coolea uses unpasteurized milk with traditional rennet, and to speed up acidity the cut curds are washed twice, to remove some of the lactose. This creates a cheese with a sweeter and denser flavor. The curds are scalded twice during a two-hour period, continuously stirred by machine, then molded and pressed over six hours, followed by brining for around four days. As with all Gouda-type cheeses, the outer surface must be kept free of molds, and in order to do this, as well as to promote ripening (cheeses ripen from the outside in, by the way), the cheese is sprayed with a food-grade melted paraffin wax coating that dries into a hard, shiny skin.

The cheese is usually matured for a minimum of six months for the smaller wheels, and up to two years for larger cheeses—in fact, the longer the better.

Gabriel & Desmond SCHULL, CO. CORK

Bill Hogan and Sean Ferry have together created two amazing cheeses. In the old days, I used to have to call the post office at Schull and speak to the postmistress, who took our order for the cheeses. Nowadays, things are more structured, but the cheeses are still made to a traditional Swiss recipe (developed with Bill's mentors and Swiss cheese experts, Joseph Dubach and Josef Enz), in specially imported copper vats and other equipment. Made with unpasteurized summer cow's milk and traditional rennet, the cheeses are aged for more than a year.

The microclimate in the southwest corner of Ireland and the lush pastures give the cheeses their unique flavor. Gabriel is like a Sbrinz or Parmesan, with its hard, gritty texture and deeply savory, herbal flavor, while Desmond is also a dry, hard cheese, but is less gritty, with a hard, fudgy texture. It is more fruity than Gabriel, which has a slight acidic edge. Really, though, these cheeses are both truly magical and quite unlike anything else in Ireland.

I remember meeting Bill Hogan in London many years ago, a rather larger-than-life character whose past employment as a teenager in the 1960s was as an office assistant to Martin Luther King, Jr. He was demonstrating cooking with his cheeses by making a fondue. The fondue included quite a lot of dry white wine, but it was really exceptional, with a salty, spritzy tang coming through. I think Alsace wines work very well with these cheeses and also the rare Jura white wines, too.

Dilliskus & Kilcummin CASTLEGREGORY, CO. KERRY

Dilliskus and Kilcummin may not be the prettiest-looking cheeses, but they each pack a flavor punch. Cheesemaker Maja Binder's farm overlooks the Dingle peninsula, where the roaring Atlantic sea spray finds its way onto the pastures close by and gives the cheeses their wild and herbal flavors. Dilliskus has dillisk, or dulse, seaweed flecked through the curd, which is not for effect, but rather an extension of the traditional

use of seaweed in Irish cuisine. I am reliably informed that smoked dillisk is still eaten in pubs throughout Ireland instead of potato chips, and I have to say that I could think of nothing more delicious than a hand-pumped glass of Guinness from the tiny pub on Dingle Bay, accompanied by Dilliskus cheese and soda bread!

First thing in the morning, Maja collects the milk, still warm from the parlor, from a nearby farm, and by the end of the morning she has made her cheeses. She brings the milk up to 79°F (26°C), to allow the starter culture to get the milk into its curdled state, before adding the vegetable rennet. Within an hour or so, she cuts the set curds into small pieces, before stirring, reheating, then lifting the curds out of the copper vat with the help of a cheesecloth. She then drains the curds, before placing in molds to rest overnight. The next day, the cheeses are removed from their molds and brined in a saltwater solution for several hours, before going to the maturing room.

The cheese has a distinct fruitiness from the milk being heated in copper, and a wild complexity of style that is enhanced by the brushing and rubbing of the rinds with a brine mixture during the aging period. The crusts take on a lovely dark, pitted appearance and an aroma of the cellar mingled with earth and peat. The wrapping of the cheeses is just as carefully thought out as the making; the thick brown paper is folded around the cheeses, then tied with string. This allows the cheese to breathe and the crust not to get soggy and give off an ammoniacal aroma.

These cheeses are not delicate in taste or appearance, but they give you a true sense of place with the flavors, and one must admire cheesemaking of this caliber, which is not afraid to push the boundaries by bringing the land and the sea together in the cheesemaking process.

BELOW, LEFT CHEESE Dilliskus, RIGHT CHEESE Kilcummin

Cheeses of Co. Cork

Co. Cork is considered an epicurean center and produces a wealth of delicious cheeses. The area is dotted with restaurants, with the famous Ballymaloe hotel and cookery school at its heart.

TOP LEFT Fingal Ferguson of the Gubbeen Smokehouse. TOP MIDDLE Giana Ferguson of Gubbeen. TOP RIGHT Gubbeen washed-rind cheese.
BOTTOM LEFT Jeffa Gill at Durrus. BOTTOM MIDDLE Grazing cows at Durrus. BOTTOM RIGHT The Durrus Farm.

Ardrahan 🐄 KANTURK, CO. CORK

The original recipe for Ardrahan was developed by Eugene and Mary Burns, but the farm is now run by Mary with her son Gerald. They use milk from their pedigree Friesians, which make up the oldest registered herd in Ireland. As with other cheeses from this part of Ireland, something magical happens during the cheesemaking process to produce an end product with great taste and appearance.

Ardrahan, with its pinky beige washed rind, has a wealth of flavor and is crustier and more wrinkled than other washed-rind cheeses. The key is in the ripening process, but this can be tricky because the rind can become dry and bitter if allowed to go too far. In the southwest of Ireland, the atmospheric conditions are perfect for encouraging washed-rind flora or *B. linens* to grow. (This is a culture of yeast and bacteria mixed with water, then smeared onto the cheese either by brushing or by rubbing with a cloth, to form a reddish sticky rind that develops through the stimulation of the lactic acid in the cheese.) The milk is pasteurized and reheated with a vegetarian rennet. The curds are cut by hand, and some of the whey is skimmed off and replaced with water, before it is scalded.

The curds are then ready for the molds, and the last stage involves brining in sea salt and washing twice over the following three days. These are classic procedures that are also used in the making of Munster (see page 47) and Livarot (see page 52), but, being in southwest Ireland with all the flora and cultures alive in the air, progress is quick, and in no time Ardrahan turns into an earthy, tangy cheese, with the character of the region very evident.

Gubbeen 🐄 SCHULL, CO. CORK

Tom and Giana Ferguson's farm is very close to the sea and surrounded by the sort of luxuriant foliage seen in parts of Cornwall, or even the South of France. Members of the Ferguson family have been farmers for five generations, and Giana, who is part Hungarian and was brought up in Spain, has an interesting background in food, even having made fresh cheese curds as a child. Her cheesemaking technique is quite different than other producers in this region, and this results in a distinctive, complex-tasting cheese. The milk is from a mixed herd of Jersey, Friesian, Simmenthal, and the local rare black Kerry breeds. It is unpasteurized and uses a vegetarian rennet.

The difference between Gubbeen and other washed-rind cheeses is that the whey is diluted to slow down the growth of bacteria, rather than washing the curd, which would mean draining off some of the whey. The maturing process is also very carefully monitored, with humidity and temperature being closely observed, and frequent rind washing to prevent any unwanted molds from growing. The resulting cheese has a slightly firm texture pitted with crevices, rather like the French Bethmale, with a more wrinkled, crusty rind, and a rather darker beige-pink hue. The taste is definitely more intense and earthy, with herbal flora and grassy notes.

Durrus 🐄 COOMKEEN, DURRUS, CO. CORK

Jeffa Gill makes this washed-rind cheese along Swiss lines. She uses copper vats, rather than stainless-steel ones, and a "harp" (a forklike tool) with vertical blades to cut through the curd. Vegetarian rennet is then added to the unpasteurized milk from a neighboring farm. Although Jeffa washes the curd in the same way as for Ardrahan, she sprays on the *B. linens* cultures, rather than relying on airborne flora. This may explain why her cheese is a little more subtle and delicate than the more robust Ardrahan. The rind is smoother and the texture more supple and springy, with a taste that is mellow and fruity, with a hint of apple. Durrus is delightful when young, but with maturing it livens up to become rather strong. I think a red wine or a Trappist-style beer works well with this cheese.

France

The French, I believe, have a great respect for the identity and diversity of each of their regions, but all the regions share a common approach to food—that you should eat and drink well, and that what you consume should be local, seasonal, and traditional.

This is especially true when it comes to cheese, such as those made with goat's or ewe's milk, which will not be seen year-round when made by the small artisan cheesemakers, who would never dream of freezing or drying milk during periods of greater supply, to be used in the "dry" months. The enjoyment of cheese, particularly very fresh styles, is so much more satisfying at the perfect time of year, when the animals are grazing and foraging freely, rather than attempting to reproduce the flavors all through the year using stored or dried milk.

France is blessed with a wide range of climates and weather patterns, which greatly influences the types of cheeses produced throughout its regions. The north produces chewy, dense-textured cheeses laden with the milk from cattle grazed all year on lush meadowland. The eastern regions make cheeses ranging from washed creamy types to alpine hard cheeses, while goat cheeses

are prevalent in the west. As you travel southward down the Atlantic coast, you find hard crumbly cow's and ewe's milk cheeses, as well as blue varieties. In the warmer south, there is an array of small goat's and ewe's milk cheeses, and a few cutting cheeses, with flavors that vary from spicy and crumbly to creamy and herbal.

Alongside the climate, the landscape and the soil also influence the many hundreds of cheeses that are produced in France. Limestone is the underlying mineral throughout the country, and, whether on the lush northern pastureland, the rocky southwest, or the heavy clay of the central region, the soil is conducive to agriculture and, in particular, to milk production and winemaking in varying forms.

The hills, valleys, mountains, and climate variations account for hundreds and hundreds of cheese varieties throughout the country. This infinite variety of *terroir*—that magical combination of local terrain, altitude, soil, and climate—accounts for the great diversity of cheese found in France; some of these cheeses make their only way as far as a local market, while others are shipped all around the world. This is a major industry made possible by a deep-rooted belief in agriculture and a respect for the land and what it offers.

By traveling around France through the regions and tasting some of the cheeses, it is possible to gain a little understanding of the culture, the people, and the lay of the land. There are winding back roads leading to hilltop villages, and hidden hamlets to be found by following the rivers and streams rushing beside narrow paths. Market days are at the center of life, and the produce and cheeses—if one happens to be there on market day—will always be worth trying.

Some French cheeses are sold only locally, and many have their own distinctive characteristics; for instance, some are wrapped in leaves, while others are thickly coated in herbs, or washed in brine and alcohol. The names of many cheeses tie them to and can indicate the village or particular hill or mountain where they are made, and some of these delightful place names are linked to artistic and literary works.

We all look to France as a country with a great wealth of taste when it comes to food, and there are still plenty of tiny, special places to be found where people are working and living off the land in a time-honored way.

The following chapter gives you a taste of France, taking you through the regions and highlighting local cheeses. Enjoy this journey through a country steeped in rich culinary history and regional influences.

ABOVE **Sheep at Roquefort Carles.**

OPPOSITE, TOP LEFT **Cheeses maturing in southwest France.**

OPPOSITE, TOP RIGHT **Cows during transhumance in the Pyrénées.**

OPPOSITE, MIDDLE LEFT **Sheltering sheep, southern France.**

OPPOSITE, MIDDLE RIGHT **Vineyards in the Pyrénées.**

OPPOSITE, BOTTOM LEFT **Urns at Bonnaserre Farm, Pyrénées.**

OPPOSITE, BOTTOM RIGHT **A small cellar maturing room, western France.**

Northern France

A glance across a map of northern France reveals a vast and varied landscape of sweeping farmland, orchards, and a long expanse of coastline. For centuries, this northern region has produced an abundance of seafood, apples (this is Calvados and hard cider country), and most significantly, dairy products from the lushpastures that abound here. These days, the dairy industry, which is big in this part of France, is dominated by mass production, and the small farms that once made cheeses to sell at markets now supply big cooperatives with milk.

The regions of the north showcase a hardworking land, where a wide selection of rich, buttery cheeses are produced in great quantity, which can mean that style and flavor are sometimes sacrificed. This makes it increasingly important to protect the small independent farms and cheesemakers. Cheeses synonymous with this area include Camembert, Livarot, and Pont l'Évêque from Normandy (Basse); and Neufchâtel, Brillat-Savarin, Petit-Suisse, and fromage blanc from Normandy (Haute). Île de France, the region that surrounds Paris, is famous for its Brie de Meaux and Brie de Melun, as well as Fougeru and Coulommiers.

Farther east, the regions of Picardy and Flandres produce strong-scented, chewy-textured washed-rind cheeses much like those of their Belgian neighbors, while Mimolette (see page 50), from Lille, is the French version of a Dutch Gouda. The Artois region just below inland Flandres is known for its beer, and the cheeses made there have a peculiar affinity with that drink, probably because they are washed in the stuff! Cheeses produced in the Avesnois/Thiérache area beside the Ardennes forest pick up flavors and styles that are Alsace/German.

The center of this vast region is Paris—as well as being the capital of France, it is also a city with a great food culture. It is a fact that the importance and popularity of Camembert since its inception in the early 18th century was due in no short measure to Normandy's close proximity to the capital.

RIGHT Munster
OPPOSITE Rollot

Munster ALSACE

The Alsace region is French, but has Germanic leanings. Munster cheese from Alsace has a more strident taste than those from across the border, partly due to French skill at ripening, but also in order to distinguish their cheese from German ones. The flavors are nutty and the texture smooth, with summer cow's milk producing a more earthy flavor and the winter milk a more buttery one. The orange-yellow rind is pungent from brine washings, which are brushed over the cheese, rather than rubbed in. This gives the texture a little roughness, which can dry out if not cared for properly. If your cheese has become dry, rub over a little salty water (boiled and cooled water mixed with a pinch of sea or kosher salt) with your fingertips. Wrap in wax paper and store in the refrigerator. Munster is delightful with dry, fruity white wines or Pilsner-style beers.

Rollot PICARDY

This cheese, made from unpasteurized cow's milk, was originally produced in the 17th century by the monks of Maroilles Abbey, close to the river Somme. The cheese became famous when Louis XIV stopped in the village of Orvillers for refreshment, sampled it, and gave Rollot his seal of approval. By the 1970s, Rollot had all but disappeared due to the popularity of Maroilles (see page 48); however, with the influence of hugely respected and knowledgeable cheese expert Philippe Olivier, Didier and Sylvie Potel from Marchelepot decided to make Rollot. Its pungent soft-washed rind and earthy mushroom taste are fast gaining it the reputation and respect it richly deserves. Rollot is matured for about four weeks, and it develops quite a distinctive, salty flavor. Enjoy this delicious semisoft cheese with a glass of dry white wine.

Maroilles 🐄 THIÉRACHE

The difference between a mass-produced cheese and a farmhouse one lies in the flavor. The flavor of Maroilles does need time to develop; however, because it also has a high aroma, commercial producers favor a quicker ripening process, to get the cheese on the shelves before it becomes too "aromatic."

This cheese requires a long, slow ripening and repeated brine washing in cold, damp, airy caves. The cultures in the air of the maturing rooms are alive with good bacteria that help to give the cheese its unique taste. The thick, square cheeses acquire ridged sides from the wire racks on which they sit, and take on a high, pungent aroma (it is advisable not to take this cheese on public transport!), which usually indicates a strong cheese to most people. Yet Maroilles has a surprisingly mellow, nutty, earthy taste, with a chewy texture and no hint of bitterness.

Eating it on the young side is fine, but a fully aged cheese has a different taste, and the robust, full-bodied flavor requires either a beer or a red wine with fruit and tannins—a Beaune, Châteauneuf-du-Pape, or Côte Rôtie

LEFT Vieux Boulogne
ABOVE LEFT Maroilles
ABOVE RIGHT Boulette d'Avesnes
OPPOSITE Crayeux de Roncq

sits well alongside these flavors. Coteaux du Layon, a white dessert wine from the Loire, provides a sweet finish to the strong flavors.

Like many cheeses of the region, Maroilles was first made by monks—in this case, by the Benedictines, who had an abbey in the village of Maroilles from around the 12th century. Village life revolved around the abbey, and the community was encouraged to donate milk (and their own cheeses) to the monks for cheesemaking.

Vieux Boulogne 🐄 PAS-DE-CALAIS

This is a relatively new Boulonnais cow's milk cheese, created by the cheesemaker Antoine Bernard, with the help of Philippe Olivier, whose influence in reviving northern French cheeses is legendary. In early July 1982, at an informal dinner at the Château-Musée in the center of Boulogne town, Bernard and Philippe presented the cheese as part of the cheese course. The cheese was obviously well received because it was suggested the name be "Vieux Boulogne," in honor of its place of origin.

Production is limited to three producers at present, and this is purely to keep it within the Boulogne area, thereby ensuring its uniqueness. The cattle graze on pastures not far from the coast, so there is evidence of iodine and salty herbaceous notes in the milk. The bright orange rind is washed regularly in a local beer from Saint-Leonard, and ripened for seven to nine weeks. As the cheese matures, the flavors become more pronounced and earthy, and the rind has an almost wild mushroom aroma, which some find overly pungent. In reality, this rich and dense cheese is more buttery and mellow than powerful, and a white dessert wine from the Loire, such as Coteaux du Layon, with its honeyed sweetness, seems a perfect accompaniment to cheeses such as this.

Boulette d'Avesnes 🐄 THIÉRACHE

A soft conical-shape cow's milk cheese, Boulette d'Avesnes is coated in paprika, to give it a reddish gold color and distinctive flavor. It is molded by hand and made with the same curd as Maroilles (see opposite), then enriched with tarragon, parsley, crushed cloves, salt, and pepper to produce a strong, definitive taste. This cheese requires a good beer, or even gin, as an accompaniment.

The cheese is also made in the shape of a dolphin, which some say symbolizes the dauphin in the court of Louis XIV, although the marine mammal has strong biblical connections, too. There is a story that the monks of Maroilles Abbey were banished from their monastery and as they fled, taking what they could, some cheeses were dropped in the herb garden. When they returned, the cheeses were found nestled in among the herbs, and on tasting the cheeses the monks discovered that the herbs had imbued the cheeses with a herby, savory quality. They decided to dedicate the herb-infused cheeses to the dauphin, by making them in the shape of a dolphin.

Crayeux de Roncq 🐄 HAUT ARTOIS/FERRAIN WEPPES

This is a modern-style washed-rind cheese from a small family-run farm not far from Lille. Cheesemakers Thérèse-Marie and Michel Couvreur of Ferme du Vinage devised this cheese with the help of Philippe Olivier, a man who has made it his mission to revive cheesemaking in this part of France.

The marshy land in this area has many canals and tributaries, much like parts of Belgium and the Netherlands, and there are even windmills dotting the landscape of patchwork fields.

The brick-shape cheese is made with rich, buttery cow's milk, and could be very bland, but the *affinage*, or ripening process, gives this cheese its full flavor. The cheeses are matured for up to eight weeks in cold, damp, airy cellars, with frequent washing in a mixture of water, salt, and local beer. As the weeks progress, the rind turns orange, and the aroma becomes more fruity.

This cheese is delicious when partnered with Chimay, which is a strong beer with a fragrance of fresh yeast. It has a light, flowery touch that accompanies the full flavors of Crayeux de Roncq perfectly.

Crayeux is always a surprise because it sometimes arrives at La Fromagerie with its rind a supple, pale pink, with an earthy mushroom taste, and at other times the rind is dark, the texture drier, and the flavors deliciously big and powerful.

Mimolette of Flandres

The lush, green fields of Flandres produce this delicious cheese. Mimolette is a cheese with an interesting history, which has had an influence on the development of its flavor.

Mimolette FLANDRES

This French version of a classic Dutch cheese grew in popularity when General Charles de Gaulle mentioned that Mimolette was his favorite cheese, a fact that was subsequently quoted in the formal government publication *Journal Officiel* in 1966. Following this statement, both the French and the Dutch claimed that it was their version of the cheese to which he was referring.

It is an interesting cheese due to the fact that it has a kind of double life When young, its softer texture makes it a perfect breakfast cheese; however, the more aged or super-aged versions are often chosen by wine and cheese experts as a good match for fine wines because its waxy yet crisp texture lends itself to wines with age and dry tannins, and even to dry sherry. Tasting the matured cheese with a wine, giving a mouth-puckering dry edge and an austere taste, magically opens up the fruit flavors in the wine.

Mimolette emerged during the reign of Louis XIV, who wanted a French version of the Dutch cheese Edam (this was swiftly counteracted by the Dutch, who brought out their own version). To make Mimolette distinct from Edam, the French cheesemakers infused carrot juice in the cheese curds, turning it orange—probably a snub at the Dutch royal house of Orange—and latterly using annatto natural coloring derived from the soft pulp around the seed of the South American achiote tree. At the time, Dutch cheeses were very popular with French consumers, which irked the king and prompted a ban on their importation. Its original names were Boule de Nord or Boule de Lille, or Vieux Hollande, and these are sometimes still used in northern France, but Mimolette is the modern name. The name is a reconstruction of the word *mollet*, which means "soft" or "supple" in French; the cheese curd is soft when first formed into balls, and only after the maturing process does the crust develop and the cheese within become harder and harder.

Mimolette has certain characteristics that set it apart from the Dutch cheese. The size of the cheese is 8 inches (20 cm) in diameter. Also, unlike the Dutch version, which is essentially an orange Edam recipe not restricted to a particular region of the country, the French cheese is made to a traditional recipe in the Flandres and Weppes pockets of the region, with La Meuse being a particularly good area to find the cheeses. Look for the Maison Losfeld label—its Mimolette is very impressive.

The crust of this cheese is fascinating. Microscopic cheese mites are brushed onto the rind, to encourage the burrowing of tiny holes that allow the cheese to "breathe" and develop. As the cheese ages, its crust becomes pitted and dry. It needs constant attention, with brushing and tapping to get rid of as much of the ever-growing cheese dust as possible. Neglecting the crust means that it becomes very thick and dusty as the mites burrow farther into the cheese. Very aged cheese has the appearance of a cannonball, which is the nickname it has been given, and it is this very aged version that is most prized, not only for its flavor, but also for its ability to complement beer, wine, or even Madeira or Port. It is truly a refined-tasting cheese.

THIS PAGE Cows grazing in Flandres.
OPPOSITE Mimolette

LEFT Coeur de Neufchâtel
OPPOSITE, TOP LEFT Camembert Fermier Durand
OPPOSITE, TOP RIGHT Brillat-Savarin
OPPOSITE, BOTTOM LEFT Livarot
OPPOSITE, BOTTOM RIGHT Pont l'Évêque

Coeur de Neufchâtel 🐄 NORMANDY

Produced in the shape of a heart or tile, this cow's milk cheese has a rind with a downy, velvety bloom, while the interior is close-textured, with a soft crumble and a gentle salty tang. Made using a very old recipe, the curds are slowly drained, and a small amount of the previous day's curds are added to the following day's. Coeur de Neufchâtel is best eaten young because the fresh mushroom aroma and light nutty flavors can become sharp and aggressive if allowed to ripen for too long.

The gentle rolling countryside around Forges-les-Eaux is the best area to find this cheese. In the past, women were the cheesemakers, while men tended the herds. As a gesture of love and devotion, the women made the cheeses in a heart shape, especially when the men went to war; a cheese was carefully wrapped and placed in a departing soldier's breast pocket.

Camembert Fermier Durand 🐄 NORMANDY

This is a traditional cheese, handmade with unpasteurized cow's milk from the village of Camembert in the territory of Orme. The maker, François Durand, with his wife and son, is the last remaining independent producer of Camembert in the village of Camembert; the other farms that produce this cheese are now part of cooperatives or much bigger producers taking milk from numerous farms in the area. The cheese comes to us at La Fromagerie quite young, but after two weeks of maturing in our temperature- and humidity-controlled rooms it acquires a beautiful soft and pliable texture, with a surprisingly lighter and nuttier aroma.

Cider and Calvados producers abound in this area of France, and a glass of dry hard cider is lovely with this cheese, but a light red Gamay-style wine, or indeed a local blonde beer, is equally good. Camembert is sometimes soaked in Calvados and covered in crumbs, which makes a delicious finale to a meal (see page 231).

Brillat-Savarin 🐄 NORMANDY

This cow's milk cheese was named by Henri Androuët, a very famous *maître fromager*. Brillat-Savarin replaces a cheese called Magnum, which ceased to be made in the early 1970s by a small family producer Dubuc located near Forges-les-Eaux, a beautiful spot in the heart of Normandy. Brillat-Savarin is made in Normandy, as well as the Île de France, using a similar recipe to Magnum of whole milk with cream added and *Penicillium candidum*, which gives it a bloomy white rind and a flaky, buttery interior. This cheese is rich and silky eaten fresh, when there is a lactic earthiness to its taste. If allowed to mature, the texture becomes more dense and nuttier in flavor. It is particularly good with a vintage Champagne, but even a blonde beer works well with the creaminess of this cheese.

Livarot 🐄 NORMANDY

A semisoft cow's milk cheese, this has an orange washed rind that is gently ridged from the wire racks and bound with five strips of raffia. The raffia is more decorative than practical, but in the past the cheese was bound in this way to prevent it from breaking apart.

It has a springy texture, with scattered pinholes, a pungent aroma, and a spicy taste. The flavor is achieved by allowing the milk to "ripen" naturally in large "baths" for 24 hours before being heated, after which the rennet is added. Curds are large for easy drainage. Once they are in the mold, salting and brining process follows, before ripening for three to four weeks. Livarot comes from the Pays d'Auge area, and this pocket of Normandy also produces Calvados, which marries well with the cheese, although it is also particularly good with robust wine from Burgundy.

Pont l'Évêque 🐄 NORMANDY

Reputedly the oldest Norman cheese still being made, modern versions of Pont l'Évêque are often pale in comparison and tend to be somewhat bland. The supple-textured cow's milk cheese has a ridged crust, with a delicate bloom that is a pinky beige. It has a chewy texture that is very tender and an almost earthy aroma.

The best-tasting cheeses are those made by smaller dairies. Look for cheeses made by the Ferme du Bours because it uses only milk from its own herd. Production is kept small, and the cheese is totally handmade from start to finish, with the salting adjusted according to the time of year and the creaminess of the milk.

Pont l'Évêque remains a favorite due to the fact that it works well presented on a cheeseboard and matches both wine and beer, especially the lighter styles.

Abbaye de Trois Vaux 🐄 HAUT ARTOIS

This is a handmade unpasteurized cow's milk cheese created by the nuns at the abbey, who work alongside the Trappist monks at the neighboring monastery at Mont des Cats. The history books and tapestries show that cheesemaking was the main source of income for the monasteries, which may have been because the religious orders encouraged the farming community not only to grow crops, but also to make cheese from the milk, rather than simply sell it. The Trois Vaux cheese is one of the "boutique" cheeses to evolve from the ancient Mont des Cat recipe—which is a somewhat interesting way for a religious community to further its expertise in self-sufficiency. The dark red-brown rind is washed in local beer, and the tender, supple texture of the cheese is not overwhelming or bitter, although a definite "hoppy" flavor comes through. The taste is nutty and savory, and the cheese is delightful as a light meal or snack, served with fresh, crusty bread.

It is important that the cheeses do not hang around too long to mature because the revenue is vital. The monastery cheeses have a big, almost "meaty" taste because they are often washed in brine, liquor, cider, or beer, to give them a powerful taste, as well as causing them to mature at a faster pace. In addition to the cheeses being sold commercially, they are served at the abbey, where they are surely much appreciated because the usual meals in religious orders are very simple, and the cheese course is therefore the highlight of the meal. A wine may be lost against the flavors coming through from this cheese, and my preference would be for a full-bodied local beer.

Explorateur 🐄 ÎLE DE FRANCE

This cow's milk cheese is very rich and creamy, with a light, soft, fudgy texture and a bloomy, downy white rind. Explorateur was invented in the 1960s, to honor the explorer Bertrand Flornoy, who was mayor of the town of Coulommiers and a lover of good cheese. He

LEFT Abbaye de Trois Vaux
ABOVE Explorateur

also helped to create the annual Foire aux Fromages in La Capelle. This is a magnet for cheese lovers, and there is a competition for ladies with a prize of 30 bottles of Champagne for the one who eats the most fromage blanc!

Its earthy, gentle mushroom taste is enhanced by the addition of cream to the milk, which also increases the fat content to 75 percent. It is a good accompaniment to hard fruity-tasting cheeses, and it is also especially good partnered with a chilled glass of Champagne.

Fougeru 🐄 ÎLE DE FRANCE

Although it has the same shape as Coulommiers, the Fougeru is thicker, with a flaky texture and a rich flavor. It requires careful ripening because of the cheese's thickness and size; otherwise, the tender, bloomy rind can become too soft, with the cheese too runny around the edges closest to the rind, yet too solid at the center. The unpasteurized cow's milk Fougeru is better in flavor, less pronounced than a Camembert, and at its best with the edges only just melting and the soft texture almost to the center, which should be just flaky. This is the perfect way to enjoy the cheese. Topped with a frond of bracken, or *fougère* (where it gets its name), this is a good cheese to select as a party centerpiece.

Olivet 🐄 NORTH ORLEANNAIS

These small (half the size of a Camembert), soft, creamy cow's milk cheeses with a bloomy white rind, are either plain or have coatings of cinders, hay wisps, or black peppercorns. They are simple in taste and style, but, when served with a Beaujolais, they are a wonderful lunchtime snack, especially those with a gritty crunch of cinders before one reaches the cheese within.

Although made all through the year, it is the spring cheeses that are particularly noteworthy, when the fresh grass gives the flavors a lovely lightness, rather than the more dense and earthy ones found in Brie (see pages 56–57) or Coulommiers (see page 57) cheeses.

ABOVE Fougeru
RIGHT Olivet with hay wisps, peppercorns and cinders

Brie de Meaux  ÎLE DE FRANCE

Brie is a big wheel of dense curds made from cow's milk, and originally the preferred way was to eat it fresh, with only a hint of the bloomy rind appearing; as it became more known and admired, the cheesemakers further developed their skills. A little of the *Penicillium candidum* is mixed into the curds, before placing the cheese in its mold; after draining and salting, some more is brushed on top. It takes several weeks' maturing in varying degrees of cold in high-humidity cellars before the bloom starts to cover the outside of the cheese. These delicate molds need careful attention, and the humidity levels are adjusted in order to avoid those nasty black spots developing if the rind is too wet. The outside bloomy rind is a vital part of the cheese: if it is too wet, it imparts a bitter taste; if too

dry, it lends no pleasure to the flavor. Some people like to cut away the rind, but you are effectively taking away all the flavor profile, which is a pity, because cheese ripens from the outside to the center. If the rind is not in perfect condition, however, it should be removed.

If you cut through a Brie to create two wheels, you can see how the curds have been loosely cut to form fat chunks, which gradually meld with ripening. While Camembert curds are simply scooped out of the pan, ladled into molds, and drained, the Brie curd is drained, then cut, before being layered into the molds. By comparing the two, you see the difference in the style of the pâte, which also tells in the taste of the two cheeses, too. Camembert has a distinct earthy mushroom flavor with a somewhat mellow cream texture, while Brie has a sharper, almost fruity tang from the fermentation process of the milk (as well as the final draining on the straw/reed mats, before going to the maturing room), which is often mistaken for ammonia on the nose. There is a difference: The light, fermented, acidic aroma will not make your eyes water like a full-blown ammonia hit.

Brie de Melun   🐄 ÎLE DE FRANCE

Brie de Melun, alongside Brie de Meaux, obtained Appellation d'Origine Contrôlée (AOC) status in August 1980, and this controls how and where the cheese is made. The strict rules mean that the more esoteric cheesemakers in the region have disappeared because they cannot call their cheese "Brie," unless it is made exactly to the guidelines. This is a little sad, since cheesemakers like to imprint their own quirks and style when making cheese.

The Brie de Melun can often be too salty because of the AOC recipe. At certain times of year, especially at the transition from winter to spring feed, the milk can create problems for cheesemakers, and the salting has to be controlled. If it is not controlled properly, then the result is a Melun with a very soft texture and salty flavor. You have essentially two problems: one being the bloomy rind and the other the curd. The rind should not dry out too quickly, but the cheese, being a shallow disk of soft curds, will ripen or even dry to a solid mass. I have found that winter cheeses are often more successful than spring cheeses because the feed has more hay and legumes in it. Spring feed has very fresh grass, which produces milk of varying quality and cheese that is difficult to ripen. It is somewhat easier to control with the 6½-pound (3-kg) Meaux, but trying to get that soft velvety texture inside and out in a 3⅓-pound (1.5-kg) Melun is often a problem.

BELOW LEFT Brie de Melun
BELOW RIGHT Coulommiers
OPPOSITE Brie de Meux

I always prefer to eat this cheese slightly immature, with the "heart" of the cheese still flaky, unless I test the cheese first by "ironing." I can determine how far to take the ripening process by inserting an elongated metal instrument into the cheese, to release a small cylindrical section for tasting, before replugging into the cheese. The flavors of Melun are more nutty and assertive than the Meaux, and are especially good with a Beaujolais wine.

Coulommiers   🐄 ÎLE DE FRANCE

There is no comparison between a *fermier* Coulommiers handmade with unpasteurized cow's milk and those made by cooperatives and large-scale producers. The soft, bloomy rind should cling to the fat, juicy interior, where the flavor is rich and buttery, yet not quite as fruity as a Meaux or Melun (see opposite and left). It is a great size for a party because it presents well on a cheeseboard with six or seven other cheeses; for a dinner party of eight to ten people, it could be the single cheese served with thin slices of walnut bread.

A bloomy rind cheese does need a little attention because, if it becomes too dry and cracked around the edges, the inside will not be pleasant. Conversely, if the rind is wet with patchy black or brown molds, this will impact on the cheese. Always check the rind or crust (*croûte*), to make sure that it is velvety and the aroma is pleasantly earthy and mushroomy. A slightly acidic ammoniacal aroma is not bad because it means that the cheese is at the height of its ripening; however, if it is too strong, the cheese is past its best.

When you get the cheese home, do not be tempted to wrap it in plastic wrap; cover it in a double layer of wax paper, then newspaper, and put into the bottom of the refrigerator or in the salad crisper. Newspaper is a good way of incubating the cheese, and it will retain moisture and help to keep the cheese in good condition.

THIS PAGE, LEFT CHEESE Chaource, RIGHT CHEESE Charolais

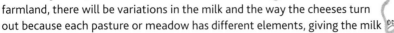

The tributaries, canals, and waterways are an interesting way of journeying through this central area of France, and they are still very much a part of life, whether for transporting livestock, grain, or produce. This is a useful and less stressful way of working with animals, and interesting, too, from a cheesemaking point of view. When cattle are moved from one field to another by canal, and even within the same farmland, there will be variations in the milk and the way the cheeses turn out because each pasture or meadow has different elements, giving the milk its contrasting character.

We are zigzagging across this terrain following the rivers as one did in the past because the river system holds the key to how the regions survived and developed, and also to how the cheeses evolved. In the Burgundy and Berry regions in the heart of France, the soft, creamy-textured cheeses were made to be consumed quickly and sold within weeks or even days. In Orleannais, for instance, the coatings of ash, hay, or leaves were used to protect the delicate creaminess of the cheeses. The region's cheesemakers looked to Camembert as a guide because that was such a popular cheese, and they developed their own Orleannais versions.

Once you enter regions such as Franche-Comté and Savoie/Dauphiné, however, you see the importance of the large wheels of hard cheeses so necessary to feed the people throughout the long, harsh winters. Cheese was both food and currency in the past, and even now the aged cheeses are savored not only for their taste, but also for the good return they provide for hardworking cheesemakers.

France's rich and checkered history is written in the influences found in French cheeses of other countries' cheesemaking styles. There are Swiss and Northern Italian styles in Savoie and Franche-Comté, for instance, and Southern Italian and Spanish styles in the Pyrénées.

Chaource 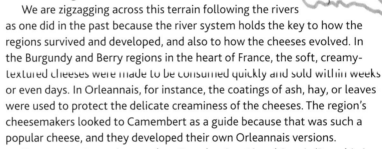 CHAMPAGNE

This drum-shape solid cow's milk cheese with a flaky texture and a white bloomy rind is produced very close to the border of Burgundy. Chaource has a bitter nutshell-like flavor, with an earthiness reminiscent of the style of the wine here, and you would think that it would be a perfect match for the cheese. You should be careful to find the perfect flavor partner, however, because the cheese is also on the salty side. The solid shape often means that the cheese does not ripen all the way through, and trying to push this can make the rind bitter, causing the center, which is still intact, to become overpowered by these flavors. This is no fault of the cheese because the milk is allowed to ripen at the first stages at its own pace, before the rennet is added to separate the curds. When you do have the chance to taste the real thing with a glass of dry, crisp Champagne, it is a wonderful marriage.

Charolais BURGUNDY

This goat's milk cheese is a chubby drum-shape cylinder, with a close-textured, crumbly pâte. The rind is natural and slightly dry in texture, with patchy gray, blue, and white molds, and the taste is rich and sophisticated, with a fine, clean mineral nuttiness. There is a slight taste of salt, as well as a mildness that develops on the palate. Charolais is unlike goat cheeses of the west coast, with their salty, herbal freshness; the beauty of this cheese is that the more ripened and dry, crumbly textures are perfect with fine full-bodied white wines and some of the region's red wines, such as Santenay, as well as a vintage Champagne. The designated zone for making these cheeses is not littered with cheesemakers, but several sell from their farms. One farm called Earl de Guillaumin in Neury-Granchamp, run by Sylvie and Gilles Aurousseau, concentrates on just the Charolais and maybe one other small cheese.

Fromagerie Gaugry

The Gaugry family has been in the cheesemaking business since 1946. Its raw cow's milk cheeses are produced using a fusion of traditional and modern techniques.

Époisses 🐄 BURGUNDY

Fromagerie Gaugry is one of two certified larger producers of Époisses and Ami du Chambertin, and they also make their own version of Soumaintrain and a Petit Creux with a craterlike top in the Langres style. These washed-rind cheeses from the heart of Burgundy are as much a part of the region as the beef breed Charolais, Dijon mustard, and the fine wines. This is a soft, tender cow's milk cheese with a brine-and-Marc-washed rind that turns deep apricot, with a wrinkled finish.

There are two schools of thought as to how to enjoy this cheese: either ripened all the way through until it is almost running away; or almost melting with the center of the cheese still intact. Smaller than a Camembert (see page 52), but not as stout as an Ami du Chambertin cheese (see opposite), this cheese is easier to ripen, and the almost

Soumaintrain 🐄 BURGUNDY

A pattern emerges with cheeses from this region—they tend to be rich and buttery, with a little mineral acidity coming through in the flavor. They are also perfect for the fine wines of the region, and a close partnership such as this makes the learning process of food matching not only enjoyable, but also enduring. Consider why you like that cheese with that wine, and why it did not work with another one.

This cow's milk cheese is the same size as an Époisses, but the natural bloom on Soumaintrain has patches of annatto, or *rocóu* (an orange vegetable extract from the South American achiote tree). This natural extract is used in other cheeses, to add color both inside and outside, and its flavor is slightly peppery, with a sweet warmth. Once it has been sprayed on the outside of the cheese, a soft bloom forms, giving the cheese a pretty color, and the flavor within is rich, mellow, and fruity, almost like a clotted crème fraîche.

Ami du Chambertin 🐄 BURGUNDY

Wtih a distinctive glistening, wrinkled orange rind, and more stout in appearance than Époisses, this cow's milk cheese has almost melting edges through to a fudgy center. The cheese was perfected by Raymond Gaugry in 1950 because a more crumbly textured cheese in the Époisses style was deemed to be better for tasting the fine, rare wines of Burgundy. The aroma is pungent due to the Marc de Bourgogne liquor wash on the outside, but inside the cheese is buttery and rich, with a little saltiness to sharpen the senses. Fine red wines are the obvious choice of accompaniment. The orange color is the result of a reaction that occurs when the Marc liquor meets the milk enzyme in the high humidity of a cold cellar.

Langres 🐄 CHAMPAGNE

A small drum-shape fudgy-textured cheese, purchased from Fromagerie Gaugry, Langres has a soft, bright orange natural rind that needs to be kept cool, but not so cold that it hardens. The texture of this cow's milk cheese is crumbly, and its taste is rich, with a spiciness that is more earthy resin than hot. There is a craterlike depression in the top of the cheese, which can be filled with a Marc or dry white wine, which soaks slowly into the cheese. An excellent match for Langres is the specialty of the region—Champagne. The younger cheeses beautifully partner a rosé Champagne, while the more ripened versions complement the dry style.

juicy, rich flavors are a rare treat. The brine-and-liquor washing on the rind imparts the characteristic pungent aroma of this cheese. The milk is hand-ladled and drained like Camembert and the ripening period in the cellar is four weeks before selling.

If you are traveling with this cheese, or want to prevent the aroma from escaping, the trick is to wrap it first in wax paper, before then wrapping in a thick layer of newspaper. This way the cheese aromas are contained within the "pulpy" paper.

Époisses is a perfect cheese on a board of mixed flavors and styles, and is especially good with a dry red wine such as Savigny le Beaune.

Given the delicate balance between transforming the milk to cheese, and the numerous washings to produce the shiny, moist rind, a lot can happen to the milk's bacterial growth. In the past, there were problems with rinds being almost "alive" with bacteria, which led to the cheese nearly being banned completely. There is now a very strong association, however, to which the Gaugry family belongs, and the rigorous checking and monitoring at every stage of production ensure that all the cheeses are in perfect condition before sale.

ABOVE LEFT Pouligny-Sainte-Pierre **ABOVE RIGHT** Valençay

LEFT CHEESE Sainte-Maure
RIGHT CHEESE Selles sur Cher

Pouligny-Saint-Pierre 🐐 BERRY

The area's proximity to the Poitou border, with its scrubby heathland and flinty minerality in the water, gives the flavor of this cheese a true goaty identity that is enhanced with ripening (the famous Sancerre white wine also comes from this region). A tall, tapered pyramid with a small squared-off top (think of the Eiffel Tower), this cheese has a natural rind that becomes more blue with aging. Its texture is close and crumbly, and a little dry, with a herbal nuttiness to the flavor. Pouligny-Saint-Pierre is perfect served with dry white wines.

Valençay 🐐 BERRY/INDRE

A pyramid with a flat, square top, this cheese is supposedly made this way because an angry Napoleon sliced the top off the cheese in a fit of fury. Valençay follows the flavor profile of the region, with its nutty, slightly earthy, and acidic taste. The natural rind is dusted with charcoal, and white bloom appears as the cheese dries and matures. The texture is slight and fudgy when young, and becomes closer and denser with ripening. Although Valençay is available all through the year, the spring through to the summer cheeses showcase the flavors best. The white and rosé wines of the region are the perfect accompaniments for this delicious cheese.

Selles sur Cher 🐐 LOIRE/CHER

A perfect shape for a cheeseboard, this small cylinder of 3¼ inches (8 cm) is coated in charcoal, with scatterings of bloomy white molds. The cheese within is bright white, with a fine, crumbly texture, and the taste is fresh and lemony. All goat cheeses from this region seem to link to each other; some, such as Sainte-Maure (see below), have more earthy notes, while others have a salty, nutty flavor. The wines of the regions have a true affinity with the cheeses, however, and show just how well *terroir* can work in providing harmony.

Sainte-Maure 🐐 TOURAINE

This famous log-shape cheese is from a region known for its white wines, and is right next door to Anjou, which is renowned for its rosé. The soil is rich in minerals, with slate and stone containing chalk, sand, and lime, which contribute to the goat's diet. A straw is placed through the center of the cheese, to aid handling in the first stages, when the log is at its most delicate and soft. To avoid too many molds appearing, charcoal ash is dusted on, and as the cheeses dry out patchy white molds appear. It is important not to let these get too thick because they can detach themselves from the inner cheese; gentle patting down of the outside molds achieves a thin rind closely adhering to the cheese. The handmade versions are not as salty as the more industrial cheeses, where the charcoal is mixed with salt. The flavors are nutty and rich, and perfect for dry white Sauvignon wines.

Crottin de Chavignol 🐐 SANCERRE

This is a small, flattened ball of crumbly-textured goat cheese, with a rich, smooth taste. The region has Berry as its neighbor, and provides a nice link for the west of Burgundy to the center of France—and the white wines of the Loire, with their flinty, chalky, stony flavors, have a true affinity with goat cheeses. The landscape of the region is irresistibly romantic, dotted with fairy-tale chateaux as ornate as wedding cakes. Looking at a matured crottin, however, whose appearance is more like goat droppings, suggests something less romantic, save for the lovely nutty flavors once tasted. Crumbly with a tart lemon acidity and nutty edge, this very versatile cheese is often broiled and used for a salad.

THIS PAGE, LEFT TO RIGHT Fresh Crottin de Chavignol, medium matured, matured

Poitou-Charentes

The Vendée waterways thread through this region and became famous for goat cheese through the Saracen invasion of southwest and western France. In the Middle Ages, armies came equipped with everything from soldiers to cattle and livestock, to literally take over countries and implant themselves lock, stock, and barrel. When the Saracen army was in retreat, everything was simply behind as the soldiers fled, and the result was that the Saracens' goats found a new home and thrived on the well-watered herbal pastures of Poitou-Charentes. There are many shapes and styles of cheese in this region, taking names from the villages or even the shape of the castle turrets; with the ideal temperate weather patterns, the goats can keep producing delicious fresh-tasting milk for cheese throughout the year.

Fleur de Chèvre 🐐 POITOU

The producers make the most of their cheeses by giving us different shapes and textures to enjoy the flavors. This soft drum-shape cheese, with its tender natural rind, is wrapped in a chestnut leaf, to ease the handling process. It is salted with the delicate, fine grains of *fleur de sel* from the famous saltpans on the Île de Re, giving the taste a gentleness quite unlike the usual goat cheeses.

Cendré de Niort 🐐 POITOU

A small, round ash-coated rind with a contrasting white goat's cheese within, it is flaky-textured, tasting fresh and herby, with a hint of salt.

Mothais 🐐 POITOU

A thick disk with a wrinkled natural rind and a chestnut leaf to help with handling. The flavors of this cheese are nutty and earthy, and with ripening become denser as the blue and white molds grow on the outside. The more mature cheeses are good with red wines.

Bonde de Gâtine 🐐 POITOU

This goat cheese takes the shape of a small, chubby drum coated in charcoal. The natural rind with scatterings of white mold and charcoal is a classic feature of cheeses in this region. This cheese, with its close, crumbly texture, but surprisingly smooth, dense bite, has a light, fruity tang and a depth of mineral richness to accompany fine wines.

Chabichou 🐐 POITOU

This natural-rinded semisoft yet close-textured cheese has a gently tapered cylinder shape. Chabichou is possibly the most well known of the goat cheeses, due to its fresh taste and lovely aromatic rind. When the cheese is allowed to ripen under proper conditions, the earthy sweetness goes all the way to its heart—the crumbly texture becomes denser as it is allowed to dry out.

ABOVE Goats in Poitou. ABOVE RIGHT A Charentes village.

TOP LEFT Fleur de Chèvre
TOP MIDDLE Cendré de Niort
TOP RIGHT Mothais
BOTTOM LEFT Bonde de Gâtine
BOTTOM RIGHT Chabichou

Persillé du Marais ⚐ VENDÉE AND POITOU

The Marais canals meander through the region to the Atlantic coast, and parts are extremely picturesque. You can see cows being transported on barges from one meadow to another. Goats, more temperamental and adventurous than sheep or cows, have to be fenced in, otherwise they fall into the water as they forage for food by the riverbank. This cheese is an intensely tasting blue cheese, with that bittersweet accent often found in very dark chocolate. A perfect complement to the sharp white wines of the region, but also the sweeter versions, too.

INSET ABOVE Persillé du Marais
THIS PAGE, BELOW Tomme de Cléon

Tomme de Cléon ⚐ PAYS NANTAIS, PAYS DE LA LOIRE

This is a semihard cheese, and its smooth, hard rind is washed in Muscadet wine, to give an aromatic, floral perfume to the cheese, as well as permeating the pâte. The smooth, white-textured pâte tastes full and fruity, and is perfect as a dessert cheese, especially after seafood.

AUVERGNE

The Massif plateau stretches across this region, with minerals of iron, bronze, silver, and gold beneath the surface—the dairy farming enjoys an excellent reputation here, as does the famous beef produced in the region. Burgundy has Charolais beef, and Auvergne has Salers. The cheeses are grand, majestic, and full of flavor—from the Cantal Laguiole to the garlic- and pepper-infused soft Gaperon. This region has a true identity and, with the Bordeaux and southwest wines, you have huge flavors that are meaty and robust.

ABOVE Grazing pastures in the Auvergne.

Sainte-Nectaire  AUVERGNE

This cheese has a coat of many colors. On first sight, it looks like a flattened boulder covered with molds of gray, brown, patches of white, and even a little blue or green shadow. The touch is soft and velvety. The aroma is like a damp cellar, with earthy farmyard underfoot, and within is a rich, dense texture and a nutty, mineral taste. It is curious, but also delicious, especially in spring and fall, which are the best seasons to eat this cheese. Always look for a farmhouse version of this cheese, which you can identify by rubbing the crust to reveal an oval dark-green plaque providing the taste sensation; the commercially produced industrial versions will be more bland.

Gaperon á l'ail AUVERGNE

If you place this cow's milk cheese in the palm of your hand, cup your fingers around the cheese, and very gently squeeze, the texture should be supple, tender, and not solid. That is how a farmhouse handmade cheese should be. The cheese is made with low-fat milk, with the addition of smoky garlic and pepper. The bloomy white molds should be patted down gently and not allowed to get too thick; they may otherwise peel away from the main body of the cheese and allow off-putting flavors to develop in air pockets. A younger cheese has a "Boursin" style, while the ripened versions are closer-textured and fruitier.

Tomme Fraîche AUVERGNE/AUBRAC

This cheese can usually be found in 10½-ounce (300-g) vacuum-packed blocks, or cut from 2¼-pound (1-kg) slabs. It is made with the freshly washed and pressed curds that make Cantal Laguiole (see page 70). With its supple, almost rubbery texture, no rind, and a light flavor, it is the vital ingredient for the regional recipes of truffade (sautéed potatoes and lardons with cheese, see page 278) and aligot (a "stretched" mashed potato, see page 284).

BELOW, LEFT CHEESE Sainte-Nectaire, MIDDLE CHEESE Gaperon á l'ail, RIGHT CHEESE Tomme fraîche

ABOVE, LEFT CHEESE Fourme d'Ambert, TOP RIGHT CHEESE Bleu d'Auvergne, BOTTOM RIGHT CHEESE Bleu des Causses

Fourme d'Ambert 🐄 AUVERGNE

This cheese is capsule-shaped and often referred to as the "connoisseur's" blue cheese because the flavors work well with other cheeses, and it is not an aggressive-tasting blue.

The crust is a thin, dry rind patched gray/white; if it does get a little wet, the flavors will become sharper. The overall texture is rich and buttery, with a subtle, mellow, nutty flavor. It is a great addition to a cheeseboard and a lovely accompaniment for fine dry red wines.

Bleu d'Auvergne 🐄 AUVERGNE

This creamy, rich blue cheese takes its style from Roquefort, but the heavier texture from the cow's milk gives it a more fatty element, which is great for cooking. It is often seen as a good addition to the cheeseboard because there is strength, but not bitterness. If partnered with the Cheddar-style hard cheeses, or even the Gruyère styles, it does not overpower, but rather adds a minerality, to cut through the heavier weightiness of the cheeses.

Bleu des Causses 🐄 AVEYRON/AUVERGNE

The defined area for production of this cheese is covered by Aveyron and some of Lozère, south of Lot. Look for the label Peyrelade from the village of the same name, which nestles in a valley surrounded by the limestone cliffs of the Gorge du Tarn. The cheese is ripened in humid caves, where *fleurines*, natural currents of air, filter into the atmosphere through the minerals via cracks in the limestone. This process further contributes to the flavors of the cheese. The milk from Laguiole cows is heated, then rennet is added. The curds are cut into large cubes, and stirred before draining, and the *Penicillium roqueforti* added. The curds are then placed in molds and stacked in the draining room for three to four days, with several turnings, before being rubbed with dry salt and left for another three days. Before entering the caves, the cheeses are scrubbed of their thick salt coating and pierced. to encourage the oxygen to thread the blue veins through the cheese. The ripening process takes place in the caves on oak shelves, with regular turnings, for three to six months. Prior to sale, cheeses weighing 5½–6½ pounds (2.5–3 kg) are wrapped in foil and marked with the AOC standard.

If you are presented with a cut cheese, look for an ivory-colored pâte (although more white in winter), with well-distributed blue molds somewhat like those of Roquefort. The texture is soft and almost melting on the palate, with flavors that are rich but not assertive, creamy, and without too much saltiness, which is often the case with some Roquefort. Cheeses from this part of France are beautifully structured and work well on a cheeseboard.

THE DAUPHINÉ & CÉVENNES

The Dauphiné, of which the Rhône-Alpes and Drôme are part, is the southern area of this large region. Here, the wines are spicier, and their dry heat complements the cheeses—mostly goat, with some soft cow's milk. In the markets, you will also see some ewe's milk and blue cheeses. The famous little Picodon of the region can be eaten fresh, or left to dry out to taste very gamy. They are available all through the year, but it is with the early summer cheeses, when the goats forage on scented leaves, bushy herbs, and flora, that you get a real sense of this part of France. Try to get to the annual Fête du Picodon held in late July at Saou, between Crest and Bordeaux, to taste cheeses from all the local farms, as well as to sample the deliciously strong and fruity local wines, such as Tricastin.

Saint Marcellin and Saint Félicien
DAUPHINÉ/ISÈRE

Nowadays, it is very rare to find the goat cheese versions of these cheeses, and more's the pity, since they are little mouthfuls of pure luxury. But goat's milk in this part of France is very seasonal and, in order to make a living, cheesemakers are producing the cheeses with cow's milk. If you get one that is properly ripened and almost melting as you break through the rind, however, its richness will reward you, especially with a lovely Côtes du Rhône wine. It is important with both of these cheeses to allow the molds to grow—they form a little protective barrier around the cheese—because airborne bacteria can infiltrate these tender cheeses. The flavor of Saint Marcellin is rich, with a little nuttiness, and the larger Saint Félicien has a slight blackcurrant earthiness to the flavors. When soft and yielding they are delicious, but at certain times of the year, when weather conditions alter the flavor of the milk, they are sometimes harder to ripen and they are firmer.

Picodon DRÔME

The name "Picodon" is derived from *occitan*, meaning "small bite." The Drôme region suffered a severe decline in farming over the years; however, the dairy cooperative has encouraged small producers to work again, and today there is a good supply of these delightful cheeses. The subtle, nutty flavors become more intense with further ripening, and you can enjoy the cheeses with the natural white bloom, or at the more robust stage, called *dieulefit*. With further washing and refining in high humidity, the rind turns a more golden beige, and the texture is drier and fruiter, partnering the southern Rhône wines perfectly. The best season to enjoy these cheeses is high summer.

Pelardon CÉVENNES

This small, thick medallion-shape soft cheese with a scraped (slightly rough) natural white crust is much better after a little maturing, when its rind is dotted with blue molds. Pelardon is a traditional farmhouse cheese, with a gentle goaty, nutty taste and a fudgy texture in the center. The best season to enjoy this cheese is late summer, with really rich and buttery cheeses appearing in the early fall. It partners perfectly with a light and gentle white wine.

FRONT LEFT CHEESE Saint Marcellin, FRONT RIGHT CHEESE Pelardon, BACK LEFT CHEESE Saint Félicien, BACK RIGHT CHEESE Picodon

Cheeses of the Aubrac

These semihard cheeses are produced on the plateau of Aubrac, an area with mineral-rich pastures and volcanic soil, environmental features that impart flavor to the cheeses.

Salers d'Estive & Cantal Laguiole 🐄 AUBRAC

What makes Salers d'Estive and Cantal Laguiole cheeses special is not only the cow's milk from Laguiole and Salers breeds, but also the terrain—the plateau of Aubrac. The breed of cow for the Laguiole is the ancient Laguiole-Aubrac, a small, sturdy cow with a pale golden/fawn coat and long upwardly curved horns. This old-established breed may not give huge quantities of milk, but the quality is ideal for cheese, and being native to the region they thrive naturally on the wild flora and rich pastures.

The Salers cow is another ancient breed, whose rich, luscious milk is used both for the cheese of the same name and the simplified Cantal.

The climate of the grazing areas on the high, vast, rough pastureland is hot and stormy in summer, and cold with biting winds and snow in winter. The grass is never cut at the higher altitudes; it is reserved for the transhumance (summer grazing) between May and the end of October. Volcanic soil, with underlying granite, is rich in phosphates, potassium, and magnesium, and a profusion of flora contributes to the flavors in the cheeses; remember this when choosing wines to accompany the cheeses because the southern Rhône wines have a particular affinity. The cheeses made on the high pastures during the summer months are labeled "Salers," and the cheeses made during the rest of the year in the lower valleys are marked "Cantal." Cantal is a very popular family-style cheese, however, and is made in both large commercial dairies and also smaller, artisan ones. It is easy to dismiss Cantal as a basic cheese, but, if you find a true artisan-made version that has been well matured, it is delicious. It has a smooth texture and a fruity, nutty taste that is not too aggressive. Salers has a firmer texture and an edge to the flavor when the cheese has been aged.

ABOVE LEFT AND ABOVE RIGHT Cows grazing on the plateau of Aubrac. OPPOSITE, LEFT CHEESE Salers d'Estive, RIGHT CHEESE Cantal Laguiole

South & Southwest France

This massive region, encompassing Provence, the Languedoc (east to west), and the Pyrénées, has the beauty and heat of the Mediterranean, and the mountains and valleys toward the Spanish border and the Atlantic Ocean.

In Provence, we find many styles of goat cheese because goats can scramble over hills to find food, and can withstand the summer heat. Some cheeses are wrapped in leaves, to preserve their rinds, and others dry out to strong, spicy-flavored morsels.

The Côte d'Azur is a summer playground for vacationers, but driving inland there is a stark simplicity to the land, broken up by the brilliant colors of lavender and sunflowers against the sky. It is heavenly, but also harsh. Given the spicy, dry, and fruity wines of the region, the cheeses are a perfect match.

Traveling to the western Languedoc, we skirt the southern parts of Aquitaine and Gascony, venturing to Béarn and Pyrénées Atlantiques, and get a completely different view of

France. In this region, you can sense the Spanish influences, not only in the people who live there, but also in the styles of the cheeses produced.

In some areas, you can see the cheese caves etched into the mountainside, where the farmers would bring their cheeses to be stored and ripened. In the summer months, the farmers and their cattle travel from the lower valleys, which become extremely hot, to the higher, lush mountain pastures to graze. This ancient tradition, known as "transhumance," has been practiced in mountain regions all over Europe in the summer months. The lead cows wear heavy bells around their necks, and herding dogs make sure that there are no strays. It is wonderful to see traditions still in place and the ways of the land respected.

The wines of this part of France are probably the best accompaniment to enjoy with the cheeses, and the gastronomy of this region is so rich and varied that you will never be bored. We taste strong, spicy, and earthy flavors that have links with British cheese styles, such as Gloucester and Cheshire, from the time of Henry II's marriage to Eleanor of Aquitaine. The wines of the southwest are bold enough to match the hard ewe's milk cheeses, and also the fine charcuterie and duck rillettes.

Banon Feuille 🐐 PROVENCE

This plump goat cheese is dipped in eau de vie and sprinkled lightly with pepper, before being wrapped in chestnut leaves and tied with raffia string. The flavor becomes more pronounced and stronger with age, and the natural rind more golden with patches of blue.

Monsieur Ripert collects nearly all the 330 gallons (1,500 liters) of milk he needs for making Banon cheeses himself. His farm is not far from the small town of Banon, announced with a sign stating "Fromage de Chèvre." Banon was originally made with ewe's milk, but as the cheese became popular it was clear that the milk supply could not cope, so cow's milk was used for many years and the cheeses sold to tourists. The goat's milk cheeses are the most sought after, however, and since the 1960s, according to M. Ripert, small farms and "chèvriers" have gradually increased in the area, and the tradition continues.

The cheesemakers have to endure the long, hot summers, with the mistral winds blowing through the region drying out the little medallion cheeses far quicker than at other times of the year. As the cheeses dry out, wrapping them in chestnut leaves provides an effective and natural form of protection, without interfering with the ripening process. They are ready to sell in three to four weeks, and the flavors are bosky and herbal, with a sharp acidity from the goat's milk. I am lucky enough to have these cheeses at my shop for a couple of months during the summer; just opening this cheese reminds me of Provence and its warm air.

RIGHT Buchette de Banon
OPPOSITE Banon Feuille

Buchette de Banon 🐐 PROVENCE

This small log-shape goat cheese is stacked on a flat wooden base, like cigarillos in a package. Its thin, wrinkled natural rind is topped with a sprig of fresh *sarriette* (summer savory), and the taste is creamy and slightly flaky, with a light fruity tang. The best time to eat these little cheeses is between mid-spring and early fall.

Bethmale ARIÈGE

This rustic farmhouse cow's milk cheese has earthy mushroom aromas that have a farmyard resonance. The supple texture to the crust is washed, giving it a rosy glow, and the pâte is semihard, with tiny pinholes. The taste is unique, with a zingy tingle on the tongue, yet mellow and nutty as an overall sensation. These cheeses are rarely seen outside their immediate region; with the wines of the Pays d'Oc, they are a perfect example of identifying a place.

Bethmale ARIÈGE

This is the goat's milk version of Bethmale. A rubbed, brushed, and lightly washed rind houses a chewy-textured cheese pitted with tiny pinholes. It has lovely earthy, floral flavors, with rustic, nutty additions to the taste. This seasonal cheese starts from early summer and goes through to fall. It is perfect when partnered with a red wine with body, fruitiness, and well-defined tannins.

Haut Barry LARZAC

This is a raw ewe's milk cheese with a lovely natural crust that has been brushed, allowing the natural molds to evolve on the rind. The texture is semihard, with tiny eyelet holes through the cheese, and the taste has a gently earthy sweetness redolent of the milk, with a fresh hazelnut bite. It makes a delicious end-of-meal cheese.

Le Gabiétout PYRÉNÉES

This supple-textured mixed cow's and ewe's milk cheese has a fruity, nutty bite and a smooth chewy texture. The rind is lightly brine-washed and rubbed, to give a pale ocher glow, and the aroma is gentle and earthy. It is at its best eaten when young; the matured cheeses have a more strident taste.

Napoleon Montréjeau HAUTES-PYRÉNÉES

The name is derived from the mountain facing the farm, which is called "Le Nez de Napoleon" because the top of the mountain bears an uncanny resemblance to Napoleon's profile. Only a small amount of this ewe's milk cheese is made and matured by Dominique Bouchait, who gives it a certain style that is quite unique—in the Ossau style (see opposite), but with a softer texture and a nutty tang.

Zelu Koloria 🐑 PAYS BASQUE

An unusual ewe's milk cheese from the mountain region of Pays Basque, it is semihard with blue veins through the dense, mellow-flavored pâte. The natural brushed crust is dry when young, but as the cheese ages it becomes a little moist, thereby giving it an extra tangy richness. It is a rare treat because blue cheeses are not normally made in this area. The spring cheeses have a lightness in taste and texture, and as the season progresses, the flavors become more intense and the texture heavier. The season ends in the fall, although a few cheeses do appear after the fall, which are fully matured and somewhat too strong.

Val de Loubières 🐐 ARIÈGE

With a washed and brushed crust encircled by a bark collar from local pine trees, this is a rich handmade creamy goat cheese with a sweetly sappy taste somewhat like a Vacherin du Mont d'Or (see page 90). It has a very limited production, but is well worth waiting for because its flavors are unique.

Anneau du Vic Bilh 🐐 PYRÉNÉES

This is like the Rouelle (see page 78) in shape but much more tender and prone to almost collapsing with softness. The flavors of the goat's milk are so sweet and fragrant, however, with an earthy nuttiness, that it is impossible not to just scoop it up with a piece of bread. It is made high up in the hills and is a very seasonal cheese, and it really only comes to market to be enjoyed in the late spring and summer months.

Tomme d'Aydius 🐐 BÉARN

This is a relatively new cheese from the Vallée d'Aspe, close to the snowline of the Béarn Mountains. A wild and rocky terrain allows the goats to graze freely. The resulting cheese is smooth and semihard, with a lovely, pale rosy hue to the brine-rubbed crust. The taste is sweetly earthy and nutty, with delicious tones of wildflowers and herbs. The main cheesemaking period is between early spring and late fall, although the cheese is available throughout the year at varying stages of maturity.

Tomme de Cabrioulet 🐐 ARIÈGE

The pinky peach, downy washed crust of this goat cheese is simply beautiful. The cheese is semisoft and gently billows, making it look very attractive. The pâte is white, with small eyelets, and tastes fresh, almost like a rich fromage blanc, with a gentle, creamy nuttiness. It is sold mostly locally, although a few cheeses do venture to larger towns and cities, but are extremely expensive.

Ossau 🐑 PYRÉNÉES

A handmade mountain ewe's milk cheese made by small, isolated communities high up in the hills, it is a semihard cheese with a brine-rubbed crust. A firm yet supple cheese, in that the hard crust holds within a cheese that crumbles and breaks down on impact, it has a complexity of tastes that tingle on the tongue. With a little age, the pâte becomes flakier and the taste more pronounced and nutty. The cheesemaking process for Ossau is somewhat similar to that of Cheshire.

BELOW, LEFT CHEESE Tomme d'Aydius, RIGHT CHEESE Tomme de Cabrioulet
BELOW RIGHT Ossau

Roquefort

This is a land where neither vineyard nor corn will grow, but thankfully the "king of blue cheeses" soaks up the limestone minerals from the Cambalou maturing caves, to enhance its unique flavors.

THIS PAGE, TOP CHEESE Roquefort Carles, **BOTTOM CHEESE** Papillon

Roquefort Carles ⚘ ROUERGUE

Jacques Carles, who joined his father's small cheese business in 1958, now runs it with his daughter. He stores thousands of wheels of cheese in damp four-level cellars cut out of the Cambalou rockface. The freshly made cheeses sit on heavy oak planks of wood, which become saturated with the water seeping out of the rocks. The oak planks are ideal for holding the cheeses and also imparting their woody aromas and flavors into them. Intense, powerful flavors and gritty texture make this a truly individual cheese.

There are numerous stories surrounding the conception of Roquefort, one being that a shepherd, sheltering from the midday sun in the entrance to one of the Cambalou caves in Roquefort, saw a lovely, young girl, and hurriedly put down his soft cheese sandwich to pursue her. His passion obliterated everything else that afternoon, and it was a while before he came back to the same shelter; there, hidden in a crevice, were the remains of his lunch! The bread had turned gray and moldy, and the soft cheese had developed a speckled blue, with a strong mineral odor. Nevertheless, he decided to taste it and was amazed at how delicious the cheese and blue mold combination was. And so it is that Roquefort was born, when dried and moldy bread was used as a base for introducing bacteria into a white cheese.

Of course, the cool, damp mineral-rich Cambalou caves also contribute to the unique flavors and textures of this cheese. Jacques Carles or his daughter Delphine can arrange a special visit to the caves, then to the production site in the village of Martrin, 31 miles (50 km) from Roquefort. Largely a wholesaler, he does not offer commercial tours, but he will explain (in French) to visitors how he makes his own *Penicillium* mold from a secret recipe based on sourdough bread. He then burrows with a "cheese iron" (an implement used to test the ripeness of cheese), deep into a round of cheese, to determine the progress of the blue mold from the edge to the center, which should be evenly distributed to indicate its perfect state. In my view (and also the view of others more expert than me), his cheese is the finest Roquefort in Roquefort.

Papillon ⚘ ROUERGUE

M. Albert Alric created the Papillon (butterfly) brand in 1906, and set high standards by working closely with the farms supplying the milk. He would not allow the sheep to be fed industrial fodder as supplements, only cereals grown organically, such as hay and legumes, and only in very small quantities in relation to fresh grass. Although up-to-the-minute machinery is used to milk the sheep, there is still no newer way of introducing the spores to the cheeses than M. Alric's invention of a machine that brushed the mold into the curd at a rate of 4 grams to the kilogram (about 100,000 million spores!). What gives Papillon its particular style are the softer, more open blue molds and a really rich, buttery texture to the white pâte. The Papillon brand is now big business, but I am sure that M. Alric is looking down from above, making sure that the ivory pâte is richly unctuous and suitably "sheepy"-tasting alongside the dusty blue molds—just as he likes it! The perfect wine to serve with this cheese is a Sauternes; in particular, look out for the names Yquem, Raymond-Lafon, and Rieussec, which are probably the best dessert wines in the world. The noble rot (a milky white film that covers the grapes) assists in the sweetly savory taste of the wine. Serve it with freshly cracked walnuts and the Papillon cheese.

Brique du Larzac 🐑 TARN

A rectangular, shallow pavé (brick-shape) ewe's milk cheese, this has a natural rind and a soft, creamy, smooth texture. The younger cheeses have a light tangy taste that is rich and sweet, and with age they develop to become drier in texture, while the flavors become fuller, with a more earthy taste.

Lou Bren 🐑 AVEYRON

This ewe's milk cheese has a golden brown natural washed crust, and a flaky almost melting texture within. The taste of Lou Bren is fruity and rich, with delicious earthy aromas and a sharp burned-caramel aftertaste.

The cheese is produced in very small quantities by artisan cheesemakers, using very traditional methods, hence its rather rustic appearance and limited availability. Lou Bren is delicious when partnered with a fruity red wine such as a Vin de Pays.

Rove des Garrigues 🐐 LOT, MIDI-PYRÉNÉES

This is a beautiful, arid area, with scrubby grasslands of wild thyme and gorse, and dense woodland of chestnut trees. The goats roam free and eat herbs and chestnuts, which give the milk its definitive herbal, bosky flavors.

The early spring cheeses are fresh and tangy, and as the season progresses their flavors become fuller. They are best eaten between early spring and early fall. Try a gentle white wine in a simple style with this cheese.

Pérail 🐑 LANGUEDOC

This cheese is a fresh, creamy shallow disk, with a thin natural rind and a rich, melting pâte. The flavor of the cheese is pronounced and delicious, with the familiar sweet earthiness of fresh ewe's milk. A light white wine with a zesty structure is the perfect accompaniment to serve with this cheese.

Lingot Saint Nicolas de la Monastère 🐐 LA DALMERIE, HÉRAULT

An ingot of pure goat's milk with a flaky, fudgy texture and a wrinkled rind. The goats graze on meadows studded with thyme, and this is clearly evident in the taste of the cheese, which is light and gently earthy, with the richness of the milk and a herbal essence at the end. It is a perfect handmade cheese, from the monastery at La Dalmerie in the heeart of Hérault, made under the supervision of Father Marcel. The season runs from spring to fall.

Rouelle 🐐 TARN

A fragile goat cheese when fresh and young, with a creamy floral tang becoming richer with ripening. In the shape of a wheel, its top is lightly dusted with charcoal or left plain white. The best time to eat it is from early spring to mid-fall.

Cabécou du Rocamadour 🐐 LOT

A small medallion-size cheese, with a thin natural rind, this goat cheese makes a velvety, melting mouthful, with a rich full taste. A perfect appetizer, it suits a red wine with some spice to its dry flavors. Available all through the year, but the best season is late summer and fall, to capture the nutty earthiness.

LEFT, TOP LEFT CHEESE Pérail, TOP RIGHT CHEESE Brique du Larzac, BOTTOM LEFT CHEESE Rove des Garrigues, BOTTOM RIGHT CHEESE Lou Bren

TOP LEFT Lingot Saint Nicolas, TOP CENTER Rouelle, BOTTOM LEFT Louvie, BOTTOM CENTER Cathare, RIGHT Cabécou du Rocamadour

Cathare ⚞ LAUREGAIS, CARCASSONNE

This cheese is approximately the size of a coffee saucer, with an ash-coated top emblazoned with the cross of the Cathars (a medieval Christian religious sect living in and around Carcassonne that was persecuted in the Middle Ages). The taste is mild and gently nutty, and should be enjoyed fresh and creamy, rather than allowed to overripen, when its flavors become too "goaty." This cheese is delicious partnered with a light and gentle white wine—try serving it with a white from the southwest of France made with the Manseng grape.

Louvie ⚞ PYRÉNÉES

A thin natural rind, with bloomy patched molds, gives this cheese a fruity, nutty taste and a crumbly texture, with the edges just melting. The richness of goat's milk is evident, but not overwhelming. These chubby drum-shape cylinders of flaky-textured goat cheese are available during summer and into fall. This area was famous for mining iron ore, as well as being known for white marble, and the mineral flavors in the cheese make a quite unique imprint on the taste buds, quite unlike those of the Loire, Provence, or the Ardèche.

Bouton d'Oc 🐐 TARN

These are tiny little pyramid "cocktail" cheeses, with a stick at the top for ease of handling. The fresh curds are simply drained and dropped into their molds, and the thin natural rind forms to hug the cheese perfectly.

This is an ideal apéritif cheese because it has a smooth yet firm texture and that thin natural rind. If allowed to mature and dry a little further, its flavors become nutty and slightly tart. This cheese works very well when served with crisp, dry white wines or even Champagne.

Pechegos 🐐 TARN

The farm is situated in the fine grazing areas of Le Causse, where goats forage in a natural meadow habitat. The cheeses have a lovely lightness, with sweet hints of flowers and herbs coming through the nutty sharpness.

There is a band of spruce encircling the cheese, to keep the soft, almost melting texture intact. The rind is brine-washed, to give an extra depth of flavor and aroma to the cheese, which is seasonal—late spring is a good time to taste it. Serve Pechegos with an aromatic, dry white wine with a citrus zest and grassy aromas, to really bring out the flavors of the cheese.

ABOVE Brin d'Amour
ABOVE TOP Bouton d'Oc
RIGHT Tomme Corse
OPPOSITE Pechegos

CORSICA

This island has been overrun by several Mediterranean cultures, including France, and these multiple influences are evident in Corsican cooking and food production. The Orezza mineral waters from Rapaggio, south of Bastia on the east coast, are prized for their medicinal properties. In fact, this east coast is where some of the best cheeses appear, and the flavors reflect the minerality and the *maquis*—the shrubby bushland of bay, thyme, rosemary, and savory, where the animals graze. In early spring, Brocciu, a light and airy ewe's milk ricotta, requires only a dribbling of dark honey to serve it as a dessert. Explore the island's narrow mountain roads and be rewarded at the end of the day with platters of roasted wild boar and charcuterie, chunks of chewy bread, and cheese washed down with a crisp local white wine.

Brin d'Amour 🐑 CORSICA

This is a relatively new ewe's milk cheese, reflecting the *maquis* with its thick coating of herbs. The cheese is simple, almost like a young pecorino, and soft, flaky, and pale in color. The herbs are augmented with chile and black peppercorns. If you allow the ripening process to include a few bloomy molds while the cheese dries out a little, the flavor is sweeter, earthier, and bosky. Brin d'Amour is produced in all the more mountainous areas, and the best season to eat this cheese is early spring until summer, when the pastures are not too parched.

Tomme Corse 🐑 CORSICA

From the area called Orientale, this cheese is not dissimilar to a Sardinian pecorino, or a Pyrénées Ossau. The best time to eat these cheeses is winter through to late spring, when the pastureland is studded with flowers and herbs from the early winter rain. The cheeses are matured for three months minimum, but are often ripened for longer, to produce semihard medium-strength to full-bodied cheeses good for grating. The flavors are rather robust and tangy, and the artisan-made cheeses partner well with strong Madiran or a robust local red wine.

Alpine

Alpine meadows and pastures are alive with the sound of cowbells. This reassuring ringing means that a long-standing tradition is alive and will continue for the foreseeable future. Summer is a perfect time to explore these vast regions of mountain pasture, which have superb grazing conditions and great hiking trails.

It is fitting to begin our odyssey in Franche-Comté because the Jura Massif straddles this region from the edge of Alsace, down to the Rhône-Alpes via Savoie, through to Switzerland, and into Bavaria in Germany. This amazing range of mountains, the national parks, and the passes are a magnet for skiers in the winter months, but only when the land returns to the farmer do we see how they are linked by agriculture.

The Italian Alpine regions start as soon as one crosses from Grenoble in France to the magnificent Gran Paradiso National Park within Piedmont and Aosta. It threads across Lombardy, to Stelvio—Italy's largest national park—which stretches into Trentino-Alto Adige/Südtirol, which, in turn, borders Switzerland, southern Germany, and Austria.

There is a common thread in the cheesemaking, too, with copper vats being used and large Gruyère-style cheeses being produced. Yet there are also very individual cheeses from the tiny isolated communities, which you have to reach on foot, rather than by car. The lower slopes and Alpine hillsides are often family-owned or, in some cases in Switzerland, owned by bank trusts and rented out to farmers and cheesemakers. This ensures protection of the areas and continued usage by farmers, as in the past.

The bucolic picture of happy cows grazing on flower-studded Alpine pastures is alluring, but, in reality, especially in times past, the work was harsh and unforgiving in the bleak colder months. Farmers barely made a living, and idled away lonely cold nights or summer evenings by carving objects to sell at local markets or to tourists and hikers. In the early 18th century, this was a serious hobby, and the fine pieces of wood carving and intricate shavings of tiny flowers and animals were greatly admired.

Ironically, this whittling led to watchmaking, and a new "industry" developed using the abundance of readily available minerals and quartz crystals in the vicinity. This meant that many young members of farming families would go to work in watch businesses, thereby putting even more strain on the agricultural sector. Local government officials finally saw sense, however, and with the new-found wealth helped farmers to regain strength. With tourism also becoming a booming business, the dairies were able to grow and develop their cheese production.

BELOW The Pillar family's high Alpine cheesemaking facility.
OPPOSITE, TOP AND BOTTOM The pastures at Käserei Boschenhof.

French Alpine

The route to Comté and Haut-Doubs is a network of farms, vineyards, and cheese cellars well worth exploring. The landscape is deeply rooted in agriculture and, driving along the winding roads in late fall, you are totally absorbed in the autumnal golds, rust burgundies, and ochers. In the commune of Les Fins, close to Morteau (famous for its delicious sausages and charcuterie), I have forged wonderful friendships and working relationships through regular visits to choose the cheeses. I like the hot, spicy flavors of Comté from the late summer months, but some of the late spring and late fall cheeses have wonderful complex qualities. Once the selection is made, the cheeses are put in the maturing rooms to await shipment. Storing cheeses in their familiar environment is a luxury and one that pays dividends—each batch received will be in tiptop condition because it has had no major changes in its surroundings that might impinge on its flavor development.

ABOVE Alps Chamrousse, French Alps.

Comté d'Estive 🐄 COMTÉ

Comté cheesemaking has been documented since the 12th century, but it has only begun to look like a dense Gruyère since the 1950s. Prior to this, the cheese was rather like Emmental, with large holes in the pâte; however, the rich milk from the Montbéliarde cows could be matured like a Gruyère, a more expensive cheese than Emmental, and it made economic sense to develop this style of cheese. The *affineurs* (cheese maturers) have reinvented this cheese as one of the most popular hard cheeses in France and, due to the long aging process, countries around the world are able to import wheels made with unpasteurized milk.

There is a strict code of practice to maintain all aspects of the cheese, and inspectors regulate on a 20-point system. For scores 15 or above, a green label is used around the outside of the cheese. Those scoring 12–15 get a red label, and any under 3 are not allowed to be called Comté. The perfect wines for Comté are Jura whites made with Chardonnay grapes or the local Savagnin grape, and vin jaune, with its almost sherrylike quality that is at once dry, fruity, and sharp—a great foil for the Comté cheese.

BELOW AND OPPOSITE Comté d'Estive

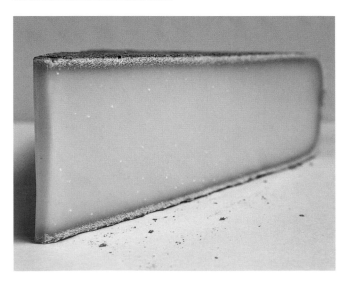

Beaufort Chalet d'Alpage

The mountain pastures, which in winter are ski runs, return to scented Alpine meadows in summer and produce the perfect grazing land for the Abondance and Tarine cows.

Beaufort Chalet d'Alpage 🐄 SAVOIE

Beaufort cheesemaking takes place in the Beaufortain, Tarentaise, and Maurienne valleys, plus part of the Val d'Arly. There are also high mountain pastures, or *alpage*. More than 10,000 Abondance and Tarine cows graze these designated areas, and it takes about 80 gallons (300 liters) of milk to make one 61–66-pound (28–30-kg) cheese. The cows are not overmilked and can produce enough milk per year for only about 300 cheeses. This not only ensures the quality of the cheese, but also, just as important, avoids overworking the pastures, which would diminish their abundance of wildflowers and grasses. Whereas Comté cheese has deep salty/caramel flavors, the Beaufort has floral, almost sweet, nutty flavors that are rich but never abrasive on the tongue—even with the aged versions. Perfect with regional white wines from Chignin and Chasselas grapes, whose freshness is bright and clear when partnered with the chewy fruitiness of the cheese.

ABOVE AND OPPOSITE Beaufort Chalet d'Alpage
LEFT Grazing cows in the Savoie.

THIS PAGE, FROM TOP TO BOTTOM Chevrotin des Aravis, Reblochon, Abbaye de Taimé, Tomme de Savoie, BACK CHEESE Emmental de Savoie Surchoix

OPPOSITE, TOP CHEESE Morbier BOTTOM CHEESE Bleu de Gex

Morbier 🐄 FRANCHE-COMTÉ

Ferme de Teigne, where Madame Chambon makes Morbier cheese, is off the beaten track. The Morbier cheeses she makes are very different than any others I have tasted. The ash stripe through the cheese seems grittier, more like the original version of the cheese, where the ash under the copper cauldrons on the embers was scraped off and mixed into a paste, before being spread over half the cheese. In this way, the morning-milk cheese could be left to settle; when the evening cheese was made, it was then poured on top, with the ash cinders providing a "mat." The cheese is mild with a nutty flavor when young, becoming richer and more pronounced with age.

Bleu de Gex 🐄 HAUT JURA

This stylish blue cheese weighing around 12 pounds (5.4 kg) has a lively taste and a rough, natural thin crust. The unwashed curds have *Penicillium glaucum* added, to encourage the blue to form. The cheese is allowed to drain naturally and is liberally pierced before going to the ripening room; this prevents the cheese from becoming too dense due to the richness of Montbéliarde cow's milk. The natural crust forms in the cold ripening room, and after about two months the cheese is ready. You can leave the maturing process for longer, but I prefer this cheese on the young side—its mild, nutty flavor mixes well on a cheeseboard with other softer cheeses of the region.

Tomme de Savoie 🐄 SAVOIE

Many cheeses are labeled "tommes" in Savoic, and this word describes the smallish round shape of the cheese. Look out for *alpage* cheeses, those made with summer milk, which have complex flavors of fruit and nut. The molds around the cheese are gray/white/blue, making it look like a small boulder. The morning and evening milk has some low-fat milk added to help with the acidity, giving the cheese a sweet milky aroma mixed with the musty earthy crust. Enjoy with the local Gamay or Mondeuse wines.

Reblochon 🐄 SAVOIE

The semisoft disk weighing 18 ounces (500 g) has a washed and rubbed pinky gold rind. The cheese has a supple chewy texture, with a lovely earthy aroma and rich hazelnut or fresh cobnut taste. The rind is all-important to the overall flavor profile; however, if the rind becomes hard or wet, cut it away because it will taste bitter. I like to add a few scoops of this cheese just before serving a fondue—it really gives it a glossy finish—although traditionally Reblochon is used in a classic tartiflette (see recipe pages 252–253).

Chevrotin des Aravis 🐐 HAUTE-SAVOIE

This is a plump goat's milk version of Reblochon, and is really delightful when properly ripened. Weighing around 10½ ounces (300 g), the white pâte should be supple and springy, not flowing or firm. The rind is washed to create

a pale peachy bloom, and the goaty taste is delicate yet still rich and floral. A perfect late spring, summer, and fall cheese, it benefits from being served with a Savoie wine, such as a red Mondeuse or a white Chignin Bergeron.

Emmental de Savoie Surchoix 🐄 SAVOIE

This 176-pound (80-kg) *grand cru* cheese has a red cross on it to indicate that it is from Savoie. It is much like other pressed and cooked cheeses—Gruyère, Beaufort—and has that familiar fruity taste, with a dense, chewy texture. The *grand cru* cheeses are more flavorful and better quality than the mass-produced versions. For cheese enthusiasts, the size of the holes is important: too big and you lose a huge amount of cheese when cutting; too small and there is a tendency toward a wet, claggy pâte. A skilled *affineur* can tell when the holes have reached the right size. Emmental is the main component of fondue, as well as being used for soufflés, sauces, and toppings.

Abbaye de Tamié 🐄 HAUTE-SAVOIE

The Cistercian monks first made this cheese in the Middle Ages; in 1861, the Abbey acquired more land and encouraged local farmers to sell their milk to the monks for cheesemaking. Now there are farms making the cheese for the Abbey, which markets the cheese. The recipe is more or less a Reblochon, but thicker, weighing about 3 pounds (1.3 kg) for the cutting cheese and 18 ounces (500 g) for an individual version. It has the same rich creamy flavor as Reblochon, with a chewy density, but is perhaps a little less nutty, yet more robust and earthy in taste. The flavor of the cheese changes with each season. In the winter, when the cows are housed in smaller enclosures and fed on hay, the cheeses have a farmyard aroma and taste. In the spring and summer, when the cows graze on the mountain pastures, the cheeses develop nutty, mossy flavors.

Bleu de Termignon  HAUTE-SAVOIE

From Haute-Savoie and weighing about 15½–22 pounds (7–10 kg), this is one of the rarest cheeses made in the high mountain pastures, at about 6,600 feet (2,000 m) in altitude. Made only during the summer months and ripened in mountain huts, this ancient cheese was almost forgotten until the early 1980s, when a determined group of cheese sellers decided to help its continuing production. There is nothing forced, added, or injected to achieve the blue—it simply forms by letting the natural bacteria in the air of the maturing cave filter into the cheeses, which are are freshly packed into their wooden molds lined with cheesecloth. Left over a period of time, the curds are pressed of their whey and spiked with needles, to create air pockets for the bacteria to work through the cheese. Once the cheeses are taken out of their molds and placed on the wooden shelves, the natural crust forms. The cheese has the texture of Wensleydale, and the nutty flavors of the blue are very different than any other blue cheese you will ever taste. The blue gives the flavor a sense of the cellar, with its slight musty mineral quality, but the sweetness of the milk hits the roof of your mouth, along with the natural blue tangle of flavors gleaned from the impact of airborne bacteria in the maturing rooms. The best wine for this type of cheese is one that is not too heavy; if you think of the lighter Rhône styles, with their well-balanced acidity, I think you will be on the right track.

This is a "particular" cheese, as I call it, special and redolent of its place of origin, which is the heart of the Massif de la Vanoise, Praz Bouchet, located in Termignon-la-Vanoise.

Vacherin 🐄 HAUT-DOUBS

I spent a morning making cheese at Le Fruitier des Jarrons, at Ville du Pont, not far from the Comté cheesemakers in Les Fins. Monsieur Rene Boissenin and his three assistants were already busy heating up the early morning milk in three vats.

The Montbéliarde cow's milk is used from midsummer until late fall for vacherin production. The milk will be particularly rich and fragrant during the months up to late fall, an ideal time for making this soft, buttery cheese, with its sappy aroma and taste from the pine-bark collar.

The short six-month season for vacherin is important to respect, and cheeses made beyond this period cannot be called Vacherin du Mont d'Or, but are given other names, such as Edel de Cléron, a pasteurized milk cheese that looks a lot like the vacherin.

The flavor of vacherin is superb with a meltingly rich, verging on clotted cream, taste. The billowy crust is washed pinky peach, with an earthy, sappy aroma. The pine bark around the cheese helps to achieve vacherin's distinctive texture and perfume.

This cheese is delicious when accompanied by a refreshing and zesty white wine. Try a Côtes du Jura, produced in the Haut Jura region, for the perfect patrnership.

LEFT Vacherin
OPPOSITE Bleu de Termignon

Tarentais ♉ SAVOIE

This drum of goat's milk cheese weighing 7 ounces (200 g) or less has a natural rind that requires careful handling; the white and gray/blue molds are encouraged, but so are the darker yellow/gold molds that cover the cheese, especially when it is at its fresher stage. This reaction to the rind can be difficult to judge. If allowed to stay in too high a humidity, it will affect the flavors, causing it to become bitter; however, if the white and blue molds flourish on top of the gold, you will have a wonderful cheese, closely packed and crumbly with a fresh, nutty taste. The goats are allowed to roam the rocky outcrops around the farms during late spring and summer, and the cheese is available only until early fall.

Abondance ♉ HAUTE-SAVOIE

This cheese takes the name of the valley, as well as the breed of cow used for the milk. The first cheeses were made exclusively in the Haute-Savoie, as early as the 14th century, by the monks of the Sainte Marie d'Abondance Monastery near the Swiss border. This high-mountain artisan cheese is made exclusively in Val d'Abondance in the north of Haute-Savoie, which stretches to the Swiss border; the farm-made cheeses are called Abondance de Savoie and are made around the Massif du Parmelan. The three breeds of cow used are Tarine, Montbéliarde, and the beautiful Abondance. Although the maturing time is around 12 weeks, if you can wait longer, the flavors are

really rich and fruity, with an almost melting quality and a bitter nut taste somewhat like fresh hazelnuts. The best season to eat cheeses made in late spring is late winter.

Besace ♉ SAVOIE

A dome-shape cheese weighing around 7 ounces (200 g) and molded in fine cheesecloth. With hardly a visible rind, this fresh, tangy, and floral-tasting cheese has a delicious light, crumbly texture. Wonderful when young, but if left to dry out a little, it becomes more dense with age, developing a mellow, nutty taste. It is available only during the late spring and summer months.

Grataron d'Arêches ♉♉ SAVOIE

In the heart of the Beaufortain area and the village of Arêches, this soft washed-rind cheese of about 7 ounces (200 g) is made with either cow's or goat's milk, although it is the goat's milk cheese that is the rarer of the two. Production is limited to spring through fall, when the goats are allowed to roam the flower-strewn pastures. The flavors of this cheese are soft but pronounced, and a zesty white wine or a light Gamay are the most suitable wine accompaniments.

Persillé de Tignes/Tarentais 🐐🐄 SAVOIE

This is a goat's milk cheese that has varying amounts of cow's milk added to supplement the goat's milk when the latter is scarce. It is available during the spring and fall while the animals are able to graze outdoors. Weighing about 3⅓ pounds (1.5 kg) and looking like a small version of Wensleydale, its crust is studded with gray and white moulds. The texture is grainy, with hints of sharp fruit and the merest shadow of blue showing through. Eaten young, the sharp crème fraîche flavours are delightful; if you allow the cheese to mature further, more strident flavors come forward and the blue will be more evident.

Grand Colombiers de Aillons 🐐🐄 SAVOIE

From the heart of the Beaufortain/Bauges region, this is another mixed goat's and cow's milk cheese, weighing around 3⅓ pounds (1.5 kg), with a lightly washed rind. Available during the summer and fall months, this cheese has a taste that is soft, velvety, and mellow. The rind should have a subtle aroma of mustiness; if it is too sticky, it will impart a bitter taste to the cheese. The well-balanced wines of the region, such as Mondeuse or a Pinot Noir, would be ideal partners. There is a little vegetal spikiness coming through the flavors of the cheese, so the clean style of these wines makes a good foil.

Swiss Alpine

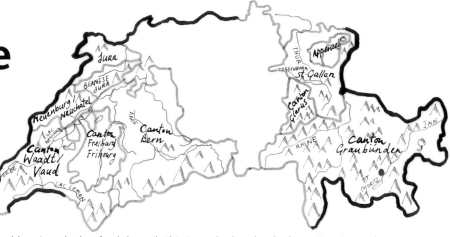

The small grazing bells Swiss cows wear on the high mountain pastures are a necessity, with each one having its own particular sound, so that the herdsman can locate every single creature. Switzerland is a landlocked country surrounded by high mountains allowing for a temperate climate, which is a satisfactory condition in which to make cheese. Mountains have pure water systems trickling down into the valleys, and valuable minerals that feed the soil. This is no doubt why the large Gruyère and Emmentaler cheeses are so delicious, especially when they are made high up in the hills during the summer months. From the 13th century onward, grazing rights and animal rights of way were complex and led to the eventual privatization of communal grazing land, driving many cheesemakers to other European plains and overseas. For many generations, the right to use an Alp has been handed down within the family, and is owned by a single family or perhaps two families, or by an Alp cooperative, which is operated and run by all the farming families of the area. All the Alps are "geyser," meaning that only a certain number of cows or other farm animals are allowed to graze during the summer, to protect the land.

ABOVE Father and son from the Pillar family making cheese, Swiss Alps.

ABOVE The view of Charmey Mountains, Canton Fribourg.

Gruyère   CANTON FRIBOURG

The high-mountain cheeses weighing 70½–88 pounds (32–40 kg) are made between June and September by small independent cheesemakers, such as the Pillar family in Charmey, using traditional methods and equipment in their mountain chalets. The flavors are savory and almost toasty because the unpasteurized milk is heated in large copper vats over open wood fires. Just two cheeses are made per day, and maturing requires a minimum of 12 months, although keeping it longer means a richer and fruitier taste to the cheese. Nearer to the village of Gruyère is Le Crêt sur Semsales, where Jean-Marie Dunand ages his cheeses up to two years, giving a fruity intensity to the flavors and a gritty crumble in the mouth. This cheese is used for a classic fondue. Or eat it on its own with a glass of white wine for an elegant finish to a meal.

OPPOSITE, TOP CHEESE Alpkäse Luven, LEFT AND BOTTOM CHEESE Gruyére, RIGHT CHEESE Alpkäse Luven

Alpkäse Luven   CANTON GRAUBÜNDEN

Dani Duerr decided to go back to his home town high up in the Alpine region of Graubünden in Luven, to make cheese just as his grandparents and father had done. He wanted to change the traditional old recipe of Toggenburg hard cheese, however, and make something with his own identity stamped on the cheese. Dani does extra brine washing to the cheeses to give a deep ocher color to the crust, and learned his craft from his father, who was a traditional cheesemaker of Emmentaler. He adapted the recipe to make a much harder, close-textured cheese weighing about 11 pounds (5 kg), and it tastes very fruity and nutty, with a much earthier taste than other Swiss cheeses. He sells his cheeses mostly locally and to one or two major restaurants in Switzerland. Hopefully he will expand the maturing area, to enable him to have enough cheeses to sell elsewhere in the world.

and so it is best eaten young, before the flavors become very tangy and earthy. The delicious wines from around Lake Geneva and Vaud provide the perfect foil for the dense, rich styles and flavors of Swiss cheese—in particular, the Henchoz family's Le Sous-Bois.

Alp Bergkäse CANTON

GRAUBÜNDEN CHUR

This is a similar cheese to Luven (see page 95), but whereas Luven is made by a single cheesemaker using his own cows' milk, Alp Bergkäse is more readily available because the collective of farmers clubs together and hires a cheesemaker for the summer season, to make the cheeses in the high Alpine huts. They are ripened for up to one year, and are really very seasonal.

L'Etivaz

CANTON VAUD

This rarity is produced in a traditional way in copper vats over open fires. In the 1930s, the collective of farms and cheesemakers around the small village of L'Etivaz decided to break away from the strictures of the Gruyère administration to make a more "authentic" style of Gruyère, using older grazing and production techniques. During the summer and early fall, the cows graze on more than 130 Alpine farms between the glaciers of Les Diablerets and the vineyards of Lake Geneva. Maturing takes place in a modern cellar. All the cheesemaking is done in mountain chalets, giving the flavors a truly complex fruity, rich, and buttery taste. Weighing about 40 pounds (18 kg) and always a little more expensive, they are really worth it.

Château d'Erguel BERNESE JURA

One of the oldest cheeses from this region, this is made at the Fromagerie in Courtelary. The Kämpf family uses the perfect Chasseral grazing areas at 4,265 feet (1,300 m), where the cows are outside for eight months of the year. In the colder months they are kept inside, but fed only hay with a supplement of dried legumes. Weighing about 15½ pounds (7 kg), the Erguel is matured for five or six months, until the spicy flavors are well developed and full.

Le Sous-Bois CANTON VAUD

Members of the Henchoz family have lived and worked in Rossinière, high up in the hills of Vaud, Pays d'En Haut, for generations. Their farm is totally organic, and they also have a herd of sheep (which is unusual to see in Switzerland). The Swiss vacherin cheesemakers think that Le Sous-Bois is very similar to vacherin, but the cheese is smaller and the rind bloomy, unlike the vacherin. The milk is unpasteurized, and the Henchoz family uses milk taken only from their own herd.

The small 5½-ounce (150-g) cheese is wrapped in a pine-bark collar, to keep the cheese intact and enhance the sappy flavors, which are rich, mellow, and nutty. The very high humidity in the cellars encourages not only the bloom on the rind, but also the ripening of the cheese,

Emmentaler ☛ CANTON BERN

Weighing in at 220 pounds (100 kg), Emmentaler is the largest cheese in the world. The more aged mountain-made cheeses have a darker rind; if you can get your hands on the 18-month cheeses from the *alpage* canton in Bern, these will taste strong and spicy, and have fewer holes than the usual versions of this cheese.

It has an almost slightly wet appearance (it sometimes looks as if little tears are oozing out of the cheese) and a chewy density with a fine, nutty texture. It is perfect for eating as a table cheese, but also one of the main components for a Swiss fondue. Eat with a lighter-style refreshing white wine with floral aromas, to really bring out the flavors of this delicious cheese.

Fleurettes des Rougemont (Tomme Fleurette)
☛ CANTON VAUD

Cheesemaker Michel Beroud, whose dairy production is based in the pretty valley of Rougemont, is something of an icon in the Swiss cheesemaking world. His little cheese is such a success that he has shown that it is not just Gruyère that is made in Switzerland. This tender 6-ounce (170 g) "squared-off" disk of soft unpasteurized cow's milk cheese has been matured for 14 days to encourage its light, bloomy white coat. The silky, almost melting cheese within is nutty in flavor, with a light earthiness coming through. It is a perfect addition to the otherwise chunky, robust, and heavier Swiss cheeseboard, and will partner both red and white wines wonderfully.

Stillsitzer Steinsalz ☛ GÄHWIL, TOGGENBURG

In the Tilsiter style, this cheese weighs about 9 pounds (4 kg). Stefan Bühler is another renegade instilling his own style of maturing and production in the cheese. Unlike other cheesemakers in Switzerland who buy in cultures, Stefan creates his own, as well as creating the rennet to coagulate the cheese. Stefan also washes his cheeses in an untreated sea salt. This is more expensive, but helps to provide the cheese's ultimate taste of rich, dense fruitiness and its slightly gritty texture.

Unterwasser ☛ CANTON ST. GALLEN

The Stadelmann family decided to split with the Tilsiter Consortium to make a cheese following organic production guidelines, at Unterwasser in the Toggenburg valley. Since then, a wide range of cheeses has been developed, one being the Unterwasser, weighing about 17½ pounds (8 kg). You might believe that all these styles of cheese would taste the same, but there are distinct differences in the milk from the different areas, and the cheesemaker himself imparts his style during the cheesemaking process, to give each cheese its unique taste. Thomas, who took control of the dairy from his father several years ago, leads his productions with passion and enthusiasm.

Raclette ☛ CANTON GLARUS

Swiss raclettes are much stronger than French, and there are two styles. Raclette Berghoff from Toggenburg has a dense texture and a supple body, enabling it to melt quickly. Alp Raclette from Alp Luser-Schlossli in the Glarus Canton is made in the high Alpine region in the Mühlebach/Engi; it has a much firmer texture, with more brine washings, and is aged for about five months. The flavors are nutty and almost smoky, and quite different in texture from other raclettes. The aroma when melting this style of raclette will be much stronger and earthier, too.

Alp Kohlschlag ☛ CANTON ST. GALLEN

Kohlschlag is just above Mels-Sargans, about one and a half hours from Zurich. This Alp is run by a cooperative, and every year it rents out the high summer pasture for cheesemaking. There are about 50 cows from different farms scattered in the lower villages and, as the season starts, the cattle are led halfway up to begin their summer idyll. As the summer progresses, the cheesemaker follows them higher up the mountain, where huts and cheesemaking facilities are situated. After a few weeks, the forms are brought down to Mels, to be matured in a large cave, where the humid environment and even temperature help the cheeses to develop right through the winter months. The high-mountain cheese is a little larger than other St. Gallen cheeses and is for sale from three months.

LEFT, FROM TOP TO BOTTOM Fleurettes des Rougemont, Stillsitzer Steinsalz, Unterwasser, cut raclette, raclette rind, Alp Kohlschlag

THIS PAGE, FROM TOP TO BOTTOM Scimudin, *Formai de Mut*, Branzi
OPPOSITE, FROM TOP TO BOTTOM Scimudin, *Formai de Mut*, Branzi

Italian Alpine

There are many national parks and protected regions within each country along the Alpine ranges. The Parc Nationale de Vanoise in the Rhône-Alpes is on the border between France and Italy, and once through the Mont Blanc tunnel you are in Gran Paradiso National Park, with the cities of Turin and Milan not too far away. Parco Veglia Devero is a natural Alpine area specifically for preserving pastureland. There are three mountain cheeses that you can find locally, but they are also transported to towns in Piedmont, as well as overseas. Parco dello Stelvio is the largest natural Alpine zone in Italy, encompassing many small towns and mountain ranges. From Bitto, with its paler pitted pâte, and the inclusion of goat's milk in the summer cheeses made in the valleys of Albaredo and Gerola and the high mountain pastures of Sondrio, to the cheeses of the Valtellina hills, this is a region of outstanding beauty.

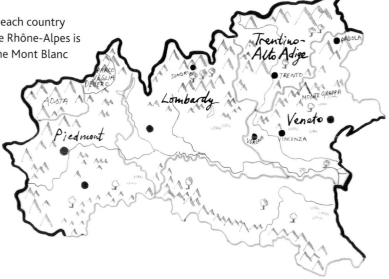

Scimudin 🐄 🐐 SONDRIO

Weighing about 2¼ pounds (1 kg), this is a soft, richly creamy cheese made all over the Sondrio area, but there are still a few farms making a goat's milk version in the Val Codera, an isolated area north of Lake Como. The milk has cream added to it before heating, then a *Penicillium candidum* added to encourage the white rind. The rich buttery texture is like clotted cream, but, if the cheese is allowed to ripen and become more fluid, a nutty sharpness will come through. The late fall cheeses are the most rich and unctuous. The Valtellina wines of the region are ideal to drink with this cheese, or a Pinot Noir with a hint of nut.

Formai de Mut 🐄 LOMBARDY

The name implies "mountain" or "alpine" in the local dialect and that is exactly what this versatile cheese is— simple and delicate, with a light floral taste in the manner of Branzi. It has a thinner, paler rind when young,

giving the cheese a more malleable texture, although with more brine rubbings during aging, the smooth rind becomes darker and very hard and the cheese becomes a delicious fruity and fragrant morsel. People from the local community use this cheese for gratins, as a topping for soups and stews, and in *fonduta*, but it is the more aged cheeses that are served at the table to end a meal.

Branzi 🐄 LOMBARDY

This is a 26½-pound (12-kg) semihard cheese that becomes more brittle with maturity. The summer cheeses are made in the high mountain dairies and dry-salted, while winter cheeses are made in valley dairies and soaked in a brine bath. The cheese has a delicate flavor and aroma when made with the winter milk, due to the cows' feed being more controlled, and in summer, when the cows graze in the open pastures, the flavors become more robust, vegetal, and aromatic. It is a lovely table cheese, but really comes into its own when used to accompany polenta because the sharp, nutty flavors liven up the dish's texture.

Franzedas Alpeggio 🐄 VICENZA/TRENTO

This is one of the rare cheeses made high up in the mountains only during the summer months. It is shaped like a flat stone, and the curds are wrapped in cloth and placed on shelves to dry out, before being hung up in the hut to mature. It has very fruity flavors and a dry, almost crystalline texture.

Asiago Pressato 🐄 VICENZA/TRENTO

This simple cheese is made in the low-lying areas of Vicenza and Trento. It has a sweet, nutty, milky flavor with a springy open texture, and weighs about 26½ pounds (12 kg). It is perfect for those who do not want an overcomplicated-tasting cheese. Asiago cheeses become drier and crumblier with age, developing salty, gritty flavors and textures.

Carnia Altobut Vecchio 🐄 PADOLA

From the municipality of Comelico Superiore, in the province of Belluno, this is an age-old mountain cheese. Mild and delicate when young, the 13-pound (6-kg) cheese will age to give a fruity, sappy flavor to the close-packed pâte, with tiny breaks or cuts in the cheese. The rind is bathed in the brine tub, then rubbed and scraped during the ripening process. This cheese is easy to keep, and could even be stored out of the refrigerator during the cooler months.

Grana Val di Non (Trentingrana) 🐄 TRENTINO

Although falling under the same umbrella as the Grana Protected Consortium, the Grana Val di Non cheese has its own special mark on the rind, to denote that it was made in Trentino.

Trentingrana is made in much the same way as Parmigiano-Reggiano, although this cheese differs in that the aged versions do tend to have scatterings of tiny "eyes" throughout the cheese. One of the main differences between Grana Val di Non and Parmigiano-Reggiano is that the cattle are allowed to graze more freely, especially those on the higher pastures of the Trentino region. ALso, the animals are not subjected to the strict dietary feeding rules applied for Parmesan.

The flavors of the Trentingrana are rich and crumbly with a fruity taste that is not as intense as Parmigiano-Reggiano. This is a very versatile cheese, and it is ideal for use both in the kitchen and as a table cheese. A sharp, dry white wine is a perfect accompaniment, or even a fully dry sparkling Prosecco.

BELOW Franzedas Alpeggio
OPPOSITE, TOP LEFT Franzedas Alpeggio, TOP RIGHT Asiago pressato, MIDDLE RIGHT Asiago pressato, BOTTOM Grana Val di Non, MIDDLE LEFT Carnia Altobut Vecchio (cut and rind)

Grasso d'Alpe Buscagna 🐄 PARCO VEGLIA DEVERO

Part of the toma family and similar to Gruyère, the Grasso, Rodolfo, and Alpeggio have rough artisan-looking crusts. Every "alp," or mountain, pasture has a cheesemaker to transform the milk into cheese, which is identified by the name of the alp. This particular grazing zone is a picturesque Alpine area for snowshoeing, rather than skiing. The tiny hamlets dotted along the way are still very much like they were hundreds of years ago. Similar in style to the Ossolana, but with a smoother texture and less rough "artisan"-style rind, this is a good cheese for snacking, as well as grating for a *fonduta* or gratin.

Toma Ossolana Alpeggio 🐄 PARCO VEGLIA DEVERO

This is another toma, weighing about 11–15½ pounds (5–7 kg). The Alpeggio, however, has a deeper color to the pâte and a real fruity edge to the flavors because it is the one made in the most basic of conditions, right down to hand milking on the mountainside.

The chewy texture of the cheese is similar to Swiss cheeses, but it has a little more oiliness, with scattered eyelets. These cheeses are made in a protected area where grazing rights are carefully monitored, to prevent the grass and flora from diminishing.

Toma Ossolana Rodolfo 🐄 PARCO VEGLIA DEVERO

In the mountain toma style, this cheese has had a longer maturing and a slightly different method of making than the Alpeggio. The mountain pastures of Valdossola are where the toma are made, and the golden straw color of the pâte has a slightly softer texture, with a chewy, savory taste and a rough-looking crust.

The cheeses weigh about 11–15½ pounds (5–7 kg) and have that simple quality can be enjoyed at the end of a meal, served with walnuts or hazelnuts instead of fruit.

Bastardo del Grappa/Morlacco del Grappa 🐄
MONTE GRAPPA MASSIF

From the Monte Grappa Massif in the provinces of Treviso, Belluno, and Vicenza, these cheeses also take their names from the river Grappa. The pastures in this region are poor, and the Burlina cow, which was used for this cheese, has almost been surpassed by Friesian or Bruna Alpina breeds because of the better milk yields. The Bastardo version is so-called because poor grazing means that milk has to be obtained from outside the Morlacco area at certain times of the year. The cheeses are made with partly skimmed milk, and formerly were made only with low-fat milk because the cream would be used for butter.

The smooth, hard, dry rind is washed in brine and rubbed in the usual mountain style, and the compact pâte has scattered pinhead holes. The cheese is ripened for a minimum of six months, but the more aged versions (ripened for up to two years) are eaten in small quantities because they have a strong taste, or even grated.

A Valpolicella red wine is good with the less mature cheeses, but I love aged versions with Recioto di Soave, a dessert wine with a sweetly savory, sherrylike taste, or a fine Amarone with its deep complexity.

Monte Veronese Grasso 🐄 VERONA

Weighing about 13–20 pounds (6–9 kg) and made with low-fat milk, the Grasso cheese is well known throughout northern Italy as being a good table cheese after six months' maturing.

It is not too strong or bitter, and will age beautifully to a crackly texture and fruity, nutty taste. The flavors of a light and fruity Valpolicella wine work wonderfully with this delicious cheese.

LEFT, FROM TOP TO BOTTOM Toma Ossolana Alpeggio, rind of Toma Ossolana Alpeggio, Toma Ossolana Rodolfo, Grasso d'Alpe Buscagna

OPPOSITE, BACK, FROM TOP TO BOTTOM Bastardo del Grappa, Monte Veronese Grasso, Grasso d'Alpe Buscagna, Monte Veronese Grasso, FRONT, FROM TOP TO BOTTOM Morlacco del Grappa, Stanghe di Lagundo

Stanghe di Lagundo TREVISO

This is a simple washed-rind semisoft cheese, made on farms around Vellau, Rio Lagundo, Rabla, Parcines, the Table Mountain and the Sole di Naturno, high up in the Treviso hills. It looks like a large rectangular loaf, weighing around 4½ pounds (2 kg), has a washed, soft pinky rind, with a musty though not unpleasant aroma—it is not as farmyard-like smelling as other washed rinds. The taste is milky and almost sweet, and perfect for thinly slicing as a sandwich filling, or melting over pasta or potatoes for a more hearty meal. It is a welcome change from all the harder cheeses of the Alpine region and is a popular family favorite.

Fontina

This is the Val d'Aosta's most famous cheese. The region has a rugged beauty and
a breathtaking backdrop of snow-capped mountains, and fertile valleys for farming and vineyards.

Fontina 🐄 AOSTA

This very well known cheese from Aosta looks as if it could
be related to French Abondance (see page 92), with its
curved "waistline" and lightly washed and rubbed crust.
An extremely popular cheese made in big quantities, it
is nonetheless the mountain dairy cheese that is more
prized, but also the most difficult to make.

Valdostana cow's milk from single milking is used, so
cheeses are made twice daily. The milk is not skimmed—
the high fat content may be one reason why this cheese is
difficult to make—and it is heated to no more than 96.8°F

(36°C) before the natural rennet is added. It is then left
to curdle for around 50 minutes, then the soft curd is
stirred, roughly broken up, and left to stand and settle.
The curds are cut again into tiny granules, then again
left to settle at the bottom of the vat, which is still warm
enough to "cook" the curds. When the curds are ready to
be removed from the vat, a cheesecloth is plunged into the
mass, and they are scooped up, lifted out, and placed in a
wooden band. The whey is pressed out—first by hand, then
with a heavy weight—for about 12 hours, and the cheeses
are turned at regular intervals, to release the whey evenly.

They are then transferred to a salting bath, before
going to the maturing rooms, where more dry salt is added
on alternate days by cleaning and brushing with brine.
The cheeses absorb about 2 percent of the salt during
the dry-salt process and continual washings in brine and
brushing, until the crust forms and the golden brown
color becomes more evident, encouraged by the humidity
and temperature of the cellars.

These maturing rooms can be in caves, grottoes,
former army bases hidden in the mountains, or even in
an old copper mine in one case; the natural flora and
minerals in the air also contribute to the flavor profile
of the cheese.

The cheese weighs about 17½–26½ pounds (8–12 kg),
and the flavors are sweet, verging on fruity and robust;
the more matured version has a texture that is chewy
and dense. Fontina is a great melting cheese for Italian
fondue, *fonduta*, and lighter red wines, such as Pinot Noir,
or similar fruity but dry-edged wines are good partners.

LEFT Fontina rind
OPPOSITE Sliced fontina
ABOVE LEFT The Aosta landscape.
ABOVE RIGHT Mont Blanc, the Aosta Valley.

THIS PAGE, FROM TOP TO BOTTOM Romadur, Bavarian Blue, Butterkäse, Alp Bergkäse, Adelegger Urberger

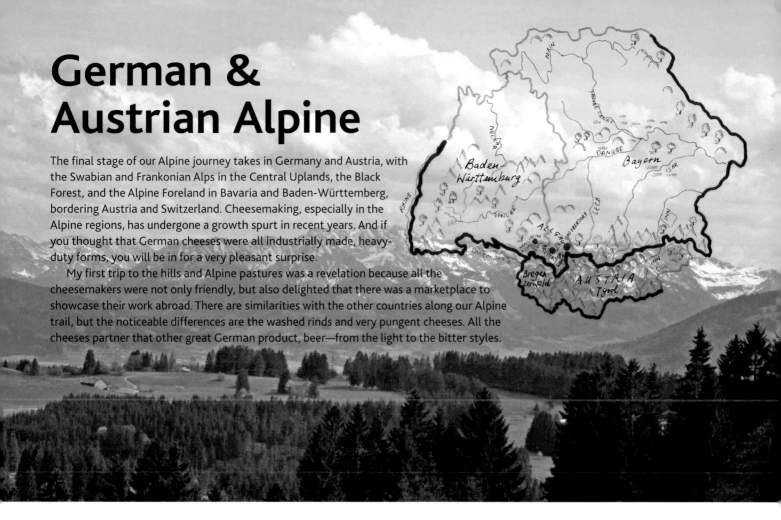

German & Austrian Alpine

The final stage of our Alpine journey takes in Germany and Austria, with the Swabian and Frankonian Alps in the Central Uplands, the Black Forest, and the Alpine Foreland in Bavaria and Baden-Württemberg, bordering Austria and Switzerland. Cheesemaking, especially in the Alpine regions, has undergone a growth spurt in recent years. And if you thought that German cheeses were all industrially made, heavy-duty forms, you will be in for a very pleasant surprise.

My first trip to the hills and Alpine pastures was a revelation because all the cheesemakers were not only friendly, but also delighted that there was a marketplace to showcase their work abroad. There are similarities with the other countries along our Alpine trail, but the noticeable differences are the washed rinds and very pungent cheeses. All the cheeses partner that other great German product, beer—from the light to the bitter styles.

Romadur 🐄 ALLGÄU

Käserei Bremenried Cooperative works with 12 local dairy farms to make an award-winning Emmentaler and a delicious Romadur. The brick-shape cheese weighs about 1 pound 7 ounces (650 g) and has the familiar pungent aroma from the copious washings of the outside rind, which produce the "Rotschmier bacteria." Basically, this is the sticky orange rind that forms on a cheese when washed in salty water and rubbed in raw salt over a period of time. The soft cheese is buttery, with a nutty tang, and is a perfect partner to beer.

Bavarian Blue 🐄 BAD OBERDORF

From the Obere Mühle Cooperative on the edge of the Alpe Engratsgund in Hindelang, this blue cheese weighing 5½ pounds (2.5 kg) has a *Penicillium roqueforti* mold mixed into the curds; the cheese was invented by Basil Weixler in 1902, to rival his favorite Roquefort cheese. Bavarian Blue is really very different, though, because it is creamier and denser with a mellow, nutty taste, making it a perfect morning cheese with toast and a blob of cherry jam, or as part of a cheeseboard selection.

Butterkäse 🐄 SOUTH WEST BAVARIA

Shaped like a loaf and without any rind, this is usually considered a melting cheese—I love it cut into small chunks, placed in the bottom of a bowl, with hot vegetable soup poured on top. The northern German cheeses are very mild and basic, while the southern version has the familiar creamy texture, but with a tart sharpness coming through. If you like raclette, but want something milder, this would be ideal. This family cheese is a staple in the high alps as well as all over Germany, but with a 50 percent fat content it should be eaten sparingly.

Alp Bergkäse 🐄 BALDERSCHWANG

At the Sennalpe Spicherhalde dairy, Fridolin Vogel has 30 Swiss Browns that graze Alpine pastures from May onward, when the whole family moves up the mountain to make cheese throughout the summer. The cheese is ready to be sold at three months, but waiting longer allows the flavors to develop further, and those high mountain meadows covered with flowers and herbs give the cheese a spicy aftertaste.

Adelegger Urberger 🐄 BAVARIA

Isny Cheeses is not only the smallest dairy in Baden-Württemberg, but also one of the best. This 15½-pound (7 kg) cheese is semihard, with a dark washed and brushed rind. When it is left to ripen over nine months, its taste becomes big and full-bodied. The long maturing process allows the flavors to develop so well, and the rind, which is washed in a brine that includes wine, also helps to deepen the taste.

Zigorome  ALLGÄU

Ulrich and Monika Leiner work together on their small farm, Ziegenhof Leiner, in Sulzberg in Allgäu. The Leiners' farm has been organic since 1989, when they received two nanny goats and two kids as a wedding present. The herd now has 60 nanny goats, and the cheeses are mostly sold locally.

Goats thrive and produce plenty of milk during bright, sunny days; in the darker months, they produce offspring and are not milked for cheesemaking, which is why true artisan-made cheeses are very seasonal. These days goats are often kept in "artificial" daylight all through the year, in barns with daylight bulbs to produce consistent milk production, but this means that you do not get the character changes in the milk as you would with goats feeding on new spring grass or late summer grass.

The Zigorome takes its name from Romadur, another washed-rind cheese, but this small 5½-ounce (150-g) cheese is sophisticated in taste, close-textured, and almost sweet, with its washed, sticky rind that seems to lend a bitter honey spiciness to the taste. Of all the cheeses from Bavaria, this one highlights the love of the animal and the land in complete harmony.

Emmentaler 🐄 ALLGÄU

This 200-pound (90-kg) cheese from the Käserei Bremenried Cooperative is quite unlike the commercial cheeses seen all over Germany. These monster cheeses require deft handling, arms of iron, and a will of steel when it comes to lifting the mass of curds from the huge copper pan. They are usually sold from three months onward, but the more aged versions give the most pleasure. The flavors are unlike Swiss or French versions because the grazing areas have natural springs, giving a very nutty and fruity intensity to the flavor.

Weisslacker 🐄 WANGEN IM ALLGÄU

From the Sibratsgfäll Cooperative (see Tilsiter, opposite), this is not a cheese for the faint-hearted—the aroma is pungent, to say the least. The secret is the 20 percent saltwater bath that the cheeses sit in for two days, before going to the warm ripening room and hand salting twice a week. It takes about nine months to complete the maturing.

ABOVE LEFT Zigorome
LEFT Emmentaler
OPPOSITE, TOP LEFT CHEESE Tilsiter, TOP RIGHT CHEESE Weisslacker, BOTTOM CHEESE Rasskass

Serve in small pieces on top of thickly buttered rye bread, with breakfast radishes and a strong beer—some people even like to dip their Weisslacker in their beer! Traditionally, it is served with hearty sausages and spätzle.

Tilsiter 🐄 BREGENZ

The Sibratsgfäll Cooperative run by Hubert Eberle collects milk from 12 dairies around this picture-postcard pretty village on the edge of Bregenzerwald, and transforms the unpasteurized milk into superdense, chewy textures with a hint of sourness that is pleasant rather than bitter. This flavor is essential because it provides heightened enjoyment, especially at breakfast with toasted whole-grain or dark rye bread, slices of cooked ham, and really firm, slightly green tomatoes. What is more, pairing Tilsiter with beer is a joy—just think of those big-flavored wheat beers or dark amber rye beers, or even a blonde—that sour hint works wonders.

Rasskass 🐄 VORARLBERG/BREGENZ FOREZ

Anton Bader of the Dorfsennerei Langenegg Cooperative produces a 14½-pound (6.5-kg) cheese that is relatively low in fat. It is similar to raclette (see page 97) when it is young, at around three months, and can be used in the same way. The cheese has small eyelets and slits running through, although the high-mountain forms are smoother.

There is that familiar strong odor and its red washed rind that is dry and easier to handle, and the flavors are strong and robust. The milk used is unpasteurized and organic, and the only feed the cows get other than fresh grass is sweet hay.

This cheese is the main ingredient used in Bregenz Forest cheese noodles (Käsespätzle, made with fresh egg noodles), a very hearty and tasty dish to serve alongside sausages from the region. It is a delicious partner to a light beer. The drinking milk and the butter from this region are also exceptional.

Italy

When I started working with cheese, I concentrated on France because I had spent so many summer vacations traveling and winter breaks skiing there. My curiosity has never dimmed, but I also became interested in finding out about Italian cheese and why, with all the quaint Italian shops in London, the cheeses looked so processed. Surely there must be farm-made cheeses? Little by little, I explored the regions and found a wealth of cheeses and producers who had never considered selling outside their immediate vicinity, let alone abroad or another part of Italy! Since my early foragings, the floodgates have opened, and we see many handmade and small-production Italian cheeses not only in the UK and USA, but also around the world.

One way to really get to know rural Italy is to stay on a farm. Agritourism is big business in Italy, and this option offers an insight into the way the farm works, as well as a chance to enjoy a region's beauty. Many of the small farms from which I purchase cheeses have these facilities, with some vineyards having very fancy accommodations, while others are more modest. They add much-needed revenue for the farms, as well as extra help should you feel the desire to get your hands dirty and do a little farmwork yourself. In France, where the gîte tradition has been going for many years, they do not offer that inspirational touch the Italians bring to the table—a welcome and a feeling of belonging right from the start, and the joy of being able to cook, taste, and buy the wonderful fruits of their labors.

LEFT An old waterwheel in Tuscany.
BELOW LEFT Maturing cellars in Trentino.
BELOW RIGHT Italian cheeses in production.
OPPOSITE TOP, MIDDLE, AND BOTTOM Mountain pastures in Trentino.

Castelmagno 🐄 CUNEO, PIEDMONT

This is an ancient cheese from the municipalities of Monterosso Grana, Pradleves, and Castelmagno, in the province of Cuneo. It comes in various weights between 4½ and 15½ pounds (2 and 7 kg), although the larger forms are more common. A semihard mold-ripened cheese, rather like a Stilton, it is pierced to allow the air to infiltrate the cheese and encourage the blue (which is only really evident in the very mature forms). It is very similar to Castelrosso (see below), but the grazing area is very specific, and the mixture of milks in the laborious recipe makes it more expensive. The very young cheeses disappoint me, and I prefer ripening them on to get that flaky texture and the earthy bitterness in the flavors. It is particularly good when paired with something special, such as a Barbaresco or Barolo red wine from the region.

Maccagnette alle Erbe 🐄 BIELLA, PIEDMONT

There are several shapes for this cheese, although nowadays it is mostly shaped like an oyster or clam shell. Its rind, once ripened, takes on this look; the cheese is scored on top to let the herbs and black pepper covering it permeate into the curd. Seen mostly around the Biella province and weighing from 18 ounces (500 g) to 2¼ pounds (1 kg), it is mostly made from cow's milk, with additions of goat's and ewe's milk when available during the year. The flavors are dominated by the mountain herbs and the pepper, which it is important not to cut away. I would suggest maybe a local beer, rather than a wine, as an accompaniment.

Toma Maccagno 🐄 BIELLA, PIEDMONT

The Luigi Rosso family from the Biella province has been making cheese since the early 19th century. This part of Piedmont is favored for skiing, and the Rossos have a hut on the slopes, to sell their cheeses to passing skiers. This lovely creamy, dense cheese weighing about 6½ pounds (3 kg) has been washed in brine, and rubbed to produce a pale peach color dotted with patches of gray and white bloomy molds. The semihard pâte is fruity and nutty, with hints of smoky sweetness. I love this cheese teamed with a zesty Gavi di Gavi, a more traditional Oltrepò Pavese red that is not too dry, or a young Barbera.

Seirass del Fieno 🐑 PIEDMONT

The word *seirass* is derived from the Latin *seracium*, which means "whey," but in Piedmont and Val d'Aosta this word also means "ricotta." *Del fieno* means that the cheese is wrapped in hay wisps, which used to help keep the cheese intact during transport. This cheese is made a little differently than other ricottas—the whey is brought to a boil, then fresh milk and salt are added, before the solids are drained. The flavors will be much more interesting and nutty if you let the cheese dry to half its size; it is an interesting cheese to serve with a dry sparkling wine.

Castelrosso 🐄 BIELLA, PIEDMONT

This is a chubby toma weighing 11–13 pounds (5–6 kg), from the Luigi Rosso family farm near Biella. It has a crumbly texture, with lovely white and gray moulds on the naturally formed crust. A moist cheese when young, and rather like a Wensleydale, it has a dry crumble, but the cheese itself has a dewy quality when you cut into it. If you let it ripen slowly, it will dry out to a flakier texture. The flavors have plenty of mineral and herbal depth, and the nutty, earthy tastes come through at the end. I really love the summer and fall cheeses. This is good with a white wine such as Gavi, or dry reds such as Resiot, from Piedmont.

ABOVE Castelmagno
RIGHT, BACK CHEESE Seirass del fieno,
FRONT CHEESE Maccagnette alle erbe

THIS PAGE, TOP LEFT CHEESE Sierass del fieno, TOP RIGHT CHEESE Castelrosso, BOTTOM LEFT CHEESE Toma Maccagno, BOTTOM RIGHT CHEESE Maccagnette alle erbe

Caprino Tartufo ⚜ PIEDMONT

From the same producer as the caprini freschi below, but this time the fresh cheeses are topped with shavings of Alba truffles. The distinct bosky aroma give a luxurious element to the flavors. If you cannot afford the high price of a knobbly truffle, crumbling this cheese into a risotto or over pasta will give a real sense of their exotic perfume, mingling with the delicate creaminess of the cheese.

Caprini Freschi ⚜ PIEDMONT

I love the cheeses from La Bottera, situated in the heart of Cuneo near Morozzo, about an hour or so from Turin. The family estate is run both on traditional lines and with modern equipment because the younger members of the family see the need to embrace both cultures in order to move forward. The resulting cheeses are always beautifully made and packaged well. The caprini freschi is delicate, just 3½ ounces (100 g) of fresh goat cheese, with no visible rind. The flavors are light and nutty, but not insipid—you do get that hint of goatiness coming through. It is perfect with Champagne or a crisp white wine.

Robiola delle Langhe ⚜ ⚜ ⚜ PIEDMONT

Coming from between Bosia and Alba in the heart of Piedmont wine country, this cheese epitomizes the richness of the milk, and the delicate flavors complement the fine wines. Robiola is famous throughout this region and uses a combination of cow's, goat's and ewe's milks, to make a fudgy, soft cylinder weighing about 10½ ounces (300 g); its thin, natural rind has a hint of white bloom.

Truffle Cheese (Tuma Trifulera) ⚜ ⚜ ⚜ PIEDMONT

La Bottera's truffle cheese is made with mixed milk and weighs 18 ounces (500 g). The crumbly textured cheese is slightly dry, but this is necessary to appreciate the truffle pieces mixed into the curd. It is earthy and aromatic.

Fiore di Langhe ⚜ PIEDMO

The smooth delicate pâte has a soft bloomy rind, to keep the cheese intact. The sweetly earthy, nutty flavors are light and delicate when young, becoming more pronounced with ripening. It is a lovely after-dinner cheese and weighs around 6 ounces (180 g).

Caprino delle Langhe ⚜ PIEDMONT

A small medallion weighing 3¼ ounces (90 g), it has a thin natural rind hugging the close-textured pâte. The Alta Langhe is in the heart of Piedmont, which is also famed for its wines, which work well with this cheese, especially when it is ripened to give the flavors a more earthy quality.

LEFT, TOP LEFT CHEESE Robiola delle Langhe, TOP RIGHT CHEESE Caprini freschi and truffle cheese, BOTTOM RIGHT CHEESE Caprino delle Langhe, BOTTOM LEFT CHEESE Fiore di Langhe
BELOW Caprino Tartufo
RIGHT, ABOVE Ricotta Carena, BELOW Grana Padano

Ricotta Carena 🐄 LOMBARDY

This cheese is produced by Angelo Carena, whose small farmhouse production is based in Piacenza, Lombardy. Angelo is famous for his pannerone cheese, which has a protected place of origin (DOP), but his other fresh cheeses are a revelation if you have been used to supermarket-bought fresh curd cheeses. His ricotta, made with cow's milk, is perhaps not as light and frothy as seirass (see page 113), but nevertheless there is no sourness to the flavors, which are rich, dense, and creamy.

Grana Padano 🐄 LOMBARDY

Piacenza is my chosen area in Lombardy for Grana. Dairy No. 205 is situated in one of the designated zones, and its Grana Padano is particularly prized for its taste and texture. Although a young cheese is often used because its Parmesan style has a creamier, crumbly texture than the grainy sharp Parmigiano-Reggiano, I like to have an aged version as well, around 18 months, to give a lovely fruity, gritty taste, but still with that creamy density. The price of this 77-pound (35-kg) cheese is not as high as Parmigiano-Reggiano because its designated areas stretch from Trentino through Piedmont and Lombardy, but nevertheless it is still a taste to be reckoned with.

Gorgonzola

Gorgonzola is produced in the Piedmont and Lombardy regions. Both regions boast fertile and sheltered areas, such as those in the Val Padana, which contribute to the complexity of flavors in the cheeses.

THIS PAGE Gorgonzola naturale

OPPOSITE, TOP LEFT "Combing" the curds.

OPPOSITE, MIDDLE LEFT "Ironing" cheese during maturing.

OPPOSITE, MIDDLE RIGHT Dairy cows in Lombardy.

OPPOSITE, BOTTOM RIGHT Gorgonzola dolce

Gorgonzola Naturale 🐄 LOMBARDY

This 26½-pound (12-kg) cheese is traditionally made as a two-layered curd, using both the morning and evening milk, which is ladled in layers into the cheese molds. The blue is from a *Penicillium roqueforti* added to the heated curds. The cheeses are brined in a saltwater solution and left for a week or two, before being pierced at the top, sides, and bottom of the cheese, to allow the blue bacteria mold to distribute evenly into well-spread blue-green veins. The taste is rich, fruity, and sappy, with earthy aromas. It is perfect for the cheeseboard, especially with a big, bold red wine, but it is also a favorite cooking ingredient.

I have tried Gorgonzola from both Piedmont and Lombardy, and there are subtle differences. While I like the rich, buttery texture of the Piedmont dolce cheeses, it is the naturale from a small production from near Piacenza in Lombardy, in the Val Padana, that strikes a good balance. Everyone expects the flavors to be pronounced and nutty for the harder naturale cheeses, but it is important that the blue does not have that aggressive, soapy attack, which can kill the taste of a wine in its tracks. If you know the famous Grana Padano from this region, with its sweetness and creaminess to the crumbly texture, you will recognize the sweet, hazelnut, milky flavor coming through with the Gorgonzola, too.

Gorgonzola Dolce 🐄 LOMBARDY

Made in Piedmont and Lombardy, the Italians call it *erborinato*—Lombard dialect for "parsley green"—which is how the molds in the cheese look. The dolce is often termed "Dolcelatte," which is a name given to a famous industrially made version, but in reality should not be associated with a true Gorgonzola. The dolce cheese is really creamy and silky, using milk from only a single milking per batch; it weighs about 17½ pounds (8 kg), and is cut into two half rounds, being such a soft cheese. The melting pâte has blue veins gently bleeding into the curd, inducing a sweet, nutty taste. As a table cheese it is sensational, but when used in cooking, such as spooning into pasta or risotto, it is delicious and unctuous.

Sottocenere al Tartufo Veneto 🐄

TREVISO

This is a compact, smooth-textured cheese has flakes of truffle mixed into the pâte, before being placed in molds. The cheese is then washed in brine after a little ripening, left to dry before being rubbed in olive oil (to prevent molds from forming), then rolled in fragrant ground spices, including cinnamon and truffle essence. Fine ash cinders are then pressed onto the cheese, to help retain all the delicious aromatic characteristics.

It is a difficult cheese to match to wine, due to all the spices, but perhaps a full-bodied dry red wine or a dessert-style wine from the region, such as Recioto di Soave, or a dry Prosecco di Valdobbiadene.

Pecorino Ubriaco 🐑 TUSCANY

(FINISHED IN TREVISO)

This is a Tuscan pecorino that is shipped up to Treviso to be ripened and washed. The cheeses, which have been aged for three months, are plunged into a vat of Cabernet grape wine pressings, or lees, giving the rind a deep purple/burgundy color. Left to marinate for at least 60 days, then dried out on wooden shelves in cool cellars, the result is a taste that is deeply fruity and rich, with a wonderful vinous aroma. There are cheeses made in this way in Tuscany and Umbria, but I believe that the Treviso ones are much more elegant and refined.

Puzzone di Moena 🐄 TRENTO

The only rind-washed and rubbed cheese in this region, and although the name of the cheese is relatively new, the recipe dates to medieval times.

Maturing lasts for a minimum of 60 days, but can go much longer—at least six or seven months. During the ripening time, the cheeses are washed by hand once a week using a water-and-salt-moistened cloth, which is massaged over the cheese. This encourages the bacteria to form on the outside of the rind, and the intense, pervasive aroma, or *puzzone* (meaning "stinky"), becomes more apparent because the bacteria also change the color of the rind to a pale golden apricot. This cheese has a chewy density and a nutty taste that is long and lingering.

ABOVE Pecorino ubriaco
OPPOSITE, TOP LEFT Sottocenere al Tartufo Veneto
OPPOSITE, TOP RIGHT, TOP CHEESE Puzzone di Moena, semi-mature, BOTTOM CHEESE Puzzone di Moena, extra-mature
OPPOSITE, BOTTOM RIGHT Taleggio
OPPOSITE, BOTTOM LEFT Strachitund

Taleggio 🐄 LOMBARDY

This is a soft, springy-textured square slab of washed-rind cheese weighing about 3¾ pounds (1.7 kg). The texture is creamy, with a rich, melting quality that is not too salty, but has a lovely sappy, floral flavor, which marries well with firm, juicy cherries from Vignola (near Modena) because they have a slightly sharper taste, but are delicious when partnered with certain cheeses. That salty—sweet grittiness to the cheese is a perfect partner to dry white and light fruity Valtellina wines.

Strachitund 🐄 LOMBARDY

The name of this cheese is partly derived from the local dialect meaning "round" (*tondo* in Italian), and it has been made in the Valbrembana area since the late 19th century. Weighing about 9 pounds (4 kg), it utilizes both morning and evening milk in the same way as Gorgonzola—the morning's milk is mixed with 25–30 percent of the previous evening's milk, then dry-salted, before maturing for two months. The cheeses are periodically turned for even ripening, and at about 40 days they are pierced, to allow a uniform growth of molds. The bluing is hardly visible at first; only after several months will you see the veining, which gives strength and nuttiness to the dry, crumbly texture. The natural crust develops its molds, which have a mottled appearance, and careful monitoring is required because they can become wet, which affects the flavor.

Parmesan

Time is on Parmigiano-Reggiano's side. The long, slow maturing stage, where the environment works with the milk to produce the layers of flavor and texture, makes this one of the world's most perfect cheeses.

Parmigiano-Reggiano 🐄 EMILIA-ROMAGNA

The fact that Parmigiano-Reggiano (Parmesan) is one of the healthiest cheeses, making it suitable for very young children, nursing mothers, the elderly, and athletes, comes as no surprise. The long, slow aging process helps the cheese to develop and disperse its goodness. Made with unpasteurized skim milk from accredited dairies within the allotted region of Emilia-Romagna, including Parma, Reggio Emilia, and Modena, the crust of Parmigiano-Reggiano is washed in brine, then rubbed with olive oil and slowly matured under strict supervision.

Only cheeses with the Consorzio Parmigiano-Reggiano markings are the true Parmigiano, and there is a definite difference in flavors and textures between mountain or hill cheeses (with high numbers) and the valley and farms closest to the river Po (with lower numbers). Some believe that the low-numbered cheeses are the most prized, but they are also the most expensive. While my preference is for the valley cheeses, mainly because I like this cheese to be at least three years of age, the mountain and hill cheeses are often sought after because their flavors are robust, but not quite as gritty and salty.

The evening milk is left overnight in long, shallow metal troughs in a warm room. The cream will slowly rise to the top and the following morning is skimmed off, then the milk will be added to the morning's whole milk and transferred to the vat, where a starter is added and the milk is heated. This procedure is the kick start to forming the curds and will also determine the flavor and texture profile of the cheese—too much or too little acidity in the starter can mean either too dry or too soft a crumble to the cheese. Next, a traditional rennet is added, and it takes 10–12 minutes for the curds to separate from the whey, ready to be "milled" in the vat into tiny lentil-size pieces. It continues "cooking" until 131°F (55°C) is reached. The curds are placed into "fascera" molds, which have the characteristic markings that imprint into the cheese, then the ID showing the code number of the dairy is pressed on the outer rind, stating where it was made, the Consortium mark, and the date of production. After the cheeses are immersed in a brine bath for 24 days, they are then ready for the maturing rooms.

I have forged connections with a small producer called San Carlo, which makes its cheeses with milk from its own herd and matures the cheeses in its own airy cheeserooms. This adds to the cost of the cheese because an inspector has to make regular visits to watch production, see that the cheeses are the right weight of 77 pounds (35 kg), and test the cheeses as they ripen. Most producers prefer to take their cheeses directly to the Consortium maturing caves, to be ripened by its professionals.

I can stipulate exactly what month and year of Parmesan I would like from San Carlo, however, and if the cheesemaker does not have what I want he will advise me what is at its peak. The butter he produces, which is made in very small quantities, is absolutely delicious—light and sweetly milky—perfect for making short pastry, and for mixing into a creamy risotto.

ABOVE LEFT The Italian countryside. ABOVE RIGHT Carpineti Castle, in Reggio Emilia. OPPOSITE Parmigiano-Reggiano

Central & Southern Italy

Once into the central regions of Italy, you sense the influence of the Renaissance when visiting its beautiful cities, but, traveling through the countryside, you can see why artists found this a paradise, and why tourists flock each year to soak up its history. The hams, salami, and famous Chianina beef are prized in the regions of central Italy, and the cheeses that evoke this part are the pecorinos—not just the hard, gritty, fruity ones, but also those that are soft and buttery, fresh and light, and others covered in ferns or vine pressings. The olive oils and wines of the region are also legendary.

The river Tiber runs through Rome and is the major river of the southern "boot" of Italy. The "ankle" is Abruzzo and Molise, and the southernmost part of Lazio; the "toe" is Calabria; and the "heel" is Apulia (Puglia), with the islands of Sicily and Sardinia off the coast. The weather is scorching in the summer, with rain and even snow in the winter—the arid, rocky terrain and hills make farming difficult and transportation not easy. The cheese production here is mozzarella from Campania, where Indian buffalo were introduced to the marshy land, and the stretched curds of caciocavallo "gourds" hanging from the beams, as well as strong and spicy pecorinos. In Apulia, you will find tomatoes and artichokes in abundance, olive groves, and spicy olive oil, and all through this particular part of Italy the wines are big and bold.

Castagnolo 🐑 TUSCAN

This is one of those oddly shaped rounds of soft pecorino with a thin natural crust, patted down to prevent too many molds from flourishing. Weighing around 2¼ pounds (1 kg), the cheese has a smooth, mellow richness, with a sweet earthy taste, and it can be matured for longer to obtain bigger flavors. The young cheeses are soft and springy, but if you ripen them quickly they become almost melting at the edges—if you are lucky enough to get them in this state, spoon some into a risotto.

Pecorino Marzolino Rosso 🐑

TUSCANY

This cheese is mostly seen with its natural rind still pristine white, achieved by placing the cheeses in cloths, then hanging them up to drain off any residue whey, and ripening. Weighing about 2½ pounds (1.2 kg), the rosso is removed from its cheesecloth bag to have its rind rubbed in tomato paste, then olive oil, before it is matured. The cheese is matured for 40 days, giving it a light, crumbly texture and a not too aggressive flavor.

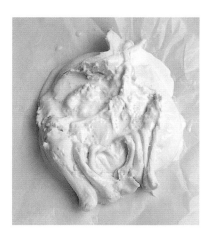

Casciotta Etrusca 🐑

TUSCANY

This is a soft ewe's milk pecorino with a supple texture and a taste of milky sweet hazelnuts. Weighing about 3 pounds 5 ounces (1.5 kg), these are seen at the farmers markets in all shapes and sizes. Melted into a sauce, or used as an accompaniment to young spring vegetables, it heralds the lighter foods for summer eating. Thinly slice the cheese onto piping hot bruschetta for a quick and tasty lunchtime snack.

Capretta di Toscano 🐐 TUSCANY

This 5½-pound (2.5-kg) goat cheese from around Maremma is very seasonal and not made in great quantity. It is a light, sweetly milky, nutty-tasting hard goat cheese, with a ridged rind rubbed in oil, to produce a deep ocher color without any added bloomy molds. It is especially good in the summer months, when the sweetness of the milk really comes through.

It should not be aged too long because the gently earthy flavors are more desirable than the harsher, more animal hints. It is good "shaved" over a green salad or onto pasta with summer truffles.

ABOVE TOP LEFT The Tuscan countryside.
ABOVE MIDDLE Burrata
OPPOSITE, TOP LEFT CHEESE Castagnolo, TOP RIGHT CHEESE Pecorino marzolino rosso, BOTTOM RIGHT CHEESE Casciotta etrusca, BOTTOM LEFT CHEESE Capretta di toscano

Burrata 🐄 MOLISE/PUGLIA

This cheese is made elsewhere in Italy, but, if you want to taste it at its best, then make sure it comes from Molise or Puglia (Apulia). The cheese is so fragile that in summer it simply does not travel the distance to London, so we do not sell it until fall.

The cheese was invented by cheesemakers wanting to use up leftover cheese from their caciocavallo and provolone. They shred the pieces, add extra cream (from the cow's milk mozzarella production), and place this in pouches made of mozzarella curd stretched into a purse shape. The top of the pouch is squeezed together and tied with string, then dipped in a hot salty brine to cook it and make it more stable, before being packed into a bag (although in the old days it was wrapped in the outer green leaves of leeks). Weighing about 10½–18 ounces (300–500 g), this is a rich and creamy confection best eaten as simply as possible.

Pecorino Tartufo 🐑 TUSCANY

Tuscany is the home of truffles, and in summer they are abundant and not too expensively priced. It is obvious that a small 18-ounce (500-g) truckle would be an ideal recipient of truffle pieces through the curd. The thin natural rind encases the cheese, which is flaky more than crumbly, but with a smooth, mellow taste. The first impact is the sweetness of the ewe's milk, with the follow-on of the truffles giving an earthy and aromatic taste. It is lovely when fresh, but when ripened in cool humid rooms it becomes richer and tastier, with the truffle earthiness coming to the fore.

Pecorino Peperoncino 🐑 TUSCANY

With this pecorino, similar in size to the tartufo, the fresh curds are mixed with chopped fresh red chiles, to give the mellow-tasting cheese a spicy hot sweetness. Always look for cheeses made with fresh, not dried, chiles because the flavors will be fresher and livelier, rather than too spicy. I love using this cheese when making pizza.

Pecorino Vilanetto Rosso 🐑 TUSCANY

This is another traditional-style cheese from Maremma, made with unpasteurized milk, to give a tangy flavor to the crumbly-textured cheese. Weighing about 6½ pounds (3 kg), the young cheeses of early spring and late fall have very different textures—spring cheeses are more crumbly and fall ones smoother.

The ewes are allowed to roam and forage for their food on pastures studded with wild herbs and flora; by late summer, the grazing areas are drier and very warm, which means that coagulation will be much quicker and the cheese will require only a light pressing. The caramel-colored crust is achieved by lightly rubbing olive oil mixed with a little tomato paste into the rind, before maturing in stone cellars. The cuore cheeses are not as gritty, with a softer, more flaky texture and flowery and fruity flavors.

Pecorino Vinaccia 🐑 PERUGIA, UMBRIA

This is a 9-pound (4-kg) farmhouse handmade ewe's milk cheese, which after a ripening period of three or four months is plunged into a vat of wine pressings, including stems, skins, seeds, etc., and left for 30–40 days to macerate. The cheeses are then taken out and the vine pressings left on the cheese, and the maturing process continues in airy cellars on wooden shelves for another three months or longer. The resulting texture is hard, with a moist crumble, and the aroma is intense, with the perfume of the wine pressings mingling with the salty-earthy cheese. The taste, as you can imagine, is strong, fruity, and nutty.

RIGHT, FROM TOP RIGHT CHEESE TO BOTTOM RIGHT Pecorino tartufo, pecorino peperoncino, pecorino vilanetto rosso, LEFT TOP AND BOTTOM CHEESE Pecorino vinaccia

Pecorino Affinato in Vinaccia in Visciola 🐑
APENNINE HILLS, UMBRIA

This 18-ounce (500-g) ewe's milk cheese has local cherries pressed on the outside rind. The Visciola cherry grows wild in Umbria and is somewhat like a Morello cherry. It is usually used to make a sweet dessert wine, but here the cheesemaker has taken the pressings after the juice is extracted and macerates three-month-aged cheeses for four weeks in the mixture. The result is a very intense fruity taste, making it strong, but not bitter. The cheeses arrive with a sticky outside rind due to the steeping process; if you find the aroma too powerful, let the cheese dry out a little by placing it on a tray in a cool room or cellar. Natural molds will develop on the outside, which can be patted down to avoid becoming too thick. The cheese will become a little drier, too, and will have a flaky texture with the flavor of the bitter cherry.

Pecorino Muffa Bianca 🐑 APENNINE HILLS, UMBRIA
From Gubbio, this 4-pound (1.8-kg) ewe's milk cheese is heated to just below pasteurization, to help eliminate any unknown pathogens because the Sopravvissana and Sardinian sheep mostly graze on open pasture land with the addition of sweet hay during the colder months. The outside molds grow naturally on the rind without any additional bacteria having to be added to the milk to encourage this process. The cheeses are aged for three months in stone caves in the hills, and the semihard texture has a lovely rounded taste, with an aroma of wild flora and mushrooms. I prefer wines with a bit of bite and acidity with this cheese, especially the dry Chianti styles and Montalcino. You definitely need something that can cope with all the wild and fruity flavors.

Pecorino Montefalco 🐑 UMBRIA
From the town of Montefalco, this 2½-pound (1.2-kg) cheese is from a small family farm producing a limited quantity of cheese from their own flock of 150 ewes. Hand milking is still valued and the traditional cheese recipe has not been altered. The cheese tastes earthy and nutty with a gentle sweetness, but with aging there is a definite farmyard intensity, so we try not to keep it too long.

Formaggio di Fossa 🐑 UMBRIA
Weighing about 6½ pounds (3 kg), this ewe's milk cheese, with additions of a little cow's milk, takes about ten months to mature completely. It is aged for five months in normal cellar conditions, then put into an Apennine *fossa* (which means "hollow") for 90 days. The cheese is then matured for another two months in normal cellar conditions, to let the deformed and softened cheese wheel reshape and develop.

This is a rare, special cheese made according to Umbrian tradition. Before it is placed in the hollow, the rind is completely covered with herbs and spices from the hills—laurel, juniper, wild thyme, mint, rosemary, and wild fennel. The cheese is then placed in a sack, ready to be matured.

The flavors of formaggio di fossa are extraordinarily complex, fruity, aromatic, sapid, and persistent. The cheeses are made in early summer, so the best time for eating is toward the end of the year or late winter. Because of the different flavors coming through with this cheese, you need a well-structured red wine, such as a Brunello di Montalcino or a Rosso Riserva from Chianti, as an ideal accompaniment. Eat the cheese simply chipped into small pieces with a knife.

LEFT Formaggio di fossa

OPPOSITE, FROM TOP TO BOTTOM CHEESE Pecorino Affinato in Vinaccia in Visciola, pecorino muffa bianca, pecorino Montefalco

LEFT Provola di Bufala Affumicate

OPPOSITE, TOP LEFT AND RIGHT Provolone
del Monaco

OPPOSITE, BOTTOM RIGHT Mozzarella
di Bufala

OPPOSITE, BOTTOM LEFT Ricotta Salata

shapes, rather than put into molds. Very fresh mozzarella that is just 24–48 hours old has a tighter, more chewy texture; if you want to eat it this fresh, you should keep the cheese at room temperature, in its own whey, so that you will taste the light, delicate qualities. Keeping the cheese for longer is not to be sniffed at, however, because it becomes softer and creamier, and even after five or six days is still delicious. Just remember not to keep the cheese too cold—it is a hardier cheese than you think.

Provola di Bufala Affumicate

CAMPANIA

These small 10½-ounce (300-g) scamorze-style cheeses are made by heating the buffalo milk and adding the rennet and whey starter culture from the previous cheesemaking session. The curd is cut with wooden knives, to expel as much whey as possible, and pressed together before slicing with steel knives into strips. After 24 hours, the strips are placed in boiling-hot water, and large wooden spoons are used to stretch the cheese, before it is shaped, then dropped into a brine bath. The balls are tied with string made of wheat straw. They are then smoked over wood chips, whereupon the outside rind becomes a beautiful dark ocher color. The aroma is intensely smoky, and the taste is light and earthy, with sweet oak-smoked flavors.

Provolone del Monaco NAPLES, CAMPANIA

This is an unpasteurized cow's milk cheese from Vico Equense, weighing 6½ pounds (3 kg) and made from single milking. The cheese is formed into its pear or cylinder shape, tied with string, and left to hang in a cellar for 4–18 months, with washing in brine occurring in between. The rind is smooth and mottled, with a few gray moulds, and the flavors are sharp and herbal, with a chewy density, redolent of the region in both taste and aroma.

Mozzarella di Bufala CAMPANIA

The humidity around the ancient town of Paestum and in the Salerno province is perfect for the buffalo because they love to wallow in the muddy, swampy "baths." The term *mozzare* comes from a Neapolitan word meaning "to cut," and the stretched curds are cut into rounds or other

Ricotta Salata PUGLIA, SICILY, SARDINIA

This is essentially a ricotta that has been pressed of its whey and shaped into conical cylinders, and is without any visible rind. Ricotta salata's salty, dried, firm texture makes it a good cheese for grating over pasta or as a filling for tortelloni. It is mainly made with ewe's milk, but also with buffalo's and cow's milk. The cheese weighs about 10½ ounces (300 g).

Pecorino Siciliano Peperoncino 🐑 SICILY

The addition of black peppercorns really spices up the flavor of the pecorino, and the locals love this cheese with a glass of red wine. It is delicious shaved over roasted artichokes, or even served in thin slices melting on top of barbecued meats. It epitomizes summer, and toasted slices of country-style bread such as ciabatta with tomatoes and slivers of this cheese are a great lunchtime snack.

Pecorino Siciliano 🐑 SICILY

The strong and spicy-flavored pecorino, weighing about 22–26½ pounds (10–12 kg), is typical in Sicily, and one farm, Casalgismondo, situated close to the Greco-Roman site of Morgantina, in the center of Sicily, produces an excellent cheese. The whole farm is run on organic principles, and the diet of the animals is supplemented by grain and hay grown on the farm. Maria Rita d'Amico and her dairymen make very traditional cheeses, and this is the perfect example of how a sharp, salty pecorino should taste. The semi-staggionati cheese is the one I offer when asked for a romano style. The locals eat this cheese with a typical rough wine, but there are other ways of enjoying the cheese as a culinary ingredient. The staggionati, which is very strong and salty, is lovely grated over pasta or vegetables instead of Parmigiano, and little nuggets with wine make a lovely appetizer before dinner.

Pecorino Siciliano Fresco 🐑 SICILY

The younger cheeses from Maria Rita d'Amico are really good as a simple snack, to chip away and serve with a full-bodied "meaty"-style red wine, especially those from the alluvial soil of Etna. The crumbly texture, with the outline of the reeded basket molds just visible on the rind, is salty and sweetly earthy, yet has not acquired that aggressive "catch-in-the-throat" acidity of the older cheeses.

Formaggio Piacentinu Ennese 🐑 SICILY

Casalgismondo also make Piacentinu Ennese, an interesting local cheese weighing about 9 pounds (4 kg), which takes on a deep gold or saffron color from the infusion of saffron threads. The curds have black peppercorns mixed in, then are strained into rush containers and placed in hot whey to cook. They are drained and covered with a weighted lid, then left for two or three days to continue the draining, before being dry-salted for a month and then matured. It is best eaten fresh, to experience the flavor of the saffron together with the hit of peppercorns; pair with a sweet Sicilian dessert wine, although Nero d'Avola red wines will also go well.

Ragusano 🐄 SICILY

This 22–35-pound (10–16-kg) squared-off loaf of stretched curd cheese is quite unique. Made in the same way as provolone or mozzarella, the cheeses are made from late fall to spring, although winter-made cheeses are deemed to be the best. The grass is not so scorched and dry as in summer, and the air is cooler, making this a perfect environment for the Modicana cows, a local breed, to graze. Because of the increased production, there are also Swiss Brown and Holstein cows, to help keep up with the quota of milk required. The curds are worked by hand or with a stick and shaped into a ball, pulling and reshaping to begin the stretching and splitting process.

LEFT, TOP CHEESE Pecorino siciliano peperoncino, RIGHT CHEESE Pecorino siciliano, LEFT CHEESE Pecorino siciliano fresco
BELOW LEFT Ragusano
BELOW RIGHT Formaggio Piacentinu Ennese

ABOVE, LEFT AND RIGHT, FROM TOP TO BOTTOM CHEESES Caprino sardo al caprone, pecorino tinaio moresco, pecorino saraceno

All this turning and smoothing, and rubbing in a little oil-and-vinegar solution, gives the surface of the cheese its lovely smooth ocher finish. Best eaten at 8–24 months, it has complex flavors and aromas that improve with time. You will sense fresh earthy mushrooms, toast, bitter orange, fresh-mown grass, and all the Iblei mountain flora coming into play, together with the typical sharp and slightly wild herbal flavors.

Caprino Sardo al Caprone 🐐 SARDINIA

The season for goat cheeses from Sardinia is very limited due to the scorching hot summers and often very cold, blustery weather in the winter. The aged cheeses from Oristano are some of the loveliest I have ever tasted; the spring, summer, and fall cheeses matured for three to nine months have gentle sweet flavors ranging to those with a more "feral" scent. The cheese has the typical "donkey-back" shape (flat top and bottom, and vertical sides), with a smooth, dark brown rind from rubbing with olive oil and cinders to prevent thick molds. The compact texture with little eyelets gives an intense and persistent taste, with an aroma of dry grass and earthy farmyard. The 4½-pound (2 kg) cheese is available up to Christmas, when we get aged versions. This is probably the most stylish hard goat cheese I have ever tasted.

Pecorino Tinaio Moresco 🐑 SARDINIA

This cheese is from Oristano on the west coast of Sardinia, where the land is irrigated by Sardinia's largest river, the Tirso, which gives the grazing pastures a mineral richness. The full-flavored pecorino has a lovely salty sharpness and fruity edge. The cheeses are washed in brine for the first 48 hours, then rubbed in oil and tomato paste, to prevent outside molds from appearing. The crust develops an ocher hue, and the flavors of the milk come through with a tingle on the tongue. This is a perfect table cheese, but you can also shave it over salads and risotto.

Pecorino Saraceno 🐑 SARDINIA

There are matured, semimatured, and fresher versions of pecorino, but the ones from the rugged mountain areas in the middle of the island of Sardinia have really powerful flavors. The versions with a blackened crust have been oiled and rubbed, then matured in mountain caves. There is a sweet mocha style in the fruity flavors, and dry red wines with mouth-puckering tannins work well with this cheese. The younger cheeses with more golden rinds have a smoother texture and are less gritty; you taste the sweeter, floral favors, which are delightful with both white and red wines. The artisan cheeses come in odd sizes, which can vary from 6½–13 pounds (3–6 kg).

Spain & Portugal

The Iberian Peninsula (with Spain and Portugal making up a vast proportion of the landmass) has an unusual position on the world map—it is on the southwestern edge of the European landmass, with North Africa within sight at its narrowest point. Its geographical location exposes it to a huge variety of climatic conditions. The peninsula has a coastline of more than 2,050 miles (3,300 km). Humidity from the Atlantic Ocean to the north and west sweeps over the limestone peaks, while the Mediterranean Sea to the hot east and south carries warming air. The dominant features of the central plateaus and mountains provide temperature extremes, as well as differing precipitation levels.

The biggest rainfalls happen twice a year, and the summers are exceedingly hot, causing droughts—these extremes of alpine climate in the Spanish Pyrenees and Sierra Nevada to the subtropical Canary Islands are reflected in the styles and flavors of the cheeses and are in tune with the terrain. The central plateau, where the most extreme temperatures occur, is referred to by Castilians as *nueve meses de invierno y tres meses de infierno*—"nine months of winter and three months of hell." Over the years, the soil has been improved by diverting water sources. For the small independent farmer and cheesemaker, however, life is still subject to often harsh climatic conditions.

There are many rivers coursing through Spain and Portugal, but a substantial number are dry for most of the year. The longest river, the Tajus, starts off in the picturesque mountain region of Albarracín in Aragon, and flows right through Spain to its outlet in Lisbon, the capital of Portugal. The Duero commences in Picos de Urbión in the province of Soria and flows out at Oporto, in northern Portugal. In Andalusia, the Guadalquivir (its name derived from the Arabic translation of the "great valley") is of immense importance to the irrigation of the "fertile valley" of this rich agricultural area; it begins in Jaén and ends in Cádiz.

Spain was slow to develop a modern approach to agriculture, and, unfortunately, its civil war and World Wars I and II intervened up until the 1950s. Following this changes started to happen, albeit slowly until 1975, when a more open attitude toward farming and the communities became possible. Hardship may have existed, but the farmers and cheesemakers have held on to their cheesemaking traditions and produce a diverse range of cheeses throughout the country.

The northern and western coastal regions and valleys have cattle grazing, with some mixed farming, while the hills and mountain areas concentrate on goats and sheep. The burgeoning wine market, where land is being nurtured, has meant that farms benefit from better grazing conditions. The cheeses from the northern regions are diverse and of differing textures and styles, while the more arid, mountainous areas of the west and the Canary Islands have goat's and ewe's milk cheeses with strong, spicy flavors. The archipelago of the Azores, with its microclimate created by its situation in the Atlantic about 930 miles (1,500 km) from Lisbon, produces the famous São Jorge (St. George) cheese (see page 148), a strong Cheddar-style which, when fully matured, gives Cheddar a good run for its money.

The reason for grouping the two countries together is not only their close proximity, shared geography, and climatic conditions, but also the similarity of some of the cheeses. Northern Portugal has rugged mountainous terrain, while the south is open and hilly, with the extreme heat of summer restricting the styles of cheeses being made. Although the cheeses of Portugal are not as widely exported as Spain's, the few that are regularly shipped abroad have made an impact, particularly alongside Portuguese wines and cured meats.

The wines of both countries are exceptional, but it is the fortified wines, such as sherry and port, that are so distinguished and somehow fit perfectly with the food. These wines became very popular in England in the 18th century, and the port trade has British names, such as Cockburn, Croft, Dow, Gould, Campbell, Graham, Sandeman, Taylor, and Warre. Try a chilled white port or dry sherry as an apéritif with a wedge of Manchego (see page 144) or a scoop of Serra da Estrela (see page 147) for the unique tastes of these countries. Both Spain and Portugal have great seafaring and exploring traditions, and, when the Spanish and Portuguese migrated to new lands, their cheesemaking skills went, too; this influence can be seen in the New World.

OPPOSITE, TOP LEFT Mountain sheep in the Spanish Pyrenees.
OPPOSITE, TOP RIGHT A Pyrenean artisan cheesemaker.
OPPOSITE, MIDDLE LEFT Empty churns await milking time.
OPPOSITE, MIDDLE RIGHT Cheeses collected from a mountain maturing cave.
OPPOSITE, BOTTOM A rushing stream in the Pyrenees.

North & Northeast Spain

From the Spanish Pyrenees, with its alpine climate, to the Mediterranean warmth of the east and the verdant "green" north with its Atlantic influences, the terrain in northern Spain is varied and dramatic.

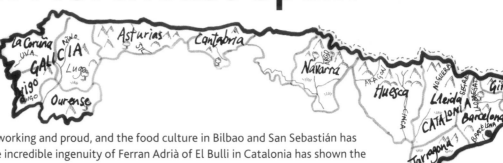

The people are hardworking and proud, and the food culture in Bilbao and San Sebastián has rocketed to stardom, while the incredible ingenuity of Ferran Adrià of El Bulli in Catalonia has shown the world a new way of cooking. Yet the cheesemaking here is so simple, with styles and flavors that embrace the land and appeal to the eye, with some cheeses resembling craggy rocks and others smoky mounds. From the rugged beauty of the mountains and the seaside cliffs to the lush pastures straddling the rivers, the cheeses in this part of Spain really do reflect the land that has produced them.

Garrotxa 🐐 CATALONIA

The once-isolated and neglected hills close to Girona have now been reclaimed, and a community of farmers makes this semihard 2¼-pound (1-kg) cheese. Garrotxa, with a thin natural crust rubbed in charcoal, then matured to produce a soft velvety coat, is also known as Pell Florida (pressed flower). I visited the Bauma farm because I wanted to see how they had managed to establish the dairy in what was barren wasteland. The simple stone and wood building has been in existence since 1980, and the herd of goats has been increased year by year. As the area is more alpine in temperature than Mediterranean, the cheese is subject to limited production during the winter months.

The process of making cheese is quick, and the day I visited we spent the morning heating the milk, then curdling to form large pea- or hazelnut-size grains, before draining off the whey, replacing it with hot water, and draining off again. This practice is important because it keeps the texture of the cheese firm and moist, and reduces the acidity slightly, which helps the texture and taste. The high humidity not only in the dairy, but also outside, together with the cooler air, highlights how careful you have to be to get the texture right. As soon as the cheeses are out of their molds after the final draining, they are rubbed in charcoal ash, then placed in a cold room with fans, to dry them very quickly and "set" the rind. Once they have had an hour or so in the drying room, they go straight to the maturing cellars to ripen.

The rinds are closely watched, and patted and turned to encourage an even growth of molds, but also to encourage close contact with the cheese. The crumbly, flaky texture adds a sweetness to the gentle goaty flavors, and the cheese has a wonderful bosky flavor because the animals are allowed to roam on scrubby grasses, as well as flowers and wild herbs. I enjoy the younger cheeses; the aged versions require a very robust red wine as the more wild goaty flavors evolve. I think this is where I first tasted the fine Spanish red wine Priorat, accompanied by a fully matured Garrotxa cheese—a great combination.

OPPOSITE Garrotxa
ABOVE Herding cows in the Spanish Pyrenees.

Montsec 🐐 CATALONIA

This is a classic northern Spanish cheese, especially prized because of the fear that artisan cheeses would become extinct. It is a credit to Enric Canut, a pioneer who reestablished cheesemaking skills in Catalonia, then helped to revive traditional cheeses all over Spain. The air in the northern mountains is humid, encouraging natural molds; on cheeses such as the 10½-ounce (300-g) Montsec, the flaky, light texture is dusted with ash, to let the molds grow evenly, but also to dry the rind a bit, so that unwanted spores do not develop. It has a creamy, nutty flavor that is not too strong.

Turo del Convent 🐐
CATALONIA

I came across cheesemaker Formatges Monber in Agramunt, when I was exploring the Spanish Pyrenees. Its cheesemaking facilities are next door to the shop and café serving its cheeses with local wine. The setup smacks of Enric Canut's aspirations for this region, being young, enthusiastic, and eager to bring traditional cheeses back into circulation.

This delicious 14-ounce (400-g) cheese with a white bloom has a close, crumbly texture and a clean, floral taste. The younger cheese (aged three weeks) is gentle and lemony-acidic, but with additional maturing it becomes more goaty and assertive with a definite edge to the flavors.

Roncal 🐑 NAVARRE

The fertile landscape that takes in Navarre to the border of Aragon is the traditional zone for this cheese, using the milk of the local Latxa and Rasa-Aragonesa sheep breeds. The hard, close-textured cheese has a smooth rind from washing and rubbing to inhibit the growth of molds. The 2¼–6½-pound (1–3-kg) tome (cylinder) must be ripened for at least four months before selling.

The dense texture is pitted with tiny eyelets or cracks in the pâte, and the pale straw/cream color makes it look delicate, but, in fact, the flavors are nutty, with a dried-fruit salty sweetness coming through, which reflects the milk style from the local breeds. Serve this cheese with slices of coarse cured sausages and a glass of dry red wine with a robust edge.

Vall de Meranges Cremos 🐄 CATALONIA

From Lérida in the Spanish Pyrenees, this cheese is made following a traditional country recipe. The smooth rind has been rubbed with brine, to create a pale glow, and the sweetly earthy, floral flavor becomes more intense with age and takes on a smoother, creamier texture. The season to eat this cheese is late winter to early spring, and cheesemaker Albert Pons matures the handmade cheeses on wooden shelving in cool cellars.

Bauma Madurat 🐐 CATALONIA

This cheese is from Borredà in the mountainous alpine part of the region, which becomes more Mediterranean in climate on the coast. It is a large, rectangular 2¼-pound (1-kg) "log" cheese, with an ash rind that develops white patchy molds as it matures. The taste is light and sweetly nutty, with a crumbly texture. Although the outside rind suggests a spicy and strong cheese because the aroma can be forceful, the surprise is that there is a delicate milky quality coming through. An aromatic dry white wine is the perfect accompaniment.

Idiazábal 🐑 BASQUE/NAVARRE

The smoked version is seen in the higher mountain area encircled by the Aralar and Urbia ranges, while the valley areas around Navarre have the unsmoked version. This is a cheese that should be allowed to ripen and mature because the flavors will improve immeasurably given time. The milk from the Latxa (pronounced *lacha*) or Carranza breeds of sheep has high acidity and low fat, giving the cheese a sharp, crumbly taste and texture. The unsmoked cheese is lighter and more delicate, whereas the smoked has an earthy sweetness to the flavor.

San Simon 🐄 GALICIA

A cone-shaped cheese weighing 13 ounces (375 g) to 3⅓ pounds (1.5 kg), formed using a special mold in a process similar to that of tetilla (see below), but this cheese is smoked over birchwood, which is native to the region. The flavors are not too strong or bitter, rather nutty, and sweetly earthy, and it is popular throughout Spain. I love to partner this cheese with a pale, dry, or even semisweet sherry because the flavors match perfectly.

Tetilla 🐄 GALICIA

A cone-shaped cheese similar to the Arzúa (see below), but a little more supple and scattered with a few small holes. Its origins are in La Coruña, but nowadays it is made all over Galicia, and the milk from the local breed of Rubia Gallega cattle has had to be supplemented with other, bigger milk sources, to keep up with the demand. The 13-ounce (375-g) to 3⅓-pound (1.5-kg) cheeses are mild, and loved by children because tetilla is almost spreadable. This versatile cheese is used in tapas—it complements olives, cured meats, and roasted vegetables. It also melts beautifully, so is often used for gratins.

Arzúa Ulloa Arquesan 🐄 GALICIA

This is very typical of western Spanish cheeses, with its tubby shape, convex sides, and its smooth washed and rubbed rind encircled with a cloth binding. The milks of Rubia Gallega, Friesian, and Brown Swiss cows are used for this cheese, which has a protected stamp of origin, because this northwestern region has such good pastureland. The cheese, weighing between 1 pound 2 ounces (500 g) and 5½ pounds (2.5 kg), is washed in brine to allow the rind to remain smooth and golden, and care is taken to prevent cracking of the rind by rubbing in a little olive oil. The cheese within is smooth and not as strong as you would find with goat's or ewe's milk, but there is a nutty complexity to the flavor from the brine washings. If matured, the cheese becomes hard and has a stronger flavor.

LEFT, LEFT CHEESE Roncal, RIGHT CHEESE Idiazábal

ABOVE LEFT, LEFT CHEESE San Simon, RIGHT CHEESE Tetilla, FRONT CHEESE Arzúa Ulloa Arquesan

OPPOSITE, TOP AND MIDDLE LEFT CHEESE Vall de Meranges Cremos, BOTTOM LEFT CHEESE Bauma Madurat, TOP RIGHT CHEESE Montsec BOTTOM RIGHT CHEESE Turo del Convent

Peralzola Azul 🐑 ASTURIAS

This is a relatively new cheese, made with ewe's milk. The style is leaning toward a French Roquefort, but is less aggressive on the palate, with nutty blue veins to give acidity. This delightful blue is excellent served with Pedro Ximénez, a dessert sherry, or port. Weighing about 4½ pounds (2 kg), and with a slightly higher fat content because it is made entirely with ewe's milk, it is a welcome addition to the other Spanish blue cheeses. Although not actively exported yet, with increased production, this cheese will be seen farther afield.

Cabrales 🐄🐐🐑 ASTURIAS

This 5½-pound (2.5-kg) blue cheese is produced only in the village of the same name and three other villages. Principally a cow's milk cheese, but with additions of goat's and ewe's milk in spring and summer when available, the texture is soft, but with a crumble that breaks down into a velvety pâte. The cheeses are drained naturally, and salting is done by hand, according to how the cheesemaker wants the flavors to expand. The cheeses are laid out in cool, airy cellars for three to four weeks, before being transferred to limestone maturing caves that have a higher humidity than those of the Picos de Europa. The spread of the blue takes longer and can often be seen around the edges of the cheese, not all the way through. In this way, you taste the metallic notes together with the salty, gritty crumble, which is piquant and powerful. Match with the dessert sherry Pedro Ximénez for an amazing tasting experience.

Valdeón

The taste of this cheese reflects the landscape from which it springs. The limestone caves found in Cantabria that are used for maturing, the peaks of the Picos de Europa, and even the trees in this mountainous region all influence the flavors of the cheese.

Picos de Europa (Valdeón) 🐄🐐🐑 CANTABRIA

The rich, creamy pâte of this cheese, with well-spread blue molds, has a mineral tanginess enhanced by the fruity zing from its sycamore-leaf wrapping. These are clues to the terrain of the majestically beautiful Picos de Europa mountains that cover the north and central section of the Cantabrian range. The peaks El Cornión to the west, Los Urrieles in the center, and Andara to the east are now part of the Spanish national park system, and therefore protected, enabling tourists to explore the picturesque landscape. Limestone caves, where the cheeses are matured, are key to the flavor profile of the blue cheeses from this area, and Picos de Europa is less intense than Cabrales, its other cheese. The leaf wrapping around the cheese creates the most stunning effect on a cheeseboard.

Picos de Europa is mostly made with cow's milk from sturdy Tudanca, Pardo-Alpina, and Friesian breeds, with additions of goat's milk from the Pyrenees and Picos de Europa breeds during the spring and summer months. This is supplemented by a little Latxa ewe's milk, which can be detected in the flavors of the cheese. The cheese is dense and buttery with just cow's milk, while more intense, sharp, and spicy flavors are evident when the mixed milks are used.

Once the 5½-pound (2.5-kg) cheeses have been made and molded, they are salted by hand, then pierced, to encourage the growth of blue veins from *Penicillium roqueforti*, which was added to the curds. They are then wrapped in the leaves, before being placed to ripen in the limestone caves, with their natural humidity and cool temperature.

Allowing the cheeses to age for more than three months will encourage bigger flavors, with a little more salty grittiness coming through. Drink a bold red wine with good tannins with this cheese, or even a port or Muscat if you want to end a meal with just this cheese and a dessert wine.

THIS PAGE Picos de Europa
(Valdeón)

OPPOSITE, TOP CHEESE Peralzola
Azul, MIDDLE AND BOTTOM CHEESE
Cabrales

Central & Southern Spain

The climate in this area ranges from continental, then Mediterranean, with a little alpine in the mountainous areas, to semiarid along the southeast corner. The Balearic and Canary islands, although hot and sultry at certain times of the year, also enjoy good rainfall. For this reason, the cheesemaking, especially on the Canary Islands, with their rich volcanic soil, is very successful, and their semihard goat cheeses have gained good recognition. The dusty Sahara winds and humidity inland, with the sparse grazing areas, do not see many cheeses produced in central Spain, although what is available works very well with the great cured hams and meats. The southern zone, including the islands, also produces some very fragile, soft fresh cheeses, which are really delicious, especially when served with strawberries or even peaches.

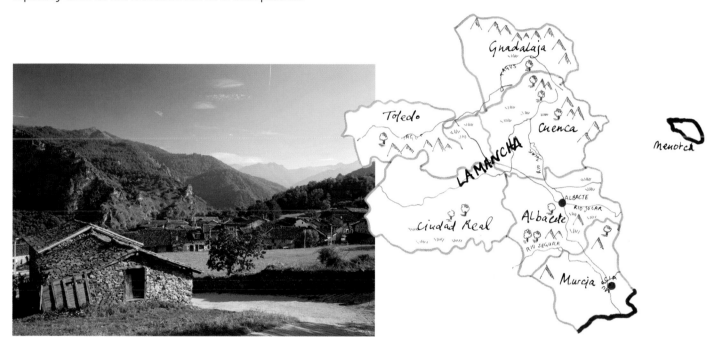

Murcia al Vino 🐐 MURCIA

The high milk quota from the Murciano-Granadina goat breed enables many styles of cheese to be made in Murcia. This traditional semihard close-textured cheese weighing about 5½ pounds (2.5 kg) is made with both a plain brine-rubbed rind and one dipped in wine and vine pressings, to create a beautiful dark-red coating. The sweet flavors of the milk come through instantly, but having the wine wash means that there is fruit and acidity, too. There are many hard and semihard goat cheeses in Spain, but this one is among the most popular with my customers.

Mahón 🐄🐑🐐 MENORCA

The island of Menorca has a microclimate responsible for lush pastureland, and cheese producers are able to graze cows, as well as a few sheep and goats. If you want to taste an interesting version of this cheese, look for those from

OPPOSITE, TOP AND MIDDLE CHEESE Murcia al Vino, BOTTOM CHEESE Mahón

the hills named "Llumena." The artisan cheeses, weighing about 5½ pounds (2.5 kg), are made with raw milk from the unique Menorcan breed and Friesian cows, although goat's and ewe's milk are added at certain times of year when quantities are available.

The curds are wrapped in a cloth, suspended to drain off the whey, then placed on a table and pressed of any remaining water. The bag is then swiftly placed in a brine bath, before being transferred to the maturing rooms. The odd shape of the rounded edges and markings of the cloth on the cheese denote the real artisan cheeses. I love the younger *tierno* cheeses of summer, with their paler crust smooth from being rubbed in oil to prevent molds from growing. In fall, I cannot wait for the aged, or *curado*, cheeses, with their toasted hazelnut flavors and salty, gritty texture, to enjoy with the season's new crop of apples. The fresh, semisharp, and sharp cheeses are also rubbed in paprika, to produce a darker finish to the rind, although I do not believe that this adds to the flavors.

Manchego & Membrillo

The matching of a ewe's milk cheese, such as Manchego, with the sweet density of slow-cooked fruit such as quince (membrillo) really enhances the flavors of the cheese. The milk used in Manchego is rich and earthy, with an almost lanolin silkiness, which, when made into a hard cheese, almost cries out for something sweet to highlight the richness, but also temper the "animal" flavor profile.

Manchego 🐑 LA MANCHA

The whole of La Mancha is devoted to Manchego, from the provinces of Albacete, Ciudad Real, Cuenca, and Toledo. With its protected origin in place, this cheese is recognized throughout the world, and the increased demand for it has placed the regulatory body under pressure to change the specified areas of the designation of origin.

This harsh, arid, rocky landscape was named "Al Mansha," meaning "waterless land," by the Moors when they were here; this describes exactly the extremes of climate—from freezing winters to unbearably hot summers, with little rain and variable wind patterns—found throughout the vast expanse of plains. The Manchega sheep are acclimatized to the extreme climate and have adapted to a diet based on the scrubby vegetation and grasses, along with what little vegetable and cereal fodder is grown for them. They are natural foragers, and take refuge under trees during the scorching heat of the day or in makeshift shelters and caves in the winter.

The cheeses are ripened to varying degrees of strength; to enjoy the experience of Manchego, you should buy a mild and medium, or medium and strong, or even a little of all of the types, so that you can explore the flavor profiles. Shops often sell only one Manchego, which is a pity because the distinctive tastes evolve with maturity.

The cheesemaking process is slow. The fresh milk is cooled, before being transferred to the heating vats, where the rennet is added and the milk gently warmed. The curds are cut into very small ricelike "grains," then heated again before the whey is drained. The curds are then placed in the molds with the familiar basket pattern, and pressed to drain off any remaining whey. Once scored with the Manchego seal, the cheeses have another pressing, then are removed from their molds, turned upside down, and returned to the mold for still another pressing. The cheeses are plunged into a saltwater bath for two to four days, depending on the quality of the milk, the season, and the fodder. Maturing takes place in cool rooms with high humidity, and the cheeses are turned and rubbed, to avoid unwanted molds growing on the surface rinds.

The smaller cheeses, weighing about 3 pounds 5 ounces (1.5 kg), will take about 30 days, and larger forms around 60 days. The fully matured cheeses, however, can take two years to reach their ultimate taste. Once you cut through the hard rind, the cheese is a pale, creamy yellow, with a few eyelets and cracks formed during the maturing. The aroma is sweetly earthy and sharp, and the flavor is not buttery, but savory with hints of caramel and hazelnuts.

This cheese is copied all over the world, even down to the decorative outside pattern, but do not be confused because only Manchego will have the name emblazoned on top of the cheese.

The perfect accompaniment for Manchego is membrillo, a quince paste. The fruit is sharp and bitter when eaten raw, but if cooked down slowly with added sugar it turns into a shiny, dark red-brown jam or paste, with a taste that is fruity with a good acidity. It is excellent served alongside cheese or cured meats.

THIS PAGE, ABOVE The Manchego stamp.
THIS PAGE, BELOW, LEFT Block of membrillo, or quince paste RIGHT Manchego
OPPOSITE, ABOVE LEFT The maturing caves for Manchego.
OPPOSITE, ABOVE RIGHT The fields of La Mancha.

THIS PAGE, TOP CHEESE Serra da Estrela,
BOTTOM CHEESE Terrincho
OPPOSITE The landscape on São
Miguel, in the Azores.

Portugal

Portugal is split by its major river, the Tejo (or Tagus, in Spanish). This serves as a clear demarcation of the landscape. The northern terrain, where rivers course through the valleys, is mountainous, while the south features a rolling landscape of plains and hills, and a hotter, drier climate. The summer weather in the mountainous areas is very arid and blazingly hot, with the animals huddling under what trees or bushy shelter they can find for shade. The islands of the Azores and Madeira produce fine cheeses, as well as the famous dessert wine, and the Duoro wines from the north, with their rich style and savory sweetness, are great partners for the cheeses. Although Spain is so closely connected, the cheeses of Portugal have distinct flavors and textures of their own, and the volcanic soil composition, rich in minerals, produces grazing areas that add a really interesting structure to the milk. Portuguese cheeses have a very definite identity—they are sharp yet rich, but with a herbaceous tingle unlike that of other European cheeses.

Serra da Estrela 🐑 NORTH

This cheese is named after a mountain between the Dão and Mondego rivers, a landscape of rugged natural beauty, spreading down to fertile orchards and vineyards that produce some of Portugal's most popular table wines. The cheese is probably the most famous with a protected place of origin (DOP) and, while similar cheeses are produced in Spain, it is the Portuguese Serra da Estrela that most stands out. This is because of its delicous and unique flavor, and the very small designated area where this cheese can be made.

Local Bordeleira or Churra sheep provide the milk, and the spring cheeses are rich and herbal, whereas the late winter versions are more intense and dense. The curdling of the milk is not done with the traditional rennet, but with cardoon thistles (Cynara cardunculus), which grow wild in this region. This imbues the cheese with a peculiarly earthy, lemony, bosky herbal flavor that is very unusual, and it is absolutely delicious when paired with a fortified wine such as port, or a Duoro red wine. There are similar cheeses found in other regions of Portugal, probably due to the migration of shepherds to warmer climates in deep winter.

Good hygiene is particularly important at this crucial transforming stage because the milk is unpasteurized. The milk is strained and heated, and the cardoon rennet is added to curdle the milk. The whey is drained, and the curds are washed a little, then broken down by hand, before being placed in cheesecloth-lined molds and slowly pressed by hand, which gives a dense, elastic texture to the cheese. They are rubbed with salt and left overnight, before being placed in the cold but humid maturing rooms. The cheeses are ready after 30–45 days for the Amanteigado or buttery-textured style, and after at least six months for the matured, or velho, style.

Terrincho 🐑 UPPER DOURO VALLEY

Weighing 1¾–2½ pounds (800 g–1.2 kg), this protected place of origin cheese is made entirely of milk from the local Churra da Terra Quente ewes. It is popular throughout Portugal for its strong, vegetal flavors and harder texture, which is a foil for the softer-style spicy cheeses. It is ripe after 30 days, although the flavors are more pronounced in cheeses aged for 60 days or more. The brine-rubbed rind is sometimes worked with paprika, to add another dimension to the flavors.

Cabra Transmontano and Quinta dos Moinhos Novos Serrano 🐐 VILA VERDE

New developments from the company Quinta dos Moinhos Novos include the cabra log, which has a French-style bloomy rind that tastes surprisingly sweet and nutty, given the almost melting edges hugging the rind. The serrano is a close-textured hard cheese still retaining a juicy crumble, which is either presented with a simple smooth white rind or washed in wine, to give a lovely fruitiness to the flavors. Both these cheeses suit the local light, sparkling white wine perfectly.

São Jorge 🐄 AZORES

One of Portugal's rare cow's milk cheeses, as well as the largest, this is a magnificent-tasting hard cheese. Unpasteurized cow's milk is mostly used for São Jorge cheesemaking from late spring to summer. The hard cheese has a sort of waxy texture, but it is somewhat like a Cheddar, with sharp, nutty flavors and a crumbly texture; if aged for more than a year, it is really delicious. If you make a Portuguese fondue, use this as the base cheese, and add softer cheeses at the end of cooking.

Graziosa 🐄 ILHA GRACIOSA

Ilha Graciosa, called "White Island," is known for its wines, as well as meat and agriculture. The semihard cow's milk cheese is similar to São Jorge (see above), but simpler and rustic, with a sharper, fruitier quality that almost tingles on the tongue.

Serpa 🐑 SOUTH ALENTEJO

These protected place of origin cheeses vary in size from 4–18 ounces (120–500 g). This cheese is made predominantly with Lacaune ewe's milk, although there are still a few local Merino herds. The heated milk is passed through a cloth filled with salt, which means no other salting process is needed; the thistle liquid is added, then after about 40 minutes the curd is ready to be cut, drained, molded, and ripened. The Amenteigado (softer) curd is often thought to be the more preferred way of eating this cheese (like spooning out a Serra da Estrela). If you let the Serpa mature to a harder consistency, the flavors develop to become powerful, strong, and spicy.

Évora 🐑 ALENTEJO

This ewe's milk cheese, with its protected place of origin, is produced in small rounds of 4–7 ounces (120–200 g); traditionally, the cheeses are placed in a stoneware pot filled with olive oil, to preserve them through the year. Today, however, there are very tiny, softer cheeses to be eaten at a fresher stage; the larger versions are aged 60 days or more, to produce a dense, almost brittle texture, with scattered holes due to the slow draining procedure. They have a strong, spicy, tangy taste, making the cheeses suitable as an *entrada*, or appetizer.

Azeitão 🐑 AZEITÃO

This is another cheese with a protected place of origin, which includes the areas of Palmela, Sesimbra, and Setúbal. The cheeses are ripened for 23 days, to form a semisoft creamy texture and smooth, full, rich fruity flavors. The Assaf breed of sheep is used for the milk and cardoon thistle for the coagulant; the curds are shaped by hand, to form the rounds, and pressed of as much whey as possible, before going to the ripening rooms, where additional moisture reduction will take place. The 9-ounce (250-g) cheeses are eaten with a spoon, and the taste is sweetly earthy and not too strong.

Castelo Branco 🐐 🐑 CENTRAL

Similar in style and flavor to the Serra da Estrela (see page 147), these cheeses are a little more yellow in color. The true artisan cheeses are made from ewe's milk, using thistle flower as rennet, while the mixed-milk cheeses, using both the ewe's and goat's milk, are similar in style and appearance, but called Beira Baixa Amarelo (medium, 40 days' maturing) and Beira Baixa (strong, 120 days' aging) and use traditional rennet. The region around Castelo Branco is protected by a microclimate, giving the pastures a lushness that is evident in the flavor of the cheese.

Nisa 🐑 ALENTEJO

Weighing about 10½ ounces (300 g), these cheeses have a protected place of origin. The area, with its vast open countryside, a softer, undulating landscape and rich fertile soil, is commonly known as the "bread basket" of Portugal. The cheeses have the cardoon thistle coagulant, and the flavors have a somewhat sweeter and less fermented sour taste than other similar-style cheeses.

Barrão 🐑 ALENTEJO

These little cheeses weighing about 5½ ounces (150 g), with the familiar yellow waxy-smooth rind and "sheepy" aroma, are very similar in flavor to neighboring cheeses, such as Nisa (see above). Being smaller, however, they are harder and therefore stronger—a perfect apéritif cheese to serve with a chilled white port. The Monte Barrão, in the northernmost part of Alentejo, is well suited to cattle rearing, and sheep and goats can also be seen grazing on the open plains or gathered under the trees.

OPPOSITE, TOP LEFT, BACK CHEESE Novos Serrano, FRONT CHEESE Cabra Transmontano

OPPOSITE, TOP RIGHT, TOP CHEESE São Jorge, BOTTOM CHEESE Graziosa

OPPOSITE, BOTTOM RIGHT, BACK CHEESE Castelo Branco, MIDDLE CHEESE Nisa, FRONT CHEESE Barrão

OPPOSITE, BOTTOM LEFT CHEESES, FROM TOP TO BOTTOM Évora, Évora second round, Serpa, Azeitão

The Rest of Europe

The distinctive cheeses from the following European countries serve as symbols of identity for those nations included and have also had a great influence on New World cheesemaking. Cross-border movement of people in Europe has often resulted in cheese being made in one country that is evocative of and influenced by the taste and style of cheeses produced in neighboring countries.

The land and climate obviously play a big part in the style of cheeses produced by these different countries, but the necessity to produce food that will keep well from the land to the table also has a role. These countries do not produce a vast array of styles like France or Italy, but somehow the cheeses, through their shapes and flavors, give you an instant snapshot of the places, the people, and their cuisines.

THE NETHERLANDS

Protecting the land from flooding has always been a priority in the Netherlands. Reclaimed marshy areas demonstrate how the land can be managed and adapted for dairy farming and agriculture. Cheese plays a huge part in the country's economy, and there are five main cheese markets: one in Woerden, with a modern commercial format, and four that are still based on the traditional way of selling from stalls in Alkmaar, Gouda, Edam, and Hoorn.

Gouda 🐄 GOUDA

The name "Gouda" has never been registered or trademarked and is, therefore, used throughout the world wherever this style of cheese is made. Gouda accounts for about 50 percent of the cheese production in the Netherlands and is done on a huge commercial scale. By contrast, the handmade *boerenkaas*, or farmer's cheese, is made from unpasteurized milk from the dairies' own herds, with additional milk from no more than two other farms operating on similar lines. This ensures the hands-on production and slow aging of the cheeses.

The cheeses take on an amazing range of flavors as they age. A seven-month-old cheese (or *belegenkaas*, meaning "young cheese") will have a smooth texture with a gentle, nutty flavor and creaminess to the light, salty, tangy taste. This is a perfect cheese for breakfast or for shaving into slices onto toasted whole-grain bread topped with tomatoes. In a two-year-old cheese, the texture is a little more dense and has hints of crystallization, where the proteins in the milk create a salty tang. This is a delicious lunchtime cheese to serve with slices of baked ham and pickled cucumbers, as well as good on a cheeseboard. These cheeses are *oude kaas*, or old. At four years old, the cheese becomes darker and more solid, with the crystals of protein more evident, and the flavors are caramelized and rich, with a brittle texture. This super-aged cheese is great with fine red wines from Bordeaux.

Some Goudas have cumin, nettles, and mustard seed added to them and are eaten younger, but aging gives the flavors a bigger spicy taste. The flavored Goudas are complex and interesting, and a perfect companion to beer.

In recent years, goat's milk Gouda has appeared, and the sweetness of the milk is totally different in style to any other goat cheese. There are also Goudas with truffles incorporated into the curd, giving the milk a gamy taste that is delicious with a glass of dry Champagne.

THIS PAGE, TOP LEFT CHEESE Two-year-aged Gouda, TOP MIDDLE CHEESE Cumin Gouda, TOP RIGHT CHEESE Four-year-aged Gouda, WHOLE CHEESES, FROM TOP TO BOTTOM Nettle Gouda, mustard Gouda, two-year-aged Gouda, seven-month-aged Gouda, BOTTOM LEFT CHEESE Goat truffle Gouda

SCANDINAVIA

The term "Scandinavia" is commonly used for Denmark, Norway, and Sweden, and all have long cheesemaking traditions. The Scandinavian climate is varied: ranging from typical western European weather for Denmark and southern Sweden, and along the west coast of Norway, to humid continental weather from Oslo to Stockholm in the center, and subarctic conditions farther north. The areas with dairy farming have perfect grazing conditions and clean, clear air, giving the grass a marked sweetness that is reflected in the milk and the cheese.

Svecia 🐄 SWEDEN

This is a semihard cheese weighing about 26½–33 pounds (12–15 kg), with a waxed rind that is wrapped in foil. The smooth, firm paste has a soft, buttery, dense texture and a lovely mellow taste, yet sharp, nutty finish. Svecia is a typical cheese from the low-lying areas all over Sweden and is sometimes seen with added cumin or cloves. This is a low-fat cheese at 28 percent and is particularly favored at breakfast on a dark rye bread, or as part of a meal with Swedish herring dishes and a glass of schnapps.

Greve 🐄 SWEDEN

This is a semihard cheese weighing about 33 pounds (15 kg), somewhat like the Norwegian Jarlsberg, although it also is similar to a Swiss Emmentaler (see page 97). The dense texture has scattered cherry-size holes and is best eaten at around 10 months, when the flavors will be rich and buttery, but also have a zingy, tangy finish. This style of cheese suits beer and crisp, clean lagers perfectly, but a fruity zesty white wine also works very well with this cheese.

Kryddost 🐄 SWEDEN

This is a semihard cheese weighing about 26½ pounds (12 kg), with a softer paste that is densely packed with cumin and cloves. It is a real delicacy in Scandinavia,

OPPOSITE, FROM TOP TO BOTTOM CHEESE Svecia, Greve, Kryddost, Havarti

where it is served as part of a buffet-style meal with pickled vegetables and herring, other fish, and meat, but also thinly shaved onto dark rye bread. These styles of cheese can be eaten young, but if matured will become very tangy and spicy in flavor. Try serving this cheese with a glass of strong schnapps for the perfect accompaniment to the flavor profiles.

Havarti 🐄 DENMARK

There are lovely old stories surrounding Havarti, which was originally created by Hanne Nielson in the 19th century as a cottage industry on her family's farm Havarthigaard in Øverød, north of Copenhagen. She had traveled around Europe and wanted to try to create a cheese that was somewhat like a semihard Swiss style. Today, this cheese is sold as a major commercial brand both plain and with all kinds of flavor additions; when you find a more artisan version, you will be pleasantly surprised by the flavors.

The cheese has a really sticky orange rind and a high aroma, but straight from the refrigerator the texture will be dense and the flavors quite mellow. I prefer it at room temperature, with the edges starting to melt and the taste becoming nutty, sharp, and tangy.

Serve this cheese with a selection of smoked and cured fish and meats, and thinly sliced rye bread with unsalted butter. It works perfectly with a glass of light fruity red wine or a Pilsner-style beer.

POLAND, GREECE, & GERMANY

Agriculture accounts for more than 60 percent of land use in Poland. The cheeses produced are influenced by other European countries, although Poland has its own traditional cheeses. Greece, in the Mediterranean, is a diverse country, with mountains as a backdrop and the beauty of its islands. From north to south, Germany is a cheese country. A third of the production is exported, and influences from neighboring countries have resulted in a diversity of cheese styles.

Ser Korycinski "Swojski" 🐄 NORTHEAST POLAND

A traditional family-style cheese, it was mainly produced by the Jewish population until World War II, and sold throughout the country. Nowadays, this local cheese is made in bigger quantities, yet still retains its "homey" appeal of uncomplicated clean, light flavors.

The cheese is mainly served fresh without any visible rind and has a flaky texture like a pressed ricotta, either plain or with herbs or black peppercorns. It can be spread on rye bread with a sprinkling of sea salt or kosher salt, or is used to make fillings for a salty cheese pastry, as well as being an ingredient for a drier-textured cheesecake.

Feta 🐑🐐 GREECE

The wide, fertile plains of Thessaly are one of the seven protected regions for feta production, and each region has its own unique tasting style. The Peloponnese feta is harder, drier, and more salty than the one from Thessaly, while Macedonian feta is much creamier and mild in flavor. This is also due to the individual production style and, if you have previously thought the cheese to be a rather uninteresting salty affair, then search out the barrel-aged cheese, which is far superior.

The time of year will define whether more ewe's or goat's milk is available, although the ewe's milk will give a richer, earthier, and more complex taste profile, and the goat's milk a lighter, lemony, sharp style. The perfect accompaniment to have with this cheese is a delicious fresh icy cold retsina, because this is a wine that copes beautifully with the salty, sharp flavors of the cheese.

Bachensteiner 🐄 GUNZESRIED COOPERATIVE, GERMANY

The influences on many cheese styles from Germany have associations with surrounding countries. For instance, Tilsiter and mild Gouda have a Dutch ancestry, and Limburger is related to both the Netherlands and the Belgian Herve. Monasteries were instrumental in creating recipes for cheeses as well as in the brewing of beer, and cheeses such as Bachensteiner, with their washed rind, are typical. This brick-shape washed-rind cheese of 7 ounces (200 g) has the familiar aroma typical of smear-ripened cheeses, but the chewy, soft texture is very mild and buttery, with a mellow finish. You can cut Bachensteiner into small squares or shave it into long, curled slices and sprinkle over caraway seeds, and use to top rye bread. A blonde beer works well with the flavors of this cheese.

Münster 🐄 ZURWIES COOPERATIVE, GERMANY

Near the historic city of Wangen im Allgäu in southeast Baden-Württemberg, this biodynamic dairy makes a classic Münster cheese, both large—18 ounces (500 g)—and small—7 ounces (200 g).

Unlike its French counterpart, the German cheese has a lighter, more delicate taste, almost like soft, fresh bitter almonds. The sticky washed rind can be further enhanced by massaging a Gewürztraminer wine into the cheese, then letting it stand for a day or two, until it becomes very aromatic and gives the cheese a lovely nutty richness to the flavor profiles.

Some people can be put off tasting this cheese because it has a very strong aroma. This is due to the reaction of the rind washing and the damp, cold cellar conditions used to encourage the development of the rind. This process creates the beautiful, warm orange-apricot glow to the outside of the cheese, but also a very marked, almost "farmyard" odor. Münster is a perfect example of not judging a cheese by its smell because in reality this cheese is rich and mellow, and its strength really only lies in its scent on the outside rind. Dry Riesling and aromatic, flamboyant Gewürztraminer wines are good matches, as are Pinot reds or even a northern Rhône.

Limburger 🐄 ZURWIES COOPERATIVE, GERMANY

Making a Limburger that is very different than the mass-produced cheeses has been a work in progress for Anton Holzinger, and it has paid off. The simple-style cheese, weighing 7 ounces (200 g), is great as a morning snack, or for lunch with a thick slice of smoked ham, but it is only when tasting an artisan version of such a well-known cheese that you get the real pleasure of the flavors.

This cheese has a high aroma due to the bloomy rinds coming into contact with the salty brine solution. The flavors of the cheese are mellow, rich, and creamy. Partner with a rich, dry Chardonnay or other full-bodied white wine.

OPPOSITE, TOP LEFT, LEFT CHEESE Bachensteiner, TOP RIGHT CHEESE Small Münster, BOTTOM RIGHT CHEESE Large Münster

OPPOSITE, TOP RIGHT Ser Korycinski "Swojski"

OPPOSITE, BOTTOM RIGHT Barrel-aged feta

OPPOSITE, BOTTOM LEFT Limburger

USA & Canada

There is a cheese revolution taking place in North America—a pastoral movement where a spirit is rippling through an already substantial cheesemaking tradition. I realized that the times were a-changin' when I tasted the prototype Vermont Shepherd cheese from the Major's farm, Putney, Vermont, back in 1993. It was a revelation; it was only a matter of time before I would be hearing more about new cheesemakers and the vivid response to the usual bland and ordinary offerings.

Every time an American customer came into my shop in London and bemoaned the fact that their country's cheeses could never be compared to European counterparts, I defended farmstead cheesemaking, and guided them to the best cheese shops in their particular neck of the woods. The incredulity that such things existed highlighted how shopping had become a weekly trawl in a supermarket, rather than a daily visit to local shops and a weekend forage in a farmers market. Although farmers markets have been going for many years in rural areas, it is only recently that urban dwellers have taken them to heart—even in the center of Manhattan. Shoppers can now indulge in the joy of buying local, seasonal, and reasonably priced foods at farmers markets in cities all over the United States. A favorite market takes place in Union Square, in New York, where you can find an incredible selection of salads and vegetables, as well as cheeses coming in from small farms just outside the city.

These new American cheesemakers have a definite entrepreneurial mind-set—some have left the fast lane to return to their country roots; others just want to get back to the land and see what nature provides. Some producers have big operations, then decide to scale down with another small artisan dairy alongside, to make a completely different style of cheese. My initial expectations of North American cheeses were modest, but what I have found are myriad flavors and really good maturing practices.

In order to assess the cheeses of the United States and Canada, I needed to understand how the countries are divided by culture. In Canada, the early European settlers were French and Scottish, while along the West Coast of the United States they were Italian and Hispanic. The Midwest was settled by the Germans, Scandinavians, Dutch, Welsh, and Cornish, and the East Coast by the British, French, and Dutch, as well as the Amish, Greeks, Armenians, Eastern Europeans, and Italians. It is interesting to note that in the 1960s and 1970s, when new irrigation techniques were implemented, the explosion of artisan or farmstead cheesemaking began in earnest.

There are literally hundreds and hundreds of cheeses, and what I have detailed here are just some of the notable varieties made by both artisans and larger producers. I cannot wait to return to search out more cheeses. It is indeed miraculous what is now available not only at local farmers markets, but also in delis and supermarkets.

BELOW LEFT The fields at Andante Farm, Petaluma, California.
BELOW RIGHT Sheep at the Three-Corner Field Farm, Shushan, New York.
OPPOSITE, TOP LEFT Sheep sheltering under a barn at Three-Corner Field Farm.
OPPOSITE, TOP RIGHT A goat at Rawson Brook Farm, Massachusetts.
OPPOSITE, BOTTOM RIGHT Sheep in the barn at Three-Corner Field Farm.
OPPOSITE, BOTTOM LEFT The barns at Three-Corner Field Farm.

West Coast

Along the west coast in California, great swathes of desert precluded any agricultural farming, until irrigation brought water for grazing and pastureland. Fruit and vegetables were the first major crops, and dairy farming started thereafter. Nearly everyone thinks of California as sunny and hot, but in the north it can be mountainous and bitterly cold. From Los Angeles to San Francisco and farther north, however, cheese production has blossomed, and the temperate climate is perfect for producing some of the best goat cheeses you will ever taste.

Moving into Oregon, the valley around the Willamette River in the western part of the state is where most agriculture can be found. The Pacific coastline is gloriously scenic and windswept, with huge Douglas firs and redwoods, which contrast with the rugged Cascade mountain range just to the east. The weather along Oregon's coast is mild and there is good rainfall, but, in the northern and eastern regions, the winters are bitterly cold and summers are dry and hot.

The most northwesterly of the states (except for Alaska), Washington is a land of contrasts, from the temperate rainforests of the Olympic Peninsula to the semidesert found east of the Cascade Range. The mostly temperate climate and good rainfall have helped dairy farming to flourish for more than 150 years, but cheesemaking is relatively new, although making a big impact with quality and stylish flavors and textures.

CALIFORNIA

California is bordered by Oregon to the north, Nevada to the east, Arizona to the southeast, Baja California (Mexico) to the south, and the Pacific Ocean to the west. The major rivers serving the Central Valley flowing out to the Pacific are the Sacramento and San Joaquin, and in the north the Klamath, with the Colorado to the southeast. Cheese production in California is expanding, and the goat cheeses, in particular, are excellent.

BELOW Goats in the fields at Andante Farm, Petaluma, California.
OPPOSITE, TOP AND BOTTOM Vella Cheese Company, Dry Jack Special Reserve

Dry Jack Special Reserve 🐄 VELLA CHEESE
COMPANY, SONOMA, CALIFORNIA

Much of the milk comes from Mertens Farm, which
is close by, and, although the majority of the milk is
from Holstein cows, this cheese also contains at least a
30 percent Guernsey milk for its rich, buttery qualities.

Dry Jack Special is a more aged version of Vella's
original Jack cheese, which was produced to take account
of the new refrigerators available from the late 1930s
onward and housewives wanting to be able to keep cheese
longer. When the Italian population grew in the 1950s, a
drier, harder version was made so that it could be grated
in the style of a Parmigiano. It is the super-aged versions,
however, that are gold-medal winners. The long, slow aging
gives a big hit to the flavors and a dry, almost crystalline
crumble. The 8-pound (3.5-kg) cheese is brined and left
to dry naturally for some days, before being covered in a

special mixture of oil (soy or safflower, but without color
or flavor), unsweetened cocoa powder, and black pepper.
After about 18 months or even longer, these shiny brown
wheels reveal their lovely fruit and nut flavors, but never that
slightly bitter sharpness of Cheddar. This cheese is perfect
for both white and red wines, especially Zinfandel.

Fiscalini Farms 🐄 STANISLAUS COUNTY, CALIFORNIA

The farm is situated comfortably between the Sierra
Nevada mountains to the east and the California coastal
range to the west, producing a perfect climate and
environment for the Holstein cows to graze.

San Joaquin Gold is a 15-pound (12.27-kg) cheese with a
natural rind that has been bandaged to hold back the
mold growth. It has a Cheddar style, but it was supposed
to be based on a fontina recipe, with a smoother, chewier
texture. Ultimately, it falls between the two, and is a
delightful snacking cheese, with nutty, buttery flavors.

Clothbound 18-Month Aged Cheddar On cutting, this cheese
is mature and has a good crumble to its golden pâte, with
a nutty, almost sweet, and toasted balance of flavors. This
52-pound (24-kg) cheese is not in competition with
British Cheddars because it has enough personality of its
own. Look for the imprint of the cow stamped on top of
these cheeses, and enjoy with a Californian Pinot Noir.

Point Reyes "Original" Blue 🐄 POINT REYES, CALIFORNIA

The Giacominis run a family farm and use only their
own milk for cheesemaking. They developed their famous
blue with the aid of Monte McIntyre, who refines the 5½-
pound (2.5-kg) cheeses for five or six months in humid
cellars aided by the salty Pacific breezes that sweep across
the farmland. The flavors are strong and meaty, with
richness to the moist, almost gritty texture. A strong, full-
bodied wine would be best, but this cheese is also a perfect
component for a blue-cheese butter or in a dip.

Cowgirl Creamery 🐄 POINT REYES STATION, CALIFORNIA

Peggy Smith and Sue Conley left their former jobs in
catering to become cheesemakers; their milk supply, which
comes via the farm of Bill Straus, goes into making all the
cheeses and fresh curd, crème fraîche, fromage blanc, and
quark. The two cheeses listed below are the best known,
and have received numerous awards. These are perfect
partners to hard, sharp cheeses and buttery blue cheeses,
as well as the myriad choices of Californian wines.

Red Hawk is a 9-ounce (250-g) triple-cream brine-washed
cheese, with a buttery richness and top notes of savory
meat juices. This is no mean feat because washed rinds
are notoriously difficult to ripen without them becoming
too sticky and rancid-tasting. This cheese is a must on a
cheeseboard selection that brings together hard, fruity-
tasting cheeses and blues, and softer, sharper cheeses.
It is all about achieving a balance.

Mount Tam is a 9–10½-ounce (250–300-g) rich, buttery cheese whose bloomy white rind is a cross between a thick, chunky Coulommiers and the chewiness of a Pont l'Évêque. Being a *Penicillium candidum* rind, however, it has an earthy mushroom aroma—the best way of enjoying the cheese is with the rind still white and downy, with a hint of beige ridges coming through from the shelf racks, and the cheese within still springy, with scatterings of tiny eyelets.

Bellwether Farms 🐄 🐑 PETALUMA, CALIFORNIA

Since 1992, the Callahans at Bellwether Farm have been making ewe's milk San Andreas, which has a very seasonal production, and a buttery, dense Jersey cow's milk cheese called Carmody. Both of the cheeses are the result of trips that the Callahan family took to Italy, where they were inspired by the cheeses. Petaluma is situated just 12 miles (20 km) from the coast, giving the grazing land whiffs of iodine and sea spray that, in turn, give the cheeses their

salty sweetness. As with many small dairies in the United States, the Callahans make a selection of other dairy products—crème fraîche, fromage blanc, yogurt, ricotta, and a peppercorn cheese are available in small quantities.

San Andreas has the definite sweet earthiness of a pecorino. It has a smooth, full flavor and is delicious with red wine, fresh crusty bread, and olives.

Carmody, with its washed and rubbed-smooth rind, has a chewiness, along with the rich creaminess of younger-style Italian cheese, especially the Reserve. This particular cheese is a simple table or family cheese, and can be enjoyed as part of a cheeseboard. Carmody was named after the road that runs adjacent to the farm.

Goat's Leap 🐐 SAINT HELENA, CALIFORNIA

In the heart of the famous wine country of Napa Valley, Barbara and Rex Backus live out their dream, which started back in 1972. Their small herd of sturdy LaMancha goats, a breed developed in Oregon in the 1930s, thrives in the Californian climate, and all the cheeses have a lovely sense of flora and herbs as background flavors.

Barbara thought up the cheese names, which relate to her passion for all things Japanese, and the toppings really do reflect their style. The milk is slowly pasteurized, to retain all the flavors of the milk; by using a traditional rennet, all the cheeses reveal a clean taste, with a subtle and zesty tang.

Goat's Leap is a small producer, so you will see these cheeses locally and at farmers markets, as well as good restaurants. Alongside the ones listed, they also produce a hard tomme style with a natural dried crust called Carmela, and very fresh small cheeses made to order.

Eclipse is a chubby drum with a bloomy coat clinging to the ash-dusted covering, topped with a whole dried star anise. Cut into the cheese, and you will see a vein of ash running through the center of the cheese, which explains the name—Barbara and Rex likened it to the sight of a lunar event in the sky. The flavors of this cheese are bright and lemony, perfect for the crisp, fruity local white wines or softer reds.

Dafne is a delightful 7-ounce (200-g) chubby cheese, with a slightly flattened top. It has a pale, almost translucent *Penicillium candidum* mold rind, in the French style. The topping of bay leaves gives a clue to the name, but it also indicates the herbal and floral notes of the cheese, a result of the goats grazing on the open, unpolluted hills around the farm for as long as the season allows.

Kiku is a seasonal "Banon"-style cheese, with a covering of fresh vine leaves that have been dipped in Sauvignon Blanc, wrapped around the cheese, and tied with raffia string. This gives the cheese a really tangy taste, with edges that are just melting. This cheese is a perfect summer cheeseboard choice.

Sumi is a lovely truncated 7-ounce (200-g) pyramid, with an ash coating covering the downy, bloomy white rind. Once cut, the sparkling white interior has a flaky, dewy texture and lovely nutty, crisp flavors.

Hyku Noir is a delicious cheese dusted with ash and topped with a pomegranate blossom. This opulent flower motif is an unusal topping for a cheese—toppings of this nature are rarely found on European cheeses. It does add a beautiful element of surprise, however, as well as reflecting the landscape.

Hyku is like a large crottin (see page 63), with patchy bloomy white molds and a fudgy texture that will start to melt further after cutting. If it becomes too soft, its flavors will be compromised and become a bit bitter. This is a perfect cheese to enjoy with a Pinot Noir, particularly those of the region.

Redwood Hill Farm and Creamery 🐐

SONOMA, CALIFORNIA

Jennifer Bice and her partner, Steven Schack, are leading breeders of dairy goats and have been making cheese since 1978. The farm is located in Sebastopol, which is right in the heart of wine country, with a beautiful green landscape of apple orchards, forests, and meadows, as well as the world-famous vineyards.

Their breeds include Alpine, Nubian, and Saanen goats, which all produce good quality and quantity milk. The goats are left to roam and forage outside during the fine weather; when the rain and wind become uncomfortable as the season changes, the animals are brought inside to keep warm.

Jennifer and Steven produce a large selection of cheeses in small batches, mostly in a fresh, zingy style, but there is a lovely creamy one, too. Apart from the softer cheeses, they also make a goat's milk Cheddar-style cheese that is aged for five to six months and is good for broiling and as a table cheese. In addition, they produce a smoked version of the Cheddar, a feta-style cheese, and a new cheese called Gravenstein Gold, which has a "smear," or washed, rind, using a local cider made with the Gravenstein apple variety.

Fresh Chevre can be literally scooped out of its packaging; these 5½-ounce (150-g) cheeses can be spread on crackers or bread, and taste light and gently earthy. A lovely young cheese, which you can use in cooking for cakes or as a filling for pasta, it is also a perfect introduction to goat cheese. By letting the cheeses ripen and age further, the bloomy rind dries, and the texture within becomes crumbly and nutty. The more aged cheese is perfect for light red wines and dry whites.

Camellia is a Camembert-style cheese weighing about 7 ounces (200 g), with a soft, white *Penicillium candidum* mold with a downy-fluff style. There is a yeasty and creamy taste coming through in the flavors of the softer, riper cheeses, while the younger cheeses are somewhat gentle and can be a good appetizer cheese for those who want to avoid "goaty" flavors. I would eat the rind and all with this cheese because the light, nutty flavor of the crust is a good foil for the mild, creamy interior.

California Crottin, a multiple award-winning cheese, weighs about 5½ ounces (150 g) and has a fudgy yet crumbly texture that dries out beautifully to a small hard ball and is perfect for grating. The flavors of lemon zest are gently earthy and you can either eat as is or perhaps dust with a little freshly ground black pepper and broil to serve on top of a mound of baby salad greens.

OPPOSITE, TOP CHEESE (with star anise) Goat's Leap, Eclipse; SECOND ROW Goat's Leap: LEFT CHEESE (with bay leaves) Dafne, RIGHT CHEESE Kiku; THIRD ROW Goat's Leap: LEFT CHEESE Sumi, MIDDLE CHEESE (with flower) Hyku Noir, RIGHT CHEESE Hyku; FOURTH ROW Redwood Hill: LEFT CHEESE Camellia, MIDDLE CHEESE California Crottin, RIGHT CHEESE Fresh Chevre

Andante Farm

Petaluma still retains its old world charm, and the countryside around Andante Farm is unspoiled, quiet, and lush, even though it is only 32 miles (51 km) from the cosmopolitan city of San Francisco.

Andante Farm 🐄🐐 PETALUMA, CALIFORNIA

Soyoung Scanlan has a musical background, and it is no surprise that the names of her cheeses express this part of her life. I met Soyoung when she visited London, and she spent a day or two in our cheese room tasting some of her favorite French cheeses. What marks out her cheeses from among many others are the finesse and delicacy of not only the inner cheese, but also the rinds. The milk is pasteurized due to the 60-day minimum ripening required in the United States for unpasteurized milk cheeses, but this does not detract from the flavors; according to Soyoung, it is the starter cultures that give the milk curds their flavor and texture at this vital first stage.

Soyoung has an academic and methodical way of working, and production is small, so she sells locally and also at a few favored restaurants. Her cheesemaking facility is based next to the Volpi farm, where she sources the goat's milk, while she gets the Jersey cow's milk from Spring Hill farm in Petaluma. There is nothing high-tech about her cheesemaking—it is pure and simple, and relies entirely on her expertise and delicate touch.

Cavatina is made as small and larger goat's milk logs, with ash coating, similar to a Sainte-Maure (see page 62) from Touraine, but with a lighter crumble to the texture. I am bowled over by this cheese, mainly due to the fine rind and the scattering of the soft, downy white bloom.

Cadence is a mixed cow's and goat's milk cheese, with extra cream added. This cheese is similar in style to Saint Félicien (see page 69) and is perfect for the cheeseboard. The flavors are rich and creamy, with a little tangy aftertaste from the goat's milk addition.

Minuet is a goat's milk cheese with cow's milk crème fraîche added at the curdling stage, to give a rich density to the texture. The light, bloomy white rinds give a gentle earthy aroma to the cheese. Match with a Chenin Blanc white wine, to help cut through the density of the cheese with a crisp, refreshing zing.

Figaro is a mixed cow's and goat's milk cheese, wrapped in fig leaves that have first been dipped in white wine. It is available only during the summer, when figs are in season. The texture is rich, and the flavors have an astringent quality from the wine-soaked leaves.

THIS PAGE, ABOVE, Andante Farm: CLOCKWISE FROM TOP LEFT CHEESES
Minuet, Cavatina (large and small), Cadence (two cheeses), Figaro, Cavatina
THIS PAGE, BELOW The barns at Andante.

OPPOSITE, TOP LEFT Cheesemaking at Antante. OPPOSITE, TOP RIGHT AND BOTTOM LEFT
Goats at Andante. OPPOSITE, BOTTOM RIGHT Cheesemaker Soyoung Scanlan.

Sierra Mountain Tomme 🐐 LA CLARINE FARM, SOMERSET, CALIFORNIA

This farm is the perfect setting for cheesemaking and now the vineyard that encompasses this 10-acre (4-ha) enterprise. Caroline Hoël, who trained in France as a cheesemaker, and Hank Beckmeyer have the right attitude toward farming and cheesemaking. Their classic 4½-pound (2-kg) hard goat cheese is sweet, nutty, and full of the flavors of the meadows and pastures. The crust forms naturally over the minimum three months' ripening, and the crumbly, pure white pâte is perfect just on its own or maybe grated or shaved over salad or vegetables. The crust is beautiful, with patches of white and pale gray molds, and beats European cheeses in terms of purity of flavors.

Cypress Grove 🐐 MCKINLEYVILLE, CALIFORNIA

Much has already been written about Mary Keehn because she is a pioneer of the Californian artisan cheese phenomenon, and her signature cheese, Humboldt Fog, still looks as unique today as it did in the late 1980s, when it suddenly jumped into the spotlight. Today, Mary does not have goats herself, but the same care and consideration go into every batch of cheese she makes and, like most American small producers, she makes numerous cheeses of different styles. Humboldt County, where her operation is located, is a huge redwood-encrusted area close to the ocean that is renowned for its natural beauty.

Truffle Tremor is a white, bloomy-rind cheese weighing 3 pounds (1.3 kg), and it provides a sophisticated tasting sensation, with the scattering of black truffles through the curd. The flavors are light and frothy, with that earthy quality of the truffle giving a truly decadent taste.

Humboldt Fog is stunning, with its ripple of ash through the center of the flaky, crumbly white cheese, and the ash coating on the outside, thickly scattered with white molds, is like the wafting mists and fog that filter through the woodland. The edges of the cheese just begin to melt, and that contributes to the lemon-zest tang of the flavors.

St. George 🐄 MATOS CHEESE FACTORY, SANTA ROSA, CALIFORNIA

Joe and Mary Matos hail from the island of São Jorge in the Azores. The famous cheese of the same name that is produced on the island (see page 148) gave them the inspiration to make their own version when they made their home in Santa Rosa in the 1970s. St. George, weighing 11–22 pounds (5–10 kg), has that familiar sharp taste and crumbly texture. The salty Pacific breezes give definition to the flavors, much like those of the Atlantic do with their Portuguese counterpart. This cheese always wins prizes, mainly because it has such depth to the flavors, which are both rich and spicy. Match St. George with local wines, such as a spicy, full-bodied Zinfandel red.

RIGHT Matos Cheese Factory, St. George

ABOVE, Cypress Grove: LEFT CHEESE, Truffle Tremor,
RIGHT CHEESE Humboldt Fog

OPPOSITE La Clarine Farm, Sierra Mountain Tomme

OREGON

Oregon, in the Pacific Northwest, is partly bounded by two major rivers, the Columbia to the north and the Snake to the east, but it is in the lush and fertile valley of the Willamette River that most of Oregon's population and agriculture—and its cheesemaking—is centered. The eastern region of the state, meanwhile, has evergreen forest and pine and juniper woodland, and a semiarid scrubby landscape and prairies, which stretch from central Oregon.

Rogue Creamery 🐄 CENTRAL POINT, OREGON

A big investment in time and effort went into creating the custom-built maturing caves at Rogue Creamery, to ensure the right degree of cold and humidity.

Smokey Blue, one of the notable cheeses of Rogue Creamery, is made to the original Oregon Blue recipe (the first blue cheese made on the West Coast), then cold-smoked over hazelnut shells for 16 hours, giving a sweet, caramel nuttiness to the sharpness of the blue.

Rogue River Blue is wrapped in local Syrah and Merlot vine leaves that have been marinated in a pear brandy. The year-long aging gives the flavors a big, fruity twang and a creamy, dense texture. This cheese is made with late summer milk only and availability is therefore limited.

Up In Smoke 🐐 RIVER'S EDGE CHÈVRE, THREE RING FARM, LOGSDEN, OREGON

Cheesemaker Pat Morford makes up to 20 different styles of cheese, and the herd of goats grazes on 12 acres (5 ha) of pasture and woodland. Up In Smoke is a small 5½-ounce (150-g) hand-molded rindless cheese, wrapped in maple leaves that have been smoked and dried. The cheeses are smoked over alder and hickory chips, but first the outer leaf wrappings are sprayed with a little bourbon, which keeps the leaves moist and imparts a smoky flavor.

BELOW Rogue Creamery, Rogue River Blue

Juniper Grove Farm 🐐 REDMOND, OREGON

Pierre Kolisch's farm enjoys a climate of cool nights and sunny days, with mineral-rich volcanic soil, clean air, and pure water from the Cascade Range, contributing to the perfect environment for the herd of 110 goats. As well as the ones listed, Pierre, like many farmstead cheesemakers, makes a range of cheeses.

Bûche is a 5½-ounce (150-g) log with a straw of wheat, complete with ear, through the middle. The close texture and crumbly mouth feel are perfectly ripened, and the flavors are rich with complex nutty and tart combinations. The rinds on all the cheeses that I tasted were absolutely right, and I suggest you do not cut them away.

Tumalo Tomme is a 3-pound 5-ounce (1.5-kg) semihard cheese in the French mountain style, with a natural crust that has been rubbed during ripening. The texture of the cheese is slightly moist and crumbly, with scattered eyelets from the drying during ripening. The flavors have a sense of the wild flora, with full-bodied, earthy qualities.

Pyramid is a 5½-ounce (150-g) classic in the style of Pouligny-Saint-Pierre, with a perfect thin and delicious rind that really comes into its own when ripened for eight to ten weeks. The drier, crumbly style has an elegant, almost restrained taste that is perfectly suited to dry white wines.

Pholia Farm 🐐 ROGUE RIVER, OREGON

What is important to this cheesemaking team is their commitment to the land and to their animals. Letting the goats forage and graze in the open pastureland means that the animals have an ever-changing choice of food.

Elk Mountain is much like a Pyrénées Tomme d'Aydius (see page 75), with its washed and rubbed rind giving a smooth finish to the crust and patches of natural white bloom. The 5½–6½-pound (2.5–3-kg) cheeses need three or four months of slow ripening to reach their potential.

Hillis Peak looks very much like a Spanish hard cheese, with a herbal acidity and a gentle, salty tang. The basket-mold pattern on the outside rind, which has been rubbed with oil and Spanish smoked paprika, acquires a dusting of white bloom during the six- to eight-month ripening period.

Pondhopper 🐐 TUMALO FARMS, BEND, OREGON

This semihard pressed cheese weighing 9 pounds (4 kg) has a smooth texture, with scattered eyelets, due to the addition of the local microbrew made with Cascade hops. The waxed outside rind holds the flavors intact; the ripening and daily rub help to develop the hoppy yet sweet flavors.

ABOVE LEFT, MIDDLE CHEESE
Rogue Creamery, Smokey Blue;
VINE-WRAPPED CHEESES River's
Edge Dairy, Up In Smoke

ABOVE RIGHT Juniper Grove: TOP TO
BOTTOM CHEESES Bûche, Tumalo Tomme, Pyramid

BELOW LEFT Pholia Farm: TOP CHEESE Hillis Peak,
BOTTOM CHEESE Elk Mountain

BELOW RIGHT Tumalo Farms, Pondhopper

WASHINGTON

The landscape in this state is varied, with rain forests, dense conifer forests, and impressive mountains, the highest being Mount Rainier. The climate west of the Cascades is temperate with abundant rainfall, which has encouraged successful dairy farming, and there are now also some very interesting cheeses coming out of Washington.

ABOVE LEFT Mount Townsend Creamery, Seastack ABOVE RIGHT Sally Jackson Cheeses OPPOSITE Beecher's, Flagship Reserve

Flagship Reserve 🐄 BEECHER'S, SEATTLE, WASHINGTON

This is a clothbound truckle weighing about 16½ pounds (7.5 kg), and is my cheese of choice for that humble classic, macaroni cheese! Although in looks and crumble Flagship resembles Cheddar, it pushes the nutty aroma and creamy texture forward and lessens the tangy sting you sometimes find in Cheddar because the culture used is reserved for Gruyère and Emmental.

Seastack 🐄 MOUNT TOWNSEND CREAMERY, PORT TOWNSEND, WASHINGTON

Matt Day and Ryan Trail have been making cheese only a few years, but the clean flavors and Matt and Ryan's terrific way with ripening rinds have given their cheeses an elegance and depth. Seastack is one such cheese. It is a 5½-ounce (150-g) disk covered with charcoal ash, then ripened to allow the white *Penicillium candidum* molds to blend in with the ash. It is obvious that the cheesemakers are taking inspiration from France, but giving the cheese a few more weeks' ripening will let the earthy and nutty flavors come forward.

Sally Jackson Cheeses 🐄🐐🐑 OROVILLE, WASHINGTON

Sally Jackson and her husband, Roger, are pioneering spirits who exactly reflect the commitment and energy required to not only master artisan cheesemaking, but also allow it to develop modestly.

Sally is self-taught and does not follow a strict regimen of rules and formulas, preferring to use her eyes, rather than reading from a technical book. Her cheeses are wrapped in locally collected chestnut and vine leaves, and the molds are made by a local potter. The cheese production is small, because they only have around 25 sheep and goats, and a few dairy cows.

The round cow's milk cheese weighs about 2¼ pounds (1 kg). The goat's is smaller, weighing about 10½ ounces (300 g), and the ewe's milk is a hexagonal shape of 10½–14 ounces (300–400 g). The flavors of Sally's cheeses are fruity and bosky from the leaf wrapping, but the milk has a gamy sweetness to it, reflecting the farm's environment of grasses, edible weeds, and alfalfa. I would serve a bold and dry, fruity red wine with these cheeses because it would complement the flavors perfectly.

Central United States

From the Great Lakes, across the Great Plains, to the Rockies, there is a huge diversity of climate and geography. Good dairy farming and cheesemaking abound in such far-flung states as Wisconsin, Minnesota, Iowa, Illinois, Indiana, and Colorado. The many styles of cheesemaking reflect the origins of the settlers from all over the world who have made these states their home.

WISCONSIN

Known as America's Dairyland, this north-central state is considered part of the Midwest, bordered by Minnesota to the west, Iowa to the southwest, Illinois to the south, Lake Michigan to the east, Michigan to the northeast, and Lake Superior to the north. The land is rich if somewhat rocky, and the weather patterns suit dairy farming, with an emphasis on cheese. Blessed with a good river system right through the state, and lakes Michigan, Superior, and Winnebago, all the elements for good dairy farming are present, and there is a justifiable pride in the way this is supported by the various associations offering information, tours, and festivals all to do with cheese. Settlers from all over Europe who plunged their roots into the soil of Wisconsin have left their traditions and styles stamped on the cheesemaking, and it is hard not to fill an entire book with cheese from just Wisconsin, but here is a good selection.

Bleu Mont Dairy 🐄 BLUE MOUNDS, DANE COUNTY, WISCONSIN

About 30 miles (50 km) from Madison, the dairy is situated between Blue Mounds State Park and Brigham County Park, where Willi Lehner and Qui'tas McKnight have honed their craft. Willi learned cheesemaking from his father, who first gained experience as a cheesemaker in his native Switzerland. The milk that is used to make the cheeses is supplied by local organic farms utilizing a rotating pasture system for feeding the cattle.

Bleu Mont Cloth Cheddar This is a perfect example of farmhouse cheese, with its distinctive musty aroma on the crust, which has been brushed free of any tiny cheese mites that gather during the long aging process. The crumbly texture is perfect, not too dry, and not too moist and acidic, and there is a sweetness and nuttiness, with a long, lingering finish. The more aged cheeses have that crystalline density somewhat like Parmesan, but, even so, there is no hint of bitterness coming through, just lovely, beefy caramel flavors. The 11-pound (5-kg) cheeses are wrapped in fine cheesecloth in the traditional manner, then brushed with a solution of clean water mixed with molds from the rinds of aged cheeses, to seal the wrappings. Once the cheeses are in the maturing room, with its high humidity and cool temperature, the natural airborne bacteria filter into them.

Lil Wil's Big Cheese is a Swiss-style cheese with a smooth, dense texture and a brine-rubbed rind. The 2¼-pound (1-kg) cheese is washed in brine using the method of mixing soil from the farm with fresh water, then filtering. The cheese itself is a Havarti style, with a rich texture that is almost melting at the edges. After the brine washing, the cheese is rubbed, then placed in the maturing rooms for ripening, where a white bloom grows on the rinds. A beer from a Wisconsin microbrewery works well with this cheese.

OPPOSITE, TOP LEFT, TOP CHEESE Bleu Mont Dairy: Lil Wil's Big Cheese, BOTTOM CHEESE Bleu Mont Cloth Cheddar

OPPOSITE, TOP RIGHT Bleu Mont Cloth Cheddar

OPPOSITE, BOTTOM Inner workings and outside view of Bleu Mont Dairy.

Fantôme Farm 🐐 RIDGEWAY, WISCONSIN

Anne Topham and Judy Borree, with their herd of 12 goats, make just enough cheese to sell at the local Dane County market. Goat cheese is not a familiar sight in Wisconsin, so it is to their credit that the cheeses have made such an impact, gaining medals at prestigious cheese awards.

Fleuri Noir is lightly dusted with charcoal; the curds are hand-ladled and left to drain in cheesecloths, then are salted and whipped, before placing into molds. The sparkling white cheese is light, almost frothy, and fresh in taste, with a clean acidity.

Small Plain Chevre is delightful as a very fresh cheese, or you could allow it to ripen a little, to dry out the texture and give a flakiness. It has very simple crème-fraîche acidity and creaminess.

Ridgeway Ghost, with just a hint of speckled ash, is perfect fresh or, if left to dry out a bit, becomes more dense. A perfect end of meal cheese.

Moreso is completely coated in dark ash, which gives a nutty flavor to the cheese, and would ripen well to produce a more complex taste. All these cheeses would be perfect with a white Sauvignon wine.

Brunkow Cheese Co-op 🐄 DARLINGTON, WISCONSIN

Karl Geissbuhler's family has been associated with dairy farming in Wisconsin since 1899, and today Karl and his partner Greg Schulte work with the help of more than 30 dairy farmers, who form the cooperative.

The Brunkow Cheese dairy used to churn out staple cheeses for the mass market, but it has diversified to produce new artisan cheeses that are handmade and matured on wooden boards in an underground cellar, such as those given below.

Avondale Truckle, made with unpasteurized milk, is a 20–22-pound (9–10-kg) clothbound truckle, aged for 6–18 months to develop layers of flavors that are fruity, dry, earthy, and vegetal when mature, although more buttery when young. It has a lovely crumbly texture, and dry, full-bodied red wines are a good match, although beefy beers and ales are good partners, too.

Little Darling is a 3-pound 5-ounce (1.5-kg) truckle, aged for six weeks, that has naturally evolved outside molds and a lovely grassy aroma with a rich, flaky texture that is sweetly earthy. A red wine that is fruity and round, rather than robust, would work, as would craft-style beers.

Dunbarton Blue 🐄 ROELLI CHEESE HAUS, SHULLSBURG, WISCONSIN

The Roelli cheesemaking tradition started with Adolph, who hailed from Switzerland, and three generations later Chris has taken over, producing Emmental, Havarti, Cheddar, Gouda, Jack, and other styles. In 2007, Chris developed a blue Stilton-style, Dunbarton Blue. On tasting it, you find a creamy richness with a fine crumble, and the blue is not intense, but adds a nutty mineral quality. I would like to keep it a little longer to see how the flavors develop. Enjoy with a glass of dry red wine.

Ten-Year Aged Cheddar 🐄 HOOK'S CHEESE COMPANY, MINERAL POINT, WISCONSIN

Tony and Julie Hook's award-winning, ten-year aged cheese, weighing 44 pounds (20 kg) has a complexity of calcium crystals giving the crumble a lovely sharpness, but with a full-bodied, rich, and creamy finish. Enjoy this cheese with a red Bordeaux.

Mobay 🐐🐑 CARR VALLEY CHEESE COMPANY, LA VALLE, WISCONSIN

This dairy has been going for more than 100 years, and Sid Cook is the fourth-generation family member to run the business. The 4½-pound (2-kg) Mobay cheese is based on Morbier cheese (see page 89), but combines goat's and ewe's milk, with a stripe of emulsified grapevine ash to separate the two layers. The sharpness of the whiter goat curd contrasts with the sweetness of the ewe's milk; the hint of fruitiness from the grapevine ash stripe finishes off the taste.

THIS PAGE, CLOCKWISE FROM TOP RIGHT CHEESE Brunkow Cheese Co-op, Avondale Truckle; Roelli Cheese Haus, Dunbarton Blue (veined); Brunkow Cheese Co-op, Little Darling; Hook's Cheese Company, Ten-Year Aged Cheddar; Carr Valley Cheese Company, Mobay (with grapevine ash)

OPPOSITE Fantôme Farm: TOP LEFT CHEESE, Fleuri Noir, TOP RIGHT CHEESE Small Plain Chevre, MIDDLE RIGHT CHEESE Ridgeway Ghost, BOTTOM CHEESE Moreso

Marieke Foenegreek Gouda 🐄
HOLLAND'S FAMILY FARM,
THORP, WISCONSIN

Rolf and Marieke settled in Thorp from the Netherlands in 2002, first to become dairy farmers, then to make a proper farmhouse Gouda. The traditional recipe has the addition of fenugreek, a seed native to Asia that is much used in Dutch cooking, and has a nutty, spicy-sweet flavor. The fresh unpasteurized milk is pumped directly from the parlor to the dairy and straight into the vats. The curds are made into 17½-pound (8-kg) forms, then pressed, before being taken out of their forms and placed in a saltwater bath for 60 hours. The maturing rooms have Dutch pine planks, which are scrubbed daily to prevent molds from growing, and these help to absorb the liquids that seep out of the cheeses as they mature. For the first 14 days, the cheeses are turned daily and rubbed to prevent molds; during this stage, a waxy coat is painted onto the cheeses by hand. Further maturing continues, with the cheeses being turned twice a week until ready for sale.

Trade Lake Cedar 🐑 LOVETREE FARMSTEAD,
GRANTSBURG, WISCONSIN

Mary and Dave Falk practice a sustainability program, including creating their own crossbred sheep, in order to develop a strain that is hardy to their region, grass-fed only and still able to produce a high butterfat milk, to give the cheeses their unique flavors. The typical Trade Lake Cedar weighs around 6 pounds (2.7 kg). I was impressed by the deep, fruity flavors and the bosky aroma, due to the cheeses having a platform of cedar branches in the "fresh air" aging rooms.

Dante 🐑 WISCONSIN SHEEP DAIRY COOPERATIVE,
SPOONER, WISCONSIN

Spooner's natural wild beauty not only boasts woods, lakes, and rivers, but also hill grazing for sheep that is ideal. Dante is made with ewe's milk, which is sweet and nutty, and its texture is slightly dry, with a lovely flaky crumble. The rind has a plastic coating, somewhat like a Gouda without the waxing; it is there to prevent molds from growing and a crust forming. During the six-month maturing time, the cheeses are turned and wiped with a wet cloth, to keep the molds at bay. A light Beaujolais-style wine or a dry Riesling would be good with this cheese.

Petit Frère 🐄 CRAVE BROTHERS FARMSTEAD CHEESE,
WATERLOO, WISCONSIN

Charles, Georgee, Thomas, and Mark Crave have 950 very pampered Holstein cows, and in 2001 they decided to become cheesemakers as well as farmers. Their Petit Frère is a good attempt at a European washed rind, and the small 9-ounce (250-g) cheese comes in a box similar to a Camembert. The brine-washed rind is a deep apricot, and little patchy white molds grow, to create a delicate mottled effect. The cheese is at its best when the pâte begins to melt around the edges, and the flavor is sensational—earthy, fruity, and sweet. If you like Munster, Époisses, or Ardrahan cheeses, then you will definitely love this.

Big Eds 🐄 SAXON HOMESTEAD CREAMERY,
CLEVELAND, WISCONSIN

The Kelssig family has farmed here since the 1850s, after emigrating from Germany; the present family members run the dairy farm and the creamery, producing five different varieties of cheese, all made with unpasteurized milk. Big Eds, named after the founding father, is 15½ pounds (7 kg) of buttery texture, with a mild, sweet hazelnut taste that is instantly enjoyable. It has a joyous appeal, which is especially good for those hesitantly entering the world of artisan unpasteurized cheese tasting, and is a true family favorite. The cheese is "cooked" in the Asiago and Emmental style, pressed, and ripened for 120 days, although it can mature on for up to six months. It is very versatile as both a table and a cooking cheese.

Pleasant Ridge Reserve UPLANDS CHEESE, MADISON, WISCONSIN

Mike and Carol Gingrich, together with Dan and Jeanne Pâténaude, started the farm in 1994. The cheese is modeled on Pyrénées cheeses, such as Ossau, with particular attention to the washing and rubbing of the rinds during the maturing process, and replicating the temperature and humidity levels that you would find in the stone caves of that region.

The fresh unpasteurized milk is processed into cheese directly after the last cow has been milked, and traditional cultures are used in the coagulation into curds. The slow aging of the reserve cheese, 12 months' minimum, gives a really layered flavor profile of fruit, nut, cream, and acidity that is not only incredibly delicious, but also lingering and sweet. This is an expensive cheese, but worth every penny, and it highlights the level of expertise displayed by independent cheesemakers.

BELOW Uplands Cheese, Pleasant Ridge Reserve

BELOW RIGHT, TOP CHEESE Wisconsin Sheep Dairy, Dante; BOTTOM CHEESE Holland's Family Farm, Marieke Foenegreek Gouda

ABOVE RIGHT, LARGE CHEESE Saxon Homestead Creamery, Big Eds; SMALL CHEESE Crave Brothers Farmstead Cheese, Petit Frères

OPPOSITE Lovetree Farmstead, Trade Lake Cedar

MINNESOTA, IOWA, ILLINOIS, & MICHIGAN

Often known as the "land of 10,000 lakes," Minnesota has a soil that is full of nutrients and mineral elements, and these give the cheeses their richness and depth of flavor. The land in Iowa is generally flat, although there are several natural lakes that contribute to good soil conditions and drainage. Illinois and Michigan both have fertile land and agricultural traditions, although cheesemaking production is still small.

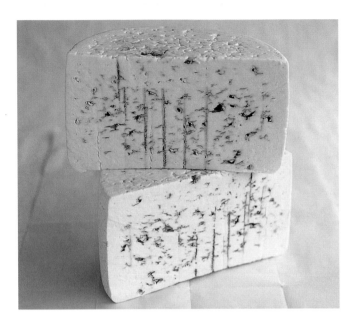

Faribault Dairy 🐄 FARIBAULT, MINNESOTA

This area is blessed with ancient St. Peter sandstone caves along the Straight River overlooking Faribault. They have been used to age beer and, since 1936, to age cheese. Faribault Dairy produces French-style crumbly blues, but they it has a new cheese to its selection, which is a Gorgonzola. Faribault still remains the only American cheesemaker to cure in natural stone caves.

Amablu, weighing 6 pounds (2.7 kg), is a rich and creamy-textured cheese, with well-defined veins. It has been aged for 75 days, to produce a good acidity and crumble, together with a strong and vibrant blue mold. As the cheeses age, salt and mineral crystals form on the outside, which have to be scraped off to allow the air to penetrate and create the blue molds. The cheese goes well with dry red wines, port, or sweet dessert wines with a savory edge.

St. Pete's Select is a 6-pound (2.7-kg) cheese aged for up to 110 days, giving it a darker yellow color and a deeper, more assertive flavor. The aging rooms burrow deep into the caves, where the cheeses mature in the murky darkness until ready for sale.

Prairie Breeze 🐄 MILTON CREAMERY, MILTON, IOWA

Rufus Musser arrived in Milton in 1992 with his wife, Jane, to start a farm. They now make numerous styles of cheese, including Colby and Cheddar, along with "squeaky" fresh cheese curds. Prairie Breeze may look like a simple large block Cheddar aged over six months, but due to the quality of the milk, and the respect for grazing and maintaining a seasonal approach to rearing the cows, the flavors of the cheese are really delicious and fruity. I think that many lessons can be learned from this style of production and the results that can be achieved by a considered approach. This simple-style table or cooking cheese is great with a dry hard cider or a hoppy beer.

Prairie Fruits Farm 🐐🐑 CHAMPAIGN COUNTY, ILLINOIS

Champaign is located in an area known for its farming communities, but Wes Jarrell and Leslie Cooperband started Illinois's first farmstead cheesemaking production only in 2005. With just 50 goats, the production is small, but the range of styles diverse; they have also started to get ewe's milk from a nearby Amish dairy in Arthur, Illinois.

Roxanne is a ewe's milk cheese, with a lovely natural rind and patchy blooms, and its fudgy, crumbly texture is sweet and earthy. The pale rind develops darker patches as it matures, and the flavors become richer and nutty. This is perfect for a full-bodied white or a fine, dry red wine.

Krotovina is styled on a French truncated pyramid, and has a layer of goat's milk curd topped with a thin layer of ash, then ewe's milk curd placed on top. The cheese is close-textured, with a very delicate, bloomy rind. The sweetness of both milks and the acidity of the goat and earthiness of the ewe's milk are delicious, and I suggest a Pinot-style wine or something with a dry edge.

Little Bloom, a 6-ounce (175-g) Camembert-style goat cheese aged for four to five weeks, has a dense, creamy texture and soft, downy white rind. It is perfect with light, fruity red wines, which will not overpower the flavor of the milk.

THIS PAGE Prairie Fruits Farm: CHEESES FROM TOP TO BOTTOM, Roxanne, Krotovina, and Little Bloom

OPPOSITE, TOP LEFT Faribault Dairy: TOP CHEESE St. Pete's Select, BOTTOM CHEESE Amablu

OPPOSITE, BOTTOM RIGHT Milton Creamery: Prairie Breeze

Capriole Farmstead

Capriole is situated in Greenville, Indiana, the smallest Midwest state. The great soil conditions on the "till plains" and the flow of rivers and streams all make for great farming. In an area known as Kentuckyana, the township has the Big and Little Indian Creeks threading their way through it.

LEFT, MIDDLE, AND RIGHT The goats of Capriole Farmstead at feeding time.

Capriole Farmstead GREENVILLE, INDIANA

Judith Schad and her husband, Larry, bought their farm in 1976 and later found out that the property had once belonged to Larry's great-great-grandfather. At first the intention was to have a mixed farm without the ubiquitous horses and run on sustainable practices, until the goats won their hearts and Judith was determined to make cheese from their milk. Although Judith had vague farming roots, she is the first of the family to take it up seriously and embrace fine-quality goat cheesemaking. She and Mary Keehn from Cypress Grove (see page 166) revolutionized the thinking around artisan small-production handmade cheeses in the early 1990s. Both she and Mary traveled through France, learning along the way. By the time they returned, they knew exactly how and what they wanted to produce. Today, Judith's herd of 400 Alpine, Saanen, and Nubian goats produces a varied selection, influenced by the classic French styles, but with the flavors and aromas of the land. Outside grazing takes place for as long as it is possible, but come winter—which is harsh—they live inside and eat sweet hay. Her maturing and ripening skills are flawless, and any new cheesemaker coming onto the scene will always look to Capriole goat cheeses for inspiration.

Old Kentucky Tomme This unpasteurized white-mold rind cheese weighs 3–5 pounds (1.3–2.25 kg). It has an earthy mushroom aroma coming from the rind, and with aging of around five months develops a richness to the pâte and a smooth, mellow creaminess. It falls between a classic mountain-style tomme and the crumbly, nutty freshness of Chaource (see page 59). I would definitely partner this with a Chardonnay wine, but one that is not too oaked.

Julianna is an aged unpasteurized 12-ounce (350-g) cheese covered with herbs and spices, somewhat like a Corsican cheese, then aged to produce the lovely patches of white molds on the rind. The flavors are dense and herbal, with a sweet woodland aroma, and these cheeses are aged for around four months.

Sofia, a closely packed 9-ounce (250-g) log dusted in charcoal, grows billowy white molds that need to be patted down during the cheesemaking process, to ensure that they do not become too thick. Inside, the cheese is marbled with ash layers, which give a tangy note to the pâte's creamy texture.

O'Banon was inspired by a trip Judith and Larry took to Provence. The curds are ladled by hand for a slower, even draining, then wrapped in chestnut leaves that have been soaked in Old Forester or Woodford Kentucky bourbon. The cheese is then tied with raffia string. The 6-ounce (175-g) cheeses are made with pasteurized goat's milk because they are sold before 60 days old, but their creamy texture will become drier and more fruity in flavor if allowed to ripen for one month.

Mont St. Francis This cheese, in particular, reveals Judith's ripening prowess, with a lovely washed rind very gently attaching itself to the 12-ounce (350-g) unpasteurized milk cheese. It is important that the rind is allowed to become neither too sticky nor too dry. The flavors of the milk become sweetly earthy as the aging process continues for up to six months.

Piper's Pyramide is very much in the style of Pouligny-Saint-Pierre (see page 62), but the dusting of paprika lends a spicy, meaty note to the flavors of the cheese. Allowing it to dry out a bit will make the texture more flaky and give a lovely tartness, too.

Wabash Cannonball is a lumpy-looking crottin (see page 63), with an ash coating that is quickly covered in white fluffy molds during the ripening stage. It is always best to eat this cheese when the texture is flaky and slightly drier, in the French style.

OPPOSITE, TOP LEFT CHEESE Old Kentucky Tomme, TOP RIGHT CHEESE Juliana; SECOND ROW, LEFT CHEESE Sofia (cut), RIGHT CHEESE Mont St. Francis; THIRD ROW, LEFT CHEESE Sofia (cut), RIGHT CHEESE O'Banon; FRONT ROW, LEFT CHEESE Piper's Pyramide, RIGHT CHEESE Wabash Cannonball

Zingerman's Creamery ANN ARBOR, MICHIGAN

The name Zingerman is held in great esteem in Ann Arbor, a major university city situated on the Huron River. There is good agricultural farming and fruit growing in this region, as well as a fertile green landscape. Zingerman's was originally a super-delicatessen with its own bakery, to supply the daily sandwich production for the store. In 2000, however, John Loomis, who was working as the cheese seller in the store, was chosen to head a new venture, with a goat farm in Manchester, to make fresh cheese. The success of the fresh cheeses soon saw the dairy move next to the bakehouse, where new cheeses were created, including a cow's milk Cheshire. These much-loved and unique cheeses are just another important part of the Zingerman philosophy and, apart from being sold in their own stores, are shipped to both the East and West coasts to cheese shops and restaurants.

Garlic with Chives is a fresh rindless goat's button, flavored with garlic and topped with chives. This cheese is a perfect spreading cheese.

Manchester is a hand-ladled soft, fudgy-textured cheese, with a bloomy, snowy white rind and a rich, creamy, gently tangy taste that has had the addition of a little extra cream to the milk. It is lovely at three to four weeks, but it can be aged for another four weeks after that, at which time it becomes more solid and flaky.

Lincoln Log is a simple log-shape goat cheese with a bloomy white rind, patted close to the cheese, in order to prevent it from becoming too fluffy and separate. This is a rich-tasting morsel, with a lovely citrus edge and a little mushroom earthiness.

Great Lakes Cheshire went through a lot of trials to get the acidity levels right, and it is now a classic crumbly hard cow's milk cheese.

City Goat is a fresh button of gentle, frothy goat cheese, achieved by ladling the curds by hand, to keep them superlight; it is topped with a fresh herb motif.

Detroit Street, a small goat's milk brick shape, with a bloomy rind and coated in freshly cracked green peppercorns, tastes sharp and spicy. It is aged for 10 days to one month.

Little Napoleon is made with hand-ladled curds, to give the cheeses time to drain and develop their flavors. The bloomy white rind becomes mottled with gray/blue molds during the maturing process. The flavors of this cheese are gentle and acidic when aged for two weeks, becoming drier and nuttier, with a more goaty aroma, when matured for one month.

Bridgewater is made to the same recipe as Manchester (left), but contains black peppercorns, to spike up the flavors a little. The fluffy white bloom will become a little drier with ripening, which also increases the spiciness of the flavors.

BELOW Zingerman's Creamery: BACK ROW, LEFT TO RIGHT Garlic with Chives, Manchester, Lincoln Log, Great Lakes Cheshire; FRONT ROW, LEFT TO RIGHT City Goat, Detroit Street, Little Napoleon, Bridgewater, Garlic with Chives, and plain cream cheese on bread

COLORADO

The state of Colorado is known for its magnificent scenery, taking in mountains, rivers, lakes, and plains. The climate is one of contrasts, with high peaks sheltering the valleys. The eastern side of the state is principally made up of farmland, with many small farming communities.

Haystack Mountain Goat Dairy

NIWOT, COLORADO

This dairy is located just outside of Boulder. Cheesemaker Jim Schott started making cheese in March 1992 with just 25 Nubian goats. Today, although retired, his influence still remains, even though the goat's and cow's milk is now brought in from several nearby farms to make their Buttercup mixed-milk semihard cheese. All the goat cheeses they produce have a simple, clean-tasting style.

Queso de Mano, a 4-pound (1.8-kg) semihard cheese with delicious nutty, hearty yet sweetly herbal flavors, stands out, primarily because the mineral-rich pastures on which the goats graze add to the flavors.

Haystack Peak, a pyramid-shape cheese, has a close texture and nutty character.

Snowdrop is a 6-ounce (175-g) light and delicate cheese, with a creamy interior. It has a soft, bloomy white rind, which is edible and contributes to the flavors.

THIS PAGE Haystack Mountain Goat Dairy: TOP RIGHT CHEESE Queso de Mano, MIDDLE CHEESES Haystack Peak, FRONT LEFT CHEESE Snowdrop

The East

This part of the United States is a varied and large region, encompassing the New England states of Vermont bordered by Massachusetts to the south, New Hampshire to the east, and New York to the west, as well as Connecticut, all of which have well-established agricultural industries that stretch back to the 17th century. In the south of this region are the states of Tennessee, Virginia, and Georgia, with a climate and landscape that are very different than their northern counterparts, with hot, humid summers and coolish but not cold winters that make for ideal grazing land.

LEFT The barns at Rawson Brook Fram, Massachusetts.

ABOVE A goat roams the pastures at Rawson Brook Farm.

VERMONT

Agriculture is an important industry in Vermont, and cheesemaking, especially small-scale artisan enterprises, is very much in evidence, with many farms offering tours and tastings. The spring and summer colors of the trees and forests are vibrantly green, which is probably due to the mica-quartz-chlorite schist—that glistening decomposed shale formation in rocks. The minerals leach into the soil and rivers, which then give the flora their extremely bright colors. This is particularly evident in the fall, when flaming reds, oranges, and golds, especially the turning foliage of the sugar maples, light up the deciduous forests.

Jasper Hill Farm

The ripening rooms at Jasper Hill Farm, which are ideal for all types of cheese, are used not only by the farm, but also by other small independent cheesemakers in and around the region.

Jasper Hill Farm 🐄 GREENSBORO, VERMONT
Mateo and Andy Kehler, who started cheesemaking in 2002, have invested a huge amount to create the first state-of-the-art underground network of ripening rooms in the country. These serve not only their farm, but also other small independent cheesemakers in the region.
Constant Bliss is a bloomy white-rinded cheese similar to the French Chaource (see page 59), weighing about 7 ounces (200 g), and made using the naturally cooled milk from Ayrshire cows, which produce a rich milk if not a huge yield. Using unpasteurized milk, the cheese has to be ripened for 60 days by law, and in that time the outside rind will become closely matted to the cheese, with some gray/blue molds appearing. The flavors are rich and dense, but with lovely floral, grassy tones.

Bayley Hazen Blue is made every other day with only morning milk because the fats in the Ayrshire milk are lower at this milking. This facilitates the ripening process, which takes four to six months, and gives a drier texture to the pâte, as well as bringing out the full flavors of the milk, rather than the overpowering minerality of the blue molds. A red wine with body and not too powerful tannins would be ideal to drink with this cheese.

BELOW RIGHT Jasper Hill Farm:
LEFT CHEESE Bayley Hazen Blue,
RIGHT CHEESE Constant Bliss

Weybridge ≡ SCHOLTEN FAMILY FARM, MIDDLEBURY, VERMONT

This cheese is produced by the Scholten family, whose approach to farming combines environmentally friendly practices with good husbandry and family values. The Scholten's small herd of Dutch Belt cows and Holstein-Friesians (both native to the Netherlands) produces the single cheese Weybridge, which is taken to the Jasper Hill cellars (see page 185) for ripening. It weighs about 8 ounces (225 g), has a delicate, bloomy white crust, and houses a rich, almost melting, buttercup yellow cheese within. The cheeses are ripened for up to 30 days. They have the nutty, earthy taste of a Camembert, but are more fluid and lighter in texture and depth, which works well with the mushroomy aroma of the rind.

Vermont Ayr ≡ CRAWFORD FAMILY FARM, WHITING, VERMONT

The Crawfords are fourth-generation farmers, and their 330-acre (134-ha) farm overlooks the Adirondack and Green mountains in the fertile Champlain Valley. They have 60 Ayrshires, 24 of which are milked for cheesemaking, and a historic barn with an original slate roof, which has been converted as a parlor with a small maturing room. The farm produces just one style of cheese, based on an Alpine tomme and made by hand.

Vermont Ayr weighs about 4 pounds (1.8 kg) and is made with unpasteurized milk; only a small quantity of rennet is added to the milk to form the curds, which are cut and stirred by hand for an hour while the vat continues to heat the whey. The curds are placed in molds lined with cheesecloth, lightly pressed, and turned every few minutes, before being removed from the molds and salt-brined overnight. They are aged slowly for several months, forming a natural crust with a light white bloom. The flavors are earthy and nutty, like fresh, milky sweet hazelnuts, and perfect with crisp white wines or light reds.

Sarabande ≡ DANCING COW CHEESE, BRIDPORT, VERMONT

Steve and Karen Getz moved from eastern Pennsylvania in 2003, to become dairy farmers and raise their family in Vermont. After winning awards for their high-quality organic milk, they decided to make cheese. As their success grew, they teamed up with Jasper Hill Farm (see page 185) in 2007, to use their cellars to age their cheeses, as well to enable Steve and Karen to reach new markets and increase sales. The pair has now diversified into other farm-made products, to add to their three cheeses—Menuet, a semihard tomme style; Bourrée, a semisoft washed rind; and Sarabande.

Sarabande, weighing about 8 ounces (225 g), is an unpasteurized single-milking cheese in a truncated pyramid shape, and is lightly washed. The golden pâte has a slightly chalky center, and the flavors are of dewy, sweet grass and fresh nuts, with a little earthy complexity, which comes from the ripening time in the high-humidity cooled rooms. This is a perfect cheese for red wines with light tannins and forward fruit flavors.

Cabot Clothbound Cheddar ≡ CABOT CREAMERY, CABOT, VERMONT

Cabot Creamery is a dominant feature in this part of Vermont. Started in 1930 as a collective, it has developed into a major conveyor-belt-style dairy, churning out basic cheese seen in all the supermarkets and shops. Times change, however, and cheesemaker Marcel Gravel decided to have a separate unit to make a clothbound Cheddar-style cheese. With help from Jasper Hill Farm (see page 185), with its fine aging facilities, the dairy has, quite magically, created a magnificent cheese in Cabot Clothbound Cheddar, weighing 38 pounds (17 kg). There have been a few tweaks along the way, notably to turn the sweeter flavors into more robust, fruity ones. The traditional wrapped cheese is rubbed in lard, to resist mold growth, but this also allows the cheese to breathe through the cloth during its 12-month maturing process at Jasper Hill.

OPPOSITE, TOP CHEESE Dancing Cow Cheese, Sarabande; MIDDLE CHEESE Crawford Family Farm, Vermont Ayr; FRONT CHEESES Scholten Family Farm, Weybridge

RIGHT Cabot Creamery, Cabot Clothbound Cheddar

Twig Farm 🐐 MIDDLEBURY, WEST CORNWALL, VERMONT

Michael Lee and Emily Sunderman are first-generation cheesemakers who have made a concerted effort to understand their surroundings and what they have to offer, but have also chosen to be very hands-on in their approach. The people who farm in these parts are called "flatlanders" locally, for the most obvious of reasons, but Twig Farm is hidden down a track through what is like a magic forest of tall, spindly pines and scrubby bush. Here, the goats wander and forage on the stone ledges and outcrops. With just 25 goats of their own, Michael and Emily supplement milk supply with goat's milk from a farm in Bridport. They produce three simple styles of cheese that reflect the skills of the cheesemaker. I would choose either a dry hard cider or a straightforward country-style red wine to serve with all three of these cheeses.

Twig Farm Square is an unpasteurized goat's milk cheese (using milk from only the farm's own herd) weighing 2 pounds (900 g). It is an irregular square, due to it being wrapped in cheesecloth, then having the ends tied in a knot in the middle of the cheese. After weighting down and pressing, it takes on its simple shape; it is then aged for 80 days, during which time pretty molds form on the natural crust. The flavors of this square cheese are earthy and nutty, and there is a real taste of "foraged" fodder, such as leaves, twigs, and ferns.

Twig Farm Washed-Rind Wheel is an unpasteurized 18-ounce (500-g) goat's milk cheese, with additions of cow's milk from Joe Severy's farm in Cornwall, Vermont, at certain times of the year when the goat's milk yield is low. It is aged for 80 days and, during the ripening process, a whey brine is used to wash the cheeses, which gives a pale apricot glow to the sticky surface rind. The rind, with its pungent aroma, and the fudgy-textured cheese, which is almost melting at the edges, have a full-bodied earthy, rich, and sweetly savory flavor.

Twig Farm Tomme is an unpasteurized 2¼-pound (1-kg) cheese using milk from the Twig herd and from Dan Robertshaw's herd in Bridport. It is aged for 80 days, forming a lovely natural crust mottled with bloomy molds from the ripening rooms, which have high humidity and cool, even temperatures. The clean, bright interior of the cheese has a flaky, semihard texture and a nutty, slightly sharp rusticity, with a lingering finish.

Vermont Shepherd ☙ VERMONT
SHEPHERD FARM, PUTNEY, VERMONT

This 6–8-pound (2.7–3½-kg) cheese has inspired cheesemakers to develop European techniques and incorporate them into their surroundings, especially with underground ripening rooms. Cheesemaker David Major has lived on the farm all his life, and his 250 sheep are on rotational pasture, with special care shown toward improving the soil, pastures, and water resources. The simple shape of the cheese is achieved by packing the curds into two domestic-style colanders and pressing them together. This unique example of the sweetly earthy, almost feral quality of the milk requires a wine with good body and depth, such as Madiran.

Tarentaise 🐄 THISTLE HILL FARM,
NORTH POMFRET, VERMONT

This 20-pound (9-kg) wheel is matured for a minimum of four months, but can be further ripened for a year, to give the sweet, hazelnut creamy texture and rich fruit flavors more depth. The cheeses are made from spring to fall, and the grazing cows have only a little homegrown organic hay and grain supplement added to their diet, so you get a true taste of the *terroir*.

RIGHT Thistle Hill Farm, Tarentaise
TOP RIGHT Vermont Shepherd
OPPOSITE, LEFT CHEESE Twig Farm Square,
RIGHT BACK CHEESE Twig Farm Tomme, RIGHT
FRONT CHEESE Twig Farm Washed-Rind Wheel

Summertomme 🐑 WILLOW HILL FARM, MILTON, VERMONT

The unique maturing cave at Willow Hill is 8 feet (2.5 m) underground and has a wall of natural bedrock that allows water to seep through the cracks, thus creating moisture and humidity in the air. This helps the rinds on Willow Hill's cheeses to develop beautiful molds. This 8-ounce (225-g) ewe's milk cheese has a delicate, crumbly texture, with the sweet, earthy, almost emulsified flavor of the pâte mingling with the floral herb coating.

Boucher Blue 🐄 BOUCHER FAMILY FARM, HIGHGATE CENTER, VERMONT

Weighing 3 pounds 5 ounces (1.5 kg), this unpasteurized cow's milk cheese has a smooth texture, with a mellow blue hit like a Fourme d'Ambert, on which the recipe is based. Enjoy this with a sweet dessert wine or a fruity red.

Two-Year Cheddar Block 🐄 SHELBURNE FARMS, SHELBURNE, VERMONT

Although this is a 2¼-pound (1-kg) block style with a waxed coating, all the elements of Cheddar are present, and the acidity is forward with this handmade unpasteurized milk cheese. There is a nutty richness from the milk, with its distinctive tangy finish on the aged cheeses.

Vermont Butter & Cheese Company 🐐 WEBSTERVILLE, VERMONT

Allison Hooper started the business with colleague Bob Reese in 1984. She is a maker of cheese, not a farmer, with a network of 25 family farms supplying the milk. I would serve a fine Sauvignon Blanc with these cheeses. **Coupole,** weighing 6½ ounces (185 g), is dense yet creamy with a full-bodied flavor achieved right at the start via a warm drying room, then a cool ripening room. It can be ripened for up to eight weeks.

Bonne Bouche weighs 4 ounces (115 g) and has an intriguing mixture of light mousse textures at two weeks when young, becoming more dense and dry after 45 days of ripening. The rind is achieved by high temperatures in the drying room immediately after making, and then aging at a lower temperature to develop the wrinkled appearance and bring the flavors forward. The ash and salt spread on top of the cheese prevent the rind from becoming too thick, which would affect the natural drying as it ages.

Bijou is a goaty, gamy button of 2 ounces (55 g) similar to Coupole. When young, it is citric and floral, while the aged cheeses are dense but creamy in the middle, with pronounced goatiness.

Fresh logs are frothy fresh, mild, and not yeasty cheeses, and should be served young, given their lack of salting at the curd stage, to keep the purity of the milk. The coatings of peppercorn or herb give added dimension, and are lovely in a salad.

LEFT, LEFT CHEESE Boucher Family Farm, Boucher Blue; MIDDLE CHEESE Willow Hill Farm, Summertomme; RIGHT CHEESE Shelburne Farms, Two-Year Cheddar Block

OPPOSITE Vermont Butter & Cheese Co.: TOP LEFT AND MIDDLE LEFT CHEESES Coupole; RIGHT TOP AND CENTER CHEESES Bonne Bouche; RIGHT MIDDLE AND BOTTOM CHEESES Fresh logs; BOTTOM LEFT CHEESE Bijou

ABOVE Consider Bardwell Farm: LEFT CHEESE Pawlet, BACK RIGHT CHEESE Dorset, FRONT RIGHT CHEESE Manchester

Consider Bardwell Farm 🐄🐐 PAWLET, VERMONT

The name of the farm is taken from the original founder, Consider Stebbins Bardwell, who set up in 1864. More than 100 years later, Angela Miller, Russell Glover, Chris Gray, and cheesemaker Peter Dixon continue the tradition of farmhouse cheesemaking with milk from their herd of 100 Oberhaslis goats and cow's milk from Lisa Kaimen's herd. Nine different styles of cheese are made, ranging from Alpine-inspired and Italian toma to unpasteurized goat's milk feta-style cheese and aged cow's milk and goat cheeses. The goats graze on organic pastures in rotational fashion, and all the cheeses are handmade in small batches.

Pawlet is an unpasteurized 10-pound (4.5-kg) Jersey cow's milk cheese, with a lightly washed rind and scattered white molds. The texture is supple and chewy like an Italian-style toma, with a sweet richness that is perfect for sandwiches or for melting on toast. It makes a great appetizer to serve with a floral white wine or blonde beer.

Manchester is an unpasteurized 2½-pound (1.2-kg) semihard tomme, with the flavors of the farm coming through and a nutty, earthy finish. The cheeses are aged to give perfect patchy gray and white molds to the crust, and I think a dry hard cider would be a good partner.

Dorset is an unpasteurized Jersey cow's milk cheese of 2½ pounds (1.2 kg), with a washed rind. The aged cheese has a rich, buttery texture and a deep savory taste, and is perfect for Riesling-style wines. The aroma from washing the rind will be more pungent at certain times of the season, according to what the pastures offer.

Dunmore 🐐 BLUE LEDGE FARM, SALISBURY, VERMONT

Greg Bernhardt and Hannah Sessions have a mixed herd of 75 Nubian, Alpine, and LaMancha goats that graze outside all through the year, coming inside only when the cold becomes too intense. The unique flora and fauna of the Champlain Valley, together with the wetland and woodland pastures, are organically managed, with a rotational grazing system to allow nature's resources to flourish. Although the goats produce milk for 10 months of the year, the milk is supplemented during the busy Christmas season from nearby Burnell Pond Farm. Dunmore is an 18-ounce (500-g) soft, buttery-textured cheese with a bloomy white rind that is barely able to contain its almost Brie-like contents.

It has a lovely richness, yet a slightly sharp, nutty flavor, too. Eat the rind with this cheese to get the full effect of the milk's herbaceous qualities combined with the mushroom earthiness of the rind. This is a perfect cheese for Rhône-style wines.

Woodcock Farm 🐄🐑 WESTON, VERMONT

Mark and Gari Fischer's flock of East Friesian sheep grazes on 45 acres (18 ha) of lush organic pastures. As soon as the snows cover the grazing pastures, the sheep are brought indoors to rest, recuperate, and produce their lambs—an important hiatus in their working year.

The Fischers buy in cow's milk from Taylor Farm nearby. Several cheeses are made, including a Bulgarian-style unpasteurized milk feta-style cheese, and the Fischers have established themselves as cheesemakers of individual styles, textures, and flavors. Their cheeses require a somewhat robust-style wine.

Summer Snow, at about 7 ounces (200 g), is an oozing, melting ewe's milk Camembert-style cheese, available only during the summer months. The thin, bloomy white rind is perfect and adds a lovely mushroom earthiness to the rich, sweetly fresh nut flavors of the cheese.

Timberdoodle is a new cheese, made according to milk availability with either cow's and ewe's milk, or just cow's milk. Weighing about 1¾ pounds (800 g), it is produced in the Havarti style, with a washed rind and a chewy, dense texture with scattered holes. The flavors are earthy and nutty, with a tangy sharpness coming through the buttery finish. This is a good addition to the cheeseboard.

Weston Wheel weighs about 5 pounds (2.25 kg) and is made with unpasteurized ewe's milk. It has a natural washed and rubbed rind and is aged up to six months. This distinctive-tasting, award-winning cheese, with its earthy, nutty, and almost dark caramel salty sweetness, has a long finish to the flavors, and is perfect for partnering with well-structured red wines.

MASSACHUSETTS

This pretty New England state lies on the Atlantic Coast. To the east is the Atlantic Ocean, and the large sandy peninsula of Cape Cod, while to the south lie the fashionable vacation islands of Martha's Vineyard and Nantucket Island. The historic city of Boston is at the innermost point of Massachusetts Bay, at the mouth of the Charles River. Although Massachusetts is a small state, there are significant climate differences between the eastern and western sections. The entire state has cold winters and warm summers, but the west experiences both the coldest winters and the coolest summers.

Hillman Farm ⚲ COLRAIN, MASSACHUSETTS

Carolyn and Joe Hillman have what is termed a microproduction of goat cheeses, with 40 American, French Alpine, and Nubian goats grazing on a 45-acre (18-ha) organic farm—a perfect sheltered environment for the animals to explore the woodlands and rocky ledges. The cheeses are made from spring to fall, both soft and matured, using simple farmstead techniques. This includes using a 1945 Cherry-Burell pasteurizer that Joe rebuilt into a cheese vat, which heats the milk at a low, slow rate, so that it sets overnight to a lactic fermented curd. This curd is then ladled by hand into different shapes or cheesecloth bags to drain.

Harvest Cheese is a hard goat cheese, and this 8-pound (3.5-kg) washed-and-rubbed rind cheese has toast in the flavours, sweet on first impact, then the body of the milk comes through with a myriad of fruit and herbal notes. The cheeses are matured for four to six months, to acquire these nutty, grassy flavors, and further ripening will let the flavors become richer, sweeter, and earthier. I think even an off-dry white wine may work with this cheese.

Birch Hill Cakes are 8-ounce (225-g) cheeses dusted with charcoal prior to ripening; they acquire their scattered bloomy molds during the stages of development. There is a lovely earthiness to the aroma on the rind, and once opened the cheese has a rich, creamy texture that is nutty and goaty. It can be ripened further to a dry, crumbly texture, where the sweetness of the milk and the complex goat's milk structure come forward. It is worth trying a microbrew beer, as well as dry red wine, with this cheese.

Flora Pyramid is a 6-ounce (175-g) truncated pyramid, with a mixture of *Geotrichum candidum* and *Penicillium candidum* cultures used to grow white molds on the dewy, moist fresh cheeses, which have first been dusted with charcoal. The cheeses are aged to become firmer and crumblier; they taste nutty when young, becoming more goaty and strong in flavor with a little maturing.

Ripened Disc is a 5-ounce (140-g) round that gathers its molds not only from the *Penicillium candidum*, but also from the natural flora in the air of the ripening rooms. The flavors are goaty and nutty—in early spring and summer, the milk is sweetly sensitive to the acidity, but by fall deeper, more fruity flavors will be coming through the milk.

Maggie's Round 🐄 CRICKET CREEK FARM, WILLIAMSTOWN, MASSACHUSETTS

The Sabot family bought one of the region's oldest active dairy farms in 2001. When Jason DeMay and Amy Jeschawitz took over as cheesemakers, they added their own herd of Brown Swiss to the farm's Jerseys. This is an unpasteurized semihard cheese weighing 18 ounces (500 g) and aged for four months, to give a supple, buttery, rich texture with a mellow, nutty flavor. The crust has beautiful striated sides, with woven patterns from the molds in which the curds are put prior to draining and pressing. This is in the Alpine or even Manchego style and, as the natural crust forms, molds grow in the grooves, creating a very decorative pattern. I would suggest a lighter red wine with clean Pinot grapes and soft tannins.

Great Hill Blue 🐄 GREAT HILL DAIRY, MARION, MASSACHUSETTS

On the shores of Buzzard's Bay, south of Boston, Tim Stone makes this cheese using the rich buttery milk from his outstanding herd of Guernsey cows. The unpasteurized as well as unhomogenized milk is also sourced from other local farms. Once the milk is heated and turned into curds, the molds are filled by hand, to ensure proper draining of the whey and that the delicate curd structure is kept intact. The 6-pound (2.7-kg) cheeses have a good scattering of blue veins, not overly dense, and release their lovely nutty, mineral flavors through the rich, buttery texture of the cheese. A classic match for this cheese would be a fine Burgundy with medium tannins.

Classic Blue Log 🐄🐐 WESTFIELD FARM, HUBBARDSTON, MASSACHUSETTS

Debbie and Bob Stetson started making cheese in 1996, when they took on the working farm. Even without previous cheesemaking skills, they quickly learned how to make delightful goat cheeses, as well a few cow's milk cheeses. They obtain milk from local farms because they concentrate on making cheese, rather than rearing the animals, too. Located just a few hours' drive from Boston, in 20 acres (8 ha) of unspoiled land, the Stetsons' beautifully preserved clapboard farmhouse dates back to the first Pilgrim settlers. This 4½-ounce (125-g) small log has a very interesting "coat." It is soft, almost like a pashmina scarf, with a gray-blue mold, which is actually a Roquefort blue mixture. This gives the cheese a unique intense flavor to the rind, but within is a soft, velvety-textured cheese that is tangy and fresh, with a bright, clean finish. This is a very individual style of cheese that I would partner with a full-bodied dry white wine or a Pinot Noir.

ABOVE Cricket Creek Farm, Maggie's Round
BELOW, TOP CHEESE Great Hill Dairy, Great Hill Blue, BOTTOM CHEESE Westfield Farm, Classic Blue Log
OPPOSITE Hillman Farm: CHEESES CLOCKWISE FROM TOP Harvest Cheese, Flora Pyramid, Ripened Disc, Birch Hill Cakes

Rawson Brook Farm

Just three hours from Manhattan, and down a gravel drive, there is a little bit of heaven right here on earth. Rawson Brook Farm may be close to the metropolis, but it could not be more remote and tranquil.

Rawson Brook Fresh Chevre ✍ RAWSON BROOK FARM, MASSACHUSETTS

Susan Sellew retreated from the rat race to become a "homesteader" on a farm in Massachusetts, just three hours from Manhattan. This desire was discovered during a trip to France. Susan stayed on a farm and was taught the cheesemaking process by a Frenchwoman who made fresh goat cheeses from her small herd, which were just for her family's use. It did not take Susan long to realize that she loved not only goats, but also the simplicity of life on a farm, and she found Rawson Brook tucked away in the Berkshires in Massachusetts, where she had been brought up. She transforms the milk very quickly into fresh curd, either plain or with herbs or garlic, and you can buy her cheeses at the farm door or at local stores, and you may even be lucky enough to see it in Manhattan and Boston.

What makes this cheese very special is the care that Susan brings to her work. There are about 70 goats, mostly American and French Alpines, but also several white-haired Saanens and one Nubian, with around 12 babies in a low-fenced paddock—a sort of kindergarten. The milkers are let out on the pastures during the day, but need to return to the safety of their paddock and barn in the evening, although they are free to graze wherever they want to roam during daylight—close to the farm or foraging further afield.

The key to the fine milk quality is the milking, which is done three goats at a time, causing no stress to the goats and no heavy-handedness by the milkmaid. While being milked, the goats nibble some grain that is kept in old army helmets at each milking station. As soon as the milk is in the pail, it is taken through to the parlor and poured into the vats, heated, then cooled slightly, then heated again, until the curds have formed. The curds are then lifted out into cheesecloths, to be hung up to drain out the whey. It is as simple as that. The light, sweet-tasting curds are packed into 7-ounce (200-g) or 1-pound (450-g) containers and are delivered for sale within 48 hours of being made.

THIS PAGE Rawson Brook Fresh Chevre, whole and spread on bread
OPPOSITE, FAR LEFT Fresh curds draining in cheesecloth bags.
OPPOSITE, TOP RIGHT A grazing goat at Rawson Brook Farm.
OPPOSITE, MIDDLE RIGHT The entrance to Rawson Brook Farm.
OPPOSITE, BOTTOM RIGHT The milking parlor.

NEW YORK & CONNECTICUT

The landscape of New York state consists of farms, forests, rivers, mountains, and lakes, and the climate is governed by two continental air masses—a warm, humid one from the southwest and a cold, dry one from the northwest—producing long, cold winters and warm summers in the higher elevations, turning to very warm, almost sultry conditions with high humidity farther south around New York City. Connecticut's landscape varies from colonial green belt to hills and mountains, as well as industrial areas, including stone quarries of both limestone and granite, which indicate that the soil is rich in minerals and well drained. The climate has seasonal extremes on the coastline; inland, the winters are cold, the summers are hot and humid, and the fall is mild, with sunny days ablaze with color right across the state.

Cato Corner Farm 🐄 COLCHESTER, CONNECTICUT

Elizabeth MacAlister and her son Mark have been making cheese since 1997; they have 13 different styles, which are seen in cheese shops and restaurants on the East Coast. **Brigid's Abbey** is a 3-pound 5-ounce (1.5-kg) monastery-style cheese with a lightly rubbed rind, and is aged for two to four months. The flavors are mellow and buttery when young, and mature to a nuttier flavor. As with all cheeses using milk from grass-fed cattle, the taste and texture change with the season. I suggest a Pinot Noir with this cheese. **Hooligan** is a 1-pound 5-ounce (600-g) salt-washed rind cheese. It has a lovely rich, buttery texture to the pâte and patches of white and gray molds on the rind. The pungent aroma on the orange, slightly sticky rind gives way to the sweet and savory flavors. I suggest an Alsace-style wine. **Drunken Hooligan** is available in winter, when the 1-pound 5-ounce (600-g) Hooligan cheeses are dipped in a bath of grape must and young red wine from Colchester's Priam Vineyard. The vinous aroma is not quite as gamy as the Hooligan, but the flavors of the vine definitely come through, to give this cheese a unique taste.

Old Chatham Sheepherding Company 🐑 🐑

OLD CHATHAM, NEW YORK

With 1,200 East Friesians, of which there are 400 milkers, this may be the largest sheep herd in the United States. The farm is run by Tom and Nancy Clark along traditional lines. **Ewe's Blue** is a Roquefort-style cheese using pasteurized ewe's milk and weighing about 3 pounds (1.3 kg); sharp blue veins mingle with the sweet earthiness of the milk. The crumbly texture is perfect as a partner to dessert pears

BELOW Cato Corner Farm: BACK CHEESE, Brigid's Abbey, FRONT RIGHT CHEESE Hooligan, FRONT LEFT CHEESE Drunken Hooligan

BELOW Old Chatham Sheepherding Company: LEFT CHEESE Nancy's Camembert, RIGHT CHEESE Ewe's Blue

and sweeter white wines; it is also good crumbled into a salad with toasted pecan nuts or with ripe figs.

Nancy's Camembert is a 2-pound (900-g) cutting Camembert-style cheese made with ewe's milk from the farm and a neighboring farm's cow's milk. Its rich creaminess, coupled with savory hints of the ewe's milk, has a slightly denser texture than traditional Camembert.

Nettle Meadow Farm 🐄🐐🐑 THURMAN, NEW YORK

Lorraine Lambiase and Sheila Flanagan make these two cheeses and a variety of fresh goat cheeses.

Kunik is a triple-cream using both goat's milk and Jersey cow's milk cream, to give a richness, but also a tangy flavor. The soft, downy rind has the merest whiff of mushroom, and the 9–10-ounce (250–275-g) cheese is a perfect foil for sparkling wines or a dry hard cider or perry (pear cider).

Three Sisters are small 4-ounce (115-g) cheeses made with cow's, goat's, and ewe's milk, and with a bloomy thin rind; the earthy, nutty taste has a definite tang at the finish. I would pair this with a fruity dry wine.

Sprout Creek Farm 🐄🐐 POUGHKEEPSIE, NEW YORK

This 200-acre (80-ha) working farm was founded by nuns in the late 1980s as a place for children to enjoy the countryside and agriculture. Today, the cheesemaker Colin McGrath produces award-winning cheeses with a herd of grass-fed Jersey, Guernsey, Milking Shorthorn, and Brown Swiss cows, as well as a small goat herd.

Sophie is a 7-ounce (200-g) goat's milk cheese available from spring to early fall. It has a delicate alabaster pâte and a soft, downy white rind. The flaky, fudgy texture is fresh and tangy, with a light herbaceous taste perfect for Sauvignon white wines or a lighter red.

Rita is a 7-ounce (200-g) cow's milk cheese available fall to spring, with a soft, downy rind that is well balanced with the rich, buttery texture. The earthy aroma on the rind offsets some of the dense texture, with the tang providing a lovely finish.

Three-Corner Field Farm

The hamlet of Shushan is just outside Salem in the eastern region of the state. It is the very essence of rural charm, preserving its history, with agriculture remaining a vital part of the area's economy.

Three-Corner Field Farm 🐑

SHUSHAN, NEW YORK

Karen Weinberg and Paul Borghard's farm lies in an unspoiled area in the Battenkill River Valley, close to the Green and Adirondack mountains. The farm is much as it was when the original settlers farmed the land in the 1840s, and even the Revival farmhouse largely unchanged, with the cellars now turned into the maturing rooms. The family began farming by giving a loving home to a few sheep and, before she knew it, Karen had learned to become a farmer and cheesemaker. Today, the 150 sheep and more than 300 lambs provide cheese, meat, and other products, and, by living "light on the land," Karen and Paul offer a healthy natural environment for the animals, not overfarming and keeping the approach simple. I watched the gathering of the ewes for milking, then the transforming of the milk into curds in the cheesemaking room, which is really no bigger than a large kitchen. Karen chatted away as she stirred the curds, then cut them, broke them down, drained them, and packed them into their molds.

Battenkill Brebis is aged in the cellars below the farmhouse, to acquire its wondrous live cultures, which go to making the crust of this 6-pound (2.7-kg) cheese. The unpasteurized milk curds are prepared meticulously, with some of the whey removed and water added during the cutting process; the curds are broken down by hand, to form the right-size nuggets, before being packed by hand again into the molds. This gives a lightness to the texture, and the flavors are sweetly earthy, with a brace of mineral and grassy flavors. It is a perfect example of a farmhouse-made cheese and can be enjoyed with either a fruity dry white or red wine, or even a dry hard cider.

Shushan Snow is an 8-ounce (225-g) or 20-ounce (600-g) Camembert-style cheese that has a delicate, bloomy white rind hugging a dense, richly creamy interior. The pasteurized milk is heated slowly, to retain as much character as possible; if ripened, the cheese becomes soft and creamy, with the flavors a little more earthy and bold against the wild mushroom aroma on the rind. This is definitely a cheese for a red wine with character.

Feta is really worth trying. Made with unpasteurized ewe's milk, it is ripened in a brine bath for 60 days. The taste is quite unlike any other feta you will buy in a supermarket, and is perfect crumbled over a salad or served as an apéritif with olives and a crisp, dry white or rosé wine.

THIS PAGE The barns at Three-Corner Field.

THIS PAGE, INSET Three-Corner Field Farm: BACK CHEESE Battenkill Brebis, RIGHT CHEESE Shushan Snow, LEFT CHEESE Feta

OPPOSITE TOP Breaking down the curds in the vat.

OPPOSITE BOTTOM The gathering of the ewes for milking.

TENNESSEE, VIRGINIA, GEORGIA, & CAROLINA

The state of Tennessee is close to the Appalachian Mountains and Valley, where the spring is warm, followed by hot, humid summers and warm, pleasant fall months. Even the winter is mild, only getting the odd snow shower. This area was also known as "marble country," so the soil has good minerals for grazing pastures. Virginia is Blue Ridge Mountain country, and much of the state has a subtropical climate, with very humid summers and very mild winters. The weather in Georgia is glorious through spring and summer, with the fall and winter months temperate and cool, but never freezing, making ideal conditions for grazing and agriculture.

La Mancha 🐐 LOCUST GROVE FARM, KNOX COUNTY, TENNESSEE

This is an unpasteurized 6½-pound (3-kg) cheese based on the Spanish Manchego, with the familiar striated "basketweave" pattern from the cheese molds. The handmade cheeses are slightly sweeter than their namesake because the starter used gives a more rounded complexity and brings out the flavors of the sweetly scented grass, especially in the more aged versions.

Grayson 🐄 MEADOW CREEK DAIRY, GALAX, VIRGINIA

This unpasteurized milk slab of washed-rind cheese weighs 4½ pounds (2 kg); its golden-yellow pâte is derived from the high betacarotene content in the milk, as well as the diversity of flavors from the grazing pastures through the season. The inspiration for the recipe came from a visit to Wales and Ireland in 2000, and, while it is similar to Taleggio, there are distinct flavor comparisons with Livarot, Reblochon, and Durrus. I think this is one of the most perfect cheeses for a cheeseboard selection, with its earthy farmyard flavors and soft, chewy texture.

Everona Dairy 🐑 RAPIDAN, VIRGINIA

Dr. Pat Elliott turned part of her kitchen into a dairy laboratory and learned how to make cheese. By 1998, a small dairy had been built, and she had taken on a couple of helpers, with Carolyn Wentz as head cheesemaker.
Shenandoah Dr. Pat and Carolyn created this in 2008, using a Swiss-style recipe, to give a tangy flavor with that familiar chewy crumble and long, lingering finish. Dr. Pat is eager to tell you that ewe's milk is special because it has twice the protein, twice the vitamins, twice the solids of cow's or goat's milk, and good, medium-chain fatty acids.
Everona Piedmont has a beautiful nutty flavor. It weighs about 4½ pounds (2 kg) and, with the French cultures, it has a lovely chewiness to the texture and a nutty, floral, sweet earthy style showing all the fine aspects of ewe's milk.

Sweet Grass Dairy 🐄🐐 THOMASVILLE, GEORGIA

This beautiful 140-acre (57-ha) farm surrounded by woodland is farmed by Al and Desiree Wehner. In 2005, Jeremy Little, their son-in-law and chief cheesemaker, and his wife, Jessica, bought the farm and continued the good farm practices, including rotational grazing pastures.
Hopeful Tomme is an unpasteurized 5-pound (2.25-kg) mixed cow's and goat's milk cheese, with lovely natural molds on the crust in the style of a Pyrénées tomme. The process involves salting by hand, using Atlantic sea salt, and actually came about when a storage tank failed to keep at the correct temperature and all the milk had to be used quickly. They hoped that it would work and, to everyone's relief, it did, which resulted in a new cheese style. Accompany with full-bodied white wines, as well as dry reds.
Thomasville Tomme is an unpasteurized cow's milk Pyrénées-style tomme, with a natural crust mottled with delicate molds and a buttery, mellow flavor from the higher butterfat content in the milk. The layers of flavors are perfect for a cheeseboard and will partner a fruity red wine.

Goat Lady Dairy 🐄🐐 CLIMAX, NORTH CAROLINA

In 1995, Steve Tate and his sister Ginnie decided that goat cheesemaking would be successful in North Carolina. This pioneering spirit has been so successful that they have had to supplement with milk from other local farms, to increase the supply.
Old Liberty is an unpasteurized milk tomme-style semihard cheese weighing about 3 pounds 5 ounces (1.5 kg). It retains a lightness, with a lovely crumble to the texture, which is not too dry. The aroma on the rind is quite powerful, but the cheese within is sweetly savory.
Sandy Creek The pasteurized milk has been slowly heated to retain the nuances of the milk, and its bloomy rind thickly coats the grapevine-ash outer rind. Within, the denser texture still retains its softness and flavors of dry fruit. I would suggest a Pinot-style wine.

TOP LEFT Locust Grove Farm, La Mancha

TOP RIGHT, BACK LEFT CHEESE Meadow Creek Dairy, Grayson; BACK RIGHT CHEESE Everona Dairy, Shenandoah; FRONT CHEESE Everona Piedmont

BOTTOM LEFT Goat Lady: LEFT CHEESES Sandy Creek, RIGHT CHEESE Old Liberty

BOTTOM RIGHT Sweet Grass Dairy: TOP CHEESE Thomasville Tomme, BOTTOM CHEESE Hopeful Tomme

Canada

The second-largest country in the world in terms of area, Canada has a vast expanse of land, with a huge diversity of terrain and landscape. The climate is very harsh in some areas, but the large expanse of the land across the southern belt of the country is dedicated to agriculture. The Atlantic provinces of Prince Edward Island and Nova Scotia have a strong farming and fishing heritage. Quebec and Ontario are the most populous provinces, with well-developed agriculture along the St. Lawrence Seaway and the Great Lakes, with orchards and market gardening, as well as animal husbandry and dairy. Quebec, in particular,

with its French heritage, has many dairies producing some of the most interesting and diverse cheese styles. While the prairie provinces are largely used for grain and cattle production, Canada's west coast has a mild climate that has encouraged dairy farming and artisan cheesemakers.

Many of the cheeses reflect those of France, Great Britain, and the Netherlands, and are not just faint copies, but true artisan-made forms that highlight the traditional recipes and embrace the *terroir*, with the flavors and textures derived from mineral-rich soils fed by the purest water.

OPPOSITE, ABOVE LEFT That Dutchman's Farm: TOP CHEESE Gouda, BOTTOM CHEESE Old Growler, FRONT CHEESE Dragon's Breath Blue

OPPOSITE, ABOVE RIGHT Fromagerie du Pied-de-Vent, Pied-de-Vent

OPPOSITE, BELOW LEFT Cow's Creamery: LEFT CHEESE, Avonlea Clothbound Cheddar, RIGHT CHEESE Cow's Creamery Extra Old Block

Cow's Creamery

NEAR CHARLOTTETOWN, PRINCE
EDWARD ISLAND

Following a visit to the Orkney Islands, Scott Linkletter decided to produce a true artisan-made cheese with head cheesemaker Armand Bernard. They tweaked the recipe with excellent results. Prince Edward Island has an iron-rich red soil, from the soft, rich sandstone composition, which is suitable for huge agricultural activity and provides great pastures for grazing.

Avonlea Clothbound Cheddar is a 22-pound (10-kg) Cheddar-style cheese aged for a minimum of one year, using unpasteurized milk and a vegetarian rennet. The cheeses are cloth-wrapped in the traditional way, and rubbed with lard or butter, to seal and prevent unwanted molds from growing on the rinds. You can taste the briny sea and the earthy richness of the soil mingling with the crumbly texture in the cheese. It is wonderful matched with a full-bodied dry red Bordeaux wine or a bold, hoppy beer.

Cow's Creamery Extra Old Block is the other side of the coin for the Creamery, where the block Cheddar-style cheese, made with unpasteurized cow's milk is sold as deli packs at about 7 ounces (200-g) or as slicing blocks of about 5 pounds (2.25 kg). The texture may not be quite as crumbly and intense as the Clothbound Cheddar, but it still has a lovely sweetness with a chewy density, making it perfect for either regular or grilled cheese sandwiches.

That Dutchman's Farm UPPER ECONOMY, NOVA SCOTIA

Maja and Willem van den Hoek arrived in Canada from the Netherlands in 1970. This rural community is a perfect setting to make their Dutch cheese.

Gouda is the heart of their business. A 13-pound (6-kg) Farmstead Gouda is made following an old recipe, using unpasteurized local milk. It is aged on wooden shelves in maturing rooms, with the air filtering through naturally.

Old Growler is an aged version of the Gouda, weighing 12 pounds (5.4 kg), and is really exceptional. The density of the texture, with the crisp, almost crystalline flavors and that briny hit of grassy freshness, takes you by surprise. I always love blonde beer with Gouda.

Dragon's Breath Blue is a small 10-ounce (300-g) black-wax-coated cheese that is supposed to be a blue; while definitely pungent like a blue, on opening, the cheese it is quite wet and almost weeping out of the pâte. The texture is soft and crumbly, and the flavors are strong and persistent; I suggest that you eat this on the young side, accompanied by a strong beer with a rye bread.

Pied-de-Vent FROMAGERIE DU PIED-DE-VENT, ÎLES-DE-LA-MADELEINE, QUEBEC

Jérémie Arseneau brought to his Pied-de-Vent farm the only breed of cow developed in North America—the almost extinct stocky, hardy Canadienne, a cross between Norman and Breton stock. His 50 milkers provide enough milk for 90 wheels of cheese per day. The grass-fed cattle get added hay and fodder produced on the island, which gives the milk its unique flavors. The cheese weighs 2½ pounds (1.2 kg) and has a piquant taste, with a chewy texture and a robust, aromatic washed rind.

Fromagerie de L'Abbaye St. Benoît 🐄🐑

SAINT-BENOÎT DU LAC, QUEBEC

The abbey is situated on the west shore of Lake Memphremagog, in the picturesque southernmost part of the Eastern Townships community in the Chaudière-Appalaches region. The Benedictine monks work by hand to make several cheeses, and visits and tours of this architecturally interesting abbey are really worthwhile.

Bleu Bénédictin is a pasteurized 3-pound 5-ounce (1.5-kg) cow's milk blue and is stronger than the abbey's other blue, Ermite, but has a soft, almost melting center and a long, lingering taste. The natural rind, with its wild mushroom aroma, is a perfect foil for the mineral intensity and richness of the cheese. A classic Burgundy or a dessert wine would be good with this cheese.

Frère Jacques is a 3-pound 5-ounce (1.5-kg), pasteurized cow's milk washed-rind cheese that has a chewy density that almost "squeaks" between your teeth. The milky sweet hazelnut flavors and aroma are similar to those of Reblochon, but the mildness of the cheese makes it perfect for breakfast. Alternatively, Frère Jacques is fantastic for melting on toast.

Le Moutier is a pasteurized goat's milk cheese weighing 2¼ pounds (1 kg) and is similar to the abbey's cow's milk version, St. Benoît. But the sweet lightness of the milk, together with the almost springy open texture and its irregular holes, makes this a perfect cheese for children and adults alike. The monks make a wonderful cider that would partner all these cheeses very well.

Ewenity Dairy Co-Op 🐑 CONN, ONTARIO

Elisabeth and Eric Bzikot formed this cooperative in 2001, with a small group of ewe's milk producers, and the membership has grown, along with Elisabeth's knowledge of cheesemaking. It is now the largest sheep dairying cooperative in Canada.

Eweda Cru is an unpasteurized ewe's milk cheese that is based on a Gouda recipe and aged for a minimum of nine months. Each 6½-pound (3 kg) green wax-coated cheese has a marking identifying the farm where the milk came from, and the rich, savory flavors mingle with the earthy, sweet, and nutty aroma.

Sheep in the Meadow is a freshly pasteurized (aged for just two weeks) 10-ounce (280-g) cheese, with a light bloomy rind covered with herbes de Provence; rosemary and thyme are the dominant aromas. There are hints toward the Corsican Fleur de Maquis, but the texture is like Camembert. The young cheeses taste sweet, with the herbs still green and fresh, while with a little ripening the texture will become richer and smoother, and the herb coating a little more earthy.

Brebette is a lovely 9-ounce (250-g) pasteurized milk cheese with bloomy rind, again aged for only two weeks, but it can be further ripened. It is delicate on first impact, becoming really sophisticated and luxurious in flavors and textures, and is a perfect cheese for a fine red wine or even Champagne.

Mouton Rouge, or "red sheep," is a delightful play on words for a cheese. The washed-rind unpasteurized milk cheese is ripened for 60 days; the 2¼–6½-pound (1–3-kg) cheeses have a pale pâte, with small holes scattered through the creamy texture. The washing imparts a grassy aroma and contrasts well with the richness of the sweetly earthy cheese. It is a lovely cheese for fresh, dry white wines.

LEFT Salt Spring Island Cheese Company: CHEESES CLOCKWISE FROM BACK TOP Montaña (cut), marinated fresh goat cheeses (with truffle, basil, and peppercorn toppings), Romelia, Blue Juliette; MIDDLE CHEESE Marcella

ABOVE LEFT Ewenity Dairy Co-Op: BACK CHEESE Eweda Cru, RIGHT CHEESE Brebette, LEFT CHEESE Sheep in the Meadow

ABOVE RIGHT Ewenity Dairy Co-Op, Mouton Rouge

RIGHT Fromagerie de L'Abbaye St. Benoît: LEFT CHEESE Bleu Bénédictin, RIGHT CHEESE Frère Jacques, FRONT CHEESE Le Moutier

Salt Spring Island Cheese Company 🐑🐐 NEAR

RUCKLE PARK, SALT SPRING ISLAND, BRITISH COLUMBIA
Tucked between Vancouver Island and the mainland of British Columbia, Salt Spring is the largest of the Gulf Islands. The temperate climate all year round enhances its pastoral setting, and the quiet, rural life is enjoyed by both the residents and many visiting tourists. When David and Nancy Wood started the cheesemaking in 1994, they concentrated exclusively on ewe's milk, but they now make wonderful goat cheeses, too, in many different styles.

Montaña is a 9-pound (4-kg) semihard ewe's milk (with a little goat's milk added) cheese, matured for three to eight months, similar in style to pecorino or Manchego, but is probably more in tune with Pyrénées cheeses. It has a slightly dry crumble to the texture, with a fresh, nutty, and lighter taste than the more artisan mountain cheeses, partly due to the milk being pasteurized.

Marinated Fresh Goat Cheeses Weighing 5 ounces (140 g), these pasteurized goat's milk cheeses have a tangy, light, almost frothy texture from the gentle handling of the curds into the molds. They are ready after just two days, and are either plain or packed into a clear plastic container with a little olive oil and toppings of truffle paste, basil leaf, peppercorns, or even flowers, chile, or roasted garlic.

Romelia is a delightful 7-ounce (200-g) washed-rind pasteurized goat cheese with high aroma on the orange smear rind. The goat's milk gives a really tangy edge to the flavors. It is good with beer.

Blue Juliette is a Camembert-style pasteurized goat's milk cheese of 7 ounces (200 g), but mixed with the bloomy white molds is a *Penicillium roqueforti* blue mold. It does not penetrate into the cheese because it is brushed only onto the rind. What you get in flavor is a fudgy center and tangy taste, with the edges softer and just starting to melt, giving the flavor of the blue and white molds a spicier finish.

Marcella is a crottin cheese weighing just 3½ ounces (95 g), with a close, bloomy white rind. It has a tartness from the goat's milk, which is quite prominent.

Australia and New Zealand are the most recently settled, major landmasses in the southwestern Pacific Ocean. The first Europeans known to have landed were the Dutch in 1642 and the British in 1768–71. The influences of these countries are evident in Australia's prolific Cheddar production and very good Gouda. A large proportion of Australia is desert or semiarid land, and not abundant in fertile soil; however, rainfall has slightly increased over the past century, with the southeast and southwest corners having a temperate climate. New Zealand's climate corresponds closely to that of Italy in the northern hemisphere, but its isolation from continental influences and exposure to cold southerly winds and ocean currents give the climate a much milder character.

Australia & New Zealand

The New Zealand Food Safety Authorities have been discussing the option of making unpasteurized milk cheese, as well as importing unpasteurized cheeses from Europe. This matter is also under government discussion in Australia. While this is not universally applauded, it is of immense importance to those cheesemakers interested in experimenting with new starters and cultures in their techniques. Agriculture has been and continues to be the main export and, hopefully, as Australia and New Zealand work closely together, they can bring a more diverse structure to the cheese industry.

This is especially relevant as cheese cultures emerge in Japan and China. In particular, Kyodo Gakusha Shintoku Farm in Japan, who produce exceptional artisan varieties, and Yellow Valley Cheese Dairy in China's Shanxi province, who make a delicious Gouda.

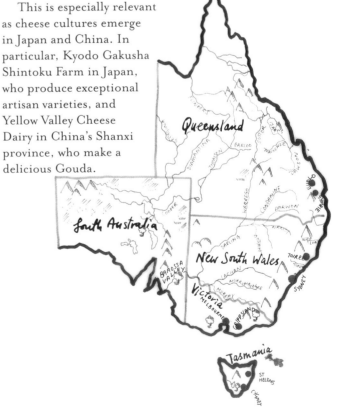

AUSTRALIA

La Luna 🐐 HOLY GOAT, SUTTON GRANGE ORGANIC FARM, CENTRAL VICTORIA
Ann-Marie Monda and Carla Meurs, having gained experience in Australia and Europe, set up their organic goat cheese dairy in 2000. The land is harsh, being made up of granite and sandy loam, but they supplement the natural grazing with additional grasses and vitamins. La Luna is a 5½-ounce (150-g) doughnut-shape white-mold, soft cheese that is fast gaining an iconic status. Accompany it with a sharp, dry white wine.

Ironstone 🐄 PIANO HILL FARM, GIPPSLAND, VICTORIA
Cheesemaker Steven Brown has trained in Switzerland, Italy, and New Zealand, which has paid dividends in the development of his Ironstone cheese. It is an 11-pound (5-kg) Gouda-style hard cheese, made from the biodynamic milks of his Friesian herd, with a fruity and earthy flavor.

Marrook Farm 🐄 NORTHWEST OF TAREE, MID NORTH COAST, NEW SOUTH WALES
Cheesemakers David and Heidi Marks started their biodynamic farm on the Bulga plateau in the mid-1980s.
Brinawa This is a 6½-pound (3-kg) washed and rubbed Swiss-style cheese that is "hand hooped," pressed, and washed before maturing. There is an intensity to the flavors, with a Swiss sweetness and a slightly softer texture.

ABOVE TOP LEFT Marrook Farm: TOP CHEESE Brinawa, BOTTOM CHEESE Bulga
ABOVE TOP RIGHT Piano Hill Farm, Ironstone
ABOVE Holy Goat, La Luna
RIGHT Woodside Cheese Wrights: TOP CHEESE Edith, BOTTOM CHEESE Etzy Ketzy

Bulga A 22-pound (10-kg) Gruyère-style cheese that uses a similar hand production, and aging of 8–12 months. It highlights the grazing pasture, which is rich in rye grass and clover; grassy elements can be detected in the flavor.

Woodside Cheese Wrights 🐄🐐 ADELAIDE HILLS, SOUTH AUSTRALIA
Cheesemaker Kris Lloyd has given style and modernity to her cow's and goat's milk cheeses.
Edith A 9-ounce (250-g) soft goat cheese with an ash coat and patches of white bloom. It has a rich, tangy flavor.
Etzy Ketzy This 4½-ounce (125-g) mixed Friesian cow's and goat's milk cheese is lightly washed. There is a clean floral yet earthy nuttiness to the flavors.

ABOVE TOP, FROM TOP TO BOTTOM CHEESE Fromart CHEESES: Gruyère, Tilsit, Raclette, Magoth, and Mutschli

ABOVE BOTTOM Ballycroft Cheeses, Annwn

Annwn 🐄 BALLYCROFT CHEESES, GREENOCK, BAROSSA VALLEY, SOUTH AUSTRALIA

This tiny farm is based in a vineyard and run by two sisters, Tracey Skepper and Sue Evans. Annwn is a 2¼-pound (1-kg) pressed cheese from Jersey and Holstein cow's milk. The rind is rubbed with salt, then placed in the ripening room, where it has regular washings with a mixture of Shiraz lees over a two-month period.

Cheddar 🐄 PYENGANA CHEESE DAIRY, NEAR ST. HELEN'S, TASMANIA

Four generations of Jon Healey's family have farmed in this fertile dairy-farming region since the 1890s, making it the oldest specialty cheese producer in Australia. This stirred-curd Cheddar-style cheese made with a traditional rennet has a sweet earthy taste to the layers of herbal, grassy flavors. The clothbound cheese comes in various sizes from 2¼ pounds (1 kg) up to 32 pounds (14.5 kg). The laws in Australia prevent the cloth from being rubbed in lard because it is an animal fat, so they use an oil.

Tongola Goat Dairy 🐐 NEAR CYGNET, WATTLE GROVE, TASMANIA

Hans Stutz and Esther Haeusermann migrated from Switzerland to become farmers in the Huon Valley of Tasmania. They raise and hand-milk their 30 hardy long-haired Toggenburg goats on the 15 acres (6 ha), either on open mixed pasture and brush, or in wooden shelters during cooler months.

Billy At four to six weeks, this 5½–9-ounce (150–250-g) cooked curd cheese has been washed in brine, to produce a pale golden rind flecked with white molds, and it has an aromatic pungency that is not too strong. The cheese is smooth, with a dense and fudgy texture, and the rind is also delicious.

Big B This is the 1¾-pound (800-g) larger version of Billy, which is matured between three and six months to become richer, more aromatic, and fuller flavored.

Capris At just 4½ ounces (120 g), this cheese is in the Curdly style, but with added salt. It is somewhat like a Camembert with its white bloomy rind, but the texture is a little more tender. This cheese is perfect as part of a cheeseboard.

Curdly A very fresh small cheese with a light, frothy lemony taste. There is no added salt, so this cheese is great for both sweet and savory dishes. It should be eaten young.

Fromart 🐄 EUDLO, QUEENSLAND

Situated in the foothills of the Glass House Mountains, Christian Nobel started out in 2006 buying Holstein and Guernsey milk from a local farm to make his traditional Swiss-style cheeses. Fromart cheeses include a Gruyère, Tilsit, Magoth (Appenzell style), the traditional melting cheese raclette, and a young 1¾-pound (800-g) semisoft washed-rind cheese they call Mutschli. The richness of the milk certainly gives a unique flavor profile.

Gympie Chèvre 🐐 GYMPIE FARM CHEESE, GYMPIE, QUEENSLAND

Cheesemaker Camille Mortaud hails originally from the village of Archigny, near Poitiers in West France, a region famous for its goat cheeses, such as Chabichou (see page 64) and Mothais (see page 64). Initially, he made cheese with his mother, before emigrating to Australia and starting his cheese business in 1999. The dairy has now moved to Conondale, approximately 54 miles (88 km) north of Brisbane on the Sunshine Coast.

The Gympie Chèvre, weighing about 4 ounces (115 g), has the typical coated rind of *Penicillium album*, to produce the patchy gray/white mold that is so desirable for goat cheeses to enhance the flavors and texture. The flaky, rich texture with nutty aftertaste is very good and, as Camille reflects, it would be even better if he were allowed to make his cheese with unpasteurized milk.

ABOVE, LARGE CHEESE Pyengana Dairy, Cheddar; Tongola Goat Dairy CHEESES FROM LEFT TO RIGHT Billy, Capris, Big B, Curdly

LEFT Gympie Farm Cheese, Gympie Chèvre

NEW ZEALAND

Curio Bay Pecorino 🐑 BLUE
RIVER, SOUTHLAND, SOUTH ISLAND
Just to prove a point that big is
also beautiful, Blue River are
probably the biggest operators in
New Zealand. They have a herd
of East Friesian sheep, with some
crossbreeding with tougher breeds
to withstand life in the southern
climes. They make some of the
best pecorino-style cheeses in the country, as well as a
great feta-style cheese. Their head cheesemaker is Maxi
Robertson and, with his 35 years' experience, he produces
a fine selection of styles. Curio Bay Pecorino is made
from pure ewe's milk and matured for at least six to eight
months. A thin natural rind forms around the pale straw-
colored pâte, to produce sweet, earthy, and floral flavors.
This cheese will mature for another year, developing a
gamy caramel style that is magnificent.

Gouda 🐄 MERCER CHEESE, NORTH WAIKATO,
NORTH ISLAND
Alfred Alfrink makes the cheese and his wife, Ineke, takes
care of their small shop, where his 22-ton annual output
sells as fast as it is made. The farm is situated in a large
caldera (the shallow ring of alluvial soil from a time of
volcanic eruption), which has created a gorge on the land,
with a waterfall running down to the river Waikato. Often

flooded, the land around the farm
is not unlike that of Alfred's Dutch
homeland, which perhaps explains
the wonder of his cheese. His farm
covers 20 acres (8 ha) of land, and
production is limited to what he can
physically make himself. The milk
is from local farms, and the cheeses
vary in size from 2¼ pounds (1 kg)
to 26½ pounds (12 kg). Although
Alfred has to pasteurize his milk, he
is hoping that he will be able to use
unpasteurized milk in the not too
distant future, which will give his cheeses more complex
flavors. In addition to the plain Gouda, his cheeses
include cumin and fenugreek Gouda and Edam.

Rich Plain & Cumin Gouda 🐐 AROHA ORGANIC GOAT
CHEESE, TE AROHA, WAIKATO REGION, NORTH ISLAND
This delightful farm is situated at the foot of Mount Te
Aroha in the Thames Valley region. The farm is run
by John and Jeanne Van Kuyk, who make a selection of
cheeses in the Gouda style.

Te Aroha is the center for dairy farming in this region,
with its very fertile land and famous thermal springs. The
herd of Saanen goats graze freely on open pastures, and
there are plenty of shelters dotted around—they are not
fond of the rain! The flavors of these simple cheeses are
sweet and nutty, with the additions of traditional Dutch
spices, such as cumin, fenugreek, and nettle, as well as a
more unconventional chile and mixed herbs addition.

Cloudy Mountain Cheese 🐄
PIRONGIA, WAIKATO REGION,
NORTH ISLAND
Cheesemakers Cathy and Peter Lang
have a small farm, situated 6 miles
(10 km) to the west of Te Awamutu,
on the banks of Waipa River, near
Mount Pirongia. They produce a
few very interesting cheeses, each
in a different style and with a care
and commitment that showcase not
only the purity of the milk, but also
their hands-on approach. Cathy is
predominantly self-taught, but her
background in microbiology and
laboratory diagnostic skills in her
previous career in animal health have
proved useful tools in transforming
the milk into cheese.

ABOVE Blue River, Curio Bay Pecorino
LEFT Mercer Cheese, Gouda

Joie A Camembert-style cheese, it has a smooth and creamy pâte and white bloomy rind.

Pirongia Blue This is a dense, rich, and soft blue cheese almost bursting out of its thin natural rind.

Kaipaki Gold This cheese has a wonderful rich and melting pâte with a washed rind, which gives a pungency to the aroma and a kick to the flavors.

Ricotta 🐃 CLEVEDON VALLEY BUFFALO COMPANY, NEAR CLEVEDON, AUCKLAND REGION, NORTH ISLAND

Helen and Richard Dorresteyn have persevered since 2006 in creating and naturalizing their herd, after importing a few animals from Shaw River in Australia. Their hard work has paid off. Not only are they responsible for producing what is considered to be New Zealand's first buffalo-milk mozzarella and ricotta, but also their cheeses are seen to be as good as anything from Battipaglia in Campania, Italy. The weather conditions and climate are ideal for the Riverine breed (they give a richer milk for cheesemaking) to thrive. The herd grazes on open pasture in this idyllic southwest corner of Auckland, and the silky, mild, and delicate cheeses have been a huge hit. The ricotta has a dewy freshness and lightness that can only be achieved by making and selling the cheese as soon after milking as possible, and the sweetness of the milk is a real pleasure. The cheeses have acquired a cult status, and it is hoped that the herd will be increased, in order to keep up with the demand.

ABOVE LEFT Aroha Organic Goat Cheese, Rich Plain Gouda
ABOVE MIDDLE Aroha Organic Goat Cheese, Cumin Gouda
ABOVE RIGHT Clevedon Valley Buffalo Company, Ricotta
BELOW LEFT Cloudy Mountain Cheese, Pirongia
BELOW TOP RIGHT Cloudy Mountain Cheese, Joie
BELOW BOTTOM RIGHT Cloudy Mountain Cheese, Kaipaki Gold

Appreciating Cheese

The cheese course is the link between the main course and dessert, although cheese is also often served at the end of the meal with a glass of port. Regardless of where you place the cheese course in the order of things, the important considerations are the styles and strengths of the cheeses and their ability to add to the overall enjoyment of the meal as a whole. This course can be thought of as the expression not only of the chosen wine, but also of the meal in its entirety.

The cheese course is where the quality of the produce shines, rather than the cooking ability of the host or hostess. A thoughtfully chosen, well-balanced cheese course is a delight for your guests and reflects the real sense of care and consideration that you have given to your guests' enjoyment. Always try to buy from a shop with a good selection and knowledgeable staff, and taste before buying to evaluate your preferences, too.

THIS PAGE Bringing cheese to room temperature; drape a clean, slightly dampened cotton cloth or dish towel over the board of cheeses after taking the cheese out of the refrigerator.

WRAPPING & STORING CHEESE

I always follow the maxim "Little and often" when it comes to buying cheese; even if you have bought vacuum-wrapped supermarket cheeses, you can help to keep them looking and tasting better by rewrapping in wax paper. Blue cheese does not mind being wrapped in aluminum foil, as well as being kept in the coldest part of the refrigerator, although I prefer to wrap the cheese in wax paper first, before covering with foil. If you have splashed out on a chunk of Parmigiano-Reggiano or similar hard cheese, then wrapping it in clean, unbleached dampened cotton cloth or several layers of cheesecloth will keep the cheese fresh in the refrigerator or pantry. You may have to check and refresh the cheese every day and make sure that the cloth is damp. Small, whole hard cheeses wrapped first in wax paper are best covered in several layers of newsprint because it is "pulped" and will hold the moisture very well in a cool environment.

For cut pieces of cheese, put the wrapped cheeses in a plastic container with a tight-fitting lid, after first spreading a slightly dampened dish towel or cloth on the bottom of the container. Do not put blue cheeses in the same container because these should be kept separate from other cheeses, to prevent the blue molds from spreading. Before closing the container, put in a few sugar cubes, which will act as a natural preservative, preventing the growth of molds and holding back oxidization, as well as distributing the humidity in the sealed tub and preventing bacteria from growing in the confined atmosphere. You will be amazed at how fresh the cheese remains; we have tested semihard and hard cheeses for up to three weeks successfully, although softer varieties last only up to a week.

ABOVE Storing cheeses with sugar cubes: a natural preservative.
BELOW LEFT Parmigiano-Reggiano wrapped in cheesecloth.
BELOW RIGHT Cheese wrapped in wax paper.

SERVING CHEESE

To serve cheese, it is best to unwrap the pieces and place on a wooden board or platter, then cover with a clean, slightly dampened cotton dish towel or cloth, and let come to room temperature. This takes from half an hour to an hour, depending on how warm or cool the room. Some washed-rind cheeses become dry on their rinds; to restore them, simply mix dry white wine or eau de vie in boiled and cooled water (say, half a coffee cup of water to 2 teaspoons of alcohol) and, with your (clean) fingertips, massage a little liquid over the rind until it looks dewy and glistening again. Think of the cheese course as a carefully thought-through selection, and do not be tempted to put too many on the board because this can be confusing to the palate. Either go with one stand-alone cheese, such as a Roquefort, with a dessert wine, or up to eight maximum for a varied selection based on the season.

CUTTING CHEESE

Cutting your cheese in the appropriate way will not only look more appetizing at the end of the meal, but also allow you to enjoy the cheese again at your next meal! Neat slices showing the central tip to the outer edge will allow for complete enjoyment of the cheese because the ripest part (and the strongest-tasting) is the outside and the more mellow flavors are in the center.

Cutting log-shaped cheeses is easy, but remember, if you are offering a selection of five or six cheeses, you do not need to cut big, chunky rounds; the maximum amount of total cheese per plate should be about 5½ ounces (150 g) or five pieces at 1 ounce (30 g) each, or the equivalent for a smaller selection.

BACK LEFT CHEESE Soft bloomy rind: Brie de Meaux; BACK MIDDLE CHEESE Log shape: Sainte-Maure; BACK RIGHT CHEESE Pyramid shape: Pouligny-Saint-Pierre; MIDDLE LEFT CHEESE Square bloomy rind: Pont l'Évêque; MIDDLE CHEESE Soft washed: Ami du Chambertin; MIDDLE RIGHT CHEESE Blue cylinder: Fourme d'Ambert; FRONT CHEESES Hard cutting: Comté d'Estive; Semi soft rind: Taupinerè

If you are using a simple cheeseboard knife, then have a couple of small pitchers or tumblers of boiled water in which to dip the knife to clean it between each cut of cheese. You do not want to have blue cheese coating a soft white cheese, or goat cheese smearing onto a hard cheese. Dipping the knife blade in hot water and drying with paper towels will ensure lovely clean, neat cuts. Very crumbly cheeses, such as Roquefort, can be cut with a long thin-blade knife or the special "guillotine"-style tool with the metal handle and a fine taut wire.

I do love the right tools for cutting cheese, and specialists make knives and cutters specifically for certain styles of cheeses. The large Gruyère and Emmental cheeses have a square-blade slicer that chops through the rind and pâte with ease, and the flat "tongue"-shape blade for soft spreadable cheeses or butter is very useful. A Parmesan knife is well worth investing in if you like chipping away at the cheese as part of a cheese course. Scandinavian and Dutch cheeses are ideally cut with a simple shaver that slides across the cut piece to create long, fine slivers. Taking the trouble at this stage of the presentation gives you immense pleasure in the way the cheese looks plated up and also cut on the board. Lastly, remember to start with the mildest cheese at the top of the plate (12 o'clock) and work around clockwise, ending with the blue cheese.

The way to cut is not to attack the whole cheese from all sides! For square-shape cheeses, such as Pont l'Évêque, or small round cheeses, cut in half and take portions from just one half, so that you can wrap the other half and store for another day. For blue cheeses that hold their crumbly texture well, such as Fourme d'Ambert, Stilton, or Gorgonzola naturale, if served in rounds (Fourme or Stilton), again take slices like a cake from each half; if the piece is a whole or half cheese, then carefully score a ½–¾ inch (1–1.5 cm) circle around the top, and cut small wedge-shape pieces (see picture opposite). For blue cheeses, cut as a wedge rather than a round; use a long thin-blade knife to avoid breaking the cheese, and slice end to end, rather than in chunks. Clean the blade to ensure that the cuts are neat and the soft cheese does not stick to the blade. For Brie, you can create a wonderful patchwork pattern (see opposite, top left), but this is because you want to try to get the outer and inner parts of the cheese on each piece for tasting—and never cut the "nose" from the pointed end because this is "bad manners" in the rules of cheese etiquette!

Once opened, very soft cheeses should be eaten quickly; they will not taste the same if kept overnight or eaten a few days later. Alternatively, cut the cheese in half and immediately return the unused portion to the refrigerator.

1 Cheese wire for cutting through large semihard to semisoft cheeses; 2 Big rectangular cutting tool for Gruyère-style and Emmental cheeses; 3 Flat blade for spreading soft curd cheese and ricotta; 4 Grater for hard cheeses; 5 Triangular cutting tool serrated on one side and sharp on the other, with a slicer in the middle (a buffet-style tool); 6 Triangular cutting tool with slicer in middle (a buffet tool); 7 Thin blade for small soft cheeses and goat cheeses; 8 Metal frame with thin wire stretched across for cutting soft blue cheeses, such as Roquefort; 9 Small fork for chopping off smaller chunks of Parmesan; 10 Small trowel for chipping off even smaller pieces of Parmesan; 11 Kitchen-style knife for harder cheeses; 12 Knife with a slightly angled handle for Brie and semisoft larger cheeses; 13 Fancy cheeseboard knife for cutting semisoft cheeses or harder cheeses in thin slices; 14 Larger Parmesan knife/trowel for cutting larger chunks of Parmesan.

WHAT TO SERVE WITH CHEESE

The ubiquitous grapes and celery can be used well if properly matched with the right cheeses, and nuts, too, have a place. Try raw almonds in their papery skins with Beaufort Chalet d'Alpage cheese, or freshly cracked walnuts with creamy triple-cream cheeses or soft goat cheeses. Spain produces muscatel raisins not only for sweet wine, but also to be eaten with all styles of cheeses; it also produces that compact fruit paste membrillo, made with quinces, which is a stylish accompaniment to Manchego or blue cheeses (see page 144).

The French board This is a typical French supper or lunch *en famille* (see picture above), and this platter of Roquefort, Brie, and Comté cheeses has all the elements for a varied and convivial meal. Sourdough wheat bread, such as pain de Poilâne or a similar wood-fired artisan-style loaf; rillettes of shredded duck, goose, or pork meat mixed with the fat, to spread on the bread; accompaniments of tart cornichons (gherkins) and a celeriac remoulade of shredded raw celeriac with grainy mustard mayonnaise—all complement the gritty fruitiness of Comté cheese very well. The meaty saucisson from the Auvergne is lovely when placed on the bread with a sliver of Brie on top. A little spoonful of wine jelly with the Roquefort provides a delicious savory-and-sweet taste, along with sweet Chasselas de Moissac grapes grown in southwest France.

The British ploughman's board The simplicity of a ploughman's lunch (bottom left) is deceiving—the bread should be white and thickly sliced, with a good golden crust, to accompany a hearty Cheddar such as Keen's; slices of crisp apple such as Cox's Orange Pippin; and celery sticks. The cheese is also served with a hand-raised pork pie, while the final flourish is piccalilli, that mustardy, spicy relish perfectly matched to the pork pie and the cheese.

ABOVE The French board: BACK ROW, LEFT TO RIGHT Pain de Poilâne sourdough, red grapes, rillettes d'oie (goose rillettes), celeriac remoulade, saucisson d'Auvergne; FRONT ROW, LEFT TO RIGHT Roquefort, Brie de Meaux, Comté, white grapes, wine jelly

LEFT The British ploughman's board: RIGHT TO LEFT Keen's Farmhouse Cheddar, hand-raised water crust pork pie, piccalilli relish, with crusty bread, apples, and celery

OPPOSITE TOP The American farmstead board: LEFT TO RIGHT New York State Cheddar, fresh goat's log, homemade chutney, cured ham

The American farmstead board This platter (above) was put together with the help of my wonderful hostess Lynda in Great Barrington, New York—the salad from her little garden plot, her homemade whole-wheat loaf, and a thick slice of her home-cured maple-syrup-basted ham. A tangy rhubarb chutney partnered the fresh goat's milk log coated in herbs perfectly. The local Cheddar-style cheese with the ham and bread are ideal for lunch.

Cured meats board The sheer variety of salamis and prosciutto from Italy is mouthwatering, along with Italy's different styles of olives, which are perfect with a cheese-and-cured-meat platter (below left). The bread is a ciabatta, and the cheeses range from creamy Piedmontese Robiola delle Langhe to a Swiss Emmentaler, three-year aged Parmesan, Cantal Laguiole from southwest France, and a Picos de Europa blue cheese from Spain. The meats—paper-thin slices of bresaola from Lombardy, to fresh soft salami with fennel seeds and truffle-infused Tuscan salami—make this a memorable meal.

Hearty Dutch breakfast board Dutch Gouda cheeses (below right) are delightful in the morning, with their chewy density and spicy flavors of mustard seeds, nettles, or cumin. They are great partnered with a dark rye bread, simple boiled ham, juicy tomatoes, crisp "hot" radishes, and celery sticks sprinkled with sea or kosher salt. There is also butter for the bread because I love buttered bread with cheese in fine shards on top. You may think that this a dairy overload, but a quality butter is one of the most perfect of simple accompaniments for the cheeseboard.

BELOW LEFT Cured meats board: BACK ROW, LEFT TO RIGHT Truffle salami, Cinte Sinese salami, mixed olives, baby gherkins; SECOND ROW Malencia beef, bresaola; THIRD ROW Fennel salami, Swiss Emmentaler; FRONT CHEESES Parmigiano-Reggiano, Robiola delle Langhe, Picos de Europa, Cantal Laguiole; FRONT ROW Mostarda di frutta, crusty bread

BELOW RIGHT Hearty Dutch breakfast board: BACK, LEFT TO RIGHT Rye bread, boiled ham, butter, radishes, tomatoes, celery; FRONT ROW, LEFT TO RIGHT Four-year aged Gouda, mustard and cumin Gouda, two-year aged Gouda, nettle Gouda

THE ULTIMATE CHEESEBOARD

On a cheeseboard, the range should always start with something light and palate-cleansing, such as a goat cheese, followed by a simple crumbly style, then something creamy, with a bloomy rind. Next should come a harder, fruitier cheese, then a washed-rind cheese with a rich full-bodied flavor and aroma. Then try something with a strong outer coating, such as herbs or vine leaves, and finally a blue cheese. This gives a rounded progression of flavors and textures, to make the tasting selection truly memorable. Here are my ultimate cheeseboards for British, American, and French cheeses. For more information on the cheeses listed, go to the relevant chapter for each country.

LEFT TOP Britain

1 St. Tola, 2 Ticklemore,
3 Berkswell, 4 Isle of Mull,
5 Montgomery's Cheddar,
6 Appleby's Cheshire,
7 Stilton, 8 Stichelton,
9 Beenleigh Blue, 10 Cardo,
11 Ardrahan, 12 Wensleydale,
13 Gorwydd, 14 Wigmore,
15 Tunworth, 16 Innes Button

LEFT MIDDLE USA

1 Cavatina, 2 Twig Farm Tomme,
3 Bleu Mont Clothbound
Cheddar, 4 & 5 Bayley Hazen
Blue, 6 Battenkill Brebis,
7 Grayson, 8 Tarentais,
9 Pondhopper, 10 Cadence

LEFT BOTTOM France

1 Selles sur Cher, 2 Charolais,
3 Ossau, 4 Comté d'Estive,
5 Beaufort, Chalet d'Alpage,
6 Fourme d'Ambert, 7 Roquefort,
8 Ami du Chambertin,
9 Camembert, 10 Val de
Loubières, 11 Brie de Meaux
(truffled cream), 12 Anneau du
Vic Bihl, 13 Banon, 14 Morbier,
15 Crottin

CHEESE & DRINKS

Wine and cheese are good partners, but matching them does require some consideration; however, once you have thought about how the wine reacts with the cheese and the flavor profiles you want to experience, it all becomes clear. If in doubt, think about the region's wines and cheeses to match.

There are no hard and fast rules when matching drinks with cheese; for instance, fresh white wines partner goat cheeses, but they can also be good with washed-rind soft cheeses, such as Munster, or hard Gruyère styles, with their sweet nuttiness. Sweet wines are generally great with blue cheeses. You can even match liquors, such as Scotch, whiskey, or even rum (try a dark rum with a triple-cream Brillat or Explorateur cheese). Other alcoholic beverages such as hard cider, beer, and sparkling wines all have cheese partners.

1 Red wine With a full body and vibrant aroma, red wines require cheeses with good acidity levels coupled with their own earthy, robust flavors. The three cheeses pictured are Camembert, Livarot, and pecorino sardo, to give you an indication of the styles, but some softer red wines can take many other cheeses, from rich and creamy to crumbly goat cheeses. New World wines are big on flavor and sometimes overpower cheeses.

①

② ③
④ ⑤

2 White wine The fresh acidity and clean, sharp flavors of these wines partner goat cheeses perfectly, but also consider Beaufort and other hard cheeses that do not want to be overpowered by red wines. It is surprising how many different cheeses work with white wines, from Riesling to the elegant Jura wines. The cheeses here are Sainte-Maure, a minerally goat cheese; Bachensteiner, which matches the Riesling; and Beaufort, for Chignin wines.

3 Port I suggest that you stick to the classic combination of Cheddar and Stilton when drinking port, served at the end of a meal. Serving a single cheese with a Spanish Picos port ends the meal on a high note. The richness of port, both red and tawny, lends itself to cheeses such as Serra da Estrela.

4 Champagne The bubbles in this wine work well with Parmigiano-Reggiano, which has a gritty, salty "fizz," as they also do with Langres. I love a mature, dry Charolais goat cheese for its nutty flavor, but also the long, lingering finish, which copes well with the wine.

5 Sauternes Sweet wines love Roquefort mainly because of the high minerality coming through from the noble rot on the grape. It is one of life's superb umami pleasures.

6 Beer Whether a dark monastery style to go with the chewy traditional cheeses, such as Abbaye de Trois Vaux, or a crumbly territorial-style cheese, or a classic hoppy beer with a yeasty aroma and flavors that partner Cheddar so well, there are many beers that work with cheese.

7 Cider This is not the overly gassy version, but rather gently petillant unfiltered pressed hard cider with a real apple flavor coming through and yeasty fermented notes. Pont l'Évêque is the perfect cheese partner.

8 Scotch whisky While it is not the obvious choice, you will be amazed when you try cheese with Scotch. For the softer styles, such as Singleton, try with Comté aged for two years. For single malts, add a splash of water and drink with salty, crumbly cheeses such as Parmesan, Isle of Mull Cheddar, or an aged Mahón, with its dense, gritty style. A matured Crottin de Chavignol is elegant with an Islay.

⑥

⑦　⑧

Recipes

There are some food aromas that are just too irresistible—for me, it is cheese the smell of cheese melting and bubbling on a piece of toast under the broiler. What is it about hot melted cheese? As much as I love preparing and creating cheeseboards, the versatility of the product in cooking is also showcased in the La Fromagerie shop and café with dishes reflecting not only the different styles of cheeses, but also the seasons. The recipes in this chapter include many from our repertoire, and reflect La Fromagerie's philosophy and commitment to bringing cheese to the forefront, rather than hiding it or mixing it up too much.

The point is that, when cooking with cheese, you should never think that you can compromise on quality and taste. The better the cheese, the better the outcome of the dish, and you will also find that you do not use as much because the best cheeses will be packed with flavor.

Making & Flavoring Cheese

There is a big difference between cheeses that are mixed with other flavors and ingredients while being made and before packaging, and the flavor sensations involved in creating homemade recipes. Making your own fresh cheese is really very simple. It is all about understanding what works and enhancing the cheese, as opposed to masking and overpowering it. Depending on the part of the USA in which you live, you may be able to access unpasteurized milk at farmers markets or even direct from the farm gate. More people are enjoying the taste of untreated (raw) milk as a drink or over breakfast cereal, but you could also make your own simple fresh cheese. It goes without saying that your supplier must be properly licensed, but, if you don't want to go this route, try organic milk instead; always ensure that any milk you use for cheesemaking is absolutely fresh.

Labneh

This strained yogurt, with its subtle, sour lemony taste, is used in all kinds of sweet and savory Middle Eastern dishes. Try to use a farmhouse–made yogurt, rather than a commercial brand, for the best flavor. You can add labneh to spicy meat dishes or serve on top of salads and roasted vegetables. It is also delicious with honey and toasted hazelnuts or pistachios, as well as with summer berries or a compote of winter fruits.

Makes 24–30 walnut-size balls
3¼ pounds (about 6 cups/1.5 kg) goat's, cow's, or sheep's milk yogurt (or a mixture)
A few good pinches of fine sea or kosher salt
Good-quality olive oil, to marinate (use a light-flavored one)
Large handful of finely chopped fresh mint leaves
Freshly ground black pepper

1 Line a large mixing bowl with cheesecloth. In another bowl, mix together the yogurt and salt, then taste to check the seasoning, adding more salt, if needed. Spoon the yogurt into the center of the cheesecloth, pick up the edges of the cloth, and tie them together at the top, to form a bundle.

2 Hang the bundle over a sink or a large bowl by suspending it from a stick or rolling pin, then let it drain (see page 229). If your kitchen is cool enough, there is no problem with leaving the yogurt out, but you may prefer to transfer the suspended bundle to the warmest part of the refrigerator. After 48 hours, most of the liquid will have drained away, and the labneh can be served at this stage (see page 229). Alternatively, for an improved taste and texture, allow the yogurt to hang for an extra day.

3 Remove the labneh from the cloth bundle, and put in a sealed container in the refrigerator. Once thoroughly chilled, preferably after 24 hours, using your hands, roll the cheese into balls somewhere between the size of an olive and a walnut.

4 In a shallow dish, pour in a layer of olive oil to a depth of about ¾ inch (2 cm). Lay the labneh in the oil, rolling each one until they are coated, then every so often spoon more oil over the cheese balls, to keep them moist. Just before serving, mix together the mint and ground pepper in a flat shallow dish, and roll the labneh balls into the mixture; serve immediately.

Cook's Note
❧ You can store the freshly made labneh balls in the oil in a sealed container or Mason or similar-style canning jar for up to 5 days.

Fresh Ricotta

The emergence of farmers markets in towns and cities has meant that there is now more choice in how we shop and we have become reacquainted with the seasonality of foods. But the most exciting thing for me is seeing small farms and cheesemakers showing their produce, and especially the chance this gives us to taste really fresh milk from single herds—sometimes even unpasteurized. What a joy, and what a revelation.

Dave Paul, who produces Hurdlebrook Guernsey cow's milk, also has the richest cream and the silkiest sour cream, and his crème fraîche is almost perfect in its consistency. Such thick, fresh milk needs to be drunk straight from the bottle—who can wait to pour it into the glass? Very naughty—but very nice!

Fresh goat's milk is really sweet and delicious. If it is available locally, try it—the fresher the better, when it comes to making ricotta-style cheeses. This fresh cheese is so simple and easy, and unbelievably takes less than an hour to make. Just follow these steps, but do make the ricotta with the freshest milk possible because most supermarket or UHT milk will not work, and the taste and texture of the cheese will not be as light and fluffy.

Makes about 2 cups (500 g)
10 cups (2½ quarts/2.4 litres) whole goat's milk
1¼ cups (300 ml) goat's cream
Juice of 1 large unwaxed lemon, preferably Amalfi
Pinch of fine *fleur de sel* or similar sea salt (optional)

1 Stir together all the ingredients, except the salt, in a large saucepan; use one with a nonreactive interior or, better yet, a copper pan if you have one. Warm the milk mixture slowly over a low heat (you may want to use a heat diffuser). Do not be tempted to stir the milk because you do not want to break up the forming curds, but gently lift the curds every now and then using a wooden spoon, to monitor the progress. As the milk reaches about 180°F (82°C) on a cook's thermometer, the "grains" of curd should be about the size of a lentil.

2 Turn up the heat slightly, and cook for another 5–8 minutes, until the curds mound on the spoon like soft white custard. When the curds start to "erupt" like a volcano in slow motion, and the temperature is just above 200°F (93°C), turn off the heat and let stand for 10 minutes.

3 Carefully tip the contents of the pan into a colander lined with damp unbleached cheesecloth, and let drain for a minimum of 15 minutes; you may want to gently squeeze out some of the liquid, then turn out the ricotta into a basin and add a little salt, if liked. Refrigerate until needed; the ricotta will last up to 4 days.

Cook's Notes
❧ This fresh ricotta can be used in the Stuffed Zucchini Flowers with Ricotta recipe, as pictured opposite (see page 284).
❧ The drained-off whey or liquid from the ricotta can be used in muffins, pancakes, or even biscuits.

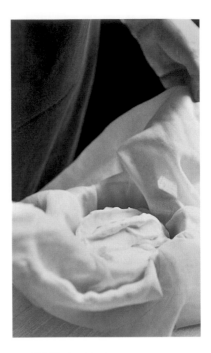

1 Beat the fromage blanc until thick. Place a fine mesh strainer lined with cheesecloth over a bowl, put the thickened fromage blanc in the cloth, and tie the cloth.
2 Let the watery whey drain through into the bowl. Pick up the cloth and gently squeeze out any watery residue.
3 When enough liquid has been released, put the fromage blanc in a clean bowl. In a second bowl, beat together the light cream and the 2 teaspoons vanilla-scented sugar until thickened and airy (it will not form peaks). In a separate, clean bowl, whisk the egg white (if using) until soft peaks form. Fold into the cream mixture.
4 Combine the cream with the fromage blanc very gently, and either use straight away or store in the refrigerator by first lining a bowl or several ramekin dishes with cheesecloth, and spooning the mixture into the cloth. Tie up the ends of the cheesecloth to encase the creamy cheese, and place the bowl and its contents in the coldest part of the refrigerator.
5 Serve with fresh berries in season and extra vanilla sugar on the side.

Cook's Notes

❦ Vanilla sugar is a useful sweetener to have in the pantry. To make, put a vanilla bean into the middle of an airtight jar of superfine sugar, close the lid, and store in the pantry to allow the vanilla to infuse the sugar. The sugar will develop a lovely scented sweetness and can be used in baking or whipped cream, or simply sprinkled over fresh fruit. The vanilla bean lasts for ages, so simply keep refilling the jar with sugar until the bean loses its potency.

❦ For a cream cheese with a lighter, fluffier texture, whisk a large egg white until it forms soft peaks, then gently fold it into the cream mixture.

Fontainebleau

This recipe takes a little organization and advance preparation: the cheesecloth should be scalded in hot water, then squeezed almost dry before using. The fromage blanc and light cream should not be too cold—room temperature is best— and, if using the egg white, remember to use a very clean bowl (if necessary, rub the inside of the bowl with the cut half of a lemon before wiping dry, to remove any greasy residue). The finished cream keeps for up to 3 days stored in the refrigerator.

Serves 8
12 ounces (350 g) whole-fat fromage blanc
⅔ cup (150 ml) light cream
2 teaspoons vanilla-scented superfine sugar,
   plus extra, to serve (see Cook's Notes)
1 free-range organic egg white (optional)

Camembert au Calvados

Philippe Olivier, whose famous cheese shop in Boulogne, in northern France, is a jewel of beautiful cheeses, especially those from Picardy, Normandy, and Pays d'Artois, invented this cheese "confection." This region in France all but lost its artisan cheesemakers during World Wars I and II, but the Oliviers have single-handedly brought them back to life by encouraging and championing their cheeses. Philippe has now retired, and his son Romain has taken up the cause. Their Camembert au Calvados is really the most delicious creation, and I have re-created it here for you to make at home.

Serves 4–6
3 slices of day-old milk bread or *pain de mie*, crusts removed

2 tablespoon Calvados or half Calvados and half Apéritif de Normande (sweet wine mixed with Calvados)

7 ounces (200 g) farmhouse Camembert, not too ripe

1 slice of dried apple or walnut half (optional), soaked in Calvados

1 Preheat the oven to 350°F (180°C). Dry the slices of bread in the oven until crisp—this will take only about 5 minutes—then crush into very fine crumbs. Put the crumbs on a small plate.

2 In a shallow bowl, pour in the Calvados or a mixture of Calvados and Apéritif de Normande.

3 Using a small sharp knife, carefully remove and discard the bloomy rind from the Camembert, then put the whole cheese in the bowl of liqueur, turning it until thoroughly coated and very wet.

4 Carefully lift out the cheese and place it in the crumb mixture, turning it over until the cheese is thickly covered on all sides. You can, if liked, dip the cheese in the liqueur and crumbs for a second time.

5 Place the apple or walnut on top of the cheese, if using, and serve. This cheese is delicious with a lighter style Rhône wine or a Gamay (Beaujolais family).

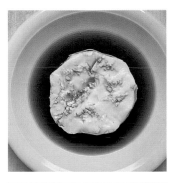

Savory Blue Cheese Butter

This flavored butter is perfect with grilled, broiled, or pan-fried steak, melted on top of a succulent hamburger or beef patty, or simply as a filling for baked potatoes.

Serves 6

4½ ounces (125 g) Bleu d'Auvergne, Roquefort, or Bleu des
    Causses (or another blue cheese with a rich, buttery texture)
½ cup (1 stick) plus 1 tablespoon (125 g) unsalted butter
Sprig of fresh sage or thyme, leaves only, finely chopped

1 Using a wooden spoon, beat together the cheese and butter in a bowl or process in a blender. Mix in the herbs until well distributed.

2 Place 2 or 3 sheets of plastic wrap on top of one another on a counter. Spoon the butter mixture onto the plastic wrap, and roll up into a cylinder like a sausage, twisting both ends to secure. Wrap the roll in foil and freeze—it is easy to cut the frozen butter into rounds as needed.

Gorgonzola Torte with Basil

This layered cheese "torte" infused with basil is really indulgent, but so much better than store-bought versions. It is important to use a really good farmhouse mascarpone—it is what makes the finished result so special.

Serves 8

18 ounces (500 g) mascarpone cheese, plus extra for coating
    (optional)
10½ ounces (300 g) Gorgonzola naturale cheese, cut into slices
    ½ inch (1 cm) thick
Handful of fresh basil leaves
Walnut bread, thinly sliced, to serve

1 Place a medium-size round mesh strainer over a mixing bowl. Line the strainer with a double layer of cheesecloth, leaving enough cloth hanging over the side of the bowl to let you tie it up.

2 Spoon a thin layer of mascarpone into the lined strainer, to cover the bottom. Put a layer of Gorgonzola in the strainer, then scatter over a few basil leaves. Repeat with another layer of mascarpone, Gorgonzola, and basil leaves until you have filled the strainer.

3 Tie together the overhanging cheesecloth to encase the cheese. Sit a plate on top, then a weight (not too heavy, just something to weigh it down sufficiently to remove any excess liquid).

4 Place the bowl in the refrigerator, and let stand for 1 hour, or until any excess liquid stops dripping through the cheesecloth. Untie the cloth, and turn out the cheese onto a serving plate.

5 Cover the dome of cheese with a layer of mascarpone, if you like, and scatter over a few extra basil leaves. Serve as a single cheese course with thin slices of walnut bread and chilled Prosecco or Vin Santo.

Triple Cream with Walnuts

This easy but luxurious idea involves steeping a triple-cream cheese in a fruit liqueur, then rolling it in coarsely chopped walnuts.

Serves 6

Scrape off the excess rind from a fresh rather than mature Explorateur (see page 54) or Brillat-Savarin (see page 52), or a similar soft triple-cream cheese.

Pour a generous 1 cup (250 ml) of your chosen liqueur—try pear, apple, or peach—into a bowl, and add the cheese, turning to coat well.

Cover, then let marinate for 30 minutes in a cool place. Toast a handful of walnuts in a dry skillet over medium heat until starting to brown; 1–2 minutes. Place on a clean dish towel, and coarsely crush with a rolling pin.

Remove the cheese from the liqueur, and shake off any excess. Put on a plate, then sprinkle over the walnuts, pressing them into the outside of the cheese until covered.

Sauces, Dips, & Soups

Simple to make but glorious to taste, these recipes are a million miles away from store-bought sauces and dips. I am very fond of soup, whether hot or cold, and a dollop of something creamy on top that you can mix in provides a wonderful finish.

Seasonal Pesto

Serve these fresh homemade pestos stirred into pasta, rice, or pilaf dishes, or place a spoonful on top of roasted, grilled, or broiled vegetables just before serving. Alternatively, bake slices of bread until crispy (as for bruschetta or crostini), and spread with a little pesto, before placing slices of mozzarella or soft goat cheese on top.

Makes 10–12 servings

FALL PESTO

This autumnal pesto is a combination of fiery Espelette peppers from Southwest France, creamy Marcona almonds, and Ossau ewe's milk cheese. Espelette peppers, a feature of Basque cuisine, arrive in early fall; you can use them fresh, or hang them up with string to dry. They are very beautiful, but deceptively hot. This pesto is lovely served with roasted or barbecued chicken.

Simply take one or two peppers, depending on how hot you want the pesto, then grind using a mortar and pestle, or process in a food processor or blender. If you can buy fresh Espelette, all the better; otherwise, use dried ones and grind everything, including the seeds.

Grind a handful of skinned Marcona almonds in a food processor until almost smooth, then add 9 ounces (250 g) Ossau cheese, and process for a minute or two until combined. Next, add the chopped peppers; process again until mixed together. Add enough olive oil to make a saucelike consistency. Spoon into a jar, cover the pesto with a thin film of olive oil, and store in the refrigerator.

WINTER PESTO

A spoonful of this winter pesto, made with toasted walnuts blended with fragrant winter herbs, can lift a risotto or pasta dish, and it goes especially well with pork.

In a small skillet over medium heat, dry-toast a good handful of walnuts for 1–2 minutes until golden; watch them carefully to avoid scorching. Grind using a mortar and pestle, or roughly process in a food processor or blender. Finely chop 1-2 sprigs of fresh sage (depending on how strong you want the flavor). Mix the walnuts into the sage, and stir in 2½ cups (250 g) grated pecorino—choose one with a good flavor, such as sardo or siciliana.

Take 1 or 2 peeled fat garlic cloves, crush slightly with the blade of a knife, and process in a food processor until smooth. Add the pecorino mixture, and process again. Add enough olive oil to make a saucelike consistency, then taste to check the seasoning and adjust to your liking, if needed—it should have a lovely toasted nut, herb, and cheese flavor, with a good hit of garlic. Spoon into a jar, cover the pesto with a thin film of olive oil, and store in the refrigerator.

SPRING PESTO

Bitter arugula leaves mixed with salty anchovies and fruity Manchego cheese work well together, while the addition of almonds give the pesto a delicious creamy texture.

Take a couple of handfuls of arugula leaves, and chop roughly. Rinse 1 or 2 salted anchovies to remove the salt, take out the backbone, then carefully take off the flesh and mash with the back of a fork. Blend or process a good handful of skinned Marcona almonds until almost smooth, then add 2½ cups (250 g) grated Manchego, the arugula, and anchovies to the processor. Blend again, then add enough olive oil to make a saucelike consistency; taste to check the seasoning. Spoon into a jar, cover the pesto with a thin layer of olive oil, and store in the refrigerator.

WILD LEEK PESTO

If you are lucky, you may come across wild leeks, or ramp, which are available for a few weeks in the spring. The long, wide leaves are delicate and pungent, and toward the end of the season the frilly white flowers are beautiful.

To make the pesto, take a handful of wild leek leaves, and process in a food processor or blender with 1½ cups (200 g) pine nuts. Add 2 big bunches of fresh basil and 2 cups (200 g) finely grated Parmesan cheese; or a mixture of Parmesan and pecorino, or Parmesan and hard goat cheese. Process again until finely chopped, then, with the motor running, drizzle in a fruity-tasting single-estate Tuscan olive oil, until it reaches a saucelike consistency. Spoon into a jar, cover the pesto with a thin film of olive oil, and store in the refrigerator.

SUMMER PESTO

The sweet and savory flavors of the peak of summer make for the perfect pesto. Serve this seasonal pesto stirred into pasta with mascarpone and a grinding of black pepper.

Briefly cook 1½ cups (7 ounces/200 g prepared weight) shelled fresh green peas (or you could use frozen) in boiling water until just tender. Drain and crush into a coarse mixture; set aside. Process or blend 2 fat garlic cloves and ¾ cup (100 g) pine nuts until almost smooth. Add a handful of chopped fresh mint and process again. Set aside.

Add 1½ cups (150 g) grated Grana Padano and pecorino toscana (half and half, or to your taste) to the processor or blender; process until still slightly gritty. Add the reserved pine nut mixture, and blend until stiff. With the machine running, slowly pour in extra virgin olive oil until it reaches a saucelike consistency. Taste and, if liked, add the grated zest of 1 lemon. Transfer to a bowl, and fold in the peas. Spoon into a jar, cover the pesto with a thin film of olive oil, and store in the refrigerator.

Liptauer

This easy cheese spread or dip will keep in the refrigerator for up to a week. It is delicious served with crudités, or salad and fresh, crusty bread.

Serves 8–10
⅔ cup (150 g) cream cheese, softened
scant ½ cup (100 g) quark or low-fat cream cheese, softened
scant ½ cup (7 tablespoons/100 g) unsalted butter, softened
1 teaspoon English mustard powder
1 teaspoon sweet paprika (preferably Hungarian),
    plus extra, to serve
1 teaspoon salted baby capers (not in brine), rinsed and gently
    squeezed dry
2 anchovy fillets, rinsed, patted dry, and very finely chopped
1 shallot, very finely chopped
½ teaspoon caraway seeds
Coarse sea or kosher salt and freshly ground black pepper
To serve:
Vegetable crudités
Thin crisp crackers

1 In a bowl, cream together the cream cheese and quark or low-fat cream cheese, then beat in the butter until smooth. Beat in the mustard powder, paprika, capers, anchovies, shallot, and caraway seeds, then season with salt and pepper to taste.
2 Cover the bowl with plastic wrap, and chill for a day to allow the flavors to develop. Serve the cheese dip with vegetable crudités and/or thin, crispy crackers.

Cook's Notes
 Instead of vegetable crudités, serve the liptauer with a ramekin dish of baby "cornichons," or gherkins, and a platter of various rye breads.
 An alternative way to prepare the cheese is to wrap it in plastic wrap to make a round, then let stand for a day to allow the flavors to meld. Before serving, unwrap the mound of cheese. In a small bowl, mix together a little paprika with peanut oil or sunflower oil, then brush the surface of the cheese with the mixture to give it a light gloss.

Cervelle de Canut

This cheese is also known by the name Claqueret Lyonnais, which refers to the wooden spoon used to mix shallots, soft fresh herbs, and garlic into the silky-smooth cheese curd.

Serves 6–8 as an appetizer
18 ounces (500 g) fresh curd cheese, or strained fromage blanc
1 tablespoon crème fraîche
1 shallot, very finely chopped
1 garlic clove, very finely chopped
1 tablespoon very finely chopped herbs, such as parsley, chervil,
    thyme, dill, fennel fronds, or chives, or any combination
2–4 tablespoons verjuice or light white wine vinegar
1–2 tablespoons extra virgin olive oil
Coarse sea or kosher salt and freshly ground black pepper
To serve:
Crusty sourdough or rye bread
Gherkins or other pickles

1 In a mixing bowl, beat the curd cheese or fromage blanc with the crème fraîche until smooth. Add the shallot, garlic, and herbs. Season with salt and pepper, then taste and add more, if needed.
2 Cover the bowl with plastic wrap, and chill for 2 days to allow the flavors to meld. Add the verjuice or white wine vinegar and the olive oil—start with the smaller quantity first, adding more, if liked. Store in the refrigerator.
3 Serve with sourdough or rye bread and gherkins or pickles.

Sweetcorn Soup with Crème Fleurette

As soon as we see the early fall sweetcorn appearing in our local farmers market, this soup in turn appears on the menu in La Fromagerie. The corn ears fold back to expose plump kernels that ooze out their milky sweetness when squeezed between your fingers. The sweetness of this soup is absolutely from the corn—no other sugar is added.

Serves 4–6
½ cup (1 stick) plus 1 tablespoon (125 g) unsalted butter
2 large white onions, finely chopped
1 large leek, finely chopped (I like to include some of the
    green top)
2 celery stalks, finely chopped
6–8 fresh corn cobs, kernels removed
8½ cups (generous 2 quarts/2 litres) boiling water, or half stock/
    half water, if preferred
Coarse sea or kosher salt and freshly ground black pepper
To serve:
Crème fleurette or crème fraîche, drained to remove some of the
    "watery" residue
Cornbread, sliced or cubed (see page 294)

1 In a large, heavy saucepan, melt the butter over medium heat until foaming, then sauté the onions, leek, and celery for 10 minutes, or until softened and just turning golden. Season with a little salt. Mix the corn kernels into the softened vegetables, then cook for another 2–3 minutes.
2 Pour over the boiling water/stock to cover the vegetables completely, then bring to a boil. Turn down the heat to barely a simmer, and cook for 5–7 minutes (depending on the size of the corn kernels), until tender. Press the soup through a fine mesh strainer, or purée in small batches in a blender or using a handheld stick blender.
3 Adjust the seasoning to taste, and ladle into warm bowls. Top each serving with a spoonful of crème fleurette or crème fraîche, and serve hot with the cornbread.

Pumpkin Soup with Gorgonzola Walnut Toast

This is a favorite soup, simply because it has such a satisfying and honest flavor. The color is beautiful, the texture creamy and silky, and the addition of a blue cheese and the walnut bread turns it into such a lovely meal.

Serves 4–6
scant ¾ cup (1 stick plus 3 tablespoons/150 g) unsalted butter
2 large onions, finely chopped
2 large leeks, finely chopped
4 garlic cloves, roughly chopped
2 medium pumpkins (firm orange flesh or Potimarron pumpkin),
    skinned, seeded, and cut into small cubes
8½ cups (generous 2 quarts/2 litres) chicken stock (see below)
    or vegetable stock
A few sprigs of fresh thyme and 1 bay leaf, tied into a bundle
Coarse sea or kosher salt and freshly ground black pepper
To serve:
Walnut bread, sliced
3½ ounces (100 g) Gorgonzola dolce cheese, thinly sliced

1 In a large, heavy saucepan, melt half of the butter over medium heat until foaming, then sauté the onions, leeks, and garlic for 10 minutes, or until softened and just turning golden. Add the pumpkin, and cook for another 5 minutes.
2 Add the stock with the herb bundle, then bring to a boil, taste, and season lightly with salt and pepper. Turn down the heat to a simmer, and cook gently until the pumpkin is very tender. Take out the vegetables with a slotted spoon, and purée in batches in a food processor or blender. Return the purée to the rinsed-out pan with the stock. Stir, taste, and season again, then stir in the remaining butter, to give the soup a lovely gloss.
3 Meanwhile, preheat the oven to 350°F (180°C). Put the slices of walnut bread in a single layer on a baking sheet, and bake for about 10 minutes, until just crisp. Top with slivers of Gorgonzola dolce, then heat until melted on top of the warm toast; serve alongside the soup.

Chicken Stock

This flavorsome homemade stock makes about 3¼ quarts (3 litres).

In a large heavy saucepan, melt 3½ tablespoons (50 g) butter with 2 tablespoons olive oil until foaming but not browned. Sauté 2 finely chopped large red onions until softened, then stir in 2 finely chopped large carrots. After a couple of minutes, add 2 finely chopped celery stalks and 2 finely chopped leeks. Sauté the vegetables until softened.

Add 1 rinsed chicken carcass, and cover with 12¾ cups (3¼ quarts/3 litres) water. Create a herb bunch with a few sprigs of fresh flat-leaf parsley and thyme, and 1 bay leaf. Tie into a bundle with string, add to the pan, and bring to

a boil. Carefully skim off any scum that rises to the surface with a slotted spoon, and turn down the heat to a gentle simmer. Add a pinch of salt and a few white peppercorns.

Turn the heat down to a bare simmer, cover the pan with a lid, then cook gently for at least 2 hours. You can add a little more boiled water if the liquid appears to be reducing too quickly. Strain the stock, discarding the solids, to make a wonderful broth.

Allow to cool, then store in an airtight container in the refrigerator (or in the freezer for up to 3 months). To defrost the stock, let stand in the refrigerator overnight, skim off any fat, then use as desired.

Beet Soup with Labneh Balls

The sweet earthiness of red beets lends such a different taste to the usual root vegetable soups. The rich red color alone is exotic (or you could try yellow beets), and the addition of the fresh cheese balls is really delicious. You may think that the amount of butter used here is excessive, but it adds flavor, as well as a silky texture.

Serves 4–6
1¾ pounds (800 g) red beets, trimmed and scrubbed
½ cup (1 stick) plus 1 tablespoon (125 g) unsalted butter, plus extra, to serve
1 onion, coarsely grated
1 carrot, coarsely grated
1 fennel bulb, coarsely grated
Juice of 2 large lemons
1–2 tablespoons superfine sugar (you may need a little more or less, according to taste)
6½ cups (about 2½ pints/1.5 litres) chicken stock (see page 238) or vegetable stock, or use low-sodium bouillon cubes, if necessary
Coarse sea or kosher salt and freshly ground black pepper
Labneh Balls (see page 227), to serve

1 Preheat the oven to 400°F (200°C). Put the beets in a deep roasting pan. Pour in water to a depth of about 3 inches (7.5 cm) water, then cover with foil, fitting it tightly around the rim of the pan. Roast in the oven for 45–60 minutes, depending on the size of the beets, until they are tender all the way through when pierced with a skewer.

2 When the beets are cool enough to handle, rub off the outer skins using your thumbs (wear kitchen gloves, otherwise you will stain your hands), then cut the flesh into bite-size pieces.

3 In a large heavy saucepan over medium heat, melt the butter until foaming. Sauté the onion, carrot, and fennel for 10 minutes, or until softened and just turning golden. Stir in the beets, the juice of 1 lemon, and half of the sugar, then pour in the stock and bring the mixture to a boil. Taste and add more lemon or sugar, if needed.

4 Season with salt, then add a few twists of black pepper; taste again to make sure that you are happy with the seasoning. Cover the pan with a tight-fitting lid. Turn down the heat to barely a simmer, and cook gently for 25 minutes or so, until the beets are completely soft and crushable (test by mashing one with the back of a fork).

5 Remove from the heat, and process in a blender or food processor to a coarse or fine purée, depending on taste. Return to the rinsed-out saucepan and, over the lowest heat possible, whisk in a good knob of butter, to give the soup a lovely gloss. Check the seasoning, and serve warm in summer and hot in winter. Pop in 1 or 2 labneh balls just before serving.

Fresh Pea Soup with Herb Fromage de Cervelle

This is a summer soup for when fresh green peas are in abundance, but if you are in a hurry you can use frozen peas, although this does ruin the fun of the shelling. If you are making a vegetable stock, simply throw the pea pods into the stockpot, and any pea shoots attached to the pea pods make a delicious addition to a salad. If you must use frozen peas, then 1 large bag will suffice.

Serves 4
3¼ pounds (1.5 kg) fresh, unpodded green peas (about 2¼ pounds/1 kg prepared weight), shelled
2 Boston lettuces, sliced
1 medium-thick slice cooked ham
2 cipolotti onions or large scallions, finely chopped
8½ cups (generous 2 quarts/2 litres) water, or half stock/half water, if preferred
Scant 1 teaspoon superfine sugar, or to taste
3½ tablespoons (50 g) unsalted butter
Coarse sea or kosher salt and freshly ground black pepper
Herb Fromage de Cervelle:
12 ounces (350 g) fromage frais, drained, or Petit Suisse
1 tablespoon finely chopped fresh herbs, such as chervil, chives, flat-leaf parsley, thyme, or mint, or a mixture

1 Put the shelled peas in a saucepan with the lettuce, ham, and onions. Cover with the water/stock, bring to a boil, then reduce the heat. Cover with a lid, and simmer gently for about 15 minutes, until the peas are soft.

2 Press the soup through a fine mesh strainer, or purée in small batches in a blender or using a handheld stick blender. Return to the pan, and adjust the seasoning (be careful with the sugar because the amount you use depends on how sweet the peas are). Bring back to a boil, then beat in the butter.

3 Meanwhile, to make the Herb Fromage de Cervelle, drain the cheese in a strainer to remove as much liquid as possible, put the cheese in a bowl, and add the herbs. Season with salt and pepper, and mix together until evenly combined. Pour the soup into warm bowls, and top each serving with a spoonful of the herb mixture.

Light meals

Cheese is the perfect food and ingredient element for lighter meals because it is a whole food in itself and with just a few added elements becomes a meal. The combinations are thoughtful rather than a mishmash of ideas, and remember that the better the quality, the better the finished result.

Cheese Club Sandwiches

Club sandwiches are not usually made with cheese, but try experimenting with different types of cheese and breads, using all the knowledge you have gained from this book!

WHITE BREAD
- Cheddar, cut into rough shards, Branston pickle or similar relish, and crisp salad greens
- Cheddar, cut into rough shards, Marmite, and watercress

BAGUETTE
- Emmental, sliced ham, Brie, sliced salami, and arugula
- Fresh goat cheese, sliced roasted beets, finely chopped thyme leaves, and arugula

WALNUT BREAD
- Comté, sliced cooked Morteau sausage, sliced white endive, and celeriac remoulade mixed with crème fraîche and grainy mustard
- Garrotxa goat cheese, cut into slices, bell peppers roasted in garlic, olive oil, and peppery salad greens

DARK RYE BREAD
- Triple-cream cheese, melon and grapes in a vinaigrette, and watercress
- Rove des Garrigues fresh goat cheese, smoked salmon (lox), cucumber salad tossed in a sweet dill vinaigrette, and trevise
- Tilsiter, crispy broiled smoked bacon, cream cheese or quark, and pickles

Croque Monsieur

I never usually advocate freezing, but you can do this successfully with this recipe, and therefore make a few at a time and have them ready whenever the urge takes you.

Makes 10

20 medium-thick slices of *pain de mie* or milk bread (this can be day-old bread)

20 medium-thick slices cooked ham, from your local butcher or delicatessen

3 cups (300 g) each grated Emmental and Gruyère, mixed

Béchamel Sauce:

½ cup (1 stick) plus 1 tablespoon (125 g) unsalted butter

1 cup (125 g) unbleached all-purpose flour

2 cups (500 ml) whole milk, plus extra just in case

1 tablespoon whole-grain mustard

Freshly grated nutmeg

Coarse sea or kosher salt and freshly ground black pepper

1 To make the béchamel, melt the butter in a heavy saucepan over medium heat until foaming. Sift in the flour, and cook the roux mixture over medium-low heat, stirring constantly, for 3–4 minutes to remove the raw taste of the flour and until it turns a very pale color and smells toasty; this is important.

2 Meanwhile, warm the milk in a pan. Pour the milk into the roux in a steady stream, beating continuously to form a smooth, very thick paste similar to the texture of cream cheese. Stir in the mustard and a few gratings of nutmeg, then season with salt and pepper. Pour the béchamel into a bowl, and leave to cool.

3 Spread a slick of béchamel over a slice of bread, follow with a slice of ham and a sprinkling of grated cheese, and top with a slice of bread and thick sprinkling of cheese. If storing, wrap in plastic wrap and foil. Repeat to make more croques and freeze them, uncooked, for future use if liked (see below).

4 Preheat the oven to 350°F (180°C). Place the croque on a baking sheet, and bake for 10–15 minutes until the top is golden and the cheese bubbling.

Welsh Rarebit

Welsh rarebit was once considered a poor man's dish.; however, it has become a trendy snack, with many variations.

Preheat the broiler to medium-high. Toast one side of a slice of bread—this can be white, wheat, whole-grain, or even sourdough. Butter the untoasted side lightly, and spread over a thin layer or either Dijon, grainy, or English mustard. Top with thick shards of aged Lincolnshire Poacher cheese (like Cheddar but with its own savory bite). Place under the broiler until the cheese is bubbling and golden. Serve at once.

Pagnotta Toasts with Lardo, Porcini, & Truffle Pecorino

Pagnotta is a very large round loaf traditionally baked in a wood-burning oven. Its crust is hard and crispy, and the texture of the bread is chewy and open. If you cannot get hold of it, a sourdough, rustic-style bread, or even a crusty baguette will work.

Fresh porcini mushrooms arrive in the stores in early fall, and sometimes even in late August. If you want an alternative, then chanterelles are fine, or even cremini, but it is really the meaty flavor of the porcini that makes this recipe so special.

Lardo is the thick layer of fat found immediately below the skin of a pig. It is cured in herbs and spices in marble bathtubs, or "conche," as they are called in Italy. The most famous area for this delicacy is Carrara in the northwest of Italy, although Aosta in the Italian Alps is another region known for this delicacy.

Serves 2 as an appetizer

In a skillet, heat 2–3 tablespoons good olive oil over high heat, then add a small handful of sliced fresh porcini or other mushrooms. Let sizzle for a minute or two. As soon as the sizzling stops, the mushrooms are ready; if you cook them for too long, water oozes out and they toughen.

On a piece of hot toasted bread, lay slices of wafer-thin lardo until entirely covered, spoon over some porcini, and crumble a young truffle pecorino cheese over the top.

Season with freshly ground black pepper, and serve the toasts with a side salad of mixed hot peppery salad greens dressed in extra virgin olive oil and a drizzle of good-quality balsamic vinegar.

Cook's Note
🌢 Instead of the truffle pecorino, try a fresh goat cheese or a young Parmesan, or even a young Wensleydale, but it is the delicious truffle taste in the pecorino that partners both the porcini and lardo so well.

Michon Franche-Comté

This is a take on toasted cheese and is a specialty of the Bouchoux plateau area at the southern end of the Franche-Comté region of France. Serve warm, cut into wedges, with a glass of Jura wine made with Chardonnay grapes, or a German Spätlese using the same grape style. This is a lovely snack or apéritif, and certainly one of the oldest recipes I have come across.

Serves 6–8

Mix together scant 2½ cups (300 g) unbleached all-purpose flour and enough water to make a soft, floppy paste. Season sparingly with salt, especially if using an aged Comté. Stir in 12 ounces (350 g) thinly sliced Comté cheese.

Brush a pat of butter over the bottom of a hot skillet, and put the doughy cheese paste in the skillet, spreading it out like a thick pancake. Fry the paste as you would a crêpe, until the cheese bubbles and the bottom is light golden. If you feel confident enough, flip it over; otherwise, flash the top under a hot broiler to brown.

Serve the Michon Franche-Comté cut into 4–6 wedges.

Cook's Note
🌢 The Comté region utilizes its cheeses in many recipes from classic chicken with a creamy cheese and morel (*morille*) mushroom sauce to morbiflette, which is a traditional potato dish with melted Morbier, and raclette using Bleu de Gex (a blue cheese with a distinct but not too strong a taste). The region's tarte au fromage is probably the best version of a cheese flan using Comté cheese, eggs, and cream for the custard filling.

Flambéed Banon de Chèvre

Provence in Southeast France is famous for its small medallions of goat cheese, and Banon is one that is covered in chestnut leaves. Before wrapping, the cheesemaker brushes over a little eau de vie to heighten the flavor of the cheese. This dish makes an end-of-meal savory treat. When choosing the Banon, you want one that is neither too ripe—oe it may split—nor too hard, so be careful to choose one that is just right! This is served with a salad of bitter leaves with toasted crushed hazelnuts.

Serves 2 to share

Remove the outer chestnut leaves of the Banon, and leave the cheese to reach room temperature.

Brush the tiniest amount of peanut or other flavorless oil over the bottom of a small pan, and heat. Add the cheese and gently cook on both sides, being careful not to split the tender skin of the cheese.

Pour about 1 tablespoon eau de vie into a metal ladle, then hold the ladle over the bare flame of a gas stovetop, gently heating it first, and before you know it the alcohol will be alight. Being very careful, slowly pour the flaming liquid over the cheese in the pan (remove the pan from the heat first and have a lid on hand in case you need to douse the flames), and let the flames "lick" the cheese. When the flames have died down, lift out the cheese and put it on top of some salad greens. Sprinkle with toasted crushed hazelnuts, and serve immediately.

Cook's Note
🐾 When making the bitter leaf salad, be careful not to use a strong-tasting vinegar because it will not agree with the cheese—or, to be more blunt, with your digestive system, which sometimes starts gurgling when a mixture of soft, creamy cheese and vinegar meld together. Dress the salad in a light olive oil with lemon juice, verjuice, or a light white wine vinegar.

Baked Vacherin

There are a few simple but necessary rules when baking a whole vacherin. One is that the cheese has to be at room temperature; if it is not, you will be waiting hours for it to cook. Secondly, keep it simple because it is really all about the cheese mingling with a little wine, and not about garlic or herbs.

The loveliest accompaniments are steamed whole new potatoes, steamed broccoli, toasted slices of baguette, cooked or cured (or both) smoked ham, and a green salad that has been simply dressed in walnut oil and a squeeze of lemon juice.

The small boxed cheeses can serve two people for a light meal or one if it is a main course; this is just such a warming and friendly way of eating, especially in the winter.

Serves 2 to share

Preheat the oven to 425°F (220°C). For each baby-boxed vacherin, take off the lid and rub the rind with dry white wine, massaging it in well. Pop the lid back on, then cover the whole box with foil.

Place the box on a baking sheet, and bake in the preheated oven for at least 25–30 minutes. Check after about 20 minutes by carefully opening up the foil, lifting off the lid, and prodding the rind to check how hot and soft it is—when ready, the cheese should almost be erupting out of its rind. If not ready, replace the lid and foil, and return to the oven.

When cooked, unwrap the foil and remove the box lid, then push back the top "skin" of the cheese, which should slide off very easily. Pour in a little more white wine, season with freshly ground black pepper, and serve immediately with your choice of accompaniments.

1. Preheat the oven to 350°F (180°C). Cut the top off each garlic bulb, and maybe a little from the bottom so that it will stand upright in a baking pan. Stand the bulbs snugly in the pan, spoon over the chicken stock or water, and pour over the wine, verjuice, or white wine vinegar. Season liberally with salt and pepper, then top with the bay leaves or myrtille and the thyme.

2. Cover the pan with foil, and place on the middle shelf of the oven. Roast for 30 minutes, then remove the foil and continue roasting until the garlic becomes golden and the liquid reduces slightly. Test with a skewer (the garlic should be tender), then remove from the oven; let cool to room temperature.

3. To serve, drizzle olive oil over a slice of crusty sourdough or lightly toasted white bread, and place on a plate with a couple of tablespoons of fresh curd per person, then lightly season with salt and a grinding of black pepper. Next, put a garlic bulb on each plate, and spoon over a little of the syrupy juices.

Cook's Note

🖤 You can also use new-season fennel, available in early summer, to make this recipe. Cut the fennel into chunky quarters if large (or halve if smaller), put in a roasting pan, and spoon over the wine or verjuice. Next, sprinkle with 1 chopped red chile pepper and fresh herbs such as thyme, marjoram, oregano, or cilantro. Roast for 30 minutes, until tender and golden.

Slow-Roasted Garlic with Fresh Curd Toasts

New-season Italian garlic arrives at the beginning of March. They are quite unlike the bulbs usually found in stores and markets because they look similar to large, thick-stemmed scallions. They are pungently sweet, however, and wonderful to slow-roast in olive oil, or alternatively in a glass of white wine or stock, then serve warm with toasted sourdough and a light, frothy goat's milk or ewe's milk curd—this really does herald a new season with its fresh yet robust flavors.

Serves 6
6 whole heads of new-season garlic
1 cup (250 ml) chicken stock (see page 238) or water
scant 1 cup (200 ml) dry white wine or verjuice, or light white
    wine vinegar
3–4 fresh bay leaves or myrtille (which is a smaller version with
    a sweeter flavor)
3–4 sprigs of fresh thyme
Coarse sea or kosher salt and freshly ground black pepper
To serve:
Good-quality extra virgin olive oil
Sliced crusty sourdough or white bread
9 ounces (250 g) fresh curd (goat, cow, ewe, or buffalo),
    at room temperature

Gravadlax and Petit Suisses

Homemade gravadlax does take time, but once you have made it a couple of times you will find it really is easy and a great centerpiece for a party or as an appetizer for a holiday meal—it is always served at my table on festive occasions.

Serves 10–12

5 pounds (2.25 kg) whole salmon, gutted, filleted, and pin-boned, head and tail discarded

2 tablespoons coarse sea salt, plus extra to taste

2 tablespoons granulated sugar

2 tablespoon white peppercorns, lightly crushed

2 tablespoons coriander seeds, roasted in a dry skillet, then crushed

Grated zest of 2 large unwaxed lemons

At least 3 handfuls of fresh herbs, including dill, cilantro, and chervil

½ cup (125 ml) vodka

½ cup (125 ml) white wine

To serve:

Petit Suisse pistols, serve 1 per person

Freshly ground black pepper

Lemon wedges

1 Lay a long sheet of plastic wrap across a large serving dish. Place one half of the salmon, skin-side down, on the plastic wrap. Put the second side of salmon on a separate dish, skin-side down.

2 Mix together the salt, sugar, white pepper, coriander seeds, and lemon zest, and spread the mixture evenly across each piece of salmon. Divide the mixed herbs between the salmon, and press them into each fillet. In a small bowl or pitcher, combine the vodka and wine, and pour over the salmon.

3 Carefully place one of the sides of salmon, not on the plastic wrap, but on top of the other piece, flesh-side down, so that the fillets are sandwiched together; pour over any excess liquid.

4 Wrap the fillets tightly in plastic wrap. Press down, and place a plate large enough to cover the salmon on top, followed by weights (cans are ideal). Store the salmon in the refrigerator overnight. After 12 hours, unwrap and turn over each side of salmon. Spoon over any excess juices, then rewrap and weigh down again. Repeat this procedure every 24 hours for the next 3 days.

5 On the fourth day, unwrap the salmon and remove most of the herb and pepper topping, although you can leave a little because this is tasty, and drain off any excess liquid. Using a very sharp kitchen knife, slice the salmon very thinly at a slight angle, being careful to remove the skin (you don't want to slice through the skin).

6 Serve each portion with a Petit Suisse and wedge of lemon. Season the Petit Suisse with salt and pepper.

Main meals

An entrée or main meal with cheese as a component really does not need a big appetizer or, indeed, a heavy dessert to follow. The cheese is in itself filling, so lighten up the rest of the menu with a simple salad appetizer, and finish with stewed or poached fruit and shortbread.

Fondue

Try experimenting with your favorite cheese combinations when making this fondue. Many of the cheeses mentioned in this book, especially those in the Alpine chapter, are suitable. Even Irish and British cheeses work beautifully.

When making a fondue, there are a few important points to remember: use a good-quality cheese and ensure that it is at room temperature; grate the cheese before starting to cook; use a heavy saucepan; and stir the fondue in a figure-eight motion to ensure that it is evenly mixed.

To calculate the amount of cheese required, reckon on about 12 ounces (350 g) per person, with rind removed. My favorite cheese combinations include: Comté aged at least 2½ years (see page 84) or aged Gruyère (see page 95); aged Beaufort Chalet d'Alpage (see page 86); Emmenthaler (see page 97); and Reblochon (see page 89).

1 Grate the Comté or Gruyère, Beaufort Chalet d'Alpage, and Emmenthaler. Keep the Reblochon to one side, and mix together the other cheeses in a bowl. I always start the fondue on the stovetop because this is quicker and you can control the melting process much better. Rub the inside of a large heavy saucepan with a large peeled garlic clove, crushing it against the inner surface. Discard any large chunks of garlic, but leave the smaller pieces in the pan.

2 Turn on the heat to medium, and pour in a couple of large glasses of dry white wine, about 1¾ cups (400 ml) for 6 people. Heat until the wine starts to bubble, then mix in the grated cheese, a handful at a time, stirring it in with a wooden spoon using a figure-eight motion (see above). Once the cheese has melted, add another handful, until all the cheese is used and the sauce is thick enough to coat the back of the spoon—pour in more wine if the mixture looks too thick.

3 Finally, add the Reblochon, which you can scoop out with a spoon after removing the rind on top of the cheese. This final addition will add a lovely gloss to the fondue and lend an even more velvety texture. Season with salt and freshly ground black pepper to taste, then pour into the fondue pot that you have warmed through in the oven in readiness. At the table, place the fondue pot on its little stove, then stir in a slug or two of Kirsch liqueur. To serve, dip cubes of day-old baguette, bite-size steamed potatoes, with skin on, and steamed broccoli florets into the fondue.

Raclette

Raclette is not only the name of a cheese, but also a dish that began as a peasant-style meal and somehow turned into a gourmet offering, especially at ski resorts. Raclette is a derivative of the word "racler," which means "to scrape," and traditionally a whole cheese was cut in half and placed in front of an open hearth, and the melting cheese was scraped off onto thick wedges of bread or boiled or steamed potatoes.

Here are a few tips for when serving raclette:

1 If using presliced cheese, brush over a little white wine before placing under the broiler; if you have an electric tabletop raclette grill, place slices in the little pans, or "coupelles," and brush with a little wine before placing on the hotplate or griddle. If you are using a traditional machine, prepare the quarter or half cheese by rubbing the outside rind with white wine—massage it into the rind well, so that it is a little sticky but not soaking. Cook for a few minutes until bubbling.

2 Have ready all the accompaniments that go well with raclette: slices of Bayonne or other cured ham; speck, a smoked cured ham; different types of salami; thin slices of crusty bread; steamed vegetables such as broccoli florets and new potatoes; small gherkins called cornichons are also good; as well as small pearl onions roasted in olive oil and balsamic vinegar. Another serving idea is to pour the melted raclette over a baked potato.

3 If using a quarter or half cheese, you must use it all; otherwise you will be left with a sorry-looking molten mess that will harden as it cools and be inedible.

Tartiflette

This hearty winter dish is perfect for a family lunch with a green salad on the side.

Serves 4–6

4½ pounds (2 kg) floury potatoes, scrubbed and skins left on
1 tablespoon olive oil
2 large onions, finely sliced
18 ounces (500 g) thickly sliced pancetta, cut into small cubes
1 small glass of white Savoie wine or similar dry,
    fruity white wine
1 large garlic clove, peeled
½ cup (125 ml) crème fraîche
2¼ pounds (1 kg) Abbaye de Tamié cheese or Reblochon cheese,
    rind removed if dry and cut into long slices
3½ tablespoons (50 g) unsalted butter
1¼ cups (125 g) grated Comté cheese
1¼ cups (125 g) grated Parmesan cheese

1 Steam or boil the potatoes for 15–20 minutes, until cooked all the way through but not falling apart. Drain the potatoes, then, when cool enough to handle, peel them and cut into slices ½ inch (1 cm) thick. The potatoes should not crumble, but don't worry if some do; set aside.

2 Preheat the oven to 400°F (200°C). Heat the oil in a skillet over medium heat, and sauté the onions for 5 minutes until golden. Remove from the pan with a slotted spoon, and set aside. Add the pancetta to the skillet—there is no need for any extra oil—and sauté over medium-high heat until golden but not too brown. Remove with a slotted spoon, drain on paper towels to remove any excess oil, and set aside.

3 Put the potatoes and onions back in the skillet, and cook for about 2 minutes, gently shaking the pan, then pour over the white wine; cook over medium-low heat for a minute or two.

4 Select a square casserole or ovenproof dish, and rub well with garlic, squeezing the clove to crush it. Spoon a slick of the crème fraîche over the bottom of the dish until lightly coated (set the rest aside), then add a layer of the potato-and-onion mixture, a sprinkling of pancetta, and slices of the Abbaye de Tamié or Reblochon. Repeat the layers, finishing with a top layer of sliced potatoes and onions. There should be no need to add salt and pepper to this dish because the cheese and the pancetta should provide enough flavor—but if you want to add extra, then do so, but judiciously.

5 Dot the butter over the top, and add blobs of the remaining crème fraîche and finally a layer of grated Comté and Parmesan. Bake in the oven for 25 minutes, until the cheese is beautifully golden and bubbling.

Pasta Carbonara

This warming winter dish makes a great supper with a green salad, or it can be served as an accompaniment to roasted meats.

Serves 2

2 tablespoons extra virgin olive oil
9 ounces (250 g) smoked pancetta, cut into small cubes
1 large garlic clove, crushed
Handful of chopped fresh flat-leaf parsley
2 organic eggs, plus 2 extra yolks
generous ¼ cup (25 g) finely grated pecorino romano, pecorino
    siciliano, or Sardo Canestrato, plus extra, to serve
⅔ cup (150 ml) heavy cream
Coarse sea or kosher salt and freshly ground black pepper
9 ounces (250 g) pasta (spaghetti, tagliatelle, or penne), to serve

1 Heat the olive oil in a skillet over medium heat, and fry the pancetta for 5 minutes, until golden; remove and place on a dish. Add the garlic and parsley, and cook for 1 minute, then remove and set aside.

2 In a bowl, whisk together the eggs, extra yolks, cheese, and cream, and season well with black pepper. Set aside.

3 Cook the pasta until al dente; drain. Immediately return the pasta to the hot saucepan over low heat, and add the reserved pancetta, garlic, and parsley. Turn off the heat.

4 Add the egg-and-cream mixture, stirring thoroughly, until the pasta is coated in sauce. The egg will cook as it comes into contact with the hot pasta, but it must not get too hot, otherwise it will scramble. If the sauce is not cooking, return the pan to very low heat for a short while. Serve sprinkled with extra grated cheese.

Cauliflower Cheese

I couldn't contemplate a Sunday roast without cauliflower cheese. Cauliflower is in season during the winter months, and this is the perfect time for warming dishes such as this, as well as layered gratins with cabbage and potatoes.

Serves 4–6

1 large cauliflower, cut into large florets
scant ½ cup (100 g) unsalted butter, plus extra for greasing
2 tablespoons all-purpose flour, sifted
2½ cups (600 ml) whole milk, plus extra just in case
1 onion, peeled and studded with 6–8 cloves
1 bay leaf, torn
12 ounces (350 g) Montgomery's Cheddar or other well-flavored farmhouse Cheddar cheese, coarsely grated
⅔ cup (150 ml) crème fraîche
1 teaspoon Dijon mustard
Freshly grated nutmeg, to taste
½ cup (50 g) finely grated Parmesan cheese
Coarse sea or kosher salt and freshly ground black pepper

1 Preheat the oven to 425°F (220°C). Cook the cauliflower in boiling salted water for a few minutes, until al dente. Strain, return the cauliflower to the pan, and shake gently over medium heat until any liquid evaporates. Transfer to a buttered ovenproof dish.
2 To make a roux, melt the butter over medium heat. Turn down the heat slightly, and add the flour. Cook, stirring constantly, for 2 minutes, to "cook" out the flour taste.

3 Meanwhile, gently warm the milk with the onion and bay leaf. Strain the milk into a pitcher. Off the heat, pour a little of the milk into the roux, and mix to a creamy consistency. Put the pan back on the heat and, in a steady stream, pour in the rest of the milk, stirring until thick.
4 Sprinkle in the Cheddar, a small handful at a time, and mix thoroughly, reserving a handful for the top. Taste and season with salt and pepper, then add, off the heat, the crème fraîche and Dijon mustard, mixing thoroughly before grating over a little nutmeg.
5 Pour the sauce over the cauliflower florets in the dish. Sprinkle with the rest of the Cheddar and the Parmesan. Finish with extra grated nutmeg, and bake in the oven for about 10 minutes, until bubbling and golden brown.

Mac 'n Cheese

This American midweek staple is real comfort food. Given a little thought, you can turn a rather mundane dish into something really delicious.

Serves 4

1 pound (450 g) macaroni or elbow-shape pasta
¼ cup (4 tablespoons/60 g) unsalted butter, beef dripping, or bacon fat, plus extra as needed
¼ cup (30 g) all-purpose flour
5 cups (2½ pints/1.2 litres) whole milk, warmed
½ teaspoon salt
½ teaspoon freshly ground black pepper
generous 1 teaspoon English mustard powder
1 pound (450 g) strong farmhouse Cheddar cheese, such as Shelburne, or Lincolnshire Poacher cheese, or a mixture of Parmesan and Cheddar cheese, grated
Dry breadcrumbs (1–2 day-old bread, dried, not toasted), tossed in a little melted butter, for sprinkling
8 slices bacon, broiled until crispy, to serve (optional)

1 Preheat the oven to 400°F (200°C). Cook the pasta until al dente; drain. Toss in a little butter, and put in an ovenproof dish. To make a roux, melt the butter over medium heat. Turn down the heat slightly, add the flour, and cook, stirring continuously, for 2 minutes.
2 Off the heat, pour a little of the milk into the roux, and mix to a creamy consistency. Place the pan back on the heat and, in a steady stream, pour in the rest of the milk, stirring until thick.
3 Take the pan off the heat, and stir in the salt, pepper, mustard, and grated cheese, mixing well. Return to the heat, and stir continuously until the cheese has melted. Pour the sauce over the macaroni in the casserole or dish, and stir to ensure that the pasta is well coated.
4 Sprinkle the top with the breadcrumbs, and bake in the oven for 15 minutes. Before serving, top with the bacon slices, if liked.

Lasagna with Bologna Sausage and Fontina Sauce

We are lucky enough at La Fromagerie to have fresh sausages direct from Bologna, Italy, with their rich, almost fruity taste, but many butchers now make their own version of this pure meat sausage. I have not used garlic because the other ingredients provide more than enough flavor. Enjoy this dish with a simple bitter leaf salad.

Serves 4–6

2–3 tablespoons olive oil, plus extra for greasing

2 red onions, finely sliced

5 or 6 fresh chunky Italian sausages made with pure meat (about 18 ounces/500 g), sliced into small rounds

7 ounces (200 g) pancetta, cut into small cubes

1 cup (250 ml) red wine (something fruity!)

18 ounces (500 g) dried lasagne sheets

2½ cups (250 g) coarsely grated fontina, plus extra for topping

2½ cups (250 g) grated Parmesan cheese, plus extra for topping

Tomato sauce:

3½ tablespoons (50 g) unsalted butter

1 tablespoon olive oil

1 large onion, finely diced

1 large carrot, finely diced

1 celery stalk, finely diced

2¼ pounds (1 kg) San Marzano or canned tomatoes, chopped

1 tablespoon finely chopped marjoram, sage, or thyme leaves

Béchamel sauce:

scant ½ cup (100 g) unsalted butter

¼ cup (30 g) unbleached all-purpose flour

3½ cups (1¾ pints/850 ml) whole milk, warmed

Freshly grated nutmeg, to taste

1 torn bay leaf

Coarse sea or kosher salt and freshly ground black pepper

1 Heat the oil in a skillet over medium heat. Add the red onions, and sauté for 5 minutes until softened. Add the sausages and pancetta, and cook until they begin to caramelize, then add the wine. Let the wine gently bubble and reduce until syrupy—around 5 minutes. Take the pan off the heat, and set aside.

2 Cook the lasagne in plenty of boiling salted water according to the packet instructions, until just al dente. Put a few sheets in at a time so that they don't stick together; I sometimes add a splash of oil to the water to prevent this from happening. Remove with a slotted spoon and set aside, then repeat with the remaining sheets. After cooking, do not pile the lasagne on top of one another because the sheets will stick together.

3 To make the tomato sauce, heat the butter and olive oil in a saucepan over medium heat until foaming. Add the onion, carrot, and celery, and sauté until softened and just starting to turn golden. Add the tomatoes and, once bubbling, turn the heat right down. Season with salt and pepper, add the herbs, and cook very slowly for at least 30 minutes, until a rich, thick sauce—you want to achieve a thick purée. Set aside.

4 To make the béchamel sauce, melt the butter in a heavy saucepan, then stir in the flour and let this cook, stirring continuously, for 2–3 minutes, but do not let it brown. Gradually pour the warm milk into the roux in a steady stream, stirring all the time, until it reaches a lovely thick, creamy consistency. Season with salt, pepper, and a little nutmeg. Add the bay leaf, and continue cooking the sauce over very low heat for 15 minutes, stirring regularly.

5 To assemble, lightly oil a deep 8–12 inch x 10 inch (20–30 x 25 cm) ovenproof dish, either glass or terra cotta. Spoon a little of the béchamel over the bottom of the dish, add a layer of lasagne sheets, then spoon over half of the sausage mixture, followed by half of the tomato sauce, another layer of pasta, then béchamel; sprinkle with half of the fontina and Parmesan. Repeat this again, and finally top with a slick of béchamel and the remaining fontina and Parmesan.

6 Place the lasagna on the middle shelf of a preheated 375°C (190°C) oven, and bake for 40–45 minutes, until golden on top and bubbling.

Shepherd's (and Cottage) Pie with Potato and Lancashire Mash

I prefer a shepherd's pie to have ground beef as well as lamb, hence the combined names in the title ("shepherd" for lamb, "cottage" for beef). This family-style meal can be adjusted and changed to your taste, but this is how my family prefer it!

Serves 6–8

2–3 tablespoons olive oil
2 large onions, finely sliced
2 large carrots, chopped or grated
1 pound 5 ounces (600 g) ground beef
14 ounces (400 g) ground lamb
1 tablespoon tomato paste
Knob of unsalted butter
5 cremini or 4 portobello mushrooms, sliced
2 tablespoons Worcestershire sauce
1 tablespoon mushroom ketchup
Freshly grated nutmeg, to taste
1 tablespoon finely chopped thyme leaves
Salt and freshly ground black pepper

Mash:

3¼ pounds (1.5 kg) baking potatoes such as russet or Yukon Gold, peeled and cut into chunks
1 large celeriac, peeled and cut into chunks
1 cup (250 ml) whole milk
⅔ cup (1 stick plus 3 tablespoons/150 g) unsalted butter
18 ounces (500 g) Lancashire cheese, grated (about 4½ cups), plus generous ¼ cup (30 g) extra
⅔ cup (150 ml) heavy cream

1 Preheat the oven to 400°F (200°F). In a large skillet, heat the olive oil over medium heat, then sauté the onions and carrots for about 5 minutes until softened. Add the ground beef and lamb, and cook until browned, breaking the meat down with the back of a spoon or a fork. Add the tomato paste and cook, stirring, for a few minutes.

2 In a separate pan, melt a knob of butter over high heat until foaming, and add the mushrooms. Cook for a few minutes until liquid starts to seep out of the mushrooms, then take off the heat. Using a slotted spoon, take the mushrooms out of the pan, shaking off as much liquid as possible.

3 Add the mushrooms to the meat, then stir in the Worcestershire sauce and mushroom ketchup. Finely grate over some nutmeg, being careful at first, then taste before adding more. Add the thyme, then season with salt and pepper to taste. Turn the heat right down and, cover the pan, and cook gently for another 8 minutes.

4 While the meat is cooking, to make the mash, steam the potatoes and celeriac (rather than boiling them in water) until tender; test whether they are done by piercing with a skewer. Take off the heat, pour away the water, and return the vegetables to the empty pan to "dry" them over low heat for a minute or two—take off the heat.

5 In a small pan, heat the milk with the butter. When hot but not boiling, start pouring the mixture slowly onto the potatoes, beating as you go. Continue until the milk and butter are incorporated and the mixture is smooth. Stir in the 18 ounces (500 g) cheese, before adding the cream, then season with salt and pepper to taste.

6 Spoon the meat mixture into a 12 x 2-inch (30 x 5-cm)-deep ovenproof dish or similar, and top with the creamy mash. Using a fork, make little peaks in the potato, then scatter over the extra cheese. Bake in the oven for 25–30 minutes, until the top is golden and the meat bubbling beneath.

Veal Scallop with Taleggio and Sage

Rose veal has a delicate flavor, and is not to be confused with baby white veal, which in the past had put many people off buying it because of the way the animals were reared. This is veal with a good conscience. It has an affinity with cheeses such as Taleggio, with its salty, creamy taste, but you could easily use a goat cheese.

Serves 1

Flatten the veal scallop or escalope with a flat wooden paddle or wooden spatula. Place thin slices of cooked ham or prosciutto di Parma on top to cover, followed by thin slices of Taleggio (a young one would be best for this dish), and finally a leaf or two of fresh sage.

Roll up the veal, and secure with one or two toothpicks, to hold the filling in place. Dust the roll in seasoned flour, coating all sides and ends, then dip in beaten egg. Lift out and shake off any excess egg, then dust again in flour to coat well.

In a skillet, heat 2–3 tablespoons olive or sunflower oil and 3½ tablespoons (50 g) unsalted butter over medium heat until the butter has melted. Pan-fry the veal roll, carefully turning to cook all sides, for 5–8 minutes, until golden and cooked through.

Drain on paper towels, carefully remove the toothpicks, and serve with sautéed potatoes and green beans, or a rich and densely fruity tomato sauce. This is for one serving; if you are cooking for more people, increase the quantity of ingredients accordingly.

Alpine Sautéed Brown Trout

The monastery of La Grande Chartreuse is hidden away in the mountains of the national park of Chartreuse. It was here that the wonderfully aromatic green liqueur Chartreuse was invented by the monks. This protected area of natural beauty is a magnet for tourists at all times of the year. The rushing streams are home to trout, and a day can be very pleasantly spent fishing and picnicking. Here is a recipe of stark simplicity that says a lot about its origins.

Serves 1

1 brown trout, gutted and scaled
scant ½ cup (7 tablespoons/100 g) unsalted butter
1 slice of lemon
Small handful of fresh herbs, such as parsley, bay leaf, marjoram, or thyme
1 garlic clove
1 thick slice brioche or other sweet milk bread, cut into croutons
Sunflower oil, for frying (optional)
1 thick slice (about 3 ounces/85 g) ventrèche (French unsmoked bacon), bacon, or pancetta, cut into small cubes
Flour for dredging
⅓ cup (50 g) diced Beaufort Chalet d'Alpage cheese, at room temperature
Coarse sea or kosher salt and freshly ground black pepper

1 Rinse the trout under cold running water and pat dry. Salt the inside of the fish, and put a little butter, a slice of lemon, and a few herbs in the cavity.
2 Crush the garlic slightly with a knife. Put the garlic in a skillet over medium heat with a large knob of butter. When the butter is foaming, throw in the croutons, and fry for about 5 minutes until golden and crispy. Take out the skillet with a slotted spoon, drain on paper towels, and set aside.
3 There should be enough butter still in the skillet, but if not add a splash of sunflower oil and heat. Now, add the cubes of ventrèche or, if you cannot find this, bacon or pancetta, and cook until nicely golden with crispy edges. Take out with a slotted spoon, drain on paper towels, and set aside.
4 Add a good-size knob of butter to the pan with the juices from the bacon, and let it foam over medium heat. Lightly dredge the trout in flour, shaking off any excess. Put the trout in the skillet, and cook for about 2 minutes each side, depending on the size of your fish; spoon over the melted butter as the fish cooks.
5 Lift out the fish with a spatula, and drain off any excess fat. Place on a plate, and carefully remove the herb-and-lemon stuffing. Spoon a small amount of the buttery juices from the skillet over the fish.
6 Transfer the bacon and croutons to the pan, and quickly heat through, then, using a slotted spoon, arrange them around the trout. Finally, add the cubes of Beaufort, and serve with a chilled glass of Chignin Bergeron.

Seasonal Risottos

Risotto and cheese work so well together, and there are numerous ways of incorporating the latter into this classic Italian dish. I have given a few variations, all with a seasonal slant, but what you won't see is the addition of mascarpone cheese, which I feel is far too rich for risotto. If you use a good-quality cheese, you will not need to add mascarpone.

Spring Risotto

Around Easter, or perhaps a little later if it falls at the beginning of April, local seasonal asparagus starts appearing. Also making a welcome appearance are spring herbs, and peas and fave (fava) beans from continental Europe. Follow the method closely for this green risotto, and you will have the most wonderfully aromatic, tasty dish. Do also remember that the rice will continue to cook in hot liquid, even if you think it is not quite ready at step 4. Have faith!

Serves 6–8

6½ pounds (3 kg) fresh, unpodded green peas, shelled (about 16 cups/4½ pounds/2 kg prepared weight) (or cheat with 6¾ cups/900 g frozen green peas)

2 large handfuls of fresh fava beans, shelled and squeezed out of their hard skins

2 bundles of fresh asparagus (about 1½ pounds/600 g), trimmed and each sliced diagonally into 3 pieces

2 tablespoons finely chopped mint leaves

1 cup (2 sticks) plus 2 tablespoons (250 g) unsalted butter

18 ounces (500 g) cipolotti onions or large scallions, roughly chopped

2 large garlic cloves, finely chopped

1 pound (450 g) Carnaroli rice

6½ cups (about 1½ quarts/1.5 litres) hot low-sodium chicken stock (see page 238)

Small handful of fresh basil leaves

⅔ cup (150 ml) dry white wine or vermouth

3½ ounces (100 g) Seirass ewe's milk ricotta or buffalo ricotta, or fresh cow's milk ricotta, crumbled (see page 228)

Finely grated zest of 2 large lemons

Large handful of coarsely grated pecorin toscana or pecorino sardo cheese

Coarse sea or kosher salt and freshly ground black pepper

1 Cook the peas, fava beans, and asparagus with half of the mint in simmering salted water for a couple of minutes until tender but still with a bite (not soft). Drain the vegetables and mint, reserving scant ½ cup (100 ml) of the cooking water. Return the drained vegetables and mint to the reserved water, and set aside.

2 In a large heavy saucepan, melt half of the butter over medium heat, then add the onions, stir, and sauté for about 8 minutes, until softened. Add the garlic, then pour in the rice. Mix with a wooden spoon for a few minutes until the rice is coated in the buttery onions.

3 Now start to add the hot stock, one ladleful at a time, stirring as you go. When the rice has absorbed the liquid, add another ladleful of stock; this will take 8–10 minutes. (The rice will continue to cook in the heat of the pan.)

4 Return the peas, fava beans, and asparagus with the reserved liquid to the pan. Tear the basil leaves, and add them to the pan with the wine or vermouth.

5 Crumble in half of the ricotta, and stir in the remaining butter, then continue to cook for a few minutes, stirring, until the butter has melted into the rice. Taste the rice; it should now be tender with the center of each grain still al dente. Fold in the rest of the fresh mint.

6 To serve, divide the risotto among the plates, top with the remaining ricotta, and sprinkle over the lemon zest and pecorino. Add a final seasoning of salt and black pepper, and it's ready.

Cook's Note

❧ The mint can be replaced with nettles, but blanch them first to remove most of the "sting." Their sharp, vibrant flavor will complement the vegetables. Also around at this time of year is wild leek, or ramp, found growing prolifically by streams and in meadows in woodland areas in some parts of the United States. Its European equivalent is known as wild garlic, and both have broad green leaves and white flowers. Wild leek tastes very strong, but can be used in small quantities in risottos, especially when served alongside a roast chicken.

Summer Risotto

This version uses baby artichokes, available from late summer, which are so tender and need hardly any preparation or trimming, combined with sweet, salty, crumbly pecorino.

Serves 6–8

Make the risotto with 3 large white onions, which you have first finely chopped and sautéed in butter and olive oil until softened, then add the rice and stock, and continue as for the Spring Risotto (page 261). Just before serving, add pan-fried sliced baby artichokes or artichoke hearts with a large handful of grated pecorino Vilanetto from Tuscany, with its flaky texture and rich, creamy taste.

Cook's Note

🍴 Ricotta salata made with buffalo milk is an excellent alternative to the pecorino. This useful hard cheese has a delicious salty yet creamy taste and can be grated into the risotto. It also goes well in a tomato risotto with a lot of lovely fresh basil.

Fall Risotto

This is such a beautifully textured dish—intensely creamy with a deep golden color. The strength of the cheese makes a great foil to the sweetness of the pumpkin, and the topping of aromatic crispy sage leaves really does finish off the dish.

Serves 6–8

Roast chunks of pumpkin in the oven with a little oil, grated lemon zest, and finely chopped chile pepper. Follow the instructions for the Spring Risotto on page 261, then, just before serving, stir in the roasted pumpkin, as well as crumbled Gorgonzola naturale for a strong flavor or Gorgonzola dolce for a creamier taste. Stir the cheese into the rice, gently heating it until melted, then serve sprinkled with crispy fresh sage leaves (fried in a little olive oil until toasted).

Cook's Note

🍴 Wild mushrooms are available in abundance in early fall, and their bosky, earthy flavor and aroma work well in risotto. Porcini mushrooms have a unique flavour, but are expensive, so use in combination with chanterelle and cremini mushrooms. Stir the mushrooms into the risotto, along with a soft primo-sale or fresh cow's milk ricotta and 1 tablespoon finely chopped thyme leaves. Sprinkle with an aged Grana Padano cheese instead of Parmesan before serving.

Winter Risotto

I love cavolo nero, Italian black cabbage, with its dark, greeny-black leaves. It is a great vegetable with both meat and fish dishes, but follow the original risotto recipe on page 261, then carry on as below, and you will have a really lovely fragrant yet savory dish.

Serves 6–8

Braise thinly sliced cavolo nero in a large pan with olive oil, a splash of water, thinly sliced garlic, finely chopped fresh rosemary, and salt and pepper. This will only take a minute or two (you know when the cavolo is ready because it will stop sizzling and hissing in the pan). Work this through the risotto, adding copious amounts of finely shaved Parmigiano-Reggiano cheese before serving.

Cook's Note

🍴 January and February can be bleak months, but there are still herbs around, and trevisana (Italian red chicory) and Castelfranco (looks like a lettuce but is a beautiful speckled green and red chicory) are delicious with finely chopped fresh thyme leaves and flat-leaf parsley, diced pancetta, and a lot of tangy pecorino toscano from the last of the November cheesemaking, before the winter sets in.

Tarts

If there is one thing that the kitchen at La Fromagerie does well, it's savory tarts. Every single day several come up for lunch at 12.30, adorned with different cheeses. I can safely say that, although the word "quiche" seems kitsch, for me, the savory tart lives on forever. I suggest that you go with the seasons for the vegetable fillings and embrace the wonderful offerings.

Savory Tarts

There are endless permutations on the savory tart, but the important thing to remember when making a tart is that the cheese used in the filling should not be so strong that it dominates the flavor of the other ingredients. There are a few variations given here and on page 269, but all use the same basic recipe for the flaky pastry shell and savory custard filling.

Serves 6
Flaky Pastry:
6 tablespoons (85 g) cold unsalted butter, cut into small pieces, plus extra for greasing
1½ cups (175 g) all-purpose flour, sifted, plus extra for dusting
Good pinch of salt, sifted
1 organic egg, plus 1 egg white, lightly beaten
Savory Custard Filling:
1¼ cups (300 ml) heavy cream
2 large organic eggs, lightly beaten
¼ teaspoon coarse sea or kosher salt
¼ teaspoon freshly ground black pepper

1 To make the pastry, using your fingertips, rub the butter into the flour until the mixture has the consistency of fine breadcrumbs. Stir in the salt, whole egg, and a splash or two of water, and bring together still using your fingers. Knead lightly to form into a ball of dough, then wrap in plastic wrap and let rest for 10-15 minutes in the refrigerator. (Alternatively, make the dough in a food processor.)

2 Preheat the oven to 400°F (200°C). Lightly grease a 10-inch (25-cm) loose-bottom tart pan, then dust with flour, tipping out any excess. Roll out the dough on a lightly floured counter, and use to line the prepared pan, making sure that you do not have any cracks or splits in the pastry. Trim the top of the pastry shell, and line the bottom with parchment paper, then pour in pie weights or dried beans to cover.

3 Bake on the middle shelf of the oven for 10 minutes, then remove the weights or beans and the parchment paper. Lightly brush with the egg white (this helps to seal the pastry shell), and return the pastry shell to the oven to bake for another 3–5 minutes, until a pale golden color. Remove from the oven, and let cool before filling with the savory custard.

4 To make the filling, mix together the ingredients for the savory custard filling in a pitcher. To flavor the tart, choose one of the options either at right or on page 269.

Selles sur Cher and Tomato

I love the oval-shape San Marzano tomato because it is superb used for simple tomato sauces or roasted in the oven with herbs and olive oil, and served warm alongside steak and French fries. The flavor is really fruity and the flesh does not disintegrate; there is also no need to remove the skins—just use them whole and enjoy their wonderful taste.

5 large San Marzano tomatoes, halved
Olive oil (not a strongly flavored one), to drizzle
2 Selles sur Cher cheese (about 6 ounces/175 g each) or other fresh, crumbly goat cheese, cut into wedges
scant ½ cup (7 tablespoons/100 g) unsalted butter
2 large onions, finely sliced
Small handful of fresh basil leaves, roughly torn
1 tablespoon finely chopped fresh thyme
Coarse sea or kosher salt and freshly ground black pepper

1 Follow the instructions for the pastry shell at left. Preheat the oven to 350°F (180°C). Put the tomatoes on a baking sheet, drizzle over a little olive oil, and sprinkle with salt. Roast in the oven for 10 minutes, until softened and slightly caramelized around the edges; set aside.

2 Mash a quarter of the Selles sur Cher, then stir into the savory custard (see left) mixture.

3 In a skillet over medium heat, melt the butter until foaming, then sauté the onions for about 5 minutes until softened. Let cool a little before spooning into the pastry shell. Sit the tart on a baking sheet (this makes it easier to transfer to the oven).

4 Carefully pour half of the savory custard into the shell, then arrange the tomatoes and Selles sur Cher on top. Scatter over the basil and thyme, and season with salt and pepper. Pour over the remaining savory custard.

5 Put the baking sheet on the center shelf of the oven, and cook for about 30 minutes, until golden on top.

Broccoli and Bleu des Causses

scant ½ cup (7 tablespoons/100 g) unsalted butter
18 ounces (500 g) shallots, finely sliced
9 ounces (250 g) smoked pancetta, cut into small cubes
4¼ cups (300 g) broccoli florets, cut into bite-size pieces
10½ ounces (300 g) Bleu des Causses or other strong blue cheese, crumbled
1 tablespoon chopped sage leaves
Coarse sea or kosher salt and freshly ground black pepper

1 Follow the instructions for the pastry shell on page 265. Preheat the oven to 400°F (200°C). In a skillet over medium heat, melt the butter until foaming, then sauté the shallots until just turning golden. Add the pancetta, and sauté until the pancetta is starting to turn crispy. Add the broccoli, and sauté for a few minutes until al dente. Let cool to room temperature.
2 Arrange the broccoli mixture over the bottom of the pastry shell. Put the tart on a baking sheet (this makes it easier to transfer to the oven). Carefully pour over the savory custard (see page 265), then sprinkle with the blue cheese and sage leaves. Season with salt and pepper, and bake in the oven for 20–25 minutes, until golden on top.

Pumpkin and Goat Cheese

18 ounces (500 g) butternut squash or pumpkin, seeded and cut into bite-size chunks
2 tablespoons extra virgin olive oil
1 tablespoon finely chopped marjoram leaves, plus extra for sprinkling
1 red chile pepper, seeded and finely chopped
18 ounces (500 g) fresh spinach (about 12 cups)
9 ounces (250 g) rindless fresh caprini or Ryefield goat cheese, crumbled
Coarse sea or kosher salt and freshly ground black pepper

1 Follow the instructions for the pastry shell on page 265. Preheat the oven to 400°F (200°C). Put the pumpkin in a roasting pan, drizzle over the olive oil, and sprinkle with the marjoram and chile. Season with salt and pepper. Roast for 25–30 minutes, until the pumpkin is tender and slightly caramelized. Remove from the pan, and let cool to room temperature.
2 Heat a little olive oil in a skillet over medium heat, and cook the spinach until just wilted. Let it cool to room temperature, drain off any excess liquid, and spoon into the pastry shell. Top the spinach with the pumpkin.
3 Put the tart on a baking sheet. Pour in the savory custard (see page 265), then sprinkle with the goat cheese and a little marjoram. Season with salt and pepper, and bake in the oven for 20–25 minutes, until golden on top.

Red Pepper and Ricotta

3 large red bell peppers, seeded and thickly sliced
scant ½ cup (7 tablespoons/100 g) unsalted butter
2 large onions, finely sliced
10½ ounces (300 g) Seirass ewe's milk ricotta or buffalo or cow's milk ricotta, crumbled
Handful of fresh basil leaves, roughly torn
Coarse sea or kosher salt and freshly ground black pepper

1 Follow the instructions for the pastry shell on page 265. Preheat the oven to 400°F (200°C). To prepare the bell peppers, arrange the slices on a baking sheet, and roast in the oven for 15 minutes, until the skin is blackened. Put them in a bowl, and cover with plastic wrap. Once cool enough to handle, rub off and discard the blackened skins. Set the flesh aside.
2 In a large skillet over medium heat, melt the butter until foaming, then add the onions and sauté for about 5 minutes until softened. Let cool to room temperature, before spooning into the pastry shell. Put the tart on a baking sheet (this makes it easier to transfer to the oven).
3 Arrange the roasted peppers on top of the onions. Pour in the savory custard (see page 265), then sprinkle with the crumbled ricotta and basil. Season with salt and pepper, and bake in the oven for 20–25 minutes, until golden on top.

Leek and Beaufort

2 large leeks, trimmed of most of the green part, washed, and finely sliced
scant ½ cup (7 tablespoons/100 g) unsalted butter
4 large shallots, finely sliced
3 cups (300 g) coarsely grated Beaufort Chalet d'Alpage cheese
Freshly grated nutmeg
1 teaspoon finely chopped thyme leaves
Coarse sea or kosher salt and freshly ground black pepper

1 Follow the instructions for the pastry shell on page 265. Preheat the oven to 400°F (200°C), and pat dry the washed leeks. In a large skillet over medium heat, melt the butter until foaming. Add the shallots, and sauté for a few minutes until softened. Next, add the leeks and continue to sauté until soft and starting to turn golden.
2 Let the onions and leeks cool to room temperature, before spooning into the pastry shell. Put the tart on a baking sheet (this makes it easier to transfer to the oven).
3 Pour over the savory custard (see page 265), then scatter over the Beaufort. Finally grate over about ¼ teaspoon nutmeg or to taste, sprinkle with the thyme, and season with salt and pepper. Bake in the oven for 20–25 minutes, until golden on top.

Twice-Baked Soufflés with Mimolette

You can prepare the soufflés in advance, and freeze or chill until required, then in a matter of minutes you've prepared an impressive light supper or appetizer. I have used Mimolette, which is a hard cheese from Flandres, because its lovely orange color lends a warmth to the soufflés.

Makes 6 individual soufflés

3½ tablespoons (50 g) unsalted butter, plus extra for greasing
10 ounces (280 g) aged Mimolette cheese
scant 1 cup (225 ml) whole milk
1 small shallot, peeled and studded with 2 cloves
1 bay leaf
6 whole black peppercorns
⅓ cup (40 g) unbleached all-purpose flour
4 large organic eggs, separated
generous ¾ cup (85 g) finely grated Parmesan cheese
Fine sea or kosher salt and freshly ground black pepper

1　Brush the insides of six 3 x 1½-inch (7.5 cm x 4-cm)-deep ramekins with softened butter, using even upward strokes, then chill and repeat again. Finely grate a generous ¾ cup (85 g) of the Mimolette, then use to coat the insides of the ramekins. Chill the ramekins again while preparing the soufflé mixture.

2　Heat the milk, shallot, bay leaf, and peppercorns in a medium saucepan until it reaches simmering point, then strain the milk into a pitcher, throwing away the solid ingredients. Rinse out the saucepan.

3　Melt the butter in the rinsed-out saucepan, and add the flour. Cook over medium-low heat for about 3 minutes, stirring continuously, until it forms a smooth, pale golden paste. Gradually add the strained milk, whisking (use a small balloon whisk) until the sauce has thickened and starts to leave the sides of the pan. Season lightly with salt and pepper, and cook the sauce over the lowest heat possible for 2 minutes, stirring now and then. If you find the paste is too stiff, add a little more warm milk (be careful not to make the mixture too soft because there are the other ingredients to add).

4　Preheat the oven to 350°F (180°C). Remove the pan from the heat and let it cool slightly, before starting to beat in the egg yolks, one at a time. Coarsely grate the remaining Mimolette and add a generous 1 cup (115 g) of the cheese to the soufflé mixture; stir until almost melted.

5　In a large metal bowl, whisk the egg whites to soft peaks, then gently fold a spoonful of the stiffened egg white into the soufflé mixture to loosen it a little. Now gently add the rest of the mixture to the egg whites, using a large metal spoon in a cutting and folding motion.

6　Divide the mixture equally among the ramekins. Put them in a roasting pan placed on the center shelf of the preheated oven, then carefully pour boiling water into the pan until it reaches halfway up the sides of the ramekins. Bake the soufflés for 20 minutes, then remove them from the bain-marie to a wire rack. (It is not a problem if they sink a little while cooling because they will rise again during the second cooking.)

7　When they are almost cold, run a small palette knife around the edge of each ramekin. Carefully turn the soufflés out onto the palm of your hand, then place them the right way up on a lightly greased baking sheet. They can now be kept in the refrigerator for up to 24 hours, lightly covered with a double layer of wax paper and with plastic wrap loosely placed over the top.

8　To reheat the soufflés, preheat the oven to 350°F (180°C). Take the soufflés out of the refrigerator, and wait until they reach room temperature. Mix the Parmesan with the remaining Mimolette, and sprinkle over the top of the soufflés, then place them in the oven, on the shelf above the center, for 30 minutes until risen and golden.

Cook's Notes

There are a few tricks when making a soufflé to ensure perfect results every time:

❦ Use a large balloon whisk when whisking egg whites. Alternatively, start off with an electric mixer, then finish off whisking by hand—it does make all the difference.

❦ If possible, use a metal bowl when whisking egg whites and make sure that it is scrupulously clean and there are no traces of grease. If necessary, rub the cut half of a lemon over the inside to neutralize the surface.

❦ Preparation is key if you want your soufflé to rise. Brush softened butter using even upward strokes over the inside of the ramekins or dish. Do this once, then chill the ramekins and repeat again. Then coat the insides of the ramekins with finely grated cheese, such as Parmesan or, as in this particular recipe, a mature Mimolette. Chill the ramekins again, before filling with the soufflé mixture.

❦ Always preheat the oven in readiness for the soufflé because having the oven at the correct temperature before starting to cook is essential.

❦ To help the soufflés cook evenly, sit the ramekins in a baking pan and place on the middle shelf of the oven. Carefully pour hot water into the pan until it reaches halfway up the sides of the ramekins, to make a water bath, or bain-marie.

Tatin of Caramelized Shallots and Persillé du Marais

We make dozens of versions of this Tatin simply because they are so easy and quick to prepare. Tiny Tatins make great canapés or appetizers, while larger ones—the size of a side plate—can be served as a lunchtime dish or first course; they are rather like a fashionable pizza!

Serves 2–4
7 ounces (200 g) store-bought puff pastry
Flour for dusting
scant ½ cup (7 tablespoons/100 g) unsalted butter
18 ounces (500 g) medium shallots, halved
1 teaspoon balsamic vinegar
1 teaspoon chopped thyme leaves
6 ounces (175 g) Persillé du Marais or Roquefort cheese

1 Preheat the oven to 400°F (200°C). Roll out the pastry on a lightly floured counter, to fit snugly into a 6-inch (15-cm) ovenproof skillet (allow a little extra for pressing down the sides); set aside in a cool place.
2 Melt the butter in the skillet over medium heat and, when foaming, add the shallots and cook, turning and coating them in the butter, until they start to caramelize.
3 Pour over the balsamic vinegar. Shake the skillet until the shallots are coated, then sprinkle with the thyme.

4 Place the sheet of puff pastry neatly over the onions as you would if making an apple tarte Tatin, and press down the edges. Put the skillet in the oven on the middle shelf, and bake for 15 minutes, or until the pastry is golden. Carefully turn out onto a serving plate, and crumble over chunks of Persillé du Marais or Roquefort before serving.

Pissaladière

Typical street food in the South of France, pissaladière is simple to make and you can vary the topping depending on the season, although traditionally it is caramelized onion, anchovies, and small black niçoise olives. When ready to serve, slice into squares or triangles, but be quite generous—no dainty little portions!

Makes 9 portions
Preheat the oven to 400°C (200°F). Roll out 9 ounces (250 g) store-bought puff pastry (try to get one that is made with butter) into a thin square, and place on a lightly oiled baking sheet. Score the pastry ½ inch (1 cm) from the inside edge, to form a ridge.

In a skillet, heat 4 tablespoons (55 g) butter and 1 tablespoon olive oil until foaming. Turn down the heat to very low, and gently cook 3–4 finely sliced onions until golden and almost caramelized (the onions should be meltingly soft and tender, but not bitter from browning), then let cool. Arrange the onions in a thick layer over the pastry; you want to be generous.

Shave thin shards of Comté cheese, about 10½ ounces (300 g), over the onions—again being very generous—and bake in the oven for 15 minutes, until the pastry is golden and the topping bubbling and brown. Let cool to room temperature, then cut into wedges.

Cook's Note
❧ You can vary this recipe by crumbling a fresh young goat cheese over the caramelized onions with perhaps roasted baby tomatoes and pitted black olives. Or try fontina or Manchego cheese in place of the Comté.

Salads & Sides

The most important part of cooking is understanding ingredients and being able to mix them in a cohesive way. When it comes to salads, you may not be actually doing a lot of cooking, but you are putting together a selection of items that not only work together, but also have textures and tastes that surprise and delight the palate and look beautiful on the plate.

Castelfranco Salad with Cashel Blue and Pears

Castelfranco salad greens are grown in and around Venice, and in the past would be seen growing wild. The delicate pale green and cream leaves have red flecks, which almost look as if they've been painted on, and taste like a cross between endive and treviso (a type of radicchio), with a bitter, nutty flavor. They are delicious when partnered with sweet fruit such as pears. The Italians love "agro dolce" (sweet–savory) flavors, and this is a perfect salad to serve as an appetizer to an entrée of fish or chicken.

Serves 2

12–16 hazelnuts or fresh cobnuts, shelled
1 head of Castelfranco lettuce
2 tablespoon Ligurian or Provençal extra virgin olive oil
2 teaspoons verjuice or light white wine vinegar
1 bay leaf, torn
1 dessert pear, such as Comice, or 2 Martin Sec (a small dessert pear from Piedmont), quartered, cored, and sliced with skin on
2 ounces (60 g) Cashel Blue, Bavarian Blue, or other mild blue cheese
Coarse sea or kosher salt and freshly ground black pepper

1 Put the hazelnuts or fresh cobnuts in a dry skillet and toast for a couple of minutes until light golden. Put in a clean dish towel, to rub off the papery brown skins if necessary, then roughly crush.
2 Tear the Castelfranco leaves, rather than cut or chop them—this looks so much better and tastes better, too, because they retain more of their crunch.
3 To prepare the dressing, mix together the olive oil, verjuice or white wine vinegar, and bay leaf in a small bowl, then season with salt and pepper. Dip the slices of pear in the dressing, and arrange them on the leaves.
4 Crumble over the blue cheese, and sprinkle with the nuts. Spoon over a tablespoon or so of the dressing (discarding the bay leaf), until all the leaves are lightly coated but not swamped, and serve immediately.

Winter Leaf Salad with Orange

Just the thought of actually being able to serve a seasonal salad in the middle of December fills me with joy, and this is the kind of dish that I like to serve as an appetizer or starter for our family Christmas lunch.

Serves 4–6
1 large handful of wild watercress
1 large handful of barbe de capucin or other wild chicory
2 medium-size treviso leaves
1 large head of Castelfranco lettuce
2–3 Tarocco oranges, depending on their size, because they are not a traditionally large fruit
1 small handful of shelled hazelnuts (optional)
7–9 ounces (200–250 g) capretta semihard goat cheese, shaved
Dressing:
¼ cup (60 ml) new-season Tuscan extra virgin olive oil – new-season single-estate oils are available from December
2 tablespoons verjuice or light white wine vinegar

1 Trim the watercress and barbe de capucin of any tough stalks, and wash the leaves under running water, then shake off excess water and pat dry with paper towels. Cut the trevise into long boat-shaped wedges, and roughly tear the Castelfranco leaves. Put the salad greens in a shallow serving bowl.

2 Using a small sharp knife, remove the peel and any pith from the oranges, then cut into segments by scoring in between the membrane of the orange. Put the segments in a separate bowl, and squeeze out any remaining juice in the membrane.

3 If using the hazelnuts, toast them whole in a dry skillet, shaking the nuts occasionally, until light golden. Remove the hazelnuts from the skillet, wrap in a clean dish towel, and bash them with the end of a rolling pin until roughly broken—don't be too harsh because you want the nuts to be chunky. Set the nuts aside in a bowl.

4 To finish the salad, sprinkle over the olive oil and verjuice or white wine vinegar—enough to coat the leaves without drowning them—then turn the leaves to amalgamate them. Arrange the orange segments between the leaves, with the excess juices squeezed from the membrane of the fruit poured on top. Using a vegetable peeler or cheese shaver, shave thin slices of goat cheese on top, and as a final flourish scatter over the toasted hazelnuts, if using.

Cobb Salad

There are many variations on this famous salad, a signature dish in the Brown Derby restaurant in Hollywood, Los Angeles, named after its creator Robert H. Cobb. Here is my version, which is particularly useful after Christmas, when there are plenty of leftovers to add to it! I like the salad to be in layers, rather than mixed up together.

Serves 4

Roughly tear spinach and crisp salad greens, then put in a shallow glass salad bowl or white serving dish. Top with slices of ripe avocado (tossed in lemon juice, to prevent the flesh from turning brown) and cooked roast chicken or turkey.

Skin some tomatoes by placing them in a bowl of just boiled water for a minute or two, then scoop out of the water. Gently press the skins, and they should come away very easily. Slice the tomatoes in half, and remove the seeds, then cut the flesh into large chunks. Arrange them on top of the rest of the salad ingredients.

Make up a vinaigrette in a small bowl, with ¾ cup (90 ml) extra virgin olive oil, 1 teaspoon Dijon mustard, 3 tablespoons white wine vinegar, a splash or two of balsamic vinegar, and the grated zest of a lemon. Add some chopped fresh marjoram and thyme leaves, and season with salt and freshly ground black pepper. Whisk thoroughly, and drizzle over the salad.

Finally, roughly crumble 5½ ounces (150 g) soft blue cheese (Rogue River would be great, or Bayley Hazen Blue from Jasper Hill Farm, Vermont) over the top, and lay 6–8 thin slices of speck, baked to a crisp, across the salad.

Spring Salad of Asparagus, Proscuitto and Fava

The first of the English asparagus arrives around Easter, or just after depending on the weather, then there are Italian fava beans, fresh green peas, and purple basil all heralding the new season. What a relief, after the long, dark winter and all those delicious filling stews, to have a crisp fresh salad again. I have to tell you that I enjoy this with a glass of Prosecco because the fizz works so well with the salty and fresh flavors.

So get shelling those fresh peas and fava beans, and blanch them briefly for a minute or two. Squeeze the fava out of their thick outer skins, to reveal shiny green morsels within. Blanch the asparagus in simmering water for a matter of minutes, to retain its crisp bite; after all, this is freshly picked stuff and is equally delicious uncooked, I can assure you.

Serves 4

Toss a handful of fresh peas, fava beans, and asparagus in extra virgin olive oil, which could be a Tuscan or Provençal one, according to your preference. Next, add some chopped mint, purple basil, and delicately scented chervil, which tastes of sweet aniseed, followed by grated lemon zest and a good squeeze of fresh lemon juice; stir until combined.

Crisp up a few slices of prosciutto in the oven (the smell is almost too much to bear—it's so delicious as it wafts into the kitchen and beyond), then arrange the hot prosciutto slices on top of the salad, before finally shaving over a crumbly pecorino from Tuscany.

Marinated Feta with Watermelon, Fennel and Mint

Barrel-aged feta, which is matured for at least six months, is far removed from the plastic-wrapped versions found at the supermarket, and is a perfect example of how slow, traditional methods of cheesemaking actually make a great deal of difference to the taste and texture of a cheese.

Serves 6–8

1¾ pounds (800 g) barrel-aged feta cheese, in one piece, drained of any watery residue

Splash of sunflower oil

2 tablespoons unsalted shelled pistachio nuts

1 teaspoon nigella seeds

2 handfuls of fresh flat-leaf parsley, tough stalks removed and leaves left whole

2 fennel bulbs, thinly shaved on a mandolin or with a vegetable peeler

1 tablespoon finely chopped mint leaves

1 small watermelon (about 2¼ pounds/1 kg), skinned, seeded, and cut into 1½-inch (4-cm) cubes

Dressing:

6–8 tablespoons (60–90 ml) fruity single-estate olive oil

2 tablespoons verjuice or light white wine vinegar

Coarse sea or kosher salt and freshly ground black pepper

Marinade:

About 1 tablespoon each of finely chopped fresh herbs, including cilantro, mint, thyme, and oregano

1 small red chile pepper, seeded and finely chopped

Juice and zest of 2 lemons

6 tablespoons (60 ml) fruity single-estate olive oil

2 tablespoons verjuice or light white wine vinegar

Freshly ground black pepper

1 Put the cheese in a shallow bowl. In a separate bowl, mix together the ingredients for the marinade, season with pepper, then pour it over the cheese. Turn the cheese in the marinade until well coated. Cover the bowl with plastic wrap, and marinate in the refrigerator for an hour or two.

2 Brush a little sunflower oil over a skillet, and cook the pistachios for a few minutes, until lightly toasted (but not scorched). Remove from the skillet, and repeat this process with the nigella seeds. Coarsely crush the pistachios with the end of a rolling pin, and mix with the nigella seeds. Set aside.

3 Put the flat-leaf parsley, fennel, mint, and watermelon in a large, shallow salad dish. To make the dressing, whisk together the olive oil and verjuice or white wine vinegar, and season with salt and pepper.

4 Pour the dressing over the salad and, using your hands, gently turn the ingredients until coated. Remove the feta from the marinade, and break into large, rough chunks. Scatter over the salad, followed by the reserved pistachios and nigella seeds.

Truffade d'Auvergne

This is a traditional loose potato galette from the French Auvergne, where thin slices of Cantal cheese (a cross between Cheshire and a dry Lancashire) are placed on top of cooked potatoes before being flipped over. Don't worry if it looks a bit messy—it's all part of the charm of the dish.

Serves 4

2¼ pounds (1 kg) potatoes, peeled and thinly sliced using a mandolin or vegetable peeler

scant ½ cup (7 tablespoons/100 g) unsalted butter

3 tablespoons olive oil

3½ ounces (100 g) pancetta or smoked bacon, finely diced

1 fat garlic clove, finely chopped

6 ounces (175 g) young Cantal Laguiole, or a young tomme de Savoie, Cheshire, or aged Lancashire, thinly sliced

Coarse sea or kosher salt and freshly ground black pepper

1 Wash the potato slices in copious amounts of water, to remove the starch, then drain in a colander and pat dry with paper towels.

2 Heat the butter and oil in a heavy skillet and, when foaming, sauté the pancetta or bacon and garlic for a minute or two. Remove with a slotted spoon, and set aside. Add a little more butter and oil to the pan if you think there is insufficient to sauté the potatoes.

3 In the skillet, arrange the sliced potatoes to form a galette (a round pancake). Cook over medium heat for about 5 minutes, before turning the potatoes with a spatula to bring the golden slices to the top and the pale slices to the bottom. Add the reserved pancetta or bacon and garlic, and put a lid on the pan. After 5 minutes, turn the potatoes again and put the lid back on for another 5 minutes. By now, all the potatoes should be tender, and some should be golden brown.

4 Spread out the cheese slices over the potatoes, season with the salt and pepper, put the lid back on, and cook for another 5–10 minutes, until all the potatoes are soft. Turn off the heat, turn the potatoes again to mix in the cheese, and put the lid back on. Let stand for 5 minutes, until the cheese is all melted.

5 Serve with roasted meats or baked sausages.

Winter Roasted Vegetable Salad with Ricotta Salata

Warm winter salads are really delicious, especially when made with naturally sweet vegetables because they roast so well. Many farmers markets sell heritage carrots, which come in a range of different colors, such as purple or pink. Ricotta salata is a favorite cheese because it also serves as a condiment due to its salty flavor. It is made from either buffalo's or ewe's milk and is a hard cheese with a light crumbly texture, meaning that it is especially good sprinkled over roasted vegetables. If you find it difficult to buy locally, then substitute feta or a semihard goat cheese.

Serves 4–6
¼–⅓ cup (4–6 tablespoons/60–90 ml) fruity olive oil
 from Puglia or Tuscany
4½–6½ pounds (2–3 kg) selection of vegetables, including
 orange-fleshed pumpkin, cut into boat-shape wedges, seeded
 but with the skin on; heritage carrots, cut into long wedges;
 parsnips, scraped but not peeled, cut into long wedges; and
 red onions, peeled and cut into quarters
1 tablespoon finely chopped thyme leaves
7 ounces (200 g) ricotta salata or feta cheese, well drained
Coarse sea or kosher salt (be careful—you may not need
 much because the cheese is already salty) and freshly
 ground black pepper

1 Preheat the oven to 350°F (180°C). Brush a baking sheet with a little of the olive oil, and add the prepared vegetables, spreading them out so that they are in a single layer. Drizzle over the olive oil, to coat all of the vegetables, but not drown them.

2 Season the vegetables with salt and pepper, and top with the thyme. Place the sheet on the middle shelf of the oven, and cook for about 20 minutes—you may need to cook the vegetables for another 10–15 minutes, depending on their size—until they are tender and caramelized at the edges; test with a skewer to make sure that they are not too hard.

3 Remove the vegetables from the oven, and let cool to room temperature, or until just warm but not hot. Arrange on a shallow serving plate, and top with shavings of ricotta or crumbled feta. Serve as a side course with roasted meat or as a first course with toasted crusty bread brushed with a fruity olive oil.

Roast Beet Salad

If you are using red beets as well as the other colored types, it may be prudent to put them in a separate bowl after cooking, to prevent their color from bleeding into the others, then amalgamate just before serving.

I like to use wine vinegars from Volpaia, a Tuscan vineyard that makes its own vinegars from wine pressings. Another alternative is verjuice, which is a delicious condiment made from the unfermented juice of wine grapes, both red and white, which are picked when not fully ripe, then pressed. It lends a fresh, fruity acidity and is not as sharp as vinegar.

4–6 servings
18 ounces (500 g) mixed colored beets, including red, yellow,
 white, or candy (look out for different colored cultivars from
 farmers markets), scrubbed and green part trimmed, if needed
⅓ cup (6 tablespoons/90 ml) light white wine vinegar or verjuice
⅓ cup (6 tablespoons/90 ml) extra virgin olive oil
1 garlic clove, very finely chopped
3 tablespoons chopped fresh herbs, such as thyme, marjoram, or
 cilantro, or use a mixture
Splash of sunflower oil
Handful of halved walnuts
7 ounces (200 g) fresh rindless goat cheese such as
 Ryefield, crumbled
Coarse sea or kosher salt and freshly ground black pepper

1 Preheat the oven to 350°F (180°C). Put the beets in a roasting pan or baking dish with enough water to cover the bottom of the dish, then season with salt.

2 Tightly cover the pan or dish with foil, and bake for 40–45 minutes, until cooked through; test with a skewer to make sure that the beets are tender. Let rest until cool enough to handle.

3 Cut off the tops and roots of the beets, then peel away the skin with your fingers. Cut the beets into wedges or halves, or keep whole if small enough. Sprinkle over a few slugs of white wine vinegar or verjuice, then add the olive oil, garlic, and herbs. Season with salt and pepper.

4 Brush the merest hint of sunflower oil over a skillet, and cook the walnuts for a few minutes until lightly toasted; roughly chop. Scatter the walnuts over the beets, then top with the crumbled goat cheese before serving.

Cook's Notes

❦ Instead of scattering the goat cheese over the beet salad, serve with a crostini of goat cheese. Simply slice a baguette on the diagonal, rub with a garlic clove, and bake in the oven until crispy. Roughly mash the goat cheese, season with salt and pepper, and pile onto the crostini.

❦ Serve the beets with bitter salad greens, dressed in olive oil and white wine vinegar.

Balsamic Roasted Carrots, Red Onions, and Treviso with Beenleigh Blue

Slow-roasting really enhances the natural sweetness of carrots and onions, and when they are served as a warm salad with the addition of a sharp, tangy blue cheese, such as Beenleigh, they make a lovely appetizer, light meal, or a side dish to roasted or barbecued meats. In spring, when the small carrots appear in bunches, you can roast them whole.

Serves 4–6

4 large carrots, cut into long wedges, or 8–10 baby carrots, left whole
3 large onions, cut into quarters or sixths if very large
4 treviso leaves, sliced into 2, or 4 if very large
Extra virgin olive oil
1–2 tablespoons balsamic vinegar, to taste
2 fat garlic cloves, lightly crushed
A few fresh sage leaves and sprigs of fresh thyme
1 red chile pepper, seeded and finely chopped
Grated zest of 1 lemon
10½ ounces (300 g) Beenleigh Blue or other strong blue cheese, roughly chopped
1 tablespoon finely chopped flat-leaf parsley
Coarse sea or kosher salt (optional)

1 Preheat the oven to 425°F (220°C). Put the carrots, onions, and treviso in a large mixing bowl. Sprinkle over the olive oil and balsamic vinegar, until the vegetables are coated but not drowned. Add salt to taste, if using, and turn the vegetables with your hands to amalgamate the ingredients.

2 Spread over a large baking sheet or shallow baking pan (a deep one will be troublesome because you need to be able to turn the vegetables). Scatter the garlic, herbs, chile, and lemon zest over the vegetables.

3 Roast for 10–15 minutes, then turn the vegetables and return to the oven. They should be cooked in a matter of 30 minutes, but check every so often by piercing with a skewer to see whether they are tender. It is important that the vegetables are roasted at a relatively high heat, to prevent them from becoming leathery. Remove from the oven, and let cool to room temperature.

4 Put the vegetables and any residual juices in a shallow serving dish, and scatter over the Beenleigh Blue or other blue cheese. Sprinkle with parsley and a little salt, if using, and serve warm.

Cima di Rapa with Garlic and Pecorino Peperoncino

Cima di rapa is a type of broccoli (sometimes called broccoli rabe) with long, slender leaves and clusters of florets. It arrives in the shop from Italy in late winter or early spring. Also grown elsewhere now that seeds are available to buy online, it makes a welcome "green" relief after winter's root vegetable overload, and can be not only used as a side vegetable for roasted meats or fish, but also transformed into a lovely warm salad. If you see purple sprouting broccoli at the farmers market, this is just as good.

Serves 4–6

Wash and trim 2¼ pounds (1 kg) cima di rapa or purple sprouting broccoli, and put into a large saucepan with a splash of water; this amount will serve 4–6. Cover the pan with a lid, and cook over high heat, shaking the pan from time to time; it will sizzle at first, then settle down. Cook the vegetables until al dente, or until tender but still crisp. Remove and shake off as much water as possible.

In a large skillet, heat a tablespoon or two of olive oil (it doesn't have to be your best one), and gently sauté 1–2 very thinly sliced garlic cloves until slightly softened and turning light golden. Add the greens and toss well in the garlicky oil until coated. Remove from the heat, and pile onto a serving dish.

Drizzle over 2–3 tablespoons extra virgin fruity olive oil (your best one because this is the dressing). Using a vegetable peeler or cheese shaver, shave over shards of Tuscan pecorino studded with chile pepper—or, if you want a stronger flavored cheese, use the Sardinian or Sicilian hard version with chile.

Asparagus with Parmesan Butter Breadcrumbs

Although the British asparagus season starts around April, we start seeing Italian asparagus in early March and the French a couple of weeks later. The season is short, but by the time the continental asparagus is finishing, the British is in full swing, so it is rather lovely to be able to enjoy the vegetable from early spring until the beginning of summer. Serving asparagus simply with buttery breadcrumbs respects the flavor of the vegetable, while the addition of sharp, salty Parmesan cheese finishes the dish perfectly.

Serves 2

Preheat the oven to 350°F (180°C). Crumble a few slices of day-old bread, either pane toscana or another simple country-style white bread, into breadcrumbs. For every 1 cup (55 g) breadcrumbs, add ½ cup (50 g) finely grated Parmesan cheese. Mix together the crumbs and Parmesan, then spread out over a baking sheet. Toast in the oven for a few minutes, until the crumbs just begin to change color and are slightly crisp. Spoon the cheese and breadcrumbs into a saucepan, add a knob of butter, and cook over medium heat until the crumbs start to darken. Add another knob of butter, and stir until the crumbs are coated in the buttery juices. Blanch 2–3 bundles of asparagus (1½–2 pounds/600–900g) briefly until al dente. Pile the asparagus onto a serving plate, and spoon the buttery crumbs over the tips—eat with your fingers.

Cook's Note
🌱 After blanching, drain the asparagus and pat dry with paper towels, then sauté in a little olive oil until slightly golden.

Stuffed Zucchini Flowers with Ricotta

From early summer until fall, the flower attached to the tip of a zucchini—resembling a marigold-orange "lantern"—is much prized. It is perfect for stuffing, albeit a bit fussy, but well worth the effort. Serve as an appetizer with a little salad made with soft leaves and maybe fronds of chervil and fennel. Dress the leaves in a light olive oil and white wine vinegar or verjuice; you want it all to be fragrant and light. Another way is to serve the filled zucchini flowers as a vegetable accompaniment to roast lamb.

Make 12–16

First, if the zucchini are large, cut away the flowers, leaving a little stalk; if the zucchini are small, leave the flower attached.

Finely chop 2 tablespoons fresh marjoram (or another soft-leaved aromatic herb, say, chervil, thyme, or tarragon, or a mixture) and 1 small seeded red chile pepper. Put them in a bowl with the grated zest of a lemon and 10½ ounces (300 g) drained and strained fresh ricotta; this can be cow's, buffalo's, or ewe's milk. If you find it difficult to get really fresh ricotta, use a very fresh goat cheese without any rind or a really light cream cheese. Season with salt and freshly ground black pepper; mix.

Spoon the mixture into a pastry bag with a medium nozzle. Carefully open the petals of the zucchini flower (if you can remove the stamen, all the better; if the flower is small, though, you can leave it intact), and pipe in the filling mixture until about half or three-quarters full. Gently close the flower, twisting the top to prevent the filling from oozing out during cooking.

Lay the zucchini flowers, about 12–16, depending on their size, on a baking sheet, lined with parchment paper, and drizzle a little Provençal extra virgin olive oil (or one that is not too overtly spiky in flavor) over the top. Bake in a preheated 350°F (180°C) oven for 5–8 minutes; you want the zucchini, if still attached, to have a crunch.

Aligot

This is an ancient recipe created for the pilgrims in Southwest France. Ideally, you should use tomme fraîche, which is a Cantal cheese that is freshly made so that it does not have a rind or crust. A specialty cheese dealer may be able to order some for you.

Serves 4
scant ½ cup (7 tablespoons/100 g) unsalted butter
2 fat garlic cloves (new-season garlic is particularly good)
2¼ pounds (1 kg) baking potatoes such as russet or Yukon Gold
⅔ cup (150 ml) heavy cream (or a single, if preferred), preferably unpasteurized Jersey cow's milk
14 ounces (400 g) tomme fraîche or a young Lancashire, Cheshire, Wensleydale, or Cantal, grated
Coarse sea or kosher salt

1 Melt the butter with the garlic in a saucepan, remove from the heat, and leave to infuse—the garlic should become very soft. Mash the garlic into the butter, then set aside while you cook the potatoes.

2 Steam the potatoes in their skins until cooked through (pierce with a skewer to make sure that they are very soft). Peel off and discard the skins, and put the potatoes back in the saucepan, which should have been rinsed and dried first. Dry the potatoes over very low heat, then mash them by either passing through a potato ricer or mashing with a fork until they are almost smooth. Beat in the garlic butter.

3 Pour in the cream and, over low heat, beat the mash with a large wooden spoon, preferably with a flat round end (it may be difficult to find this kind of spoon, but otherwise just use a usual one). Use the same technique as you would for fondue, stirring in a figure-eight motion with a loose wrist action, until the texture changes and becomes creamy.

4 Continue to stir the mixture in a figure-eight motion while you gradually add the cheese, then start to lift the mixture to stretch it—it should snap back into the pan. When all the cheese has been added, taste, then add salt, if needed. Serve with roasted meats or cured ham.

a skewer to make sure that it is not hard in the center, but nicely cooked all the way through. Remove from the oven, and let stand until cool enough to handle.

3 In a skillet, melt the butter with a tablespoon or two of olive oil until foaming, and sauté the chanterelles. (You can tell when the mushrooms are cooked because the hissing sound suddenly subsides.) Remove from the pan with a slotted spoon, and set aside.

4 Grate 1¾ ounces (50 g) of the Parmesan (a scant ½ cup grated). Heat the cream with the grated Parmesan, garlic, and the remaining sage, until the cheese has melted and the cream is warmed through, but not too hot. Season with pepper.

5 Arrange the pumpkin on individual warm serving plates with the chanterelle mushrooms, then spoon over a little of the cream sauce. Using a vegetable peeler or cheese shaver, shave the remaining Parmesan over the vegetables. Serve immediately with an accompaniment of bitter salad greens and toasted bread, such as a country-style pagnotta or ciabatta, with a little olive oil drizzled over the top.

Roasted Pumpkin with Chanterelles and Parmesan Cream

The fall colors of this warm salad make it picture perfect. The marriage of the sweet pumpkin, earthy chanterelle mushrooms, and the salty–savory Parmesan give it great appeal. It makes a lovely lunch dish in its own right, or can be served as an accompaniment to roast veal.

Serves 4

3¼ pounds (1.5 kg) orange-fleshed pumpkin, skin intact, seeded and cut into wedges

1–2 tablespoons olive oil, plus extra for drizzling

2 tablespoons finely chopped sage leaves

3½ tablespoons (50 g) unsalted butter

10½ ounces (300 g) fresh chanterelle mushrooms, or other wild mushroom of your choice

5½ ounces (150 g) aged Parmesan cheese

1¼ cups (300 ml) unpasteurized (if available) heavy Jersey or similar cream

1 garlic clove, very finely chopped

Coarse sea or kosher salt and freshly ground black pepper

1 Preheat the oven to 350°F (180°C). Put the pumpkin in a roasting pan, and drizzle over some olive oil, then scatter half of the sage leaves over the top and season with salt and pepper.

2 Bake in the oven for 35–40 minutes, until the pumpkin is tender and is caramelized around the edges—test with

Desserts, Breads, & Biscuits

I love rich, creamy desserts, and I urge you to buy the best-quality cream or mascarpone, which has not, if possible, been treated in any way. Simple savory breads, biscuits, and wafers really are easy.

Tiramesù

This dessert is traditionally a combination of zabaglione (a Venetian foamy egg custard made with Marsala wine), pastry cream, mascarpone cream, and savoiardi cookies, drizzled with strong espresso coffee. I think that we can go slightly off-piste, however, and create something a little simpler, although just as rich. This dessert should be made a day ahead, in order for all the flavors to meld.

Serves 8
1 teaspoon superfine sugar, plus extra to serve
2 small cups very strong espresso coffee, left to cool
Splash or two of brandy
Savoiardi or ladyfingers (up to 24 if large; 36 if small)
Good-quality unsweetened cocoa powder (Valrhona, for preference), to serve

Zabaglione:
4 large organic egg yolks
¼ cup (50 g) superfine sugar
Small wine glass of Marsala wine (or Amaretto, if preferred)
½ teaspoon vanilla extract
Grated zest of 2 lemons

Mascarpone cream:
1 pound 10 ounces (750 g) fresh mascarpone cheese
generous 1 tablespoon superfine sugar
A little vanilla extract or a scraping of fresh vanilla seeds
scant 2 cups (425 ml) heavy whipping cream

1 Using a double boiler (or a saucepan of simmering water with a mixing bowl resting on top but not touching the water), combine the ingredients for the zabaglione. Whisk continuously over low heat for 3–5 minutes, until the custard has thickened and coats the back of a spoon. Take off the heat and let cool (it can be left overnight in the refrigerator).

2 For the mascarpone cream, put all the ingredients, except the heavy cream, in a mixing bowl, and beat together until smooth. In a separate bowl, whisk the heavy cream into soft peaks, and gently fold into the mascarpone mixture. Set aside.

3 To assemble, either make in small individual bowls or a large serving dish. In a shallow dish, mix 1 teaspoon superfine sugar into the coffee and brandy. Briefly dip the sponge fingers (one at a time) into the coffee mixture until barely coated—you don't want a soggy sponge base. Line the bowls or dish with the fingers, placing them very close together.

4 Spoon over the zabaglione in a thick layer, then arrange more fingers on top. Next, add the mascarpone cream in an even layer, and smooth the top. Chill for a few hours or overnight. Before serving, sift over a dusting of unsweetened cocoa powder, and sprinkle with a smattering of sugar, if liked.

Cook's Note
Simple desserts such as this one require the best possible ingredients. If you can find a farm-made mascarpone cheese, and you have a coffee machine at home to brew espresso, this tiramesù will surpass all expectations.

Fall Berry Tartelettes with Quark

Make the most of fall berries because their season is short and, once the frosts appear, the bounty is finished. Berries in fall are not only fruity, but also acidic and juicy. They make excellent jams and jellies, but also work well in pies and tarts. If you have time, prebake the pastry shells and freeze them, then all you need to do is fill with soft cheese and fruit before serving.

Makes 6

scant ½ cup (7 tablespoons/100 g) unsalted butter
scant ½ cup (90 g) superfine sugar
¼ teaspoon salt
¼ teaspoon vanilla extract
1 organic egg yolk
1 cup (125 g) unbleached all-purpose flour, sifted, plus extra for
   dusting
Filling:
7 ounces (200 g) quark (choose the drier version, which is similar
   to a dry curd), or a low- to semi-fat cream cheese, drained
confectioners' sugar, to taste
2 cups (300 g) blackberries, rinsed and hulled
2 tablespoons superfine sugar

1 Cream together the butter and sugar in a mixing bowl. Stir in the salt, vanilla extract, and egg yolk, then fold in the flour to make a smooth dough. (You can do this by hand or in a food processor.) Form the dough into a ball, wrap in plastic wrap, and let rest for 2 hours or overnight in the bottom of the refrigerator.

2 Preheat the oven to 400°F (200°C). Lightly grease six 3¼-inch (8-cm) loose-bottom tartlet pans or an 8-inch (20-cm) loose-bottom tart pan.

3 On a lightly floured counter, roll out the dough and use to line the tart pan(s) and prick the bottom(s) with a fork. Place a circle of parchment paper inside the pastry shell(s), and fill with pie weights or dried beans. Bake in the oven for about 10 minutes, until the sides of the pastry shell(s) are golden. Take out of the oven, remove the weights and paper, and put the tart(s) back into the oven for a few minutes until light golden. Let cool.

4 Put the quark in a mixing bowl, and sweeten with confectioners' sugar to your taste; set aside. Put the blackberries in a saucepan with the superfine sugar and cook for a few minutes, until the sugar has dissolved and the fruit has softened a little; let cool.

5 Spoon the quark into the pastry shells, and spoon over the blackberries (without the syrup). Pour the syrup from the blackberries into a pan, and heat until reduced and thickened. Let cool before drizzling over the tarts.

Plums with Quark

When I found a handmade version of quark made by Mrs. Wild's dairy in Isny, in the beautiful Alpine region of Bavaria, I was both delighted and relieved to know that a traditional version of this cheese still exists.

Quark is delicious on its own or with the addition of puréed fruit or minced nuts. Preserved or baked fruit, such as plums, are superb accompaniments because the sharp yet sweet taste of the fruit is perfect alongside the smooth, silky texture of the soft fresh cheese.

This is no ordinary plum recipe. I have discovered that a sweet fruit wine called Visciolata made with small cherries (similar to Morellos in look and taste), from the Marche region in Italy, is the perfect dessert wine to macerate the dark plums of late summer.

Fill a large bail-closure or French Kilner canning jar with plums that are in perfect condition, with no bruises or splits in the skin; choose fruit that are not too large because you don't want to squash them in the jar. Pour over the Visciolata wine to just cover, and insert a cinnamon stick and star anise into the middle of the jar. Close the jar and store in a cool, dark place.

The following day, fill up with more wine because some will have been soaked up by the fruit, then repeat this for the next 2 days. On the final day, after filling with more wine, close the jar, make sure that the rubber seal is tightly in place, and set aside for 2 weeks in a cool, dark place.

Serve the fruit with a good spoonful of chilled soft, velvety quark cheese for a simple dessert.

Brillat-Savarin Cheesecake

This triple-cream cheese has a nutty flavor and a rich, buttery texture, and is really a luxurious way of making a cheesecake. Obviously, you have to close your eyes to the number of calories, but you really do not need to have a huge slice of this rich confection. The cheese is really at its best in spring or late summer, although it is available all through the year, and is simply delicious served really cold with berries or fruit compote.

Serves 8–10

9 ounces (250 g) Brillat-Savarin cheese
3½ ounces (100 g) farmhouse mascarpone cheese
½ vanilla bean, split in half lengthwise and seeds scraped out
Grated zest of ½ lemon
2 organic egg yolks
¼ cup (50 g) superfine sugar
1 organic egg white, whisked to soft peaks
Stewed winter rhubarb or fruit compote, or fresh berries, to serve
Cheesecake base:
4 cups (200 g) graham crackers, crushed
scant ½ cup (7 tablespoons/100 g) unsalted butter, melted
1 teaspoon runny honey

1   Grease and flour the bottom of an 8-inch (20-cm) springform cake pan. To make the cheesecake base, combine the crushed graham crackers, butter, and honey in a bowl, then press the mixture into the bottom of the prepared pan in an even layer. Put the pan in the freezer for 1 hour, or overnight, if preferred.
2   Preheat the oven to its lowest possible setting. To make the filling, blend the Brillat-Savarin, mascarpone, vanilla seeds, and lemon zest in a blender for a few minutes until smooth, or beat by hand.
3   Whisk the egg yolks with the sugar, add to the blender, and process for a few minutes, or beat by hand. Pour the mixture into a bowl, let stand for a minute to settle, and then gently fold in the whisked egg white.
4   Remove the cake pan from the freezer, and place on a baking sheet. Pour the filling mixture into the pan, and bake in the oven for 30–40 minutes until set, then let rest in the oven with the door slightly ajar until cooled to room temperature, before chilling in the refrigerator.
5   To serve, place the cake pan on a cup or bowl, and gently slide down the rim of the pan to release the cheesecake. With a palette knife, slide the cake off the base onto a serving plate. Serve with stewed winter rhubarb or another sharp-tasting fruit compote, or fresh berries.

Baked Cheesecake

I could include a dozen or so different kinds of cheesecakes, but prefer to offer you this one, which is really lovely and light, and different to the indulgent one made with Brillat-Savarin, a triple-cream cheese from Normandy (see opposite). I do like cheesecakes with a crushed cookie base, but, if I have a preference, then it is for the prebaked pastry shell, which holds the cheese mixture perfectly. The secret to a good cheesecake is to mix the filling well, so that there are no lumps, and also to bake it at a low temperature, then leave the cake in the turned-off oven to cool completely—your patience will be rewarded.

Serves 8

½ cup (1 stick/115 g) unsalted butter, cut into cubes
scant 1⅔ cups (200 g) unbleached all-purpose flour
generous 1 tablespoon superfine sugar
½ teaspoon grated lemon zest
½ teaspoon vanilla extract
1 tablespoon iced water
Pinch of salt
Filling:
14 ounces (400 g) mild fresh goat cheese, such as Ryefield, rind removed, or a fresh goat curd
7 ounces (200 g) mascarpone cheese
scant ½ cup (85 g) superfine sugar, plus 2 tablespoons extra
¼ cup (4 tablespoons/60 g) butter, melted
Grated zest and juice of ½ large lemon
2 tablespoons ground almonds
¼ teaspoon vanilla extract
2 large organic eggs, separated
To serve:
Crème fraîche
Fresh strawberries (optional)

1   Grease and flour a 9-inch (23-cm) springform cake pan. Put the flour, butter, sugar, lemon zest, vanilla extract, iced water, and a pinch of salt into a food processor, and process briefly until the mixture resembles fine breadcrumbs.
2   Empty the mixture into a bowl, and bring it together with your hands, to form a smooth ball of pastry. Roll out the pastry on a lightly floured surface, and use to line the prepared cake pan. If preferred, you can slice the pastry thinly, then press the slices into the pan, using the palm of your hand to make a shell. Put the cake pan in the freezer for 30 minutes.

3 Preheat the oven to 400°F (200°C). Bake the pastry shell for about 12 minutes, until it is pale in color and dry to the touch, then remove from the oven and let cool. (Don't put the cream cheese mixture straight into the hot pastry shell.)

4 Meanwhile, to make the filling, crumble the goat cheese into a mixing bowl, then add the mascarpone, scant ½ cup (85 g) superfine sugar, melted butter, lemon zest and juice, ground almonds, vanilla extract, and egg yolks. Beat until smooth.

5 Reduce the oven temperature to 350°F (180°C). In a clean, grease-free bowl, whisk the egg whites until stiff peaks form, then gently fold in the extra superfine sugar. Fold the egg whites into the cheese mixture, and pour into the partly baked pastry shell. Bake in the oven for 45 minutes, or until the top is pale gold.

6 Turn off the oven, and let the cheesecake stand for 15 minutes, then open the door slightly and let stand until completely cool. Spread crème fraîche over the top, and decorate with fresh strawberries, if liked.

Cheese Sablés

These waferlike biscuits are simple to make, but all the more tasty if you use the best-quality Parmesan or other tangy hard cheese.

Makes 10–15
1²⁄₃ cups (200 g) all-purpose flour
1¼ cups (125 g) finely grated Parmesan or other hard cheese
Large pinch of cayenne pepper
½ cup (1 stick/115 g) unsalted butter, cubed and softened
1 large organic egg yolk

1 Preheat the oven to 400°F (200°C). Grease and flour a baking sheet. In a mixing bowl, combine the flour, Parmesan, and cayenne. Add the butter and, with your fingertips, lift and work the mixture until you have a breadcrumb consistency.
2 Mix in the egg yolk to form a stiff dough. Wrap in plastic wrap, and let rest in the refrigerator for 30 minutes.
3 On a lightly floured counter, roll out the dough to ½ inch (1 cm) thick. Cut into rounds using a wine glass or a 2-inch (5-cm) cookie cutter, and place on the baking sheet. Reroll when necessary, pressing out more rounds. Place the baking sheet in the middle of the oven, and bake for 15 minutes, or until the sablés are lightly golden.

Parmesan Crisps

These thin, lacy crisps can be made in moments, so if you run out just have some finely grated Parmesan in the freezer at hand. As an apéritif, they are hard to beat, especially when served with chilled Prosecco or white wine. The important thing to remember is that you do need to use a well-matured Parmesan because young cheeses do not taste as fruity or have as crisp a texture.

Preheat the oven to 450°F (230°C). Line a baking sheet with parchment paper. Finely grate 9 ounces (250 g) Parmigiano-Reggiano cheese (2½ cups grated). Place little mounds of the grated cheese on baking sheets or sprinkle a layer of Parmesan into a 2-inch (5-cm) cookie cutter for more even rounds; make sure that you leave enough space between the cheese rounds because they spread during cooking. This amount of cheese will make 12–15 rounds.

You can also add a little chopped fresh red chile pepper or paprika to the cheese, to give a spicier taste to the crisps, but if you use an aged Parmesan they should be sufficiently flavorful. Bake in the oven for just a few minutes until golden and lacy. Let cool on the baking sheets and, when sufficiently easy to handle, use a palette knife to transfer to a serving plate.

Cheese Straws

No need to write out a laborious ingredients list for this recipe. You just take a package of puff pastry, the best quality you can find (and preferably made with butter), and roll it out into an oblong. Grate some Parmesan, Cheddar, or similar crumbly hard cheese (or you could use a mixture) into a bowl. Sprinkle the cheese over the rolled-out pastry in a thick layer, and press it down. Season with sea salt and freshly ground black pepper.

In another bowl, mix together 1 teaspoon cayenne pepper and 1 teaspoon English mustard powder, then sift over the cheese and press down with the back of a spoon. Cut the pastry into 8 x 1-inch (20 x 2.5-cm) strips, and twist each strip into a spiral, before placing on a buttered baking sheet. Bake in a preheated 400°F (200°C) oven for about 5 minutes, until golden and crisp. Transfer to a wire rack to cool.

Cook's Note
🐾 Place a very thin length of Parma or Bayonne ham on each strip of cheese-covered pastry, then twist as before. Alternatively, sprinkle poppy seeds and caraway seeds over the cheese strips, and press them down before twisting.

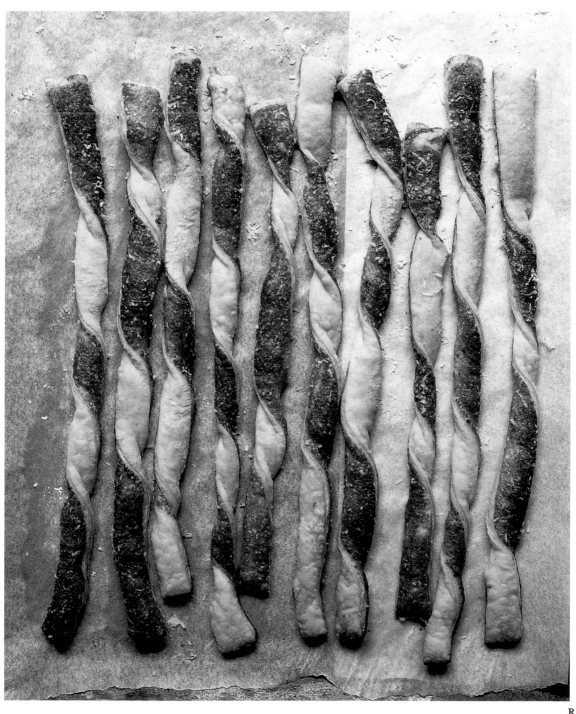

Gougères

These make a great dinner-party appetizer or party canapé, and they are also a good way of using up odd bits of strongly flavored hard cheese.

Makes about 24
½ cup (125 ml) whole organic milk
3½ tablespoons (50 g) unsalted butter
1⅔ cups (200 g) all-purpose flour, plus extra in reserve
4 large organic eggs
1 cup (100 g) grated Emmental Francais or a lighter style
   Gruyère cheese, plus extra for sprinkling
Good pinch of freshly grated nutmeg
Coarse sea or kosher salt and freshly ground black pepper

1 Preheat the oven to 400°F (200°C). Line two baking sheets with parchment paper. Put ½ cup (125 ml) water (filtered for preference), the milk, butter, and a pinch of salt in a medium heavy saucepan, then slowly bring to a boil.

2 Remove from the heat, add the flour, and beat with a wooden spoon. Return to the heat, beating continuously over medium-low heat, until the mixture forms a smooth dough. Turn down the heat to low, and cook the dough mixture until it starts to come away from the sides of the pan—this will take only a minute or two.

3 Spoon the dough into a bowl, and let cool for a minute. Now beat in the eggs, one at a time, making sure that you beat in each one thoroughly; this is important, and don't be afraid if the dough looks like it is going to separate—just keep beating and it will come together, I promise. Stir in the grated cheese, reserving ½ cup (55 g), plus a good pinch of pepper and nutmeg.

4 Put the dough in a pastry bag fitted with a ½-inch (1-cm) plain round nozzle, or a larger one if you prefer bigger puffs, and pipe little mounds onto the

baking sheets, about 2 inches (5 cm) apart. Sprinkle over the reserved cheese, and bake in the oven for 15–20 minutes, until the puffs are golden brown.

5 Serve hot straight from the oven, although you can let them cool, before storing, covered, in the refrigerator; warm through before serving.

Cook's Note

❧ You can make these in advance; pipe them onto baking sheets, then "open freeze." Once totally frozen, put them in a freezer bag—they won't stick together. To defrost, remove from the bag and place on the prepared baking sheet, then bring to room temperature. Sprinkle with cheese, then bake as above.

Cornbread with Fresh Goat Cheese

I love to use cornmeal with the husk intact to give a coarser texture to the bread. This is a lovely accompaniment to pumpkin soup or served with a simple side salad.

Makes 10–12 pieces
3½ tablespoons (50 g) unsalted butter, melted
scant 1 cup (225 ml) whole milk
1 organic egg
generous ¾ cup (100 g) unbleached all-purpose flour
1 tablespoon baking powder
Scant 1 teaspoon salt
generous ¾ cup (100 g) yellow cornmeal
1–2 red chile peppers, seeded and finely chopped
Small handful of fresh basil or cilantro, finely chopped
3½–4½ ounces (100–125 g) caprini or other soft fresh goat
   cheese, roughly chopped

1 Preheat the oven to 425°F (220°C). Grease and line the bottom of a 10-inch (25-cm) square baking pan. Pour the milk into a pitcher, and whisk in the egg; set aside.

2 In a mixing bowl, sift together the flour, baking powder, salt, and cornmeal, then make a well in the center. Pour in the milk mixture, and stir until mixed together and smooth. Next, stir in the melted butter, chiles, and herbs, then gently fold in the goat cheese.

3 Pour the batter into the baking pan, and bake for 20 minutes, or until the top is golden and a metal skewer inserted into the center of the cornbread comes out clean; if not quite ready, return to the oven for a few extra minutes. Let cool slightly in the pan, then turn out onto a wire rack to cool completely. Serve cut into slices or chunky cubes.

Parmesan Cheese Biscuits

Cheese biscuits are really easy to make and are delicious served warm for breakfast, lunch, or supper. They are perfect for picnics, too, although my favorite way of serving them is with a filling of herb goat cheese topped with salty-sweet crisp shards of speck.

Makes about 10
2 cups (250 g) self-rising flour
½ teaspoon baking powder
Large pinch of sea salt
¼ cup (50 g) finely grated Parmesan cheese
Good pinch of cayenne pepper (optional)
1 teaspoon English mustard powder (optional)
¼ cup (4 tablespoons/60 g) unsalted butter, chilled but not too hard, cut into small cubes
⅓ cup (75 ml) whole milk
⅓ cup 75 g) plain yogurt
2 large organic eggs, lightly beaten
Filling:
9 ounces (250 g) fresh rindless goat cheese or goat's milk curd
1 teaspoon baby capers, rinsed and gently squeezed dry
1 tablespoon finely chopped fresh herbs, such as chives, chervil, basil, or parsley
1 teaspoon grated lemon zest
Pinch of salt
8 slices speck or other smoked cured ham, fried until crisp

1 Preheat the oven to 350°F (180°C). Put the speck or ham on a baking sheet, and cook until crisp. Set aside.
2 Sift together the flour, baking powder, and salt into a large mixing bowl. Add the Parmesan and the cayenne and mustard powder, if using. Rub in the butter with your fingertips until the mixture resembles fine breadcrumbs, then make a well in the center.
3 In a separate bowl, mix together the milk, yogurt, and lightly beaten eggs (keeping back a little of the eggs to coat the tops before baking), then trickle it into the flour mixture, stirring as you go, to form a sticky dough. Line a baking sheet with parchment paper, and warm it in the oven for a few minutes, then set aside.
4 Meanwhile, lift the dough out of the bowl and knead lightly on a floured counter until smooth. Sift over a little extra flour, and roll out the dough using a floured rolling pin until it is around ¾ inch (2 cm) thick. Dip the rim of a 2¾-inch (7-cm) cookie cutter or glass into flour, and press out about 10 biscuits, rerolling the dough when necessary. Place the biscuits on the warm baking sheet. (Alternatively, you can form the dough into a large round, and score into triangles.)

5 Brush the tops of the biscuits with the reserved beaten egg, and bake in the oven for about 8 minutes, until risen and golden. Let cool slightly on a wire rack; they are best served warm.
6 To make the filling, mix together the goat cheese, capers, herbs, and lemon zest with a pinch of salt until smooth. Split the biscuits, and place a spoonful of filling on one half, then place a few shards of crisp speck or ham on top, followed by the other half of biscuit.

Directory of cheeses

KEY

🐄 .... Cow's milk
🐐 .... Goat's milk
🐑 .... Ewe's milk
🐃 .... Buffalo's milk
W .... Weight of cheese
F .... Fat content
P .... Page number

THE UK

Alderwood 🐄
Cranbourne Chase Cheese, Ashmore, Dorset
W4½ lb. F45% P19

Appleby's Cheshire 🐄
Appleby's Farm, Weston-under-Redcastle, Shropshire
W4½ lb. F45% P26

Beenleigh Blue 🐑
Ticklemore Cheese, Totnes, Devon
W6½ lb. F50% P16

Berkswell 🐑
Ram Hall Farm, Berkswell, West Midlands
W6½ lb. F48% P24

Caboc 🐄
Highland Fine Cheeses, Tain, Ross & Cromarty
W2 lb. 7 oz. F69% P36

Cardo 🐐
Sleights Farm, Timsbury, Somerset
W2½ lb. F45% P19

Colston Bassett Stilton 🐄
Colston Bassett Dairy, Colston Bassett, Nottinghamshire
W15½ lb. F45–48% P28

Cornish Yarg 🐄
Lynher Dairy, Liskeard, Cornwall
W6½ lb. F45% P19

Devon Blue 🐄
Ticklemore Cheese, Totnes, Devon
W6½ lb. F48% P16

Doddington 🐄
North Doddington Farm, Wooler, Northumberland
W11–33 lb. F45% P33

Dunsyre Blue 🐄
Walston Braehead Farm, Carnwath, Lanarkshire
W6½ lb. F45–48% P34

Gorwydd Caerphilly 🐄
Gorwydd Farm, Tregaron Ceredigion
W4½ lb. F45% P30

Harbourne Blue 🐐
Ticklemore Cheese, Totnes, Devon
W6½ lb. F50% P16

Hurdlebrook 🐄
Olive Farm, Babcary, Somerset
W6½ lb. F45%
Two cheeses produced: one a crumbly Caerphilly-style cheese, and the other a softer version of Cheddar with a tactile crust.

Innes Button 🐐
Innes Cheeses at Highfields Farm Dairy, Tamworth, Staffordshire
W2¾ oz. F45% P25

Isle of Mull 🐄
Sgriob-ruadh Farm, Tobermory, Isle of Mull
W55 lb. F45% P36

Keen's Farmhouse Cheddar 🐄
Moorhayes Farm, Wincanton, Somerset
W61–66 lb. F45% P20

Kirkham's Lancashire 🐄
Kirkham's Farm, Goosnargh, near Preston, Lancashire
W24 lb. F45% P34

Lincolnshire Poacher 🐄
Ulceby Grange Farm, Alford, Lincolnshire
W13–15½ lb. F45% P31

Montgomery's Cheddar 🐄
Manor Farm, North Cadbury, Somerset
W57 lb. F45% P20

Richard III Wensleydale 🐄
Fortmayne Farm, Bedale, North Yorkshire
W5½ lb. F45% P33

Shropshire Blue 🐄
Colston Bassett Dairy & Long Clawson Dairy, Nottinghamshire & Leicestershire
W17½ lb. F45% P26

Single Gloucester 🐄
Smarts Farm, Churcham, Gloucester
W7½ lb. F45% P23

Stichelton 🐄
Stitchelton Dairy, Wellbeck Estate, Nottinghamshire
W15½ lb. F45% P29

Stinking Bishop 🐄
Laurel Farm, Dymock, Gloucester
W4 lb. F45% P23

Ticklemore 🐐
Sharpham Creamery, Totnes, Devon
W4 lb. F45% P19

Tunworth 🐄
Hampshire Cheeses at Hyde Farm, Herriard, Hampshire
W9 oz. F45% P22

Waterloo 🐄
Wigmore Dairy, Riseley, Berkshire
W14–18 oz. F45% P22

Wigmore 🐑
Wigmore Dairy, Riseley, Berkshire
W14–18 oz. F45% P22

IRELAND

Ardrahan 🐄
Ardrahan Farmhouse Cheese, Kanturk, Co. Cork
W7 oz. / 3 lb. 5 oz. F45% P42

Cashel Blue 🐄
J&L Grubb ltd., Fethard, Co. Tipperary
W4½ lb. F48% P39

Coolea 🐄
Coolea Farmhouse Cheese, Macroom, Co. Cork
W2¼–22 lb. F45% P40

Crozier Blue 🐑
J&L Grubb ltd., Fethard, Co. Tipperary
W4½ lb. F48–50% P40

Dilliskus 🐄
Maja Binder, Castlegregory, Co. Kerry
W2 lb. 4 oz. F45% P41

Durrus 🐄
Durrus Farmhouse Cheese, Coomkeen, Durrus, Co.Cork
W3 lb. 5 oz. F45% P43

Gabriel & Desmond 🐄
West Cork Natural Cheese Company, Schull, Co. Cork
W13–17½ lb. F45–48% P41

Gubbeen 🐄
Gubben Cheese, Schull, Co. Cork
W3 lb. F45% P43

Kilcummin 🐄
Maja Binder, Castlegregory, Co. Kerry
W2 lb. 4 oz. F45% P41

Ryefield 🐐
Fivemiletown Creamery Cooperative, Bailieboro,Co.Cavan
W2 lb. 4 oz. F45% P39

St Gall 🐄
Fermoy Natural Cheese Company, Fermoy, Co. Cork
W9 lb. F45% P40

St Tola 🐐
Inagh Farmhouse Cheese, Inagh, Co. Clare
W2 lb. 4 oz. F45% P39

FRANCE

Abbaye de Trois Vaux 🐄
Abbaye de Trois Vaux, Haut Artois
W2½ lb. F45% P54

Ami du Chambertin 🐄
Fromagerie Gaugry, Burgundy
W7 oz. F45% P61

Anneau du Vic Bilh 🐐
Fromage de zone de Montagne, Pyrénées
W6½–7 oz. F45% P75

Ardi Gasna 🐑
Fromage de zone de Montagne, Pyrénées Atlantique
W4½–5 lb. F45–48%
Similar in style to hard Spanish cheeses like Manchego, but more brittle and gamey in flavor.

Banon Feuille 🐐
Romain Ripert, Provence
W2¼ oz. F45% P73

Bethmale 🐄
Jean Faup, Ariège
W9–11 lb. F45–48% P74

Bethmale 🐐
Jean Faup, Ariège
W9 lb. F45–48% P74

Bleu d'Auvergne 🐄
Morin, Auvergne
W5½ lb. F50% P68

Bleu des Causses 🐄
Fromagerie des Causses et Auvergne, Aveyron/Auvergene
W5½–6½ lb. F45% P68

Bonde de Gâtine 🐐
Fromagerie Bonde de Gâtine, Poitou
W6½–7 oz. F45% P64

Boulette d'Avesnes 🐄
Via Philippe Olivier, Boulogne or Fauquet Thiérache
W5½–7 oz. F45% P49

Bouton d'Oc 🐐
Pic, Tarn
W1 oz. F45% P80

Brie de Meaux 🐄
Donge, Île de France
W6½ lb. F45% P56

Brie de Melun 🐄
Rouzaire, Île de France
W3 lb. 5 oz. F45% P57

Brillat-Savarin 🐄
Ferme Lepetit, Normandy
W1 lb. 3 oz. F70% P52

Brin d'Amour 🐑
Pierucci, Corsica (Haut)
W1 lb. 5 oz. F45–48% P81

Brique du Larzac 🐑
Bergers du Larzac, Tarn
W6½–7 oz. F45% P78

Buchette de Banon 🐐
Ripert, Provence
W5½ oz. F45% P73

Cabécou du Rocamadour 🐐
SAS Les Fermiers du Rocamadour, Lot
W1½ oz. F45% P78

Camembert Fermier Durand 🐄
Ferme de la Héronnière, Normandy
W9 oz. F45% P52

Cantel Laguiole 🐄
Plateau of Aubrac, Auvergne
W77 lb. F45% P70

Casinca 🐐
Pierucci, Corsica (Haut)
W12 oz. F45%
Washed-rind semi-soft goat cheese that is delicate and fruity when young, ripening to a full-bodied robust goaty style.

Cathare 🐐
Local central market, Lauregais, Carcassonne
W6½–7 oz. F45% P79

Cendré de Niort 🐐
Fromagerie Bonde de Gatine, Poitou
W7 oz. F45% P64

Chabichou 🐐
Fromagerie Bonde de Gatine, Poitou
W6½ oz. F45% P64

Chaource 🐄
Fromagerie Lincet, Champagne
W9–16 oz. F50% P59

Charolais 🐐
Domaine de Saulnieres, Burgundy
W6½ oz. F45% P59

Chenette 🐐
Local central market, Montastruc-la-Conseillere
W6½ oz. F45%
Small brick shape goat cheese with natural rind and topped with an oak leaf (Chene). Fudgy texture and good flavor.

Coeur de Neufchâtel 🐄
Gaec Brianchon, Normandy
W7 oz. F45% P52

Coulommiers 🐄
Donge, Île de France
W1 lb. 2 oz. F45% P57

Crayeux de Roncq 🐄
Via Philippe Olivier, Boulogne, Haut Artois/Ferrain Weppes
W1 lb. 3 oz. F45% P49

Crottin de Chavignol 🐐
Dubois-Boulay, Sancerre
W2¼–2½ oz. F45% P63

Crottin Maubourguet 🐐
Fromage zone de Montagne Pyrénées
W2¾ oz. F45%
Tubby goat's milk Crottin with

a fuller flavor than the Loire version. Good with Pays d'Oc-style red wines.

Crottin Pic de Bigorre 🐐
Fromage zone de Montagne, Ariège
W3½ oz. F45%
High mountain goat's milk Crottin, with a lovely crumbly sweet flavor and texture. Good lingering finish, too, and will partner red wines.

Époisses 🐄
Fromagerie Gaugry, Burgundy
W9 oz. F45–48% P60

Estibere 🐑
Via Gabriel Bachelet, Bearn
W1 lb. 10 oz. F45%
Washed-rind ewe's milk cheese with a wonderful rich and silky texture and sweetly earthy taste.

Explorateur 🐄
Fromagerie Le Petit Morin, Île de France
W9 oz. F75% P54

Fleur de Chèvre 🐐
Fromagerie Bonde de Gatine, Poitou
W7 oz. F45% P64

Fougeru 🐄
Rouzaire, Île de France
W1 lb. 2 oz. F45% P55

Fourme d'Ambert 🐄
Morin, Auvergne
W4 lb. F50% P68

Gaperon á l'ail 🐄
Patricia Ribier, Montgacon, Auvergne
W9 oz. F45–48% P67

Haut Barry 🐑
Bergers Larzac, Larzac
W6½ lb. F45% P74

Langres 🐄
Schertenleib, Saulxures, Champagne
W5½–6½ oz. F50% P61

Le Gabiétout 🐐 🐄
Via Gabriel Bachelet, Pyrénées
W4½ oz. F45% P74

Lingot Saint Nicolas de la Monastère 🐐
Monastery at La Dalmerie, La Dalmerie, Hérault
W3½ oz. F45% P78

Livarot 🐄
Graindorge, Normandy
W1 lb. 2 oz. F45% P52

Lou Bren 🐑
Bergers Larzac, Aveyron
W4½ lb. F45% P78

Louvie 🐐
Via Gabriel Bachelet, Pyrénées
W10½ lb. F45% P79

Maroilles 🐄
Philippe Olivier/Syndicat des Fabricants de Maroilles, Thiérache
W25–28 oz. F45% P48

Mascares 🐐 🐑
Ripert, Provence
W5½ oz. F45%
A pave (square)-shape soft cheese with a natural rind. The flavors are creamy with a flaky texture, and as the cheese ripens it becomes more nutty.

Mimolette 🐄
Maison Losfeld, Flandres
W6½ lb. F40% P50

Mothais 🐐
Fromagerie Bonde de Gatine, Poitou
W9 oz. F45% P64

Munster 🐄
Siffert Freres or Haxaire, Alsace
W1 lb. 2 oz. / 9 oz. F45% P47

Napoleon Montréjeau 🐑
Bouchat, Hautes Pyrénées
W9 lb. F48–48% P74

Olivet 🐄
Fromagerie d'Onzain, Orleannais
W7 oz F45% P55

Ossau 🐑
Fromage zone de Montagne, Pyrénées
W12 lb. F48% P75

Pechegos 🐐
Pic, Tarn
W10½ oz. F45% P80

Pelardon 🐐
Co-operative de Pelardon les Cévennes, Cévennes
W2¼–3½ oz. F45% P69

Pérail 🐑
Bergers Larzac, Languedoc
W5½ oz. F48% P78

Persillé du Marais 🐐
Charente-Poitou cheese association, Vendée and Poitou
W3 lb. 5 oz. F48% P66

Picodon 🐐
Co-operative de Picodon de la Drôme, Drôme
W2¾–3½ oz. F45% P69

Pont l'Évêque 🐄
Pere Eugene/Graindorge, Normandy
W9 oz. F45% P52

Pouligny-Saint-Pierre 🐐
Syndicat des Producteurs de Fromages de Pouligny-Saint-Pierre, Berry
W9 oz. F45% P62

Rollot 🐄
Via Philippe Olivier, Picardy
W8 oz. F45% P47

Roquefort Carles 🐑
Carles, Rouergue
W3 lb. F48% P77

Roquefort Papillon 🐑
Papillon, Rouergue
W3 lb. F45–48% P77

Rouelle 🐐
Fromagerie Pic, Tarn
W7 oz. F45% P78

Rove des Garrigues 🐐
Compagnons Bergers de Languedoc, Lot, Midi Pyrénées
W3½ oz. F45% P78

Saint Félicien 🐄
L'Etoile de Vercours, Dauphiné/Isère
W6½ oz. F40% P69

Saint Marcellin 🐄
L'Etoile de Vercours, Dauphiné/Isère
W2¾–3½ oz. F35% P69

Sainte-Maure 🐐
Fromagerie Hardy, Touraine
W9 oz. F45% P62

Saint-Nectaire 🐄
Morin, Auvergne
W3½–3¾ lb. F45% P67

Salers d'Estive 🐄
Plateau of Aubrac, Auvergne
W77 lb. F45% P70

Selles sur Cher 🐐
Ets Jacquin, Loire/Cher
W5–5½ oz. F45% P62

Soumaintrain 🐄
Ferme Lorne, Burgundy
W9–10 oz. F45% P61

Soum d'Aspe 🐐
Fromage zone de Montagne, Pyrénées
W3½ oz. F45%
Tubby, cylinder goat cheese with a definite goaty flavor, natural thin rind, and crumbly texture. Made high in the hills in isolated farms.

Tomme d'Aydius 🐐
Hillside cabins in Valle d'Aspe, Béarn
W6½ lb. F45% P75

Tomme de Cabrioulet 🐐
Fromagerie col de Fach, Ariège
W6½ lb. F45–48% P75

Tomme de Cléon 🐐
Via Gabriel Bachelet, Pays Nantais, Pays de la Loire
W6½–9 lb. F45–48% P66

Tomme Corse 🐐
Pierucci, Corsica
W6½ lb. F45% P81

Tomme Fraîche 🐄
Morin, Auvergne/Aubrac
W10½ oz.–2¼ lb. F45% P67

Val de Loubières (Resineux de Loubieres) 🐐
Fromagerie col de Fach, Ariège
W14 oz. F48% P75

Valençay 🐐
Moreau, Berry/Indre
W7 oz. F45% P62

Vieux Boulogne 🐄
Via Philippe Olivier, Pas-de-Calais
W12 oz. F45% P49

Zelu Koloria 🐐
Fromage zone de Montagne, Pays Basque
W13 lb. F48% P75

ALPINE

FRENCH ALPINE

Abbaye de Tamié 🐄
Abbaye de Tamié, Haut-Savoie
W1 lb. 2 oz.–3 lb. F35% P89

Abondance 🐄
La Cooperative de Vacheresse,
Haute-Savoie
W22 lb. F48% P92

Beaufort Chalet d'Alpage 🐄
Caves Cooperatives du Beaufort de
Haute Montagne, Savoie
W61–66 lb. F55% P86

Besace 🐐
Savoie
W7 oz. F45% P92

Bleu de Gex 🐄
Syndicat Interprofessionnel du Bleu
de Gex-Haut-Jura-Septmoncel,
Haut Jura
W12 lb. F50% P89

Bleu de Termingnon 🐄
Chalets in Parc de la Vanoise,
Haut-Savoie
W15½–22 lb. F40% P90

Chevrotin des Aravis 🐐
Cooperative Thones, Haut Savoie
W10½ oz. F35% P89

Comté d'Estive 🐄
Comite Interprofessionelle de
Gruyere de Comté, Comté
W9 lb. F50% P84

Emmental de Savoie Surchoix 🐄
Syndicat des fabricants et affineurs
d'Emmentals Traditionnels, Savoie
W176 lb. F45%P89

Grand Colombiers de Aillon 🐐 🐄
Chalet huts and Ecole and Chatelard
markets, Savoie
W3 lb. 5 oz. F35% P93

Grataron d'Arêches 🐄 or 🐐
Le Groupement Pastoral du Cormet
d'Areches, Savoie
W7 oz. F35% P92

Morbier 🐄
Association des Fabricants de
Veritable Morbier au lait cru de
Franche-Comté, Franche-Comté
W6½–20 lb. F45% P89

Persillé de Tignes 🐐 🐄
Mountain chalets, Savoie
W3 lb. 5 oz. F35% P93

Reblochon 🐄
La Cooperative Agricole des
Producteurs de Reblochon, Savoie
W18 oz. F45% P89

Tarentais 🐐
Mountain chalets, Savoie
W7 oz. F30% P92

Tomme de Savoie 🐄
Fromagerie Cooperative Thones,
Savoie
W2 lb. 4 oz. F33–40%P89

Vacherin 🐄
Syndicat Interprofessionnel de
Defense du Fromage Mont d'Or ou
Vacherin de Haut-Doubs, Haut-Doubs
W18 oz.–6½ lb. F50% P90

SWISS ALPINE

Alp Bergkäse 🐄
Mountain Collective, Canton
Graubünden, Chur
W51–73 lb. F50% P96

Alp Kohschlag 🐄
Mountain chale, Canton St Gallen
W15½ lb. F48% P97

Alpkäse Luven 🐄
Dani Duerr, Canton Graubünden
W11 lb. F48% P95

Château d'Erguel 🐄
Fromagerie, Courtelary, Bernese Jura,
Canton Bern
W15½ lb. F48% P96

Emmentaler 🐄
Mountain collective, Canton Bern
W220 lb. F45% P97

Fleurettes des Rougemont (Tomme Fleurette) 🐄
Michel Beroud, Canton Vaud
W6 oz. F45% P97

Gruyère 🐄
Jean Marie Dunand, Le Crêt sur
Semsales, Canton Fribourg
W70½–88 lb. F45–48% P95

Le Sous-Bois 🐄
Henchoz Farm, Canton Vaud
W5½ oz. F45% P96

L'Etivaz 🐄
Farm collectives, Canton Vaud
W40 lb. F48% P96

Raclette 🐄
Alp Luser-Schlössli mountain dairies,
Canton Glarus
W9–11 lb. F45% P97

Stillsiter Steinsalz 🐄
Stefan Bühler, Gähwil, Toggenburg
W9 lb. F48% P97

Unterwasser 🐄
The Stadelmann family,
Canton St Gallen
W17½ lb. F50% P97

ITALIAN ALPINE

Asiago Pressato 🐄
Consorzio Tutela Formaggio Asiago,
Vicenza/Trento
W26½ lb. F45% P100

Bastardo del Grappa/ Morlacco del Grappa 🐄
Alpine and valley dairies, Monte
Grappa Massif
W13–15½ lb. F45% P102

Branzi 🐄
Cooperativa Agricola Saint'Antonio in
Valtaleggio, Lombardy
W26½ lb. F45% P99

Carnia Altobut Vecchio 🐄
Mountain and valley dairies, Padola
W13 lb. F45% P100

Fontina 🐄
Cooperativa Produttori Latte e
Fontina, Aosta
W17½–26½ lb. F45% P104

Formai de Mut 🐄
Cooperativa Agricola Saint'Antonio in
Valtaleggio, Lombardy
W17½–26½ lb. F45% P99

Franzedas Alpeggio 🐄
Mountain huts, Vicenza/Trento
W4½ lb. F45% P100

Grana Val di Non (Trentingrana) 🐄
Consorzio per la tutela del Formaggio
Grana Padano, Trentino
W77–88 lb. F35–40% P100

Grasso d'Alpe Buscagna 🐄
Mountain Huts, Parco Veglia Devero
W11–15½ lb. F45% P102

Monte Veronese Grasso 🐄
Latteria in and around Verona, Verona
W13–20 lb. F45% P102

Scimudin 🐄 🐐
Latteria Agricola Cooperativa
Livignesi, Sondrio
W2 lb. 4 oz. F70% P99

Stanghe di Lagundo 🐄
Mountain dairies, Treviso
W4½ lb. F45% P103

Toma Ossolana Alpeggio 🐄
Mountain Huts, Parco Veglia Devero
W11–15½ lb. F45% P102

Toma Ossolana Rodolfo 🐄
Mountain Huts, Parco Veglia Devero
W11–15½ lb. F45% P102

GERMAN & AUSTRIAN ALPINE

Adelegger Urberger 🐄
Isny Cheeses Dairy, Bavaria
W15½ lb. F45% P107

Alp-Bergkäse 🐄
Sennalpe Spicherhalde Dairy,
Balderschwang
W51–61 lb. F50% P107

Bavarian Blue 🐄
Obere Muehle Co-operative,
Bad Oberdorf
W5½ lb. F48% P107

Butterkäse 🐄
Co-operative Bremenried,
south west Bavaria
W13–17½ lb. F50% P107

Emmentaler 🐄
Käserei Bremenried Co-operative,
Allgäu
W200 lb. F35–40% P108

Rasskass 🐄
Dorfsennerei Langenegg
Co-operative, Vorarlberg/
Bregenz Forez
W14½ lb. F45% P109

Romadur 🐄
Käserei Bremenried Co-operative,
Allgäu
W1 lb. 7 oz. F40–45% P107

Tilsiter 🐄
Sibratsgfäll Co-operative, Bregenz
W8–11 lb. F30–60% P109

Weisslacker 🐄
Sibrtsgfäll Co-operative,
Wangen im Allgäu
W10 oz. F40–45% P108

Zigorome 🐐
Ziegenhof Leiner Far, Allgäu
W5½ oz. F40% P108

ITALY

Blu di Langa 🐄 🐐 🐑
Alta Langa, Piedmont
W2 lb. 4 oz. F50% P112

Burrata 🐄
Nuzzi, Molise/Puglia
W10½–18 oz. F60% P125

Capretta di Toscano 🐐
Azienda Agricole La Querchette,
Tuscany
W5½ lb. F45% P125

Caprini Freschi 🐐
La Bottera, Piedmont
W3½ oz. F45% P116

Caprini Tartufo 🐐
La Bottera, Piedmont
W3½ oz. F45% P116

Caprino delle Langhe 🐐
Alta Langa, Piedmont
W3¼ oz. F45% P116

Caprino Sardo al Caprone 🐐
Associazione Regionale Allevatori
della Sardegna, Sardinia
W4½ lb. F45% P133

Casciotta Etrusca 🐑
Latteria in and around Sienna,
Tuscany
W3 lb. 5 oz. F45% P125

Castagnolo 🐑
Latteria, Tuscany
W2 lb. 4 oz. F45% P125

Castelmagno 🐄
Marco Arneodo, Cuneo, Piedmont
W4½–15½ lb. F35–40% P114

Castelrosso 🐄
Luigi Rosso Farm, Biella, Piedmont
W11–13 lb. F40% P114

Fiore di Langhe 🐐
Alta Langa, Piedmont
W6 oz. F45% P116

Formaggio di Fossa 🐄
Latteria in hills, Umbria
W6½ lb. F40% P129

Formaggio Piacentinu Ennese 🐑
Casalgismondo Farm, Sicily
W9 lb. F45% P132

Gorgonzola Dolce 🐄
Consorzio per total formaggio di Gorgonzola, Lombardy
W17½ lb. F48% P119

Gorgonzola Naturale 🐄
Consorzio per total formaggio di Gorgonzola, Lombardy
W26½ lb. F48% P119

Grana Padano 🐄
No. 205 Dairy, Lombardy
W77 lb. F32% P117

Maccagnette alle Erbe 🐄
Melo Grand Renato, Bielle, Piedmont
W18 oz.–2¼ lb. F45% P114

Mozzarella di Bufala 🐄
Cooperativa Allevatori Bufalini Salernitani, Campania
W9 oz. F45% P130

Parmigiano Reggiano 🐄
Consorzio di Parmigiano Reggiano, Emilia-Romagna
W77 lb. F32–35% P122

Pecorino Affinato in Vinaccia in Visciola
Hillside dairies, Apennine Hills, Umbria
W18 oz. F45% P129

Pecorino Marzolino Rosso 🐑
Caseificio Sociale Manciano, Tuscany
W2½ lb. F45% P125

Pecorino Montefalco 🐑
Montefalco farm, Umbria
W2½ lb. F45% P129

Pecorino Muffa Bianca 🐑
Hillside farms, Appenine Hills, Umbria
W4 lb. F45% P129

Pecorino Peperoncino 🐑
Tuscany
W18 oz. F45% P126

Pecorino Saraceno 🐑
Associazione Regionale Allevatori della Sardegna, Sardinia
W6½–13 lb. F48% P133

Pecorino Siciliano 🐑
Casalgismondo Farm, Sicily
W22–26½ lb. F45–48% P132

Pecorino Siciliano Fresco 🐑
Casalgismondo Farm, Sicily
W22–26½ lb. F45–48% P132

Pecorino Siciliano Peperoncino 🐑
Casalgismondo Farm, Sicily
W22–26½ lb. F45–48% P132

Pecorino Tartufo 🐑
Latteria in and around Siena, Tuscany
W18 oz. F45% P126

Pecorino Tinaio Moresco 🐑
Hillside farms, Sardinia
W6½ lb. F45–48% P133

Pecorino Vilanetto Rosso 🐑
Caseificio Sociale Cooperativo, Tuscany
W6½ lb. F40–45% P126

Pecorino Vinaccia 🐑
Small dairies, Perugia, Umbria
W9 lb. F48% P126

Pecorino Ubriaco 🐄
Tuscany (Finished in Treviso)
W2 lb. 4 oz. F45% P120

Provola di Bufala Affumicate 🐄
Cooperativa Allevatori Bufalini Salernitani, Campania
W10½ oz. F45% P130

Provolone del Monaco 🐄
Vico Equense, Campania
W6½ lb. F45% P130

Puzzone di Moena 🐄
Caseificio Sociale di Predazzo e Moena, Trento
W20 lb. F45% P120

Ragusano 🐄
Rosario Floridia, Sicily
W22–35 lb. F45% P132

Ricotta Carena 🐄
Angelo Carena, Piacenza, Lombardy
W2 lb. 4 oz. F35–40% P117

Ricotta Salata 🐑 🐄 🐄
Latteria, Puglia, Sicily, Sardinia
W10½ oz. F30–35% P130

Robiola delle Langhe 🐄 🐑 🐐
Alta Langa, Piedmont
W10½ oz. F45% P116

Seirass del Fieno 🐑
Mountain communities, Piedmont
W4½–11 lb. F45% P114

Seirass Fresca
Fratelli Giraudi, Piedmont
W12 oz. F45% P113

Sottocenere al Tartufo Veneto 🐄
La Casearia, Treviso
W6½ lb. F45% P120

Strachitund 🐄
Communita Montana Valle Brembana, Lombardy
W9 lb. F48% P120

Taleggio 🐄
Communita Montana Valle Brembana, Lombardy
W3¾ lb. F48% P120

Toma Maccagno 🐄
Luigi Rosso, Biella, Piedmont
W6½ lb. F45% P114

Truffle Cheese (Tuma Trifulera) 🐄 🐐 🐑
La Bottera, Piedmont
W18 oz. F45% P116

Vezzena Vecchio 🐄
Caseificio Sociale di Lavarone, Trentino/Venezia
W17½–22 lb. F45–48%
A beautifully ripened, hard Asiago-style cheese with robust fruity flavors complemented by a crumbly, chewy texture.

SPAIN

Arzúa Ulloa Arquesan 🐄
Quesería Agro Despensa, Galicia
W18 oz.–5½ lb. F45% P139

Bauma Madurat 🐐
Bauma Farm, Catalonia
W2 lb. 4 oz. F45% P138

Cabrales 🐄 🐐 🐑
Small Dairies, Penamellera Alta Township, Asturias
W5½ lb. F48% P140

Garrotxa 🐐
Bauma Farm, Catalonia
W2 lb. 4 oz. F45% P136

Idiazábal 🐑
J. Aranburu Elkartea, S.A.T.Caserío Ondramuino, Basque/Navarre
W3 lb. F45% P139

Mahón 🐄 🐐 🐑
Via Ardai cheese specialists, Menorca
W5½ lb. F45% P143

Manchego 🐑
Dehesa de los Llanos, La Mancha
W3 lb. 5 oz. F57% P144

Montsec 🐐
Via Ardai cheese specialists, Catalonia
W10½ oz. F45% P138

Murcia al Vino 🐐
Via Ardai cheese specialists, Murcia
W5½ lb. F45% P143

Perazola Azul 🐐
Via Ardai cheese specialists, Asturias
W4½ lb. F48% P140

Picos de Europa (Valdeón) 🐄 🐐 🐑
Via Ardai cheese specialists, Cantabria
W5½ lb. F48% P140

Roncal 🐑
Queso Larra SL, Navarre
W2¼–6½ lb. F45–50% P138

San Simón 🐄
Via Ardai cheese specialists, Galicia
W13 oz.–3 lb. 5 oz. F45% P139

Tetilla 🐄
Via Ardai cheese specialists, Galicia
W13 oz.–3 lb. 5 oz. F45% P139

Turo del Convent 🐐
Formatges Monber, Catalonia
W14 oz. F45% P138

Vall de Meranges Cremos 🐄
Via Ardai cheese specialists, Catalonia
W17 oz. F48% P138

PORTUGAL

Azeitão 🐑
Small Dairies, Azeitão
W9 oz. F48% P148

Barrão 🐑
Small Dairies, Alto do Chão, North Alentejo
W5½ oz. F48% P148

Cabra Transmontano 🐐
Quinta dos Moinhos Novos, Vila Verde, north west Portugal
W7 oz. F45% P148

Castelo Branco 🐑 🐐
Meimoa Co-operative, Beira Baixa Central
W3 lb. 5 oz. F48% P148

Évora 🐑
Small Dairies, Alandroal and Vila Vicosa, Alentejo
W4–7 oz. F48% P148

Graziosa 🐄
Small Dairies on Island, Ilha Graciosa Azores
W22 lb. F40–45% P148

Nisa 🐑
Monforqueijo Co-operative, Alentejo
W10½ oz. F48% P148

Qunita dos Moinhos Novos Serrano 🐐
Quinta dos Moinhos Novos, Vila Verde, north west Portugal
W1 lb. 2 oz. F48% P148

São Jorge 🐄
Cooperativa de Leitaria da Beira, Sao Jorge, Azores
W17½–33 lb. F45% P148

Serpa 🐑
Small dairies, Beja, South Alentejo
W4–18 oz. F50% P148

Serra d'Estrela 🐑
Mountain communities, Parque Natural da Serra Estrela, north Portugal
W1 lb. 2 oz.–2½ lb. F50% P147

Terrincho 🐑
Small farms and dairies, Trás-os-Montes, Upper Duoro Valley, north east Portugal
W1¾–2½ lb. F48% P147

THE REST OF EUROPE

THE NETHERLANDS

Edam 🐄
Co-operative, Edam-Volendam, North Holland
W1 lb. 2 oz.–2 lb. 4 oz. F30–35%
Round ball-shape with red wax-coated rind. Semi-hard with a mellow salty taste, becoming more intense with maturing.

Gouda
Small dairies, Gouda, South Holland
W44 lb. F45% P150

Leiden
Small dairies, Leiden
W8–20 lb. F20–40%
The original Cumin cheese: look for the red rind, farm cheese with a cross-keys crest stamp.

Maasdam
Small dairies, all Holland
W33 lb. F45%
Like a Swiss-style Emmenthal, with large holes and a smooth chewy texture.

Mimolette
Small dairies, North West Holland
W6½ lb. F45%
Similar in flavor to the French cheese.

Old Amsterdam
Small dairies, North Holland
W22 lb. F45%
A Gouda but made by larger dairies than the Boerenkaas.

Smoked Cheese
Small dairies, all Holland
W9 oz.–2 lb. 4 oz. F45%
Sausage-shape cheese eaten sliced into salads or in sandwiches, or as an accompaniment to sausages.

SWEDEN

Greve
Falbygden
W33 lb. F30–45% P153

Kryddost
Falbygden
W26½ lb. F40% P153

Svecia
Falbygden
W26½–33 lb. F28% P153

DENMARK

Havarti
Havarthigaard, Øverød, Copenhagen
W10 lb. F45% P153

POLAND

Bundz
Artisans, Podhale
W18 oz.–2 lb. 4 oz. F40%
A creamy cottage cheese.

Golka & Oscypek
Artisans, Tatra Mountains
W18 oz.–2 lb. 4 oz. F40%
Made with spindle and woven basket molds, salty with a chewy texture.

Redykolka
Artisans, Tatra Mountains
W18 oz.–2 lb. 4 oz. F40%
Artisan bird-shape cheese. Similar to Oscypek in flavor.

Ser Korycinski 'Swojski'
Agnieszka Gremza, Korycin
W4½ lb. F40% P154

GREECE

Anthotiros
All Greece
W2¼–4½ lb. F40–65%
Ewe or goat's milk cheese, or mixed, mild and crumbly when young, becoming salty and drier with age.

Feta
Mt Vikos,Thessalia
W110 lb. barrel F30% P154

Formaella of Parnassos
Parnassos
W4½ lb. P33%
Ewe or goat or mixed milks. Rich and piquant semi-hard cheese, good as a table cheese or to fry.

Galotiri
Epirus/Thessalia
W4½ lb. F14%
A ewe and goat's milk mixed, or just single milk cheese, with a sharp, tangy taste, and soft spreadable texture.

Graveira of Crete
Crete
W4½ lb. F40%
Ewe and goat's milk or mixed, aged for five months, with a sweetly earthy, robust taste.

Kalathaki of Limnos
Limnos Island
W4½ lb. F25–30%
Ewe's milk, or with a little goat's milk added, and with a sour/ salty tangy taste.

Kasseri
Macedonia, Thessalia, Mitilini island, and Xanthi
W2¼–4½ lb. F25%
Ewe and goat's milk or mixed and rather like a Mozzarella texture, which can be used for topping pastry and melting, or in a salad.

Manouri
Central and Western Macedonia/ Thessalia
W2¼–4½ lb. F37%
Ewe or goat's milk, or mixed, rindless and with a smooth texture and creamy rich taste.

GERMANY

Allgäuer Emmentaler
Bremenried Co-operartive, Weiler, south west Bavaria
W176 lb. F45%
This cheese is usually sold at around five to seven months, but luckily a few are matured for 14 months, which opens out the flavors to give a rich and nutty layer of tastes.

Bachensteiner
Gunzesried Co-operative, Blachach Valley, Bavaria
W7 oz. F45% P154

Limburger
Zurwies Co-operative, Baden-Württemberg
W7 oz. F45% P154

Münster
Zurwies Co-operative, Wangen im Allgäu, south east Baden-Wüttemberg
W7–18 oz. F45% P154

BALKANS

Kashkaval
W18 oz.–2 lb. 4 oz. F45%
Typical semi hard cwe milk cheese, crumbly and salty.

HUNGARY

Liptaeur
Large production, all Hungary
W7 oz.–2 lb. 4 oz. F30–40%
A salty, creamy cheese to spread.

ROMANIA

Aldermen
Romania
W2¼–4½ lb. F45%
Buffalo milk cheese with a crumbly texture.

USA

Amablu
Faribault Dairy, Faribault, Minnesota
W6 lb. F45–48% P178

Avondale Truckle
Brunkow Cheese Co-op, Darlington, Wisconsin
W20–22 lb. F45% P174

Battenkill Brebis
Three-Corner Field Farm, Shushan, New York
W6 lb. F45% P200

Bayley Hazen Blue
Jasper Hill Farm, Greensboro, Vermont
W7½ lb. F48% P185

Big Eds
Saxon Homestead Creamery, Cleveland, Wisconsin
W15½ lb. F45% P176

Bijou
Vermont Butter & Cheese Company, Websterville, Washington
W2 oz. F45% P190

Birch Hill Cakes
Hillman Farm, Colrain, Franklin County, Massachusetts
W8 oz. F45% P194

Bleu Mont Cloth Cheddar
Bleu Mont Dairy, Blue Mounds, Dane County, Wisconsin
W11 lb. F45–48% P172

Bonne Bouche
Vermont Butter & Cheese Company, Websterville, Washington
W4 oz. F45% P190

Boucher Blue
Boucher Family Farm, Highgate Center, Franklin County, Vermont
W3 lb. 5 oz. F48–50% P190

Bridgewater
Zingerman's Creamery, Ann Arbor, Michigan
W7 oz. F45% P182

Brigid's Abbey
Cato Corner Farm, Colchester, Connecticut
W3 lb. 5 oz. F45% P198

Bûche
Juniper Grove, Redmond, Oregon
W5½ oz. F45% P168

Cabot Clothbound Cheddar
Cabot Creamery, Cabot, Vermont
W38 lb. F45–48% P187

Cadence
Andante Farm, Petaluma, California
W2¾ oz. F45% P164

California Crottin
Redwood Hill Farm and Creamery, Sonoma, California
W5½ oz. F45% P162

Camellia
Redwood Hill Farm and Creamery, Sonoma, California
W7 oz. F45% P162

Carmody
Bellwether Farms, California
W3 lb. F45–48% P161

Cavatina
Andante Farm, Petaluma, California
W3–7 oz. F45% P164

City Goat
Zingerman's Creamery, Ann Arbor, Michigan
W2¾ oz. F45% P182

Classic Blue Log
Westfield Farm, Hubbardston, Massachusetts
W4½ oz. F45% P195

Cloth-bound 18-month-Aged Cheddar
Fiscalini Farm, Stanislaus County, California
W52 lb F45–48% P160

Constant Bliss
Jasper Hill Farm, Greensboro, Vermont
W7 oz. F45% P185

Coupole 🐐
Vermont Butter & Cheese Company,
Websterville, Washington
W6½ oz. F45% P190

Dafne 🐐
Goat's Leap, Saint Helena, California
W7 oz. F45% P162

Dante 🐑
Wisconsin Sheep Dairy Co-op,
Spooner, Wisconsin
W8 lb. F45–48% P176

Detroit Street 🐐
Zingerman's Creamery, Ann Arbor,
Michigan
W16½ oz. F45% P182

Dorset 🐑
Consider Bardwell Farm, Pawlett,
Washington County, Vermont
W2½ lb. F45% P192

Drunken Hooligan 🐄
Cato Corner Farm, Colchester,
Connecticut
W1 lb. 5 oz. F45% P198

Dry Jack Special Reserve 🐐
Vella Cheese Company and Mertens
Farm, Sonoma, California
W8 lb. F48–48% P159

Dunbarton Blue 🐄
Roelli Cheese Haus, Shullsburg,
Wisconsin
W6½ lb. F45% P174

Dunmore 🐐
Blue Ledge Farm, Salisbury, Addison
County, Vermont
W18 oz. F45% P192

Eclipse 🐐
Goat's Leap, Saint Helena, California
W6½–7 oz. F45% P162

Edelweiss 🐄
Edelweiss Creamery, Monticello,
Wisconsin
W185 lb. F45–48%
After pressing and hand-
washing, these huge cheeses
are turned twice a week, with a
salt-water rub to keep the rinds
smooth. Excellent for fondue.

El Dorado Gold 🐐
Matos Cheese Factory, Santa Rosa,
California
W3 lb. F45%
A tomme that has been brine-
and whey-washed, then rubbed
form a smooth, thin rind with
scattered white molds and a
chewy texture.

Elk Mountain 🐐
Pholia Farm, Rogue River, Oregon
W5½–6½ lb. F45% P168

Everona Piedmont 🐑
Everona Dairy, Rapidan, Virginia
W4½ lb. F45% P202

Ewe's Blue 🐑
Old Chatham Sheepherding
Company, Old Chatham, New York
W3 lb. F48% P198

Feta 🐐
Three-Corner Field Farm, Shushan,
New York
W2 lb. 4 oz. F45% P200

Figaro 🐄 🐐
Andante Farm, Petaluma, California
W3½ oz. F45% P164

Flagship Reserve 🐄
Beecher's, Seattle, Washington
W16½ lb. F45–48% P171

Fleuri Noir 🐐
Fantôme Farm, Ridgeway, Wisconsin
W6½ oz. F45% P174

Flora Pyramid 🐐
Hillman Farm, Colrain, Franklin
County, Massachusetts
W6 oz. F45% P194

Fresh Chevre 🐐
Redwood Hill Farm and Creamery,
Sonoma, California
W5½ oz. F35% P162

Fresh Logs 🐐
Vermont Butter & Cheese Company,
Websterville, Washington
W3½ oz. F45% P190

Garlic with Chives 🐐
Zingerman's Creamery, Ann Arbor,
Michigan
W2¾ oz. F45% P182

Grayson 🐄
Meadow Creek Dairy,
Grayson, Galax, Virginia
W4½ lb. F45% P202

Great Hill Blue 🐄
Great Hill Dairy, Marion, Plymouth
County, Massachusetts
W6 lb. F45% P195

Great Lakes Cheshire 🐄
Zingerman's Creamery, Ann Arbor,
Michigan
W4¾ lb. F45% P182

Harvest Cheese 🐐
Hillman Farm, Colrain, Franklin
County, Massachusetts
W8 lb. F45% P194

Haystack Peak 🐐
Haystack Mountain Goat Dairy,
Niwot, Colorado
W5½ oz. F45% P183

Hillis Peak 🐐
Pholia Farm, Rogue River, Oregon
W2 lb. 4 oz. F45% P168

Hooligan 🐄
Cato Corner Farm, Colchester,
Connecticut
W1 lb. 5 oz. F45% P198

Hopeful Tomme 🐄 🐐
Sweet Grass Dairy, Thomasville,
Georgia
W5 lb. F45% P202

Humboldt Fog 🐐
Cypress Grove, McKinleyville,
California
W16½ oz.–5 lb. F45% P166

Hyku 🐐
Goat's Leap, Saint Helena, California
W5½–6½ oz. F45% P162

Hyku Noir 🐐
Goat's Leap, Saint Helena, California
W5½ oz. F45% P162

Julianna 🐐
Capriole Farmstead Goat Cheese,
Greenville, Indiana
W12 oz. F45% P181

Kiku 🐐
Goat's Leap, Saint Helena, California
W3–3¾ oz. F45% P162

Krotovina 🐐 🐐
Prairie Fruits Farm, Champaign
County, Illinois
W7 oz. F45% P178

Kunik 🐐 🐄
Nettle Meadow Farm, Thurman,
New York
W9–10 oz. F45% P199

La Mancha 🐐
Locust Grove Farm, Knox County,
East Tennessee
W6½ lb. F48% P202

Lil Wil's Big Cheese 🐄
Bleu Mont Dairy, Blue Mounds,
Dane County, Wisconsin
W2¼ lb. F45% P172

Lincoln Log 🐐
Zingerman's Creamery, Ann Arbor,
Michigan
W2 lb. F45% P182

Little Bloom 🐐
Prairie Fruits Farm, Champaign
County, Illinois
W6 oz. F45% P178

Little Darling 🐄
Brunkow Cheese Co-op, Darlington,
Wisconsin
W3 lb. 5 oz. F45% P174

Little Napoleon 🐐
Zingerman's Creamery, Ann Arbor,
Wisconsin
W2¾ oz. F45% P182

Maggie's Round 🐄
Cricket Creek Farm, Williamstown,
Berkshire County, Massachusetts
W18 oz. F45% P195

Manchester 🐄
Consider Bardwell Farm, Pawlett,
Washington County, Vermont
W2½ lb. F45% P192

Manchester 🐐
Zingerman's Creamery, Ann Arbor,
Michigan
W3½ oz. F45% P182

Marieke Foenegreek Gouda 🐄
Holland's Family Farm, Thorp,
Wisconsin
W17½ lb. F45% P176

Minuet 🐐 🐄
Andante Farm, Petaluma, California
W7 oz. F45% P164

Mobay 🐐 🐑
Carr Valley Cheese Company,
La Valle, Wisconsin
W4½ lb. F45% P174

Mont St Francis 🐐
Capriole Farmstead Goat Cheese,
Greenville, Indiana
W12 oz. F45% P181

Moreso 🐐
Fantôme Farm, Ridgeway, Wisconsin
W5½ oz. F45% P174

Mount Tam 🐄
Cowgirl Creamery, Point Reyes
Station, California
W9–10½ oz. F60% P161

Nancy's Camembert 🐑
Old Chatham Sheepherding
Company, Old Chatham, New York
W2 lb. F45% P199

O'Banon 🐐
Capriole Farmstead Goat Cheese,
Greenville, Indiana
W6 oz. F45% P181

Old Kentucky Tomme 🐐
Capriole Farmstead Goat Cheese,
Greenville, Indiana
W3–5 lb. F45% P181

Old Liberty 🐄
Goat Lady Dairy, Climax,
North Carolina
W3 lb. 5 oz. F45% P202

Pawlet 🐄
Consider Bardwell Farm, Pawlett,
Washington County, Vermont
W10 lb. F45% P192

Petit Frère 🐄
Crave Brothers Farmstead Cheese,
Waterloo, Wisconsin
W9 oz. F45% P176

Piper's Pyramide 🐐
Capriole Farmstead Goat Cheese,
Greenville, Indiana
W7 oz. F45% P181

Pleasant Cow 🐄
Beaver Brook Farm, Lyme, Connecticut
W1 lb. 12 oz. F45%
This cheese is matured for four
to five months to create a mellow
buttery, gently tangy taste. There
is a toasty hazelnut edge with the
more mature cheeses.

Pleasant Ridge Reserve 🐄
Uplands Cheese, Madison, Wisconsin
W10 lb. F45% P177

Point Reyes 'Original' Blue 🐄
Giacominis Farm, Point Reyes,
California
W5½ lb. F48% P160

Pondhopper 🐐
Tumalo Farms, Bend, Oregon
W9 lb. F45% P168

Prairie Breeze 🐄
Milton Creamery, Milton, Iowa
W20–40 lb. F45% P178

Pyramid 🐐
Juniper Grove, Redmond, Oregon
W 5½ oz. **F** 45% **P** 168

Queso de Mano 🐐
Haystack Mountain Goat Dairy,
Niwot, Colorado
W 4 lb. **F** 45% **P** 183

Rawson Brook Fresh Chevre 🐐
Rawson Brook Farm, Monterey,
Massachusetts
W 7 oz. / 1 lb. **F** 35% **P** 196

Red Hawk 🐄
Cowgirl Creamery, Point Reyes
Station, California
W 9 oz. **F** 60% **P** 160

Ridgeway Ghost 🐐
Fantôme Farm Ridgeway, Wisconsin
W 5½ oz. **F** 45% **P** 174

Ripened Disc 🐐
Hillman Farm, Colrain, Franklin
County, Massachusetts
W 5 oz. **F** 45% **P** 194

Rita 🐄
Sprout Creek Farm, Poughkeepsie,
New York
W 7 oz. **F** 45% **P** 199

Rogue River Blue 🐄
Rogue Creamery, Central Point,
Oregon
W 5 lb. **F** 45–48% **P** 168

Roxanne 🐄
Prairie Farm, Champaign County,
Illinois
W 6½–7 oz. **F** 45% **P** 178

Sally Jackson 🐄 🐐 🐑
Sally Jackson, Oroville, Washington
W 10½ oz–2¼ lb. **F** 45% **P** 171

San Andreas 🐑
Bellwether Farms, Petaluma, California
W 3 lb. **F** 45% **P** 161

Sandy Creek 🐐
Goat Lady Dairy, Climax,
North Carolina
W 4¼ oz. **F** 35% **P** 202

San Joaquin Gold 🐄
Fiscalini Farm, Stanislaus County,
California
W 15 lb. **F** 45% **P** 160

Sarabande 🐄
Dancing Cow Cheese, Bridport,
Addison County, Vermont
W 8 oz. **F** 45% **P** 187

Seastack 🐄
Mount Townsend Creamery, Port
Townsend, Washington
W 5½ oz. **F** 45% **P** 171

Shenandoah 🐑
Everona Dairy, Rapidan, Virginia
W 4½ lb. **F** 45% **P** 202

Shushan Snow 🐑
Three-Corner Field, Shushan,
New York
W 8–20 oz. **F** 45% **P** 200

Sierra Mountain Tomme 🐐
La Clarine Farm, Somerset, California
W 4½ lb. **F** 45% **P** 166

Small Plain Chevre 🐐
Fantôme Farm, Ridgeway, Wisconsin
W 2¾–3½ oz. **F** 45% **P** 174

Smokey Blue 🐄
Rogue Creamery, Central Point,
Oregon
W 5 lb. **F** 48% **P** 168

Snowdrop 🐐
Haystack Mountain Goat Dairy,
Niwot, Colorado
W 6 oz. **F** 45% **P** 183

Sofia 🐐
Capriole Farmstead Goat Cheese,
Greenville, Indiana
W 9 oz. **F** 45% **P** 181

Sophie 🐐
Sprout Creek Farm, Poughkeepsie,
New York
W 7 oz. **F** 45% **P** 199

St. George 🐄
Matos Cheese Factory, Santa Rosa,
California
W 11–22 lb. **F** 45–48% **P** 167

St. Pete's Select 🐄
Faribault Dairy, Faribault, Minnesota
W 6 lb. **F** 45–48% **P** 178

Sumi 🐐
Goat's Leap, Saint Helena, California
W 7 oz. **F** 45% **P** 162

Summer Snow 🐑
Woodstock Farm, Weston, Windsor
County, Vermont
W 7 oz. **F** 45% **P** 193

Summertomme 🐑
Willow Hill Farm, Milton, Chittenden
County, Vermont
W 8 oz. **F** 45% **P** 190

Ten-Year Aged Cheddar 🐄
Hook's Cheese Company, Mineral
Point, Wisconsin
W 44 lb. **F** 45% **P** 174

Tarentaise 🐄
Thistle Hill Farm,
North Pomfret, Vermont
W 20 lb. **F** 45–48% **P** 189

Thomasville Tomme 🐄
Sweet Grass Dairy, Thomasville,
Georgia
W 5½ lb. **F** 45% **P** 202

Three Sisters 🐄 🐐 🐑
Nettle Meadow Farm, Thurman,
New York
W 4 oz. **F** 45% **P** 199

Timberdoodle 🐄
Woodcock Farm, Weston, Windsor
County, Vermont
W 1¾ lb. **F** 45% **P** 193

Trade Lake Cedar 🐑
Lovetree Farmstead, Grantsburg,
Wisconsin
W 6 lb. **F** 45–48% **P** 176

Truffle Tremor 🐐
Cypress Grove, McKinleyville,
California
W 3 lb. **F** 45% **P** 166

Tumalo Tomme 🐐
Juniper Grove, Redmond, Oregon
W 3 lb. 5 oz. **F** 45% **P** 168

Twig Farm Square 🐐
Twig Farm, Middlebury, West
Cornwall, Addison County, Vermont
W 2 lb. **F** 45% **P** 188

Twig Farm Tomme 🐐
Twig Farm, Middlebury, West
Cornwall, Addison County, Vermont
W 2¼ lb. **F** 45% **P** 189

Twig Farm Washed Rind Wheel 🐐
Twig Farm, Middlebury, West
Cornwall, Addison County, Vermont
W 18 oz. **F** 45% **P** 189

Two-Year Cheddar Block 🐄
Shelburne Farms, Shelburne, Vermont
W 2¼ lb. **F** 45% **P** 190

Up In Smoke 🐐
River's Edge Chèvre, Three Ring Farm,
Logsden, Oregon
W 5½ oz. **F** 45% **P** 168

Vermont Ayr 🐐
Crawford Family Farm, Whiting,
Addison County, Vermont
W 4 lb. **F** 48% **P** 187

Vermont Shepherd 🐑
Vermont Shepherd Farm, Putney,
Westminster West, Windham
County, Vermont
W 6–8 lb. **F** 48% **P** 189

Wabash Cannonball 🐐
Capriole Farmstead Goat Cheese,
Greenville, Indiana
W 2¾ oz. **F** 45% **P** 181

Weston Wheel 🐄
Woodcock Farm, Weston, Windsor
County, Vermont
W 5 lb. **F** 48% **P** 193

Weybridge 🐄
Scholten Family Farm, Middlebury,
Addison County, Vermont
W 8 oz. **F** 45% **P** 187

Widmer 🐄
Widmer Cheese Cellar, Theresa,
Wisconsin
W 1–4½ lb. **F** 45%
Although this cheese may look
commercial, the flavors are
distinct, and the texture is
crumbly, due to the traditional
recipe and the commitment
to hand-crafting the cheese
throughout all the stages of
production. The flavors are
nutty and the crumble,
although a little moist, has
a good acidity level.

CANADA

Avonlea Clothbound Cheddar 🐄
Cow's Creamery, near Charlottetown,
Prince Edward Island
W 22 lb. **F** 45% **P** 205

Blue Bénédictin 🐄
Fromagerie de L'Abbaye St Benoît,
Saint-Benoît du Lac, Quebec
W 3 lb. 5 oz. **F** 48% **P** 206

Blue Juliette 🐐
Salt Spring Island Cheese Company,
Ruckle Park, Salt Spring Island,
British Columbia
W 7 oz. **F** 45% **P** 207

Brebette 🐑
Ewenity Dairy Co-Op, Conn, Ontario
W 9 oz. **F** 45% **P** 206

Cow's Creamery Extra Old Block 🐄
Cow's Creamery, Charlottetown,
Prince Edward Island
W 7 oz.–5 lb. **F** 45% **P** 205

Dragon's Breath Blue 🐄
That Dutchman's Farm, Upper
Economy, Nova Scotia
W 10 oz. **F** 45% **P** 205

Eweda Cru 🐑
Ewenity Dairy Co-Op, Conn, Ontario
W 6½ lb. **F** 48% **P** 206

Frère Jacques 🐄
Fromagerie de L'Abbaye St Benoît,
Saint-Benoît du Lac, Quebec
W 3 lb. 5 oz. **F** 45% **P** 206

Gouda 🐄
That Dutchman's Farm, Upper
Economy, Nova Scotia
W 13 lb. **F** 45% **P** 205

Le Moutier 🐐
Fromagerie de L'Abbaye St Benoît,
Saint-Benoît du Lac, Quebec
W 2 lb. 4 oz. **F** 45% **P** 206

Marcella 🐐
Salt Spring Island Cheese Company,
Ruckle Park, Salt Spring Island,
British Columbia
W 3½ oz. **F** 45% **P** 207

Marinated Fresh Goat Cheeses 🐐
Salt Spring Island Cheese Company,
Ruckle Park, Salt Spring Island,
British Columbia
W 5 oz. **F** 45% **P** 207

Montaña 🐐
Salt Spring Island Cheese Company,
Ruckle Park, Salt Spring Island,
British Columbia
W 9 lb. **F** 48% **P** 207

Mouton Rouge 🐑
Ewenity Dairy Co-op, Conn,
Ontario
W 2¼–6½ lb. **F** 48% **P** 206

Old Growler 🐄
That Dutchman's Farm, Upper Economy, Nova Scotia
W12 lb. F48% P205

Pied-de-Vent 🐄
Fromagerie Pied-de-Vent, Îles-de-la-Madeleine, Quebec
W2½ lb. F45% P205

Romelia 🐐
Salt Spring Island Cheese Company, Ruckle Park, Salt Spring Island, British Columbia
W7 oz. F45% P207

Sheep in the Meadow 🐑
Ewenity Dairy Co-op, Conn, Ontario
W10 oz. F45% P206

AUSTRALIA

Annwn 🐄
Ballycroft Cheeses, Greenock, Barossa Valley, South Australia
W2 lb. 4 oz. F45% P210

Big B 🐐
Tongola Goat Dairy, Cygnet, Wattle Grove, Tasmania
W1 lb. 12 oz. F45% P210

Billy 🐐
Tongola Goat Dairy, Cygnet, Wattle Grove, Tasmania
W5½–9 oz. F45% P210

Brinawa 🐄
Marrook Farm, North West of Taree, New South Wales
W6½ lb. F45% P209

Bulga 🐄
Marrook Farm, northwest of Taree, New South Wales
W22 lb. F45% P209

Capris 🐐
Tongola Goat Dairy, Cygnet, Wattle Grove, Tasmania
W4¼ oz. F45% P210

Cheddar 🐄
Pyengana Cheese Dairy:St. Helen's, Tasmania
W2¼–32 lb. F45% P210

Curdly 🐐
Tongola Goat Dairy, Cygnet, Wattle Grove, Tasmania
W9 oz. F45% P210

Edith 🐐
Woodside Cheese Wrights, Adelaide Hills, South Australia
W9 oz. F40% P209

Etzy Ketzy 🐄 🐐
Woodside Cheese Wrights, Adelaid Hills, South Australia
W4½ oz. F25% P209

Fromart 🐄
Fromart Cheeses, Eudlo, Queensland
W9–17½ lb. F45–48% P210

Gympie Chèvre 🐐
Gympie Farm Cheese, Gympie, Queensland
W4 oz. F45% P211

Ironstone 🐄
Piano Hill Farm, Gippsland, Victoria
W11 lb. F45% P209

La Luna 🐐
Holy Goat, Sutton Grange Organic Farm, Central Victoria
W5½ oz. F45% P209

Molton Gold 🐄
Gympie Farm Cheese, Gympie, Queensland
W9 oz. F45%
Named after the Queensland gold rush in 1867, this cheese has a buttery, melting consistency with a bloomy thin rind.

NEW ZEALAND

Curio Bay Pecorino 🐑
Blue River Dairy, Blue River, Southland, South Island
W6½ lb. F45% P212

Galactic Gold 🐄
Over the Moon Dairy, South Wakato, North Island
W8½ oz. F45%
A slab of washed-rind cow's milk cheese that looks somewhat like Pont l'Eveque, but with a richer texture. This cheese accompanies a Riesling wine very well.

Gouda 🐄
Mercer Cheese, North Waikato, North Island
W2¼–26½ lb. F40–45% P212

Gruff Junction 🐐
Greenpark Farm, Christchurch, South Island
W3½ oz. F17–25%
These large Gouda cheeses can take on some wild and strong flavors, and like all goat's milk cheeses need taming, especially during the ripening and maturing stages.

Joie 🐄
Cloudy Mountain Cheese, Pirongia, Waikato Region, North Island
W7 oz. F45% P213

Kaipaki Gold 🐄
Cloudy Mountain Cheese, Pirongia, Waikato Region, North Island
W10½ oz. F45% P213

Pirongia Blue 🐄
Cloudy Mountain Cheese, Pirongia, Waikato Region, North Island
W10½ oz. F45–48% P213

Rich Plain & Cumin Gouda 🐐
Aroha Organic Goat Cheese, Te Aroha, North Island
W1–2 lb. F38% P212

Ricotta 🐄
Clevedon Valley Buffalo Company, North Island
W7 oz. F35–40% P213

THE REST OF WORLD

JAPAN

Selection of Farmhouse Cheeses 🐄
Kyodogakusha Shintoku Farm, Shintoku Town, Hokkaido.
W9 oz.–6½ lb F35–45%
Cheesemaker Mr Nozomu Miyaiima produces five cheeses: Gouda with a light taste, Camembert, Blue Camembert, Mozzarella and a smoked cheese. The pure water from the Taisetsu Mountains and the clean air create the perfect grazing and cheesemaking environment.

CHINA

Gouda 🐄
Yellow Valley Cheese Dairy, Taiyuan, Huangzhai Region
W6½ lb. F30–40%
Dutch cheesemaker, Marc de Ruiter, makes superb cheeses, using milk from surrounding small family farms in the Huangzhai region. The cheeses follow a traditional recipe and are as good as anything you will find in Holland.

NEPAL

Chhena (Chhana) 🐄 🐃
Local dairies, Nepal, Bangladesh, and neighboring parts of India
W10½–18 oz. F30%
A fresh, unripened curd cheese that is similar to Italian ricotta. The soft, creamy cheese is used for making sweet desserts such as rasgulla, small balls of Chhena rolled in semolina and boiled in light sugar syrup.

Ragya Yak 🐂
Nomadic tribes, Nepal
W1 lb. 2 oz. F25–35%
This cheese is not too strong with a dense, slightly gritty texture and a dark beige pâte. There is a nutty, earthy aroma coming from the natural rind giving the cheese a hint of spice.

TIBET

Hand-made cheese, Yak's 🐂
Small isolated communities, Plateau Region
W7 oz. F35%
The cheese curds are pressed into molds and dried in open airy huts during production, to allow the wind and sun to filter through the cheeses. It has a very strong taste.

PHILIPPINES

Kesong Puti, 🐃
Small communities, Provinces of Laguna, Bulacan, Samar and Cebu
W10½ oz. F25–30%
Also known as Filipino cottage cheese, this simple style fresh cheese is made from the whole milk of carabao, a domesticated species of Southeast Asian water buffalo. The curd cheese is soft, salty, and sometimes a bit sour.

INDIA

Bandel (Bandal), 🐄
Small dairies or Artisan, Bandel, East India
W7 oz. F25–30%
This soft, salted, unripened cheese has a lovely aroma. During production, the cheese is shaped and drained in little baskets, then smoked. The cheeses are removed from the baskets, patted into flat circles, and sold immediately after production.

Paneer (Panir), 🐄
Small Dairies or Artisan, All regions
W3½ oz. F25%
Probably the most well known of all Asian cheeses, Paneer is a traditional, semi-soft cheese used in many recipes in Indian cuisine. Ripening or setting is done with lemon juice and the finished cheese has a similar texture to tofu or a pressed ricotta.

AUTHOR'S ACKNOWLEDGMENTS

As my publisher and friend would say, space is tight, so dear Jacqui Small, thank you. Just that. But there are also many other people to receive these two words from me. Kerenza Swift who, as Managing Editor, worked tirelessly and long into the night. I will miss the e-mails and the banter.

Lisa Linder's photography speaks for itself—simply beautiful. If you only knew the weather conditions we worked in—pelting rain, snow, wind, blazing sun—and all of this just outside my shop as we photographed in the doorway! Thank you, Lisa.

Lawrence Morton's design is not only precise but also chic and shows cheese in a whole different light. I think it is the most beautiful looking book on cheese.

It is always a bonus when free-hand drawings scatter a book, and many thanks to my daughter Kate for her talented contribution with the maps.

Wil Edwards, the photographer for the U.S. cheeses handled the brief with charm and good humor and I am truly grateful for his work. Kate Arding, my friend and American colleague, helped gather together the cheeses for the photo-shoot, and I thank her so much for her amazing skill and ingenuity in getting the U.S. and Canadian cheesemakers involved in the book.

I have good colleagues all over the world, and some close to hand, too. Will Studd in Australia has been insightful but also generous with his time and knowledge. Laurie Gutteridge's modern approach to artisan cheesemaking in Australia resulted in many interesting e-mail "discussions". Sarah Aspinwall of Canterbury Cheesemakers in Christchurch, New Zealand, gave me sound advice and opinions, as did Calum

"thecheesycurdnerd"—read his blog, it's fascinating! Also many thanks to Adrian Lander, who photographed the Australian cheeses.

Over the years I have met and become friends with many cheesemakers, producers of fine food and wine, and colleagues who help me gather and bring the merchandise to London; I have limited space, but they know who they are and I couldn't run my business or have written my book without them. Their generosity in sharing their wealth of knowledge and supplying me with wonderful produce is the anchor of La Fromagerie. Long may it continue.

Finally, I love my family—everyone who knows me will understand the importance of my family. Both my beautiful daughters, Kate and Rose, have supported me through thick and thin, and Danny, my husband and business partner, has been there right from the start. My other family, my work colleagues, are also so important to my life. Without them La Fromagerie would not exist. My general manager, Sarah Bilney, has strength to match the toughest challenge, and wit and wisdom to make each working day so enjoyable. From Cecile in accounts to my charming cheese managers and assistants, shop floor managers and assistants, chefs and kitchen and café crew, my continued thanks go out to you as you all work so hard to make La Fromagerie such a special place. Nothing sends shivers down my spine than someone I admire saying something nice about me! Who could be less than impressed to know that Jamie Oliver would step up to write a foreword so heartfelt, and so many thanks to Nigella Lawson, Nicholas Lander, Sue Conley, Peggy Smith, Rose Gray, and Ruthie Rogers for their kind quotes.